ƒP

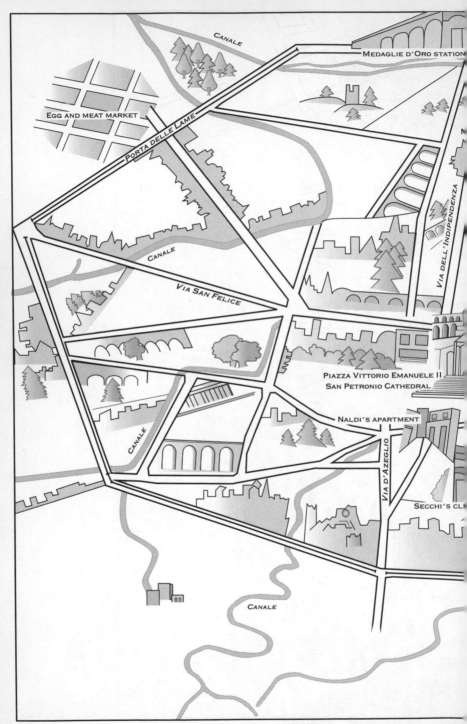

CANALE

Medaglie d'Oro Station

Egg and meat market

Porta delle Lame

Canale

Via San Felice

N

Via dell'Indipendenza

Piazza Vittorio Emanuele II
San Petronio Cathedral

Naldi's apartment

Canale

Via d'Azeglio

Secchi's cl

Canale

BOLOGNA 19

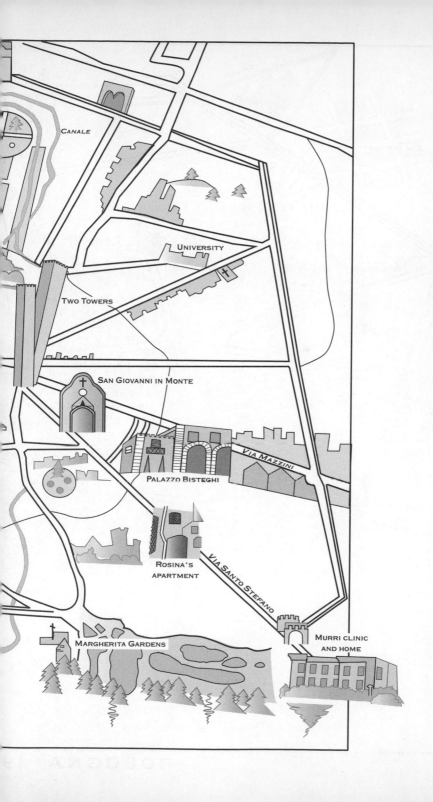

INDECENT SECRETS

THE INFAMOUS MURRI MURDER AFFAIR

CHRISTINA VELLA

FREE PRESS
NEW YORK   LONDON   TORONTO   SYDNEY

FREE PRESS

A Division of Simon & Schuster, Inc.
1230 Avenue of the Americas
New York, NY 10020

For information about special discounts for bulk purchases,
please contact Simon & Schuster Special Sales:
1-800-456-6798 or business@simonandschuster.com

All illustrations not credited to other sources are from
the author's private collection.

Manufactured in the United States of America

1   3   5   7   9   10   8   6   4   2

Library of Congress Cataloging-in-Publication Data
Vella, Christina.
Indecent secrets: the infamous Murri murder affair / Christina Vella.
p. cm.
Includes bibliographical references and index.
1. Bonmartini, Francesco, conte, d. 1902. 2. Murri family.
3. Murder—Italy—Bologna—Case studies. 4. Trials (Murder)—Italy—Turin.
I. Title.
HV6535.I83 B673 2006   3411   8868   9/06
364.152'3'094512—dc22   2005049496
ISBN-13: 978-0-7432-5046-7
ISBN-10:   0-7432-5046-X

To my special Sanitation Pirates

CONTENTS

DRAMATIS PERSONAE

FRANCESCO BONMARTINI, the murder victim

LINDA MURRI BONMARTINI, his widow

MARIA AND NINETTO, the Bonmartini children

CARLO SECCHI, Linda's lover

TULLIO MURRI, Linda's brother

ROSINA BONETTI, Tullio's lover

TISA BORGHI, Secchi's assistant and reputed lover

AUGUSTO AND GIANNINA MURRI, parents of
Linda and Tullio

RICCARDO MURRI, Augusto's brother,
uncle of Linda and Tullio

PIO NALDI, Tullio's friend

SEVERO DALLA, friend of the Murri family

AUGUSTO STANZANI, magistrate and
chief investigator of the murder

*A pronunciation guide of names, places, and terms appears
at the end of the book, following the notes.*

A NOTE

The Murri case, which lasted from 1902 until 1906, was one of the most publicized events in criminal history. Every word and gesture, and even many thoughts, of the people deposed and interviewed were recorded during the long investigation, as were the speculations of the police. The trial itself was exhaustively reported in every major newspaper in Italy. Everything described in this book—nods, shrugs, mannerisms, tones of voice—was recorded in the documents cited and in others besides; nothing written here is intentionally fictional. All the translations, however, must be blamed on me.

INDECENT
SECRETS

1. THE MURDER

Bologna, Italy, 1902

Dressed in his good suit, his vest neatly buttoned over his gray tie, and his suitcase full of soap, Count Francesco Bonmartini* stank uncontrollably. Years later, neighbors could still recall the odor that permeated all the apartments at 39 Via Mazzini and reached out to the street, where the driver of the police carriage finally had to urge his horse toward the gentler air of the next block. The smell had begun on August 30, and was so unbearable by September 2 that the manager of the building called the police and made arrangements to open the Bonmartini apartment that appeared to be the source.[1] Several officers of Bologna's public security arrived with a picklock and hammer and broke the fastening with a practiced blow. When the door swung open, the invaders were thrown back into the hall by the stench of Bonmartini. He was lying just inside the entrance. Faustino Cenacci, the manager, controlled his nausea, braced himself against the odor, and went in behind the police, following the black creek that led from the door to the body. He made for the window and opened it, gulping the outside air before he turned around to look at the rotting man.

Bonmartini was lying on his side, his hand on his chest as if to

---

*Pronounced Bone-mar-*tee*-nee. A pronunciation guide of names and places appears at the end of this book for readers not completely familiar with Italian.

touch the gaping crescent where his larynx had been and which now held a deep socket of clotted blood. There were thirteen cuts on his face, hands, arms, and chest, including one terrible hole between the second and third buttons of his vest where a ferocious stab had broken his sternum, pierced his heart, and produced the hemorrhage that covered the room with a carpet of dark crust. His jacket was open; his wallet, empty of money, lay nearby. Among the folded papers in the wallet was a note signed with an initial:

> *Dear Count, Thursday the 27th is fine for me, also the time.*
> *However, I wonder if we couldn't meet at the door on the Via*
> *Pusterla side, where we won't be seen by the tenants in the front?*
> *Meanwhile, I'm sending you many kisses and fondly remain*
> *Your B.*[2]

Bonmartini had just arrived home from Venice when he was attacked, still holding his keys, umbrella, overcoat, and yellow suitcase. A knife was plunged into his chest as he crossed the threshold. He must have tried to defend himself even while hemorrhaging on the floor—both his hands were cut from grabbing the weapon—but his desperate efforts were futile. According to the medical examiners, the lethal blow was the first one, "cutting the sternum in two," they said with amazement, "even though it is one of the densest bones in the body."[3] To finish him off, the assassin cut his throat twice, with two sweeping slices that severed Bonmartini's esophagus and a nerve bundle near his shoulder. Now the yellow nerves had spilled onto his jacket lapel. Cenacci could detect a few strands on the railroad schedule that was folded under Bonmartini's arm.

The big body had long been spoiling. Cenacci forced himself to look at the vermin swarming over Bonmartini and at the movement that had gathered in a tight party at the count's nostrils and eyes. Where do maggots come from? he remembered thinking. Are they born spontaneously as the body decays?[4]

The apartment was scarcely less horrible and fascinating than the body. A trail, black and coagulated, stretched from the body to the bathroom, where there was a full basin of blood and red-soaked towels. Two glasses and an empty champagne bottle stood on the dining room table like props left behind onstage from some previous affable play. Bonmartini's wife and two children were in Venice taking the baths. In the children's bedroom were part of a cake and two sandwiches, the remains of a simple meal. There was an imprint of a body on one of the beds and a light, dirty footprint on the other, as if someone had stepped on the coverlet. Between the two little beds, cigar ashes had spilled to the floor. The police carefully saved the ashes and dirt and measured the ghost that had dented the bed. Under a pillow on the count's bed was a pair of women's underpants, well made by machine, with delicate drawstrings and lace on the gathers under the knee. Though notably red, they were not the cheap bloomers of a streetwalker.

Bonmartini's wife, Linda Murri, was informed that the body had been discovered, and a message was dispatched to her father, a renowned doctor and the head of a clinic in Bologna. Her brother, Tullio Murri, who could hardly stand the sight of Bonmartini when he looked his best, was called in to identify his disintegrating corpse. Tullio arrived with his uncle, a lawyer, partially deaf. The two of them remained for some time in the front courtyard, the excited Tullio telling anyone who would listen, "The motive must have been robbery, because they also took Linda's jewels," a refrain repeated word for word by the uncle who, having heard only the word "robbery," would hasten to provide details. Tullio informed visitors to the commotion that Bonmartini had led a "disordered life" and was known to consort with fast women. As if to confirm his assertion, the investigation soon turned up a few long blond hairs in the count's bed and chamber pot. Bonmartini's luggage indeed contained a disordered collection of objects: a curling iron and some leather curlers, a fork, a bathrobe that was not his, a tortoise shell hatpin, two dressing gowns that would not have fit him, and a cigar case, along with many newspapers tucked into the side holders. He carried a rosary in his pants pocket, loose with his change. The eminent Augusto Murri, father of Linda and Tullio, visited the cadaver and offered his professional opinion: his son-in-law had not committed suicide, as police had first conjectured when called to the locked apartment.[5]

All over Italy journalists and their readers advanced theories about how the count died, each day's articles confirming that the rich and famous, too, have sordid and unhappy lives. It was believed for a while that the count had planned a rendezvous with a woman on his return to Bologna and that, after lovemaking, the woman opened the door to accomplices who murdered the count and robbed the apartment. The defenders of this hypothesis were hard put to explain why Bonmartini would have arisen from a bed of vice and meticulously redressed himself with all the pieces of his three-piece suit and a railroad timetable under his arm. If robbery had been the motive for the murder, why had the thieves left valuable rings on the victim's fingers? The elderly *portinaia,* doorkeeper of Bonmartini's building, said she saw the count arrive home in a carriage about 6:30 on the evening of August 28. "It would have been my duty to carry his suitcase," she explained to investigators, "but he gave me to understand that it was too heavy." She therefore unlocked the outer gate to the house, walked with him through the long corridor to the inner courtyard, and watched him go up the stairs to his apartment. She returned to her window near the front of the house just in time to see an accident: the carriage that had brought Bonmartini collided with an automobile and lay overturned at the corner. Though the evening had been eventful, the carriage driver remembered that the count was tall, fat, and young, had a black beard and wore a black hat, and that he was let down at precisely 6:20.[6] A few minutes after the count's arrival, one of the contessa's servants came by, a wardrobe mistress whom the portinaia called the Flower Lady because her hats were prinked with flowers. The wardrobe woman inquired whether the count was in, and she, too, went up the stairs but returned in a moment, reporting that he had told her to come back the next day. According to both the portinaia and a young girl who was with her in her kitchen, no one else came in or out of the front entrance that night.

"Are you certain, Grandma, that Count Bonmartini didn't leave again that night?"

"Not that night or after" came the answer. According to the old lady, he never went out the front door again until he was carried reeking down the stairs. None of the neighbors recalled hearing any disturbance coming from his apartment either on the night of the murder or during the five days afterward while he noiselessly decomposed. Nothing else of special interest was found in the apartment, except in the count's desk. One drawer contained stationery that exactly matched the rendezvous letter from the mysterious "B."

Count Bonmartini's family estate was outside Padua. A search of his bedroom there uncovered a collection of pornographic photos which the investigators examined conscientiously. His briefcase contained a revolver, ammunition, a gun license, a walking stick with a sharp, pointed end that could serve as a weapon, a crucifix, a picture of the Madonna, and letters— from a singer, and from *donne allegre* ("lively" women), along with drafts of his letters to them.

> *Your darling is late in answering you* [he explained in one] *because I'm in the country with the family and only just got your letter. I am very much against what you suggested, as I see no way of bringing you to Bologna. Your coming would be an embarrassment and, since you love me, you wouldn't want to do that to me. You know how important it is to me to fulfill my duties toward my family, and how I'd do anything not to be remiss where they are concerned.*[7]

To another he wrote:

> *Your letter gave me quite a start. It shows me that you don't understand what our relations are and must be. Given your*

relationship with [name obliterated], *which you must maintain and safeguard, and given my family constraints, we should both understand that I am not, nor could ever be, your lover.*

Bonmartini agrees, however, to give her some money that she has asked for but he cautions her:

Read this letter carefully. If we keep to the straight and narrow, we can always be the best of friends, and in that hope I embrace and kiss you with much affection.

To a third:

My dear, it is absolutely impossible for me to come tomorrow. I have a ring on my finger and am not, therefore, free to do as I please. . . . Write me here in Padua, to Dr. Piccoli [Bonmartini's extramarital pseudonym]. *Give me your home address, as it's impossible for me to take off for the Caffè Orientale in between classes* [he was attending medical school]. *A kiss to your Pomegranate Blossom.*

The newspapers published other police findings: effusive missives to Bonmartini from three women, all indicating their partiality to his eyes and his fortune.[8]

My gorgeous love, . . . I'm having a great deal of success in Trieste, but I was better off in Bologna because there I was with you. I'm dying for your kisses. I want to cover you with caresses. Really.
                                                              Your Nini

My dear, beloved sweetheart. I feel neglected and wonder if you've forgotten me. Wait, I don't know what to think——maybe you don't love me and would rather have some two-lire tramp, like those in the station. Through no fault of mine I often find myself needing money that I hope you won't refuse. This will be a new proof that you love me. I'm absolutely counting on your coming.

Kisses, Silvia

Silvia wrote again of *"that train station tramp who caused me so much torment"* but ended by *"covering those beautiful eyes with long, long kisses."*

My handsome love [wrote another, who was also waiting to kiss his *beautiful eyes*]: *The seventh of April is my Name Day. All my lovers are migrating, so I'm saving it for you alone. I love you. Kissing you everywhere, everywhere, everywhere!*

Your Clelia.

Dear, my love, my wonderful treasure, my handsome one. I'm hungering for your caresses. . . . Seeing your writing made me start to cry. . . . My mother thanks you so much for the marsala. Write me right away. Covering you with kisses, I am your very much in love,

Nini.

Dear friend . . . After your oaths I didn't believe you were false this way. But believe me, your method of doing things will cost you many tears, because, believe me, my love toward you has now changed to utter scorn. You must know that for your sake I left my [name obliterated] *and lost the 70 lire a month that he was giving me, you, with your slick ways, you made me despise that man who adored me like a madonna in order to dedicate myself completely to you who was such a fine gentleman and a liar. You should know that if you don't respond right away to this request I will wait until the end of the month and then I'll give your wife all your letters. Understand?*

Clesias

For several days, the major newspapers provided readers with delectable accounts of Bonmartini's exploits. Sightseers began gathering in front of the Palazzo Bisteghi on Via Mazzini, now that the smell had subsided. They asked sly questions in the *farmacia*, located then as now under the Bonmartini apartment; the druggist had nothing to report concerning women, but he could talk feelingly about the stink that had come through the ceiling. Bonmartini's cousin Valvassori and his best friend Cervesato tried to defend his memory; but their protests were a splash against the deluge of lurid articles and public contumely. "I knew that Bonmartini was fond of caffè singers," said a lawyer in Padua, "though he was raised to be very religious. I was shocked to read that he allowed a donna allegra in the family home. I didn't think he was capable of that." One young woman felt bound to answer the reports of the count's degeneracy by recording that she had encountered him in her territory near Via Mazzini. "Seeing that he was good-looking," she wrote, "I approached him. 'Go home to your people!' he told me."[9]

The nasty essays attacked both Bonmartini and the aristocracy in general. *L'Avvenire d'Italia,* a Bolognese daily, reported that Bonmartini had contracted a venereal disease that infected his wife.[10] The result of this contagion, the paper averred, was that Linda lost one eye to the malady and had gone to clinics abroad to seek treatment. It was suggested that the count's malodorous dead body was an apt symbol for the fleshly offenses he committed when alive. Alongside these editorials were articles recounting Linda's history of sickness and injury, and even longer reviews of her father's accomplishments. Augusto Murri was not from an old family; he was a self-made man, an exemplar of the active, educated, agnostic professionals who had been gaining ground everywhere in Europe, making independent names for themselves. The Murris were respectable and genteel. How could an event of such raw brutality happen in a decent family?

The long and sordid Murri-Bonmartini story had begun.

2. THE MARRIAGE

Francesco Bonmartini was born in 1869 in Cavarzere, on the out-skirts of Padua, near Dante's house and Donatello's glinting general sitting nobly through the centuries in the sun and snow.[1] The leafy island of Padua was surrounded by rushing water and unhurried people; its bridges reached into the surrounding farms and com-munities, but its urbanity stopped at the city gates. In the great University of Padua, the debate between religion and reason had resounded since the Middle Ages. The students who had waged it—Galileo, Copernicus, Goethe—now reposed as busts in front of the theater of anatomy. But on the agricultural estates that stretched out from the fringes of the old city, religion had long since won. Life around Padua was pervaded by the tender piety of Giotto, with his lovely frescoes bordering the tillage at one end of town, and the gen-tleness of Saint Anthony, with his seven-domed cathedral high at the other corner. Bonmartini was baptized at one of Il Santo's altars, perhaps even in St. Anthony's own chapel, where his miracles still shone bright and fresh on marble reliefs: "St. Anthony gives speech to an infant to prove its mother's innocence"; "Discovery of a stone instead of a heart in the corpse of a miser"; "St. Anthony reattaches the foot of a penitent youth"; and so forth. Less fresh, but certainly arresting, was the saint's black and stringy tongue, displayed in a gay gold reliquary; his vocal chords, too, would one day rest nearby for

Bonmartini's children to admire, if they paid the admission fees that were charged even then.[2] This happiest of churches and quietest of countrysides was the landscape of Bonmartini's youth.

Bonmartini's father died when he was very young. His mother was excessively devout, almost puritanical, according to friends too polite to call her a fanatic. Though he was heir to a conspicuous fortune, he was brought up to be modest, frugal, and credulous, guided by an older cousin, Battista Valvassori, who was a second father to him. And though educated by priests, Bonmartini was lighthearted, one of those noblemen who pass as believers by keeping quiet during discussions of religion.[3] Indifferent to hunting, cards, and most other recreations of the young provincial nobility, he loved natural science, photography, and music; he composed, and played the piano with remarkable untaught ability.

When he was fourteen, his mother died of what was discreetly called "chest cancer," leaving him alone on the estate except for an old priest who sometimes tutored him but most times did not. Young as he was, he took over the administration of his large property, displaying a genius for management, according to his cousin. His secondary schooling apparently stopped after his mother's death, when he went into the seminary for two years. Priest-ridden in adolescence, taught mainly the catechism of local superstitions, the count was hardly prepared for a life of fashionable parties, cultural sophistication, or suave small talk. He was a large, shabby, ingenuous young man. His wealth would have made him welcome in society anywhere in the region, but like the silkworms on his mulberry trees, he spent his days on the estate, a typical member of the agricultural nobility—even his most loyal defenders said so.[4] Until his death at the age of thirty-three, he was a moderate conservative, jovial, meticulous about money and indeed about everything except clothes, a man who made two copies of every good idea he heard.

In 1892, when Bonmartini was twenty-three, he met Linda Murri, the daughter of a prominent doctor in Bologna. Linda's brother Tullio had contracted typhoid. In order to remove her from that contagion—

and from another more abstract and confidential infection—her parents had sent her to stay with a friend in Padua. The friend promised to introduce Linda to all the eligible men she knew. She knew only one: Cesco Bonmartini. The Murris were "free thinkers." The vagueness of the term served them well in their university circle in Bologna, but in Padua it meant that they were anti-Church. Linda cared nothing about the local saints, had traveled abroad, expected scientific progress rather than God's favors, and worst yet, had a brother who was a leading socialist—everything to make Bonmartini's friends uneasy. Nevertheless, romance sparked between the Catholic landowner and the daughter of the bourgeois atheist. In a memoir written long after her husband's murder, Linda Murri averred that she initially found Bonmartini unlettered, bigoted, and full of country arrogance.[5] She graciously concealed those reactions when she met him. Her long, ardent letters to him during their brief courtship showed a nineteen-year-old heart completely captivated by the calm, cheerful, and somewhat old-fashioned Cesco. *"How much do I love you?"* she wrote.

Oh! I could repeat it ever so many times. My adored Cesco! You are everything to me, you are my soul! Oh! Dear, dear, I am yours, completely yours. Oh!! More love than this you could never know, Cesco my dear! During the night, my thoughts, O my Cesco, are always, always of you. I see you. I talk to you and tell you so many things that can't be said with words and lips. I dedicate my body and soul to you, all to you, the best of men.[6]

Early on, he expressed some doubts about their religious differences and whether Linda could be satisfied in the quiet world of his estate. *"I can frankly and securely tell you yes,"* she reassured him. *"I have examined myself a long time. I couldn't be happy if I misled you about one single detail."*

Linda's father investigated the young suitor's family. His grandfather had ended in a lunatic asylum. However, his father died sane, his sister succumbed blamelessly to tuberculosis, and his mother also died respectably. In a premarital interview, Professor Murri asked nothing about Cesco himself, apparently quite satisfied with the match. He did not raise the objection that both Linda and Cesco were too young: in Italy the average age for marriage was a full-blossomed twenty-five for women and twenty-nine for men. Linda herself had no reservations about their union: *"Oh, my beloved, beloved Cesco, your Linda loves you so much, so much. Oh! Cesco, Cesco dear, she lives only for you."* Her declarations went on for pages.[7]

They wed on October 17, 1892, just three months after their first meeting. On paper, Linda's dowry was 100,000 lire, but Augusto Murri never got around to paying it—a common enough circumstance in marriages where the dowry was a large monetary commitment. To the irritation of his son-in-law, who had never been known to eschew money, Murri kept the principal and gave Bonmartini the annual interest on its investment. Linda took up the delicate duties of an Italian lady and mistress of an estate—renovating and modernizing the rundown villa; setting menus for the newly hired domestics; ordering the new rugs put down in winter and the new battery fans put out in summer; visiting the *contadini* at times of birth, sickness, and death; distributing largesse.

The only servants Linda had known growing up were salaried maids and coachmen. At Cavarzere, she met peasants, tenant farmers who raised and ate their own food: beans, lard, onions, potatoes, and corn. They were Italians who hungered for salt, who had never cooked with tomatoes and rarely with meat, who drank not wine but *vinello*— mostly water—and instead of wheat bread ate niacin-deficient polenta made of maize.[8] They lived on prayers—prayers for training the vines, turning the beds, bandaging a child's finger, passing an ice seller or crossing a train track, prayers for relatives who had emigrated abroad. They were slow readers, uneasy with a pen and still likely to visit the letter writers whose desks and feather quills were set out on the sidewalks in town.[9] In the years that lay across the turn of the century, all of Italy shivered with malaria, and Linda had routinely encountered it. Malaria made half of Italy uninhabitable and, even in Rome, caused four times as many deaths each year as all other sicknesses combined.[10] But epidemic pellagra was new to the young countess. She had never before been so close to festering skin, watery stools, and wasting minds and bodies as in the houses of the contadini with their regular, wretched, springtime pellagra.[11]

She had to adjust to Padua, too. With its 81,000 rich and poor, smart and dull inhabitants, the city was progressive in some ways and primitive in others. Torture long having been abolished throughout Italy, Padua maintained a torture museum in a local prison—a fake rigged up for tourists—complete with racks, instruments of mutilation, and a crucifix device with a dried-up human hand still attached.[12] It was an amiable fraud that outraged nobody. In town, Linda could see a motion picture show and be spattered by a passing automobile; yet the city was ringed with houses where humans lived together with sheep and pigs, the farmers above and the animals below. In the miserable sharecroppers' hovels only a few kilometers from the poor box in St. Anthony's cathedral, the peasants had no animals to live with. In 1900, had she remained on the estate, Linda could have handed out the government's provision of free quinine to the contadini; but Cesco was hard put to make them net their windows against malarial mosquitoes or dig their sewage pits a safe distance from the cottages. She could visit her own dentist in Padua and preach regular tooth brushing to the house staff, but "teeth pullers" still roamed the countryside, along with witches and salesmen of every magic charm and gizmo, a countryside that came up to the very doors of the university.

Yet for all the rusticity that Linda abhorred in Cavarzere—the eager, inoffensive gestures, the mumbling and bowing before the landlord—landowning still conferred immense respectability, and Linda was not immune to the satisfactions of being Contessa Bonmartini. It was often said in the northern Italian provinces that industrialists and wealthy professionals like the Murris yearned for land, just as people who have had many love affairs end up looking for marriage and a quiet life. Linda was well liked in Padua, and Cesco was respected by everybody. The Bonmartinis were considered a happy family. Even after they were married two years and had a child—Maria, born in 1893—Linda continued to write Cesco long, effusive letters whenever they were separated even for a day. *"My Ceschetto, Dear, My treasure: We will always love each other, you are my life, my support, my well-being, my hope, my everything!"*[13]

However, relations between Cesco and the Murris were never warm. Early on, Cesco assumed that Augusto Murri would take him on as assistant in his Bologna clinic, a presumption he stubbornly clung to despite the insistent vagueness of Murri's comments on the subject. It was a reasonable hope, not especially opportunistic, for Italy was still a country ruled by a hereditary king, its society dominated by a hereditary nobility. The idea that men came into property, titles, privileges, and positions of influence "by right" was perfectly acceptable everywhere in Europe. The highest-ranking member of a family was still expected to provide his relatives with lucrative opportunities within his patronage. Industrialization had created outstanding examples of self-made men, but tradition kept strong the family networks of the old order. It was commonplace for doctors, lawyers, notaries, architects, or men in any profession with private clients to bring in their sons and sons-in-law and groom them to take over their practices. Some of these younger men had university degrees; many did not. Apprentice training was far more common than higher education for preparation in careers, as we might expect in a country where the total number of university students was only 28,000 in 1902, the year of Cesco's death. The prisons, by comparison, had an enrollment almost two and a half times as large.[14]

Doctors were frequently attached to laboratory-clinics, small or large. Here physicians worked up their own concoctions and contraptions, relieving the novel ailments that were brought to them or creating treatments for common illnesses according to a program approved by the head of the establishment. Some of these private clinical practices amounted to family businesses and produced professional dynasties. After 1894, Augusto Murri held the chair of medicine at the University of Bologna and was the suzerain of a large private clinic that was ancillary to his university professorship. The clinic trained medical students and guided doctors toward specialization while it took in patients. To Linda, old Murri protested quite reasonably that several men who had worked years in his laboratory aspired to be his assistant and all of them held medical degrees. He could hardly put Cesco ahead of them without arousing resentment. Linda's mother declared that Professor Murri was "shocked" that Cesco, lacking the minimum credentials, would hope to work alongside him. "How can he work at the University like that?" Giannina Murri wrote to her daughter. "Nevertheless, if there is one single person in the laboratory who has no medical license, Papà will make an exception for Cesco. Otherwise, no."[15]

Yet Murri encouraged his son-in-law's expectations by saying that he wanted him to become a doctor. Around Padua, Bonmartini was already addressed as *Dottore,* a term of respect that is still conceded to European men of social distinction. With a doggedness that characterized him in many areas of his life, Cesco, wealthy as he was, decided to earn the medical degree that he saw standing between him and the position he coveted. He did not go to the University of Padua where he had many connections and could have enjoyed the sponsorship of his friend Dante Cervesato, who happened to be an eminent pediatrician. Instead, he moved his family to Bologna so that Linda and the baby might stay with her parents while he went to school in Camerino, entering at the age of twenty-six the first phase of his studies. Medicine and surgery being the most popular curriculum, the country's nine thousand medical students were rotated through several schools. Besides the Ateneo di Camerino, Cesco would attend the University of Bologna, the Istituto Superiore in Florence, and the University of Rome, where he eventually obtained his physician's license. A medical degree was a four-year university program like any other and did not require attendance at a graduate school. In every place, the professors knew of him and his connection to the Murri family, since all of the country's twenty-one universities were small. The entire student body of

Padua and Bologna, the oldest schools in Europe, each numbered only about 1,500.

Linda was delighted to be back "home" and wrote to Cesco every day. *"Maria had hardly opened her eyes when she started looking for you,"* she wrote during his first absence. *"Poor little thing! All she could do was cry, 'Papà, Papà.'"* Receiving a letter from him, Linda *"read it, reread it, kissed it, and rekissed it,"* although he had been gone only twelve hours. They had been married three years when she wrote, *"I kissed your card and am kissing it again, not being able to kiss the hand that wrote it."*[16]

But exuberant hand kissing was as far as Linda's urges extended. Cesco confided to his friend Cervesato that from the first day of their marriage, Linda exhibited nothing but distaste for physical relations. Making love to her, he explained sadly, was like having sex with a dead person.[17] He coaxed her playfully in his letters. *"If your photo tells the truth,"* he wrote after receiving her picture in 1895, *"watch out when I get home!"* She responded, *"Your threats make me tremble, my dear Cesco. I will do whatever you want, but I am so afraid of another pregnancy."*[18] Sheath contraceptives made of animal gut were available in the cities, and as a medical student, Cesco could have procured them. His letters do not mention them—perhaps they were more uncomfortable than the alternative of abstinence. Nor do the letters mention *coitus interruptus,* which generally gets credit for the country's low birthrate. Italians of Linda's generation, even those with a normal interest in sex, contrived somehow not to have too many children, but no one today is quite sure how.[19]

Except for her frequent altercations with the servants, Linda was cheerful, her messages intensely affectionate and full of domestic details.[20] In 1895, their second child was born: Giovanni, nicknamed Ninetto. Even then, she wrote of missing her husband so much that she had to close her eyes and imagine he was near. The separation was bearable *"because of the joy I'll feel when you are a good and respected doctor."*[21] Her last love letter, from her parents' villa in Rimini, is wistful and heartfelt: *"Darling Cesco, When you are not here,*

I'm like some lost creature. I want you back so much, you can't even imagine it. When I'm with you, I seem to be a different woman." It is in this letter that she first mentions a Marchesa Rusconi, a woman Cesco would eventually refer to as "the caterpillar" and "that lurid animal," and who would figure in his sourest complaints.[22]

Until the middle of 1898, Cesco Bonmartini still thought he had an impressive career and a charmed future ahead. But his life changed, suddenly and irrevocably, and he would never know happiness again after that melancholy summer. The turning point was the last time he had sex with his wife, in July. From then on, she began treating him with a coldness he had never before experienced from her. What alarmed Cesco more than Linda's physical rejection of him—he had been dealing with that ever since their wedding—was that she stopped loving him, almost overnight. She stayed away from home, stopped talking, fell into spasms of depression or cried at the slightest upset. He was dumbfounded by her sudden contempt for him, a sentiment that was echoed by their acquaintances in Bologna who, one by one, let it be known that Bonmartini was unwelcome at their gatherings. On November 25, after four months of enforced celibacy, Cesco demanded sex from his wife, such as it was, and she refused. After that confrontation, all endearments stopped, the vestiges of Linda's affection vanished, and she began talking seriously about a legal separation, the limit of disunion allowed in Italy at the time. At intervals she considered the possibility of a Swiss or French divorce, although such a division would have had no legal force at home.[23] Moreover, divorce, though lawful in many countries, was not easy anywhere in Europe, particularly for a foreign petitioner.

The rupture in their relationship was undoubtedly not as sudden as it seemed to Cesco, since both he and Linda had long been ignoring their sexual incompatibility. But on the same day that he brought the issue out into the open, he wrote to a gynecologist concerning his wife's frigidity: "She has always endured conjugal relations with sufferance, and since the birth of the children, her repugnance has increased rather than diminished. It seems to me that she is not attracted to men as such."[24]

Though aspirin was not available until 1906, wives in Italy, as in every country, had long been using headaches to postpone marital obligations. Nevertheless, sexual indifference in women was not considered normal. Nor was the topic of sexuality as private as we might suppose. Advertisements in family newspapers described erectile dysfunction, menstrual irregularities, and the like, just as they do today. In Bologna bookshops, Cesco could have thumbed through the Italian version of *The Twentieth-Century Household Medical Adviser*, with its chapter on marital relations, or *The Practical Family Doctor*, popular in the U.S. and Europe, which addressed "diseases of the vulva and womb," along with "delicate and wonderful matters pertaining to the nature and relations of the sexes."[25]

In her letters, Linda never acknowledged that sex played any part in her aversion to her husband. At the same time Cesco was writing to the gynecologist, she was writing to Cesco, listing her grievances. These filled twenty pages. She began by observing that a separation would benefit him more than her. He would be free to take a woman of his choice, whereas she would still remain under certain constraints, namely, *"the constant watch that I must exercise on my conscience—free, yes, but always faithful to the scrupulous honesty that I can openly acknowledge is one of my qualities. I've told you that I feel real friendship for you, but that isn't enough for someone like me who needs love."* Linda hints at her distaste for his lovemaking, at his clumsiness, but instead of pressing the point, she digresses into a dozen other vexations.

"When I married you I loved you a great deal. I thought you were very good and very delicato. You are good, it's true, but indelicate, at least with me, and it is that which has, little by little, destroyed my love. Just recall the times you called republicans 'riffraff'; and haven't you a thousand and one times, in front of everybody,

ridiculed in the most cruel way my mother in particular, and my family in general?"

She takes him to task for being tight with money, for having incorrect ideas about wine, beans, and her friend, the Marchesa Rusconi. All this, she wrote, was making her more and more sad and sickly.[26] If in July Linda had been a "lost creature" without Cesco, by the end of November she considered any life with him a fate worse than death.

> *If you don't accept a separation, I'll come back promptly and remain the same as always. I will not charge either you or the children with my unhappiness and hope God gives me sufficient strength for the sacrifice that will mean my whole life. I will at least keep a pure conscience, having sacrificed even more than the famous martyrs, for they found a quick death and were assured of passing into a better life.*

She never gave him credit for being a brilliant father. Though he had not known his own father, Cesco had somehow become an adoring and adored Papà, a cuddler and a teaser, both whimsical and loving. Maria and Ninetto were five and three years old in 1898 and were so like Cesco that nearly every document concerning them remarks on the resemblance. Deeply hurt by his wife and angry at her family, who showed not the slightest sympathy for him, Cesco now lavished his unspent affection on the only two people who still wanted it—his children.

In September, Linda had told Cesco of encountering her first love, Carlo Secchi, at one of Marchesa Rusconi's receptions. Rusconi was rumored to be Secchi's current lover. Searching for some explanation for his wife's sudden change toward him, Cesco wondered if Linda's feelings for Secchi had reawakened. He could not understand, he said, why Linda would seek the company of the dim-witted Rusconi, unless the woman were putting her in touch with Secchi.

Cesco's old friend and counselor Valvassori wrote to Linda, "Cesco incessantly repeats that there is nothing in the world he loves more than you. He recognizes great defects in himself, but he is afraid you find these faults unbearable only because of an old passion that may have resurged."[27] Cesco, who never said anything just once, had apparently brought up the issue of Secchi already, for on December 5, 1898, Linda responded:

> That again! . . . this same discourse on the subject of some passion
> that you imagine I harbor for a man who has been dead for me for
> ten years. . . . I thought simple good sense would make you
> understand that if I had wanted to add to my suffering with a
> hidden love, I would hardly have gone back to him. I have had
> much suffering in not finding in my husband, who could have, who
> should have been everything to me, this harmony of heart and
> commonality of soul that can make marriage a paradise, or if these
> are lacking, a hell.

To Valvassori, Linda wrote, "*Cesco will never change. He seeks explanations everywhere but in himself.*"

Cesco was pacified. "*You're right,*" he wrote back to Linda, "*and not only will we not speak of it again, but we won't even think of it. Your letter has taken away all my doubts. If I have burdened you with this thing, it wasn't to torment you but to help us.*"[28]

On December 24, 1898, just as he was about to come home from school for the holidays, he poured out his heart:

> My dear Linda, Battista told me everything in his fatherly way.
> However, he was quite severe with me. The turmoil I'm going
> through keeps me from talking to you the way I would like to, keeps
> me from being able to express how hard I am going to work to
> reconquer you. If my clumsiness leads you to think I don't love you,
> I want to make amends and devote myself entirely to you. The day
> when you are satisfied with me will be the day of my utmost

happiness. But you, my Linda, help me—you who are so good and intelligent. Don't desert an unhappy man who, although he hasn't known how to show it, loves you and is hurting. Embrace our dear children and believe in the affection of your unhappy
Cesco[29]

Despite his anguished letter, Linda received him coldly when he arrived in Bologna. On a Christmas Day that held no festivity for him, he began keeping a diary. He stopped it after the eleven days of his stay at home but then resumed writing it three years later. The original diary was only a cheap notebook, small enough to fit in a pocket, with his neat penmanship covering some sixty pages. It seems likely that a lawyer advised him to keep a record of his dealings with his wife, so that if she insisted on a separation, his legal position might be strengthened. He later recopied the first part, making corrections and reducing it. The journal begins with a preface, a biographical essay on his wife, in a professorial tone, as if he were a doctor taking a medical history. Cesco is occasionally driven to confiding his heartbreak in the diary, and now and then he allows himself an outburst against his father-in-law; but he always returns to an impersonal format that shows he is collecting information for a third party. It was not a confessional journal. Nevertheless, the diary of 1898 and its companion diary of 1902 proved to be the most important and most public documents of Bonmartini's life, a handful of pages that were at the center of one of Italy's longest murder trials.[30] Bonmartini's own words about his marriage, uttered as if from the grave, captivated newspaper readers. The diary was one of the most influential elements, for both the jurors and the public, in deciding whether the defendants were lying. It is therefore worth quoting at length.

Diary of My Life with My Wife

Teolinda Murri was born September 12, 1872. Her mother not being able to breast-feed the baby, she was put with a wet nurse in Fermo, watched over by her paternal grandparents who lived there. She has

a younger brother of twenty-four, a man of lively intelligence but un-
balanced mind. She also had an older brother who died at five of con-
vulsions brought on by the mistreatment he suffered at the hands of his
parents.

    Teolinda did poorly with the wet nurse who, instead of giving her
milk, fed her herbs, polenta, etc. As a result of this horrible diet, the
baby suffered dysentery, and the grandfather, appalled by her condi-
tion, unfortunately returned her to her parents. I say unfortunately be-
cause the parents did not love their daughter, who reminded them in
one way or another of the child who had died. Her mother especially
took a dislike to her, so that even her earliest memories are of mistreat-
ment. She remembers that at two years old, when she was sitting on
her potty, her mother kicked her in the buttocks for no reason. Every
day brought blows and arbitrary correcting. Her father loved her a little
better than her mother, but only so long as his affection didn't incon-
venience him. He is a very bright man but absolutely inept at being a
husband and head of a family, so that even today he must submit to
the tantrums of his wife.

    Farming out babies to country wet nurses was a normal practice
in middle-class urban families. Some women came in from the far
rural areas to rent out their breasts in the city, but sending the babies
to the nearby countryside was also very common. In Milan, for example, a third of the babies under a year old were living with wet
nurses outside the city at the time Cesco was writing.[31]
    Bonmartini next lists the quirks of Linda's family: her grandfather
was a spendthrift; another ancestor was "an altogether odd character."
These conditions, Bonmartini concludes, resulted in Linda having a
difficult temperament, "despite an innate goodness that doesn't always show." Italians of the turn of the century, Bonmartini included,
thought of heredity the way the ancient Greeks thought of Fate—individuals were helpless against its curse; therefore, to understand any
problem, one had to find its genesis in previous generations.
    Cesco continued:

She was educated by her father, who wanted to make her a scholar. Perhaps that would have succeeded if the girl had not had opposing tendencies toward homemaking and more strictly feminine pursuits. However, at sixteen a disappointment in love resulted in her becoming so terribly anemic that her schooling was interrupted and her father spoke no more of studies.

Cesco then goes into some detail about Linda's chronic intestinal problems. They began with childhood dysentery; her father's remedy provoked the opposite problem, unremitting constipation. When Professor Murri became aware of that condition years later, he prescribed belladonna and a daily pill of podophyllin, a laxative, though, according to Cesco, he still did not realize that the earlier medication had caused the constipation.[32]

She takes that pill to this day, so that she has chronic loose bowels.

After the first disappointment in love, she married. The first years passed pleasantly enough, the bitterness of her parental home being fresh in her memory. But when the husband went to medical school, he had to move their residence to Bologna. Here the contrasts in their thinking were intensified. Father and brother are socialists; husband conservative. They saw with displeasure how Linda had adapted to her husband's ideas. The father, who had enjoyed all his daughter's affection, went around repeating what a marvel it was that with all her education, she could love a man like her husband and stoop to his level. The husband observed that after the move, the wife was not the same to him.

Cesco explains that when he and Linda finally had it out, she said she wanted a separation.

To the husband, such a proposal seemed preposterous, since there had been no violent scenes, nor cruelty, nor infidelity. He had left her the fullest liberty to go out, to spend. At first he reacted by try-

ing to make her understand how much he loved her, that he indulged her in every way while trying to reserve the right to direct the family according to his ideas. He had not been careful about letting himself denigrate his wife's family. However, his first days of anguish passed, and he realized that everything had been brought on by her intestinal condition, with the nerves and weakness that went with it.

There follows Cesco's own autobiography, in which he catalogs many suspicions but ends by revealing his complete ignorance of the true reason for his wife's loathing. He then begins the daily, sometimes hourly, record of his wife's torts against him, minutely observed and set down for permanence.

December 25, 1898. I offered for the 100th time to take her out, showing everybody that I'm happy to be seen with her. Response: that she didn't care to go out accompanied.

Cesco sees his son at Christmas Mass with their German maid and afterward remonstrates with Linda that the children must resort to the servants for their religious instruction. Linda answers that if they know their prayers in German, she sees no need for them to pray in Italian as well.

1:25 P.M. Took Maria's temperature. Has 37.8. I asked Linda if she thought we should call Silvagni [the doctor]. She answered with glacial calm that I could do whatever I wanted. After lunch, seated on the divan, she was sighing quietly. She looked up like someone who had just seen a rather hateful object. In all of her moves, there's a coldness and excessive sharpness.

I would say she almost feels disgust toward me. Yesterday evening she told me that in six years of marriage, she hasn't gotten accustomed to seeing me do for her the most humiliating service (emptying her dung anytime I am in the bedroom). I answered that it's enough for me that she accepts it as proof of my devotion. Since this summer I haven't had intercourse with her. I believe that must be due to her faulty up-bringing. Educated by a socialist father with her first disappointment in love ten years ago, and her intestines having been neglected as a baby, all that must have resulted in this neurasthenia that's so intense now. Because of my conscience, I'm doing whatever I have to for my children, being humiliated in front of her and them, letting all of them exaggerate my faults so that the children won't lose either their mother or their father.

Her father doesn't really care about her happiness. He's an egoist who, for the excitement of being popular, makes himself out to be socialistic; actually, he's a conservative of the first water. A bargainer in human flesh, making people pay 1,090 lire for each consultation. If he doesn't get his price, he's happy to let their diseases kill them.

Bonmartini was paying 1,000 lire *a year* for an elegant seven-room apartment. Unquestionably, Professor Murri's fees were ferocious. The unburdening continues:

Her brother, an anarcho-socialist, is a layabout by profession who enjoys the esteem of nobody. Her mother has an evil mind.

3:00—I begin to understand why Linda does not come out with me. Our difficulties have been made public and she is ashamed to be seen with the husband who, naturally, has been assigned all the blame.

Bologna was and is a pedestrian's city. From the Piazza Vittorio Emanuele II (now Piazza Maggiore), a few wide thoroughfares and tramways radiated to twelve city gates.[33] People could stroll across almost the entire town on terrazzo floors covered by long arcades that protected them from sun and rain. Where there were no covered walkways, the amblers took over the streets, forcing carriages and carts to wend through the crowd. Linda and Cesco were living a kilometer away from where the Murri villa and clinic would soon be established just outside one of the gates, Porta Santo Stefano. The clinic, facing what is now called Via Murri, bordered Margherita Gardens, the park where all Bologna gathered on Sundays to hear concerts, row on the pond, and eat ice cream. Italians who could afford it required constant provisions of ice cream, which, then as now, they blithely consumed anywhere they happened to be.[34] Unlike Athens or Madrid, where the men struck out alone for their evening exercise, in Bologna men routinely promenaded with the whole family, including the maid, Papà carrying the baby and stopping as *nonna* lit candles in one of the churches along the way. On Sunday and Thursday, the traditional half weekday, the parks and sidewalks, as well as theaters and caffès, were thronged with families—but not Cesco's.

The tense holiday wears on. On Christmas evening, they go to dinner at the Murris' and come home in heavy silence. He gets up with the children during the night, brings tea to Linda, empties her chamber pot, and then sits down to write his will. He leaves all his property to his children—lands worth one and a half million, with an annual income of 75,000 lire, a substantial inheritance, considering that the Bonmartini maids earned 25 lire a month. Valvassori—not Linda—was to be his executor and the children's guardian. He explains in the document that he fears his wife will yield to the untoward influences of her family in rearing the children. Cesco wanted two hundred Masses said for his soul. "Despite appearances to the contrary," he wrote, "I remain a firm believer in the apostolic Roman Catholic Church."[35]

December 26. I see that I am not going to be able to endure this life. I have loved that woman more than anyone could have. I have put up with her extravagances with singular resignation because I saw her goodness. Now I begin to doubt even that she is sick.

December 27. At the beginning of this diary I forgot to record how many times she told me she loved me so much. Why has she changed? I don't know if it's been exposure to her people with their ideas so opposite of mine, or if it's the company of friends who repre-

sent the social life that this miserable husband deprives her of. I emptied the usual pot.

The chamber pot appears in nearly every entry of the diary. Cesco is obsessed with it, and with his own abnegation in emptying it. With her self-induced diarrhea, Linda used the vessel all night. Apparently, Cesco began the habit early on of emptying it right away, perhaps to spare her and himself the unpleasantness of leaving the full pot under the bed, or in a bedside cabinet, until the servants cleaned it in the morning. After he and Linda moved into separate bedrooms, he continued to perform "the humble service," as he called the ritual disposal, whenever he heard her stirring in her room. The Bonmartini apartment, like many dwellings in Italy, was in an old house. It had electric lights, for Italy's shimmering cities were in the forefront of Europe's electrification, but not the flush toilets and gas heat that were being installed in Bologna's new buildings.

December 28. Cesco observes that Linda treats Maria coolly, and wonders if it is because the child resembles him. At lunch they discuss whether a woman who has an illegitimate child should keep the baby with her or give it to the maternity hospital. Linda believes the woman should sacrifice her own honor for the sake of the child, an opinion that pleases Cesco so much he kisses her and buys her a fashion magazine when he goes out. He is obliged to travel to Padua, or rather Cavarzere, to attend to his estate. A landlord could either take half of his tenants' harvest as rent or, like Bonmartini, he could collect a set rent in quarterly installments. He makes the trip, collects the quarterly rents from his tenants, and returns the very next day, so as not to be apart from his children longer than necessary.

January 1, 1899. The invitation came to go to dinner this evening at her family's. I asked her if she believed I should go this morning to give my best wishes to them. However, I think the less they see me, the better off they are. They are crazy, advising their daughter to lie and be immoral. I helped her try on a dress in front of the mirror.

Supper at her house. Returning home, she said, "What will '99 bring? I wish it were the last year I had to live through." Helped her undress, she took care of her necessities and I went to empty it. She told me that she wasn't sleepy but that she's very sad. We stayed a while, looking at each other and not talking. She was completely immobile, with her mouth open and her eyes staring. She didn't even seem to be breathing. I looked at her face and saw that her eyes were filling up with tears. Then with a pitiful voice she said, "If I were no longer here, would you confer with Papà in bringing up the children?" I answered that maybe I would, but I hoped she would be here. Then she began crying so violently that she started vomiting. Fortunately, there were only two spasms and she didn't throw up much. I gave her some water to wash her mouth and a little glass of anisette. She kept on crying, saying she only prayed to God to let her die, that she had put her trust in God but that God had not heard her. I answered that I really didn't understand. Here I am doing everything in my power to make myself acceptable to her because I had never stopped wanting her or wanting what is best for the children. Poor Maria in her little bed, hearing her mother talking about death, started her own torrential crying.

Cesco finally offers Linda a separation, but she rejects it because she fears he would take away the children and she would have to leave the house.

I'm a despot because I once remarked that women should obey their husbands. I'm hard with the servants; I used to be hard with the children but now I've changed; and once, some time ago, I said that when a wife enters into a family she should adapt to its customs. I answered that all that was true, that with the servants I was constrained to play the part of the padrone because otherwise, with all her kindness, we would end up being their servants. In a word, I want to be the head of my household and give the family the direction I believe in; this is my duty. Certainly, I told her, with her character, she wouldn't have wanted a man in a skirt; she would have refused to marry me.

She told me that at Padua and here I make her serve me, sending her to fetch my clothes that need washing. That is absolutely untrue, I've never done it; I see that her state of health is making her hallucinate. I told her again that I loved her, that although I knew she didn't love me, I loved her just the same; the feelings and admiration I had for her when we married had only increased with time. I kissed her, and she even took my hand and drew me to her. I kissed her face and her mouth and asked her forgiveness if, involuntarily, I had made her unhappy. She then asked forgiveness of me, telling me to have patience. I am more and more convinced that her mind has been affected by chronic, severe anemia. This very evening I told her father to give her some iron, but he said, as he always does, that it was useless.

Cesco speculates that the crisis was brought on by a letter from Professor Murri in which he told Linda he was sending her flowers to help her start a happy new year, although he was sure the year would not, in fact, turn out well. Linda kept the letter under her pillow.

Her people give her rotten advice. Instead of bolstering her and curing her, God knows what they tell her. And what am I supposed to do? Whatever I propose is rejected by her father, along with the prescriptions of every other doctor. One thing is certain: I can't go on this way. I really think the only thing for me to do is get out of this cursed Bologna. She says that she's suffered this misery for six years, but it's not true; hasn't she told me so many times that she had such faith in me and thought I was so good! How did we get from there to here?

January 2. I don't remember how it began, but she told me that if it's true that I love her, I mustn't think of taking away the children if we can't come to some agreement between us, and on and on with this drivel for an hour. She told me everyone advises her to take a lover if I don't suit her, but she is too serious for that and would rather die.

Cesco hears that Linda's father will pay half of her expenses for a trip the two are planning. "I can't trust that," Cesco writes. And in fact Murri tells him, "without beating around the bush," that he will not pay. Linda is going with her father and her colon to San Remo on the Riviera near Nice, then a quaint town of about 20,000 and a popular mountain resort for "wintering," as the seasonal pilgrimages were called.

How can this imbecile of a father advise her to travel instead of sending her to a nursing home? Cesco asks himself.

On January 4, Cesco goes again to Padua, a journey of about seventy-five miles requiring a train ride of two and a half to five hours each way, to get money for Linda's trip and to pick up some blouses for her.

How glad I would be to do these things for her if she loved me! Again, before lunch, she told me that if I loved her I would just go away and leave her the children. You call that reasonable?

On the long train ride, he grumbles to his diary:

And they are going to pay!!! Ha! Those people don't give anything to anybody—true socialist speculators.

He returns tired but plays the pianoforte to soothe Linda—the entire score of a new opera, *La Bohème*. Then he makes her some orangeade and cleans up the inevitable deposit.

January 6. As usual, she brought me coffee. I got up and gave her 1,000 lire for the trip. We had begun to talk when in comes that pain in the neck, Rusconi. I accompanied her to the station full of emotion, feeling all the while like I wanted to cry. It's no use. I love her.

Cesco closes this first diary with thoughts of his children:

And my babies, poor little things, it hurts me so much to see them leave.

Since he had to return to the university, he was not to see them again for five months.

The formal separation came at the end of the academic year. In April 1899, faced with the prospect of spending three months of summer as they had spent the eleven tense days of Christmas, Cesco and Linda parted legally. Separations were still so rare in Italy that everyone who heard about theirs felt bound to express disapproval and remark upon the terms.[36] Cesco was to maintain his own residence in Bologna where he could see the children, in addition to having them two months of the year in Padua, with Linda or without her, if she chose instead to travel elsewhere. He would pay for all their housing and expenses. In addition, he would give Linda 7,500 lire a year.[37] The judicial separation was dated October 17, 1899, their seventh wedding anniversary.

They remained apart for three years, years punctuated by bitter incidents. Cesco continued his medical studies on schedule. During breaks from school, he had dinner with his children at the Hotel d'Italia in Bologna, where he paid 1,000 lire a month for three rooms (including "light," electricity being considered an optional comfort), the cost of an entire year's rent for Linda's apartment. In all but the most luxurious Italian hotels, travelers said, the beds smelled like stables, bedbugs shared the mattresses, and soap was a high-priced extra.[38] The Hotel d'Italia, however, was lavish. Its Christmas and Easter menus were reported in the newspapers, along with guest lists of well-known millionaires who had checked in for the holidays. From time to time, Linda and Cesco discussed reconciling for the sake of the children. A flurry of correspondence would then ensue between Linda, her family, Cesco, and his two or three confidants. "Your Linda loves you well enough," Cesco's friend Gallerani wrote him after visiting the Murri parents in February 1900, "but with a higher love that is difficult to understand because it's based on sublime ideals." Cesco would have none of it.

She's happy and mocking me while I'm alone like a dog [he wrote back]. *And you want me to believe she loves me? What kind of love is that! "I love you, but don't get under my covers." Quite sublime! I don't think she even loves the children, since she's unwilling to make the least sacrifice for them. As for her father, may God annihilate him—him and that whole family of pigs!*[39]

Soon after the separation, Linda took a trip with her father to Mount Etna. Cesco, ill with typhoid, was hospitalized in Rome. On their way to Sicily, Linda and her father visited him in the hospital, went to see a play, and then continued on their southward journey. As Linda was returning on a train with the usual open windows, a volcanic cinder blew into her left eye and started a persistent infection. She eventually underwent surgery in Switzerland to remove the particle. This was the eye affliction that the newspapers would describe as a venereal disease. In July 1900, Linda stayed in a rented villa (Cesco paid the rent) in San Marcello Pistoiese, below Bologna, one of several trips that would later come under fierce scrutiny. She traveled a great deal, though her eye was inflamed and she was still inconvenienced by the intestinal irritation that no one except Cesco seems to have taken seriously. At about the time Cesco graduated in 1901, she moved to 39 Via Mazzini (now Strada Maggiore), to the nine-room apartment in the Bisteghi Palace where Cesco was to die on the threshold.

Despite the separation, Cesco still wanted Professor Murri to take him on as his assistant. In other ways, too, he seems to have been trying to force Murri into the role of a father—his father—with an obligation to pass on his name and prestige. Murri sensed the paternal solicitude that Cesco expected from him and coolly rebuffed it. In January 1902, when Cesco asked him to get Linda to modify her conditions for reconciliation, Murri wrote back:

Dear Cesco, I will do everything to promote a settlement acceptable to both you and Linda. I could not back anything unfavorable to

Linda. Although you are a son to me in a certain sense, if you two cannot come to an understanding, it is unrealistic to imagine that I would advance your objectives and oppose hers. I know you complained about me because I didn't force Linda to stay with you, therefore I wanted to clarify your position.

As Murri never passed up an opportunity to insult his son-in-law, he added nastily:

You will understand this only with difficulty, because of your atavistic notions derived from prehistoric times regarding the law and paternal love; I had hoped that the study of medicine would remove these traces from your mind, though prejudice had embedded them deeply. My studies of physiology, psychology, and pathology have taught me that at twenty years the brain attains its greatest capacity, and that by fifty years its decline has begun. Therefore, since Linda is thirty and I am fifty, she is more qualified than I am to make her own decisions.

A. Murri.[40]

Cesco was nevertheless determined to assume a position at the right hand of his father-in-law, though the old man clearly despised him and had no intention of admitting him into his professional circle. At long last, Murri stopped his tergiversations and wrote to Cesco with an explicit refusal.[41] Even then, Cesco was not ready to give up. He told his wife that since Professor Murri would not let him use the facilities of the University of Bologna medical laboratory, he needed to attach himself to the medical school at Padua and was therefore ready to move the family back to Padua, that is, to Cavarzere. So that he and Linda would have equal access to the children, he proposed putting them into a boarding school—an idea that he knew was anathema to Linda—unless, of course, his father-in-law reconsidered and hired him as assistant. He was not serious about boarding school—that was said only to pressure Professor Murri—but he did want to move back to Padua, and he had no intention of going without Maria and Ninetto.

Why didn't Professor Murri try to placate Cesco with a lower-ranking position? If Murri did not want him as his assistant or didn't even want him in his presence, couldn't some invisible and decent place have been found for him as a reward for the significant effort he had expended in getting his medical degree? Nothing of the sort was ever offered.

In spring 1902, Cesco finally consulted a professor of criminal law at the University of Bologna about the possibility of gaining legal custody of his children. Alessandro Stoppato was a paisan of Cavarzere and, at forty-six, an old friend of Bonmartini's family. Cesco complained to him that the separation left him longing for his children while the Murris were telling them that their father was dissolute, a lout, and an ignoramus. He realized bitterly that, under the Murri influence, they would grow up having no respect for him. He wanted to educate them according to his lights. He wouldn't raise them to be sanctimonious, but neither did he want them subjected to the anarchism of the Murri household. Stoppato told Cesco it would be hard to take the children from their mother without cause, and even if there were grounds, Stoppato himself could not pursue a case against the daughter of such an influential man. Stoppato referred him to three other lawyers who, one by one, rejected Cesco because they did not want to set themselves against Augusto Murri.[42]

Giuseppe Pigozzi finally took Bonmartini as a client, after first refusing to see him because he had heard that he mistreated his wife. The count was "a perfect gentleman," he reported. Other attorneys, friends of Cervesato, began offering Bonmartini informal advice. Ermolao Barbaro from Padua had known Cesco for some years. He would later testify that the count was loyal, conservative, religious, very intelligent, a fine man overall, though untidy and hardly fashionable. Rumors about Linda had reached all the lawyers, but nevertheless, they warned Cesco that he would never get legal custody of his children in an Italian court, regardless of his wife's possible infidelity. Cesco was adamant in wanting to try.[43]

Meanwhile, six-year-old Ninetto fell ill with an infected throat. Professor Murri called in the children's doctor, Luigi Silvagni, who in turn called in a pediatrician from Padua—none other than Cesco's best friend, Cervesato, who warned the family that the malady might be diphtheria. The Murris were not warm to Cervesato's presence and were even less disposed to allow the newly licensed Bonmartini to treat his son. Linda refused to allow Cesco to see his child unless she were in the room, and to be certain of being present, she got in bed with the boy and refused to budge even when Cesco threatened to call the carabinieri to throw her out.

In the midst of this roiling conflict, astonishingly, the couple reconciled. After the angry scenes at Ninetto's bedside, Linda worried that Cesco would make a serious attempt to get the children. Cesco agreed to the reconciliation simply because he missed his babies and was afraid he would not win a custody suit. He knew what it meant to long for a parent, he said.[44]

"Do you swear my wife is honest?" Bonmartini wrote to his cousin Valvassori, who urged the reunion. On Valvassori's assurance that Linda had no lover, Cesco acquiesced to Linda's terms for reuniting. Each side made a great show of reluctance in taking the other back, but in reality, no one was taken back. As two tenants of the Palazzo Bisteghi, they merely agreed to share certain comforts of the house, including the children. Linda wanted her apartment to be entirely separate from Bonmartini's, but in the end, Cesco and Linda had separate bedrooms—that was all. Cesco was to continue giving her 10,000 lire a year in addition to paying all expenses. These were enumerated: carriages, food, clothing, servants, teachers, rent, lights, travel fares, and the cost of vacation villas. He was to dismiss all of his servants and replace them with new domestics whom Linda would manage, though their salaries were Cesco's obligation. He was to be assigned a maid of his own whom the family could borrow when they needed her. Linda and Cesco would present themselves as a married couple, but she would be "perfectly free to go out night or day, to receive whomever she wishes, to go to dinner with her parents and friends," etc. The reconciliation was signed in April 1902, before Cardinal Svampa, the prestigious archbishop of Bologna and representative of the conservatives, with the couple kneeling and swearing to observe its terms. There were prayers; then curtains parting to reveal a crucifix, two candelabra, and a makeshift altar set up behind the legal documents; then repeated blessings, holy water, and a fair amount of solemn and showy ritual.[45]

After the reconciliation, Bonmartini ran into his mentor, Barbaro, at Bologna's Caffè San Pietro, together with Cervesato and a group of other lawyers. "I only did it for the children," Cesco told him apologetically. "You did absolutely the right thing," the lawyer replied. But as he later explained,

> Cervesato told us privately about the ridiculous agreement—that Bonmartini would never enter her room, that they would see each other only at dinner, and so forth. Cervesato felt bad that his friend had been forced to accept such humiliation for the sake of his kids.

Another lawyer who was present at the caffè recalled that people were a little sarcastic in congratulating the count on the reconciliation. "Bonmartini never said anything negative about his wife or her family," the attorney reported, "although everyone knew that the Murris would not even acknowledge him on the street.

> He then made the strange comment that he always took a carriage since the reconciliation, even when he was with Cervesato. In fact, they went off in a carriage to the station, That was the last time I saw poor Bonmartini.[46]

As soon as Cesco moved from the Hotel d'Italia into Via Mazzini in April 1902, Linda left for Salsomaggiore, a small, exclusive resort with saline springs and luxury hotels that was just coming into vogue. It was the beginning of the travel season for European aristocrats, the months of pleasant weather when the idle and wealthy all over the continent migrated from one recreation spot to another in search of the sea, the city, the waters, the hunt, the games (of whatever sort), or one another. Traveling was an end in itself, without any specific reason, much like the modern migrations of comfortable pensioners. Linda moved about so restlessly during the summer before the murder that the jury later analyzing her trips found it difficult to follow her back and forthing. In June, she rented a cottage in San Lazzaro for herself, the children, and servants. Cesco was permitted to come only for lunch, being obliged to occupy himself elsewhere the rest of the day and night. Though close to Venice, San Lazzaro was an island with little more than a seminary in the town; there was no easy access to anything but prayer. The next month, Cesco went to Venice with the children for two months for the baths—meaning the spas and beaches—taking servants, while Linda returned to the clinic in Switzerland. She then went to Sicily with her father for a second time. Cesco and the children remained in Venice, where Linda's brother Tullio visited for two days in August. For the rest of the summer, Linda commuted between Rimini, Venice, and San Moritz, on the Riviera, where her father was resting. Cesco also made short trips out of Venice until his murder on August 28, 1902. He was not vacationing, however, but diligently trying to find a position.

When Cesco moved to Via Mazzini on April 16, 1902, he resumed writing in his secret diary. Rejection had hardened him, and now he used the diary as a private therapeutic monologue, burning and petty, allowing him to blow off steam. When he left, he gave Linda all the furniture; but now he has to keep his underwear in the credenza in the dining room. The wardrobe woman, Maria Pirazzoli, is impudent to him. Linda is cold toward him, especially in front of the servants, and the children seem constrained to be less affectionate in her presence.

Maria was going to bed without telling me goodnight. I called her
back and gave her a kiss.[47]

For the first days, things went along fairly well. The boredom of
their lives would appear to be stressful in itself, for even distracting
chores such as shopping were assigned to the ubiquitous servants.
Cesco's main activity is recording how much money he is disburs-
ing—8,000 lire the very first day of his return. Linda's only work is
to order preparation of their various residences for occupancy or va-
cancy, arrange who will accompany her on trips, and see to it that
the trunks are disinfected against plague on their return.[48] Linda and
her mother depart for Salsomaggiore; Cesco is to keep the children.
He politely sends a carriage to fetch his mother-in-law, but she re-
fuses it. When Linda leaves, she addresses the maids, gives her hand
to everyone except Cesco,

and if I had not repeatedly called after her to say good-bye, she
would not have even looked at me.

After a few days, Ninetto develops a fever and Cesco sends
Maria away from possible contagion, to her grandmother, who had
already returned. Residential telephones were not yet commonplace
in Bologna, and Cesco was obliged to send the most reliable servant,
the German Frieda Ringler, back and forth to the Murris with messages, many messages, because of his nettling attention to detail: May
Maria come? Should he bring her himself? On Maria's return, he
sends her back with Frieda on a special trip to thank her grandmother for her hospitality.

April 28. This morning a card came from Linda addressed to the
children in which she says she will return this evening from Salsomag-
giore. I went to the station with little Maria. Hellish weather, huge rain. I
hated for Maria to be in that dampness. The train brought Queen Na-
talia, but not Linda. We returned home not knowing why she didn't ar-

rive. At eight-thirty Ettore [the Murris' manservant] *brought me a telegram from Linda addressed to the Murris that said, "Terrible weather. I'm staying. Let the children know. Many kisses." Her Highness does not deign to notify me, but instead telegraphs her people. To welcome her, I had her room ready, full of flowers that I was able to get only with difficulty and at a high price on account of the bad weather.*

More and more, the children become not only his stated reason for living with Linda but his reason for living at all. As both husband and wife search for new ways to irk each other and justify themselves, they begin exaggerating their parental attachment. Cesco complains that when he is gone for a day or two, Linda fails to send him bulletins about the children. Linda insists that in her absence, everything Cesco does with them must be reported by the maids. But all she finds out is that he buys the children geography games and spends his evenings playing with them.

May 16. Today early signs of battle. I told her that I wanted to keep the children in Cavarzere in September and October, and I would keep them. She knows I have to go, and she expects me to stay there without the children as well. She answers: "Already! Here it is, I knew it! This is the way you are, and it's better not to talk about it. Let's go to breakfast."

Cesco's estate in Cavarzere was the only source of his abundant income. Typically, a landlord provided land, buildings, implements, dwelling houses, and stock—either cattle or sheep—for his tenant farmers. He paid for seed, fertilizer, perhaps a mill, and all the taxes. The peasant's rent was based on the quality of the land he worked; therefore, the landlord had to keep his eye on changes in the yield of various plots, if he hoped to maintain harmony on his estate. The leases were typically rotated every three years, with the crops also rotated in cycles of wheat, maize, clover, and beans, along with large areas for vineyards and mulberry. It was not a system that would run itself without a careful arbiter assigning plots and crops, adjusting charges, and distributing free solicitude. Bonmartini's tenants told the authorities investigating his death that the count was a fair man, good about carrying them during bad harvest years, and that only once had he ever evicted a debtor—an impressive record of subvention.

Bonmartini had always resided on his estate until he entered medical school. He therefore felt constrained to stay near his tenants for at least a few months in summer to demonstrate an interest in their well-being, for contadini notoriously resented absentee owners. The agricultural pattern was still semifeudal, the sense of mutual obligation between landlord and peasant kept alive by frequent visits and the traditional exchange of platitudes about loyalty. Whereas in the South, the landlord took whatever he wanted from the contadini—typically, the workers kissed their lord's hand and displayed a groveling deference to anyone well dressed—in the North, the peasants were truculent: there were 629 agricultural strikes in 1900 to obtain better contracts. The peaceful estates around Padua were those where the landlord knew his tenants' parents and chronic illnesses. Having an estate did not guarantee wealth, as many big farms were marginal. Twelve percent of the people in Italy were landed proprietors, but less than two percent, Bonmartini among them, qualified as "wealthy."[49]

Since Cesco was so successful with his estate, his determination to pursue a medical career is hard to explain. He complained that his father-in-law was ruining his chances to work as a doctor; in that, he was entirely correct. At the turn of the twentieth century the humanist-physician, whose clinic reflected an individual philosophy and personality, was the prevailing model in medicine, just as today, the dominant model is a huge hospital that projects an impersonal, corporate professionalism. The leading physicians exerted an influence far exceeding the size of their institutions or the number of patients they had actually cured, just as certain modern colleges carry great prestige, even though their student enrollment is quite limited. Three hospital-clinics in Italy were known all over Europe, though they were small by our standards—only thirty or forty beds. The most famous was in Rome, directed by the Minister of Public Health.[50] For patients who could see their way to Naples, there was the eye clinic of Antonio Cardarelli. The third clinic, with many international visitors on account of its location, was in Bologna—and it was Murri's. Cesco applied to the first two and was rejected at once. He then tried the smaller clinics. In May, he went to Naples to ask a Professor Castellino to take him on as his assistant. The doctor replied frankly that he could not afford to make an enemy of Professor Murri by accepting Bonmartini in the face of his father-in-law's dispraises. Cesco was told the same thing by other doctors in Italy's three largest cities, Milan, Naples, and Rome, as well as in Bologna.[51] He was not just any applicant who could slip unnoticed into the lower levels of the medical network; Professor Murri would always know who had disregarded his eminent opinion by hiring Cesco.

Cesco came back from Naples deeply dispirited:

In my room, on the desk, I found the flower vase empty. When she returned from Salsomaggiore, I had all of her vases full of flowers.

He is nervous, too, about the family's finances:

June 19. With these service people we need to start over, tabula rasa, or, I know it better than anybody, we'll have to move back to Padua because here the house is a Babylon with wild expenses that I can barely restrain.

He discovers that Linda sent the wardrobe woman out to sell one of her dresses:

It makes me sick to think that she's making me out to be a miserly figure who doesn't give her enough cash despite all that she makes me spend. I asked her not to sell our clothes because it compromises both my dignity and hers. I told her that if 2,500 lire was in-

sufficient, I would arrange to give her more rather than have her do such things.

Early on the morning after Cesco's return from Naples, Linda dispatched the children on a train excursion with a maid. Cesco thinks "Her Highness" is keeping them away to spite him. Linda urges Cesco not to go to Venice in the summer but to spend the months with her in the Murri villa at Rimini. "That way you would make a step toward peace with my family," she says. Rimini, fifty miles from Bologna and on the Adriatic, was still a quaint provincial town in 1902, known for its anarchists and murders rather than its beaches, though that was not what bothered Cesco about the place. He had decided to take the children to Venice, he said, because of its proximity to Padua and Cavarzere, where he could attend to his affairs. Indeed, from any high tower in Venice, one could see Padua, twenty-five miles and one hour away.

For the remaining weeks, Cesco records his day-to-day irritations and the pleasure he derives from indulging Maria and Ninetto. He complains that Linda makes him the disciplinarian of the servants, putting him in the position of having to refuse their requests. He cannot resist inviting her to see the tenor Bonci in *Rigoletto* in Faenza.* Linda asks her father if he thinks it's all right to go, but Professor Murri instructs her to decline.

Tonight she came home at nine, apparently having dined at her father's. She had a muzzle a yard long and brought regards from her family—not to me, but to the German maid.

---

*Alessandro Bonci joined the Manhattan Opera the next year, providing a competitive attraction to Enrico Caruso, who would make his Metropolitan debut in *Rigoletto,* also in 1903. As an opera-goer, Bonmartini probably heard the Neopolitan Caruso before the latter emigrated. Bonci was actually a neighbor on Via Mazzini. Faenza was a city of 39,000 between Bologna and Florence, famed for a richly decorated type of Renaissance pottery, faience.

June 26. Today Her Highness asked me, crying, not to deprive her of the children next month. Seeing that she's not well, I had them call Dr. Silvagni without her knowledge.

There the record ends. As the summer wore on, Cesco thought more and more about returning to inexpensive Padua. Perhaps he was hoping to recapture the life he had with his wife before the fateful autumn of 1898. Linda, meanwhile, went to Switzerland. He thought she was with the wardrobe woman, getting a tattoo to hide the scars left by the first eye surgery, and wrote her his intention to move to a house in Padua near his estate—unless her father gave him a reason to stay in Bologna.[52] The old man, however, vowed that he would rather resign from the clinic himself than hire Cesco. He advised his daughter to seek a new separation, or perhaps even a Swiss divorce.

Cesco had high hopes when he learned that Linda's brother Tullio was coming to Venice in the middle of August, "to make peace in the family," as Linda described the purpose of the trip. Cesco assumed that Professor Murri had changed his mind and was sending Tullio with the offer of an appointment. He received his brother-in-law warmly. The two joked and bantered throughout the visit, Cesco expecting any moment that Tullio would break the good news. They piled the children and a servant into a vaporetto and went picnicking on the Lido, one of the four entrances from the lagoons of Venice to the open sea. The Lido—the "sand hill"—had an attractive caffè on a terrace overlooking the sea. On the beach, the two men engaged in a boyish wrestling match that Cesco won, despite the smaller man's best efforts. But that was the only contest Cesco won. He was bitterly disappointed when Tullio left without so much as mentioning the assistantship.

By then Linda had returned to Venice. Cesco was annoyed when a maid evaded one of his questions, causing him to suspect that Linda was conspiring with the servants against him. Overwrought after Tullio's visit, he made a gesture to fling a chair at his wife but instead threw the chair on the floor. Afterwards, according to two maids, he said, "I'm sorry I did that, Linda, but you know, I was angry." Linda accepted the apology, but she did not forget the transgression.[53] Like so many apparently minor tiffs in the marriage, it would receive intense scrutiny in the Bonmartini murder trial.

Throughout the four and a half months of reconciliation, Cesco remained as he had been for the previous three years, utterly bewildered at the way his life had fallen apart and heartsick over not being able to work as a doctor. The following week, rebuffed in his application for a post in Milan, he gave orders for the move to Padua. On August 19, he wrote to Cervesato from Venice that he was again afraid his wife had a lover. But that was not the only fear haunting him. Cesco's diary had stopped on June 26. When Linda gave the notebook to police investigators, entries for the last two months of his life had been torn out. The document that remained made no reference to the idea that dominated Cesco's last days, an issue he discussed with all of his close friends: Count Bonmartini knew that someone was going to kill him.

The preoccupation took hold of him almost as soon as he and Linda were reconciled in April 1902. Acquaintances reported that in order to avoid a possible assassin, he never walked even short distances, preferring to take a carriage. In Bologna, he carefully locked the several doors that led into the apartment each time he came in and had bolts installed on both the downstairs door leading up to his room and the bedroom door itself. He bolted himself in his room at night and went down each morning to unlock the doors so that his man, Picchi, could bring him the coffee his wife usually prepared. Cesco did not trust the servants and was particularly afraid of the wardrobe woman. Seeing a shadow outside his bedroom window, he had the window taken out. He was known to carry a revolver. [54]

One morning, he woke up itching all over because of some crumbs—his children had been munching cakes in his bed the previous night. The crumbs had fiercely irritated his skin wherever they touched him, so he gathered them up and asked Cervesato to analyze them. The doctor later conceded that the analysis had been too superficial to confirm whether or not the cakes contained a toxic substance. At the beginning of July 1902, Cesco had been deathly ill with diarrhea, weakness, fever, and drowsiness—all the symptoms of poisoning, according to Dr. Silvagni, who theorized that one of the cooking pots in the household had faulty plating and was leaching some harmful chemical into his food. As soon as he was settled in Venice, the mysterious illness cleared up—but not Cesco's suspicions. [55]

A few weeks later, in a trattoria in Padua, Cesco was having dinner with a priest, an old friend, when he broke down and confided that he was a marked man. He even told the priest who it was that was planning to kill him. Cesco had long before given Cervesato the name of the assassin, a name the distraught pediatrician would bring to the authorities as soon as he learned of the murder, just as he had promised his luckless and persecuted friend. Before he left Venice, Cesco told Cervesato again, "Remember, if they find me dead, you know who did it." [56] On August 26, two days before his death, he bought a coffin for himself and a grave site at the cemetery in Padua. [57] He was going to the Bologna house for the last time on August 28 to pay the rent for the preceding quarter year and have the place cleared out. Picchi packed his suitcase with soap, shirts, and collars. There had been no bathrobe, since Count Bonmartini did not use one, and no curling iron, since he never curled his beard. [58]

Before leaving Venice, Cesco celebrated his name day alone with his children. The cook had prepared Pasta Margherita and served the fish that Nonna Gianinna had sent the children from Rimini. Lunch was rather sumptuous in honor of the special day, and the children hugged and kissed their father even more than usual. They gave him a new wallet, purchased by the cook on Linda's orders. Exclaiming over the gift, Cesco transferred the contents of his old wallet at once. A friend remembered seeing Bonmartini at the train station and greeting him as he boarded the 3:19 for Bologna; the man waved to Bonmartini again as his car passed before him.[59] Three hours later, in Bologna, Cesco's killer rummaged through the new wallet. Brown and shiny and full of smiling photos that the count himself had taken of his children, it lay open on the floor next to him when Bonmartini's broken, rotting, and infested body was found by the police.

3. THE WIFE

*Just as focusing on a heavenly star makes the points appear
more luminous the longer one looks steadily into the sky, the
longer I focus on you the more attractions I discover in
you. . . . I would like to see you always, to hear you always.
While traveling, I feel the need to write you what I felt when
seeing you and even more what I suffered when not seeing
you. To be without you is the worst privation.*

*The thought of you obsesses me night and day; but I don't
have anything worthwhile to say, my Linda. Since we don't
make physical love, we are not making love at all if I don't tell
you with words that I love you, and that even if you were not
my daughter, I would love you just the same . . . however ineffectual this anguished love is in soothing your troubles.[1]*

Of the four men in love with Contessa Bonmartini in 1902, her father
Augusto Murri was the most esteemed and obsessed. Honored in Italy
as the healer who in former years had been the personal physician of
the Queen Mother, Margherita, the sixty-one-year old doctor was also
regarded as a scientist and teacher.[2] By the time of his son-in-law's
murder, he had mobilized a score of symposiums and sent a flotilla of
articles into the streams of medical opinion. The wealthy and infirm
came from all over Europe to his clinic, where, as Bonmartini noted
sulkily, Murri commanded shattering fees for even brief examinations;
he was one of the first consultants other doctors turned to in cases
where the patient was famous or the disease obscure. His silver jubilee

had been celebrated in 1901 with the rector of the University and the mayor of Bologna in attendance. In a field where prestige is the layman's only measure of competence, Murri's reputation was unassailable. He was respected by almost everyone who did not know him.

Linda was a little girl when Augusto Murri acceded to his throne in Bologna. In 1875, when she was three, her four-year-old brother Tullio died of what was called "eclampsia"—a quite original misdiagnosis, since that condition occurs only in pregnant women. It was decided later on that the boy's death had resulted from an epileptic seizure. "He was the luckiest of all of us," Linda remarked optimistically, "because he did not have time to taste life's disappointments."[3] Her younger brother was born three months after the funeral and named Tullio, like the dead child, but called Nino in the family.

"The day Tullio died," Professor Murri once wrote to Linda, *"you climbed up on the bed where I had taken my grief and came to me with all the tenderness a baby is capable of expressing, as if to tell me, 'I will fill the emptiness with my immense love.' Then I resolved to do my best—everything possible—to make you happy. I never succeeded. The intelligence and will of one man,"* he added wanly, *"are small things against the compulsions of nature."*[4]

The compulsive nature Linda's father was most helpless against was that of her mother, Giannina. Linda reported that Professor Murri never interfered with her mother's household tyranny, which fell harder on her than her younger brother. She described her childhood as miserable and solitary; both children were tutored at home and did not attend the schools that generally served the youngsters of the professional class. According to Linda's bitter account, Giannina Murri beat her every day, whereas Tullio fell afoul of his mother only when he tried to protect his sister. Giannina Murri's motherly care consisted of carping over petty grievances until she worked herself into an ecstasy of violent rage. She became more unstable with advancing years. The police investigating Bonmartini's murder reported that when they approached the Murri villa where the family was gathered, Signora Murri stood at the edge of the porch and screamed at them about the dead man's worthlessness.[5] Growing up, the children learned to forestall their mother's tirades by subterfuge; by the time they were adults, they were nimble liars. Moreover, clear lines of attachment had developed: Linda to her father and Tullio to his mother.

Linda eventually became the center of her father's life, his constant project, more important to him even than his work. Between Tullio and his father, on the other hand, relations were chronically strained. "What part of our life does he participate in?" Professor Murri complained to Linda.

> *Precisely nothing. He reads, writes, dances, has breakfast and lunch with us, but whatever Mamma and I hold dear is a matter of indifference to him. . . . When we were his age, the men in the Murri family were already married and taking our mamma for walks. Nino is completely alien to that sort of intimate family life. He likes going out with Tabbioni, with Dalla, the Rosinas, the dressed-up girls. Two minutes with us is enough to exhaust his small store of inquiries and responses. . . . I feel more comfortable with you and your suffering than with Nino, who's always splashing about.[6]*

To his father's remonstrances, Tullio replied that it was ridiculous to treat life as if it were a penance. "He thinks he's an excellent son," Professor Murri snickered, "because he cuts a fine figure as a gentleman."[7]

Tullio was not without accomplishments. At the time of Bonmartini's murder, he had attained degrees in both law and literature and had become one of the leaders of the socialist party in Bologna. He liked to write, had composed several verse dramas—Italians of the period having an odd preference for emotions that rhymed—and he was the editor, probably unpaid, of *La Squilla,* the socialist weekly.[8] None of this won his father's approval. *"Nino will never know your kind of deep sadness,"* Augusto wrote regretfully to his daughter in

1899, when Tullio was twenty-five, *"but neither will he know the spiritual exaltation that you reach with your fine sensitivity."*⁹

Linda, adored by both brother and father, was the intermediary between them. It was she who in 1899 persuaded her father to grant Tullio an allowance of 5,000 lire a year—up from 1,200, but usually unpaid—so that he could move out of the family home and live on his own. This was the same amount Linda herself was receiving from her father, in addition to the substantial largesse of her husband. Augusto promised Tullio the stipend so as "to give us both our freedom—freedom for him to order his life the way he wants to and freedom for me not to have to watch him."

"Only you can make him quicken and tremble," Murri commented to Linda. *"The only time he is one of us and not on the outside is when something concerns you."* Otherwise, *"he and I would have nothing connecting us but blood."*

If Murri regarded his son with detachment, he sought a kind of fusion with his daughter. *"I can't embrace you without being pierced by the thinness of your poor body,"* he wrote in 1899,

> *even though I embrace you with the rapture of a lover, with a love that grows every day because every day shows me that you are as virtuous as you are unhappy. Be courageous and steadfast, my Linda. If you live only for others, then take care of yourself, because others love you so much. Good-bye, my Teolinda; your name reminds me of the other woman (my mother) who still possesses my heart.*
>
> > *Good-bye,*
> > *Your Augusto*¹⁰

As a prominent journalist wryly observed, "These are certainly unusual letters."¹¹ When the searchlights of publicity fell on the Murri family, newspapers all over Italy posed the intriguing question of whether the letters from "Augusto" were evidence of incest between Linda and her father—whether, indeed, that guilty relationship had somehow led to Bonmartini's murder. Though the Catholic and conservative press denounced the Murris without hesitation, liberal editors resisted the idea that a great scientist, a man cherished as enlightened and good, was a degenerate. But how was one to explain a father who confessed to feeling "the rapture of a lover," expressed himself in terms of "making love," and assured his daughter that he was capable of loving her outside their filial bond, that is, loving her as a woman? In the early letters to Linda, Professor Murri is clumsy and unable to speak plainly on the subject of sex. His overweening impulses appear to be cerebral rather than carnal. He plunges into dense abstractions when discussing sexuality, as if to put at a distance a subject that is causing him conflict. If we are to believe his words— *"Since we don't make physical love"*— there was no incest, at least not in 1899.

But if the paternal embrace was not at that time overtly sexual, it was abnormal on both sides, and everybody saw it. Linda required every man she loved to be a doctor; but even then she did not allow any lover to disengage her from her absolute model and husband prototype, her father. To Murri, Linda was superbly educated (though her haphazard instruction ended entirely when she was sixteen), a goddess far more developed emotionally and intellectually than the blemished mortals who surrounded her, especially her suitors. Murri turned Linda into a surrogate wife in everything except—perhaps— sex, where he was already overburdened, although he and his wife kept to their separate bedrooms.[12] In correspondence that he and Linda took care to hide from Giannina by means of codes and false addresses, Professor Murri abandoned himself to complaining to his daughter about the sexual expectations of her mother. *"Despite the accumulated irritations of all these years, she demands that I be still on my honeymoon! What craziness!"* he exclaimed. *"To live with her means you have to constantly stifle your own thinking. If you say what's in your mind, lightning will strike. Without even considering her as a woman or wife,"* he wrote in 1900, in a remark Linda would echo word for word in discussing her own marriage, *"we are so dissimilar psychologically that through the years we have lived together she has become steadily more repulsive."*[13] Any moment she might *"blow up some trifle into a monstrous affair."* Unlike Linda, however, Professor Murri expected to die by the side of his spouse, still enduring *"a drone of grievance stopped only by eruptions of raving fury. It makes life despicable."*[14] By contrast, his daughter and confidante was perfect. All her years, Linda carried with her the superiority complex her father induced in her as a young girl, when he treated her as an equal—or better, as an extension of himself.

Only one man vitiated Linda's enthrallment to her "Augusto." Carlo Secchi was a medical student when he first saw Linda cowering behind the door of her father's study. He was twenty-seven. She was eight and in anguish because her father was shunning her. It seems her mother forced her to drink nauseating goat's milk every morning. One day a maid saw her dumping it out of a window. According to Linda's autobiography, which is by no means to be trusted, her parents questioned her and she lied even to her father about pouring out the milk. He felt so betrayed that he joined her mother in refusing to speak to her—or look her way—for an unbelievable six months.[15]

"Why are you hiding?" Secchi asked gently.

"Because Papa is angry with me."

"Poor little thing," he said, stroking her hair, "You don't have to be afraid of your father."

For decades Linda Murri would remember that first touch of Secchi's hand. Well-mannered, mild, and diffident, Secchi hardly looked like the love of anyone's life in those days, and he looked even worse later on. However, he was Murri's fondest protégé and the only one taken into the family. He visited the professor at home several times a week and eventually occupied that enviable position, Murri's assistant in the clinic. Secchi was as captivated by the little girl as she was by him. When Linda was thirteen, he began giving her daily training in gymnastics. By the time Giannina Murri noticed the attraction between Secchi and her daughter, Linda was sixteen and their special relationship, though always supervised and constrained, had been going on for eight years. Considering Giannina's reputed shrewishness, the letter she sent Secchi was a masterpiece of tact.

> *Dear Carlo,*
> *It would be contrary to my customary frankness if I didn't*
> *say that in stopping your visits you show that you understand*
> *perfectly well the unfortunate situation in which we find*
> *ourselves. . . . I wanted to thank you for having surmised our wishes.*
>   *Fondly,*
>   *Giannina Murri[16]*

The break with Secchi was somewhat protracted by several long letters exchanged between Professor Murri, who couldn't blame anyone for falling in love with Linda, and Secchi, who claimed to have only an avuncular affection for her and offered, in passing, to kill any future husband who might make her unhappy—a remark that would haunt him later on.[17] Giannina Murri finally ended the tortured discussion with a curt letter and a warning that if Secchi encountered her and Linda on the street, he was not even to greet them.

There were no encounters. Though Bologna held more than 100,000 people in those days, only a few blocks separated Secchi's quarters from Linda's. The Murri apartment looked out on the famous leaning towers, beloved by Dante, where main streets and carriages converged—but not Secchi and Linda.[18] He never saw her at the Sunday concerts in the Giardini Margherita, nor at the Saturday markets set up around the Piazza Comunale, nor at the university, where he daily passed the busts of female professors as he went in and out of the faculties spread throughout the neighborhood.[19] To Linda's pained inquiries, her mother replied that Secchi was too old for her and had evil habits. When the moping persisted, her mother reported that Secchi expressly stated he was not in love with Linda, only amused by her flirting with him; he was complaining to everybody in Bologna that her infatuation had ruined his pleasant relationship with her father. Linda stopped talking about him. After a time a rumor reached her that he was engaged to be married. Yet years later, when he was interrogated about his relationship with the young girl, Secchi said, "I never denied even then that I loved her intensely."[20]

It is not clear why the Murris dismissed Secchi as a conceivable suitor. Since he was a doctor and Professor Murri's assistant, he might have succeeded him and enjoyed a fine career. He was a man of certain ability. After leaving Murri's aegis, he developed a thriving practice and established his own clinic with fifteen beds at 3 Via Garibaldi. A number of prominent doctors—Silvagni and Gotti among them—had their offices and clinics in nearby buildings, for if sickness was everywhere in Bologna, treatment was quarantined within a few neighborhoods. Nevertheless, Secchi had been sent away in 1889, and within three years Linda was married to Cesco. Count Bonmartini was apparently more acceptable to the Murris than Doctor Secchi.

Linda claimed later that her mother talked her into going through with the marriage, coercing her with arguments such as "Haven't you looked in the mirror? You're ugly, you know. And disagreeable, with your dry manner. You have no spirit, no poise. Besides, everybody knows you ran after Secchi. Who will want to marry you after that? At least Bonmartini is from Padua and doesn't know about it."[21] But the notion that she was pressured is one of Linda's persevering fictions. Her own overheated letters to her fiancé show that she needed no urging to marry Bonmartini. If not love, then the illusion of love for the young nobleman had somehow been powerfully created.

The courtship was not smooth. Giannina Murri took a dislike to Cesco and strictly guarded the girl's contact with him. "I would like to give you to him without his even having kissed you," she was reported as saying—a peculiar idea even a hundred years ago.[22] She rained blows on Linda, according to Linda, for allowing Cesco to kiss her on the cheek, even while Linda herself was caressing his letters, the air in which she pictured him standing, the shoulder of a blouse where he had furtively laid his head.[23] Her father's feverish attachment meanwhile continued unchanged and unchallenged through her engagement and marriage. When Professor Murri was out of town, he wrote to *"my Linda, my good Linda,"* every day, *"kissing you again and again, not knowing words to express so much love."*[24]

Year after year, Tullio witnessed the ardent raddling between his father and sister without being able to participate in it except as a bystander. Rather than competing with Linda for his father's love, he seems instead to have drawn a little favorable attention to himself by assisting at the worship services Augusto Murri conducted for his daughter. Tullio's part was to induce the sad idol to laugh—or rather, to pretend that's what he was doing. In truth, all the Murris, including Tullio, cultivated Linda's moroseness like the exquisite attribute of a shade-seeking flower. *"I love her with an immense love,"* Tullio wrote to a friend, *"as much as my parents and perhaps even more, because the tenderness is bound up with infinite pity for that poor being who has no blood, flesh, or joy, who seems put on this earth only to suffer."*[25] Early on, Linda realized that suffering was what she did best, since her saturnine disposition received so much respect. She was brought up to be depressed, as other girls are brought up to be ballerinas or debutantes. "I was born out of spite," she apparently remembered, "and grew on a diet of sadness."[26] Loving Linda and her sadness was for Tullio a kind of mystic ecstasy, unhealthy to outside observers but never questioned by the family.

During the investigation of Bonmartini's murder, there was a great deal of talk about incest between Tullio and Linda. The police invited all the family's friends to give their impressions of the brother-sister relationship; those who were not interrogated opined anyway in the press.[27] Naturally, sex was easier to suspect than to prove, and nobody was able to prove anything more sordid than obsession on Tullio's side. But in the rabid publicity about incest, Tullio turned into a kind of surrogate for Professor Murri. It took courage to attack a revered scientist on such grounds, whereas Tullio, being a socialist, was in bad odor anyway with respectable people. Men who were too careful of their careers to voice unspeakable conjectures regarding Professor Murri could imply anything about Tullio without fear of alienating the young man's defenders—Tullio's friends were already alien to good society. The police went over and over Tullio's letters, trying to wring out attainting phrases; the most they could extract were a few suggestive remarks. Tullio's preoccupation with his sister, though intense and agitated, did not appear in his letters to be as morbid or unhealthy as his father's. Even when he wrote that he would like to "merge" with her so as to give her body some of his health and spirit, the statement had no erotic charge.[28] Only once in his ample correspondence, in a long letter intended to comfort her, was his closing kiss "long and interminable."[29]

Linda thus married Bonmartini with her brother's encouragement and her father's perfunctory blessing, bringing a trousseau of underwear (a dozen winter and summer corsets "for sleeping") and a promise in place of a dowry.[30] She left the fury of her parents' home knowing very little about the gentle count who claimed to love her. After Cesco's death, Linda wrote her own diary of sorts to give her side of their marital conflict. "It never passed through my mind that he was rich," she wrote of her wedding day, though she was memorably disappointed when he brought her to his "palace" in Cavarzere.[31] They were welcomed not by the butler she expected but by Don Tullio, the nursemaid-tutor-priest who had been raised by Cesco's mother and in turn raised Cesco after her death. He met them on the stairs with a trembling lamp. She was buffeted by the smell of rancid oil and old, unused rooms somewhere beyond the arc of wan light. The coachman who had driven them to Cavarzere came in, the odor of the stable clinging to him, to serve a dinner she found so affronting in its simplicity that she remembered every plate: prosciutto, antipasto, minestrone, a piece of capon, and some fruit.[32] The room was frigid, she recalled, since they hadn't even made a fire for her in the Franklin stove. Cesco had neither the substantial house that estate owners usually raised for themselves nor did he concern himself with the religious trappings—the customary fast days, the private chapels—with which the rich tried to atone for their accumulations. Besides the priest and the maid-coachman, only three desiccated servants staffed his palace. In Bologna, the Murris had been cared for by six full-time domestics and several others, such as seamstresses, who provided special services. In the 1890s, the best houses had gas heating, electricity, and running water. Cesco's ramshackle palazzo had neither heat nor light, and water did not run; it came slowly, sullenly, with a porter who dragged his feet all the way from the hand pump. But with Cesco's encouragement, Linda took possession of the old place, purchased furniture, and set about transforming it into a suitable habitation for a well-bred Bolognese bride.

She could not so easily transform her husband. "My poor Cesco," as she always referred to him after his death, "had been raised in an unrefined and narrow-minded ambience and had no practice in civility. He didn't know the simplest duties that society imposes." When visiting the Murris, "he, poor thing, committed little indelicacies at the table"—leaning toward her and whispering in her ear, for example—that quite distressed her family.[33] Such venial breaches were deplorable to Linda because her parents deplored them. Linda objected to Cesco's management of his tenant farmers. In particular, she wanted him to increase the supply of fresh water to their cottages, according to her later accounts, and to be more liberal with the house staff. She had been taught by her father to treat servants as equals, to apologize for any rudeness toward them, and to be mindful that they were not in a position to defend themselves against an employer's unkindness. She seems to have practiced these admirable principles sincerely. But it is not surprising that Bonmartini did not share her demotic ideals since, for the time and place, they were radical notions that neither the nobility nor the bourgeoisie, and certainly not the rural padroni, subscribed to. A third of the country's population were peasants, angry and explosive on one hand but also deeply conservative and orthodox. Up until a few years before Bonmartini's marriage, the contadini had paid compulsory tithes to the Church.

Of all the people in Italy, they were the least receptive to socialist egalitarianism. According to Cesco, people who were born into the landlord-tenant relationship understood its conventions, unlike those, he twitted her, who "came up from the bottom."

"I treat my tenants like everybody else does," he protested, "no worse."

"In my family, we expect to treat our dependents better than other people do," said Linda.

"Of course," he retorted. "You're socialists."[34]

All day, Cesco did nothing, Linda complained, "and if it's possible to think of nothing, then certainly, he thought of nothing," content to spend whole hours sitting near her, wherever she was working. "I never gave up . . . trying to raise that poor mind," she wrote, even while "resigning myself to the emotional inferiority of my husband."[35] Linda's parents heartily joined in disparaging him and his background. Writing to a family friend soon after Linda's marriage, Professor Murri observed, "Her not writing to you shows how very sad she must be. She is in the country near Padua just now, with relatives of her husband. Good people, to be sure, but barely above ground level either emotionally or intellectually. She is grateful to them, but one can't expect her to be happy."[36]

In 1894, the Bonmartinis' first child, Maria, was born. "I wanted to nurse her myself," Linda wrote, "but Papa would not consent to it."[37] She made do with a wet nurse and Nestlé farina. By 1896, Linda's plans for her husband's poor mind seemed to be succeeding. Yielding to the wishes of his wife and in-laws, Cesco entrusted his estate to a manager and registered at the University of Camerino, in the medical school where Augusto Murri had studied thirty-four years previously.[38] That was the end of Linda's life as a provincial noblewoman: she returned to live with her parents in Bologna. Without regret she left the olive orchards festooned with necklaces of vines, left fields of sugar cane that braced still more grapevines, never to see them again. All differences with her mother forgotten, she settled back into the second-floor apartment at Via d'Azeglio, just between the central square* and the Two Leaning Towers. Her father became father to Maria and to the second baby, Ninetto, born during Cesco's first school term. Cesco stayed with the Murris, too, during school vacations. For three years, Linda showed no desire to return to a household of her own with a husband who, though temporarily absent and permanently inferior, was her own. Cesco's country flaws were all the more visible in the glare of Bolognese society and her parents' scrutiny. "I had hoped contact with my father would civilize him," Linda said concerning the move to her parents' house. Cesco, on the other hand, looking inside the dreadful nest she had come out of, decided that Linda was a better person than he had imagined. He made the unhelpful comment that the more he observed her "thieving" family, the more her goodness seemed to him a miracle.[39]

During their infrequent sexual contacts, Linda still found "poor Cesco" loathsome. "He was too big and corpulent; his massiveness frightened me, as I was small and delicate." Coitus left her sick for three or four days. When she told Cesco that sex "brought on my sad condition, he had the generosity to renounce it completely."[40] That was in March 1898. Even then, she wrote, he was sometimes bewildered when he found her crying and tried to console her. He could not see that he himself was the cause of her despair. "Cesco's vulgarity, his crudeness in manner and speech, his lack of culture, the shabbiness of his person . . . all of these continually made me more sad, more nervous, sick in body and spirit." He was noble "only in his title," she wrote. "I was unhappy! That is the cruel truth." Before Cesco was halfway through his curriculum, she was calling connubial life her "Way of the Cross."[41]

At least that was how she later recorded the nine years of her marriage in a memoir written when she was seeking to justify herself in the face of overwhelming scorn. Like Cesco's diary, Linda's

*Piazza Vittorio Emanuele II, now Piazza Maggiore, also its name before the accession of King Vittorio Emanuele. Construction of the buildings in the piazza and the adjoining Piazza Nettuno began in the thirteenth century.

memoir was intended as a public document. But the letters she wrote while Cesco was in medical school tell a different story. *"Your letter gave me immense joy!"* she exclaimed in a typical missive. *"Such joy can't be understood except by those who love deeply, deeply, as deeply as we love each other."* She described little domestic events to him—the dress she put on their daughter for receiving visitors, a present brought by one of the guests—along with a dozen uninhibited expressions of affection: *"How awful it is to be separated. Reading your description of your suffering made me ill. I would have sent you my blood if that could have helped. If you catch even one cold, I will die of it."*[42] Linda clearly thought she loved her husband until something happened that turned her completely against him.

That something was a chance encounter with Carlo Secchi. In July 1898, Linda saw him in Rimini, but they did not speak. Then, the following September, just after Cesco left to begin his third-year studies, Linda met her old love again. They were both at a reception given by Marchesa Paola Rusconi—rumored to be Secchi's mistress—one of those meaningless little parties whereby the upper class of any society confirms its existence and surveys its membership.[43] At this meeting and in trysts that followed, Linda and Secchi sorted out the lies they had been told ten years before. She swore she never would have wed Bonmartini had she known Secchi loved her. He talked of his continuing affection for her father. Secchi was now one of Bologna's leading nose and throat specialists. He had never married; he loved her still. "He knew my soul," Linda said of him. "He was my true husband! At least *he* would have respected my father." Linda had been writing love letters to her husband almost until the day she saw Secchi again. Her letter to Cesco, *"When you are not with me, I'm like some lost creature . . ."* was sent only a week before seeing Secchi at Rimini and two months before the fateful meeting at Rusconi's.[44] Except for Cesco's lovemaking, which she had hated from their wedding night, Linda's fierce index of grievances against her husband began only after Secchi re-entered her life.

Out of his vast inexperience, Professor Murri tried to counsel his daughter. *"I don't deny the existence of this sort of passion,"* he wrote to Linda, *"I deny that it's necessary. It is like a sickness of the mind. Whoever has it is an unhappy soul, not a criminal, unable to enjoy things in life that are more real and easier to pursue. Instead, he is tormented and suffocated by desire."*[45] Professor Murri thought a consuming love was like an argument which, if shown to be counter to accepted principles, could be set aside. He thus tried to point out mistakes in Linda's reasoning. Faced with his daughter's obstinate passion for Secchi, he finally despaired of curing her "disease."

"I feel oppressed seeing that all my will counts for less than a grain of sand and that you, whom I love more than myself, are destroyed by accidental meetings, meddling friends, calculated matchmaking. If I am so powerless when confronted by evil, then life isn't worth living, as you say yourself. I kiss you again and again. . . ."[46]

Cesco came home to Bologna during his semester break at the end of 1898. It was during that unhappy Christmas vacation that he began his first woeful diary. In her own *Memorie*, Linda commented, regarding that period, "If Cesco had made one step toward me, I could have returned to him and somehow managed to find life bearable. I would not have fallen, I think, and would have kept intact my dignity as a woman; all our ruin would have been avoided. Alas! He couldn't change."[47]

In January 1899, Linda went to San Remo on the Italian Riviera with the children, ostensibly for her health. It was this trip Cesco described in his diary when he stated that it hurt him to see his children go and irked him that his father-in-law had wriggled out of sharing the expenses. After Professor Murri returned to Bologna, Secchi secretly joined Linda in San Remo. He was introduced to the children and servants as Carlo Borghi, "an engineer from Florence." Meanwhile, Linda began a correspondence with Cesco's cousin, protesting against Cesco's suspicions concerning her and Secchi, and asking Valvassori to persuade Cesco to agree to a formal separation that would leave her with custody of the children.[48]

"He [Cesco] knows my character, and now he knows what's troubling me. Why is he trying to uncover some secret guilt in my dissatisfaction with him when there are clearly so many legitimate reasons for it?" At first, she wrote, her tactfulness made her refrain from telling Cesco he was repulsive. "But now that he knows everything, can he believe that it's a small matter for a woman like me, born for love, to spend a lifetime attached and subjugated to someone who opposes all her hopes and ideals? Isn't that alone sufficient to explain the miserable state I am in, both physically and mentally?" She had one complaint against her father, "my dear, adored papa," as she called him repeatedly. It was that "he induced in me such excessively delicate feelings."

The separation came in April 1899.[49] Linda and the children moved into an apartment paid for by Cesco, while he went to the Hotel d'Italia during breaks in his university schedule. According to their recollection, Linda and Secchi did not become lovers until the following autumn, when he came to her one night after everyone else in the house was asleep. Thereafter, Secchi's nurse, Tisa Borghi, served as their go-between. Throughout that year they had been meeting at the Marchesa Rusconi's. Finally, in December 1899, both Linda and Secchi received a courteous letter from their hostess asking them not to visit again but also assuring them that she would not gossip about their relationship. The letter provoked a vicious response from Tullio:

December 1899
Signora Marchesa,
Your vile and villainous offense against my sister has been allowed to pass only because . . . your being a woman, I cannot whip your snout, as otherwise I would do.

Tullio Murri[50]

The following month, January 1900, Linda visited Cesco in the Rome hospital and contracted her well-known eye infection while returning from Sicily. By now, knowledge of the affair with Secchi was spreading. If it was difficult for the lovers to escape the notice of acquaintances, it was impossible to evade the eyes of the servants, the six or seven usually with the Bonmartinis and the Murri domestics who came in and out of Linda's house on various errands. In Bologna, the servants were given the night off or told to stay in their rooms when Secchi visited. Naturally, they figured out why. In July 1900, Linda, Secchi, and the children and servants spent thirteen days in San Marcello Pistoiese, an Apennine retreat about fifty miles south of Bologna.[51] During the vacation, Secchi lived *in famiglia,* except for the one occasion when Cesco visited without warning and Secchi was obliged to keep to his room. According to the story eagerly repeated by the servants, Bonmartini was told that no food was left for him and he would have to dine in a restaurant.

For lovers with maids, there could be no privacy, even seven and a half miles from the nearest road. Frieda Ringler knew all the habits of the "engineer," whom she described as "small, rather fat, with a dark chestnut mustache, about forty." (Secchi was actually fifty when Frieda summarized him.) Once during the San Marcello idyll, Frieda walked into a sitting room attached to Linda's bedroom and found her employer, with a florid face and bare breasts, kneeling in front of a chair where the "engineer" was seated. The maid ran trembling from the room, straight into Tisa Borghi, who had accompanied Linda on the trip. "Tisa questioned me so relentlessly that I ended up telling her what I had seen," Frieda deposed.[52] "She insisted that such a thing was impossible. She tried every way to convince me that I hadn't seen it. I thought of the things the cook had already told me about Linda and the engineer." According to Frieda, Linda called her in the next day. The twenty-five-year-old maid stood before Linda, not sure where to rest her uneasy gaze, as if she, and not her mistress, should feel ashamed.

"Who knows what you must think of me," Linda began. She then told a story of the engineer having playfully untied her blouse while she, mortified, fell to the floor.

"She had me write a note to the engineer," Frieda reported, "in which she said she would not tolerate such jokes in the future, neither with her nor with other people in the house." It seemed an epoch had passed since the time when Linda regarded sex as a curse worse than cramps.

In fairness, it is all too easy to condemn Linda's perfidy, her cruel treatment of a husband who loved her, and her carelessness in exposing her children to a sordid and risky situation. But, like the husband of Browning's Last Duchess, even Linda must have found it difficult to say outright, "Just this or that in you disgusts me" and, having said it, make it comprehensible to outsiders who never had to share her husband's bed. If there are a hundred ways a man can offend a woman of rarefied sensibilities, there are two hundred ways a sexually aroused man can do it. How could she hope to explain exactly what in his lovemaking was distasteful? She reached adulthood in a society that had never heard of Freud or Kinsey. If people were not as prudish as we imagine, neither were they comfortable about violating the privacy of marriage. The respectable lay vocabulary for sexual dysfunction was spare; there was no generally accepted way of measuring normality and no casual airing of intimate problems that were unconnected to medical conditions. Certainly something more than self-sacrifice was behind Cesco's preoccupation with Linda's bowels; he was altogether too fond of her chamber pot. Did he have other noisome quirks that might have repelled any woman not paid to cater to them? If Linda was "sick" after intercourse with Bonmartini but tolerated fellatio fairly well with Secchi, she may have had complaints about her husband that, for once, she abstained from stating openly. It is true she lied to everyone concerning her adultery; but unless she were prepared to give Secchi up, what else could she do? She could have behaved more discreetly, but then Linda was still young—twenty-eight—and reckless and in the grip of a grand passion.

Most of the people who knew about the affair with Secchi—

Linda's brother Tullio, her friends, servants, and several men in the medical community—knew that it was certainly erotic. Among the many love letters from Secchi that came to light after the murder was one deemed too obscene for publication, even in the Catholic press— though it turns out merely to contain some awkward banter that has dapper Secchi revealing himself in outdated slang. Only Professor Murri believed Linda's claims that the relationship was platonic. *"Everything in your letter pleases me,"* he reassured Linda when she first wrote to him apologetically of the romance, *"because you please me in everything."* Regarding Secchi, Murri cautioned her, *"I knew him before you and believe I know him better than you. Which one of us is deceived? But I will treat him well because I know you care for him."* In one letter he urged her not to try to hide from him her longing for Secchi. *"For as long as it lasts, we will suffer together,"* he offered.

Linda and her father endlessly discussed whether she could expect to get custody of her son and daughter if she went to Switzerland where divorce was recognized. Linda seems to have convinced her family that she was being forced to choose between living with Bonmartini and giving up her children. This was the problem that Professor Murri said was burdening her spirit and threatening her health. Yet a legal separation granting her custody was unquestionably available to Linda up until her affair with Secchi became known. Courts routinely awarded control of youngsters to the mother, as Bonmartini's lawyers warned him. In order to gain possession of his children, Cesco would have been required to prove that Linda was in some way—perhaps morally—unfit to care for them. He could not prove such a condition if Linda had no lover. Even with outright proof of immorality, getting the children away from Linda would have been very, very difficult. It was the affair with Secchi, not Cesco's insistence on having the children, that made the danger of losing them a possibility, if an unlikely one, and caused her anguish. As for her physical ills, she was apparently anemic, judging from her emaciation, pallor, and weakness. The surgery she underwent to remove the particle of volcanic ash in her eye resulted in her vision being damaged, and she was diagnosed with nephritis, which she might even have had.

The most accurate diagnosticians were experienced doctors, like Murri, with many dead patients on their souls; they were quicker than inexperienced colleagues to recognize the patterns of certain illnesses, even if they were powerless to affect them. On the other hand, they resisted new findings, just as Murri rejected Bonmartini's opinion that Linda's weakness was caused by a mineral deficiency. Though the bacterial origin of cholera was known, reputable doctors of Murri's age could not give up the notion that "noxious fumes" emanating from damp ground caused cholera and a dozen marshland illnesses.[53] They tested urine as assiduously as modern doctors test blood. To confirm a diagnosis of diabetes, rampant in Italy, the dedicated physician tasted his patient's urine to determine whether it was sweet. Treatments—Murri's or anyone else's—seem counter to any kind of logic. But then, common sense is only common to its own generation. It invariably ends where newer fences overlap the old grounds. Doctors both young and aged worked in the dim light of a period when the only wonder drug in their laboratories was quinine. To relieve the cramps of cholera, they suggested a "counter-irritation" of mustard and turpentine rubbed on the abdomen. They humanely treated diabetes—and much else—with opium, so that people who could not live in health should die in peace.

Professor Murri's prescriptions— fresh air for Linda's nephritis, and emetics, arsenic, and narcotics for everything else—were appalling but perhaps no worse than the dispensations of any other doctor. Whenever Cesco required any travel of Linda, her father came to her rescue by declaring she was too ill to leave home. After he administered his therapeutic barbiturates, she did, indeed, need her bed. Often, however, he ordered a change of air to distract her from her sad meditations. Father and daughter took many long trips until Bonmartini's death ended her restorations.

Linda's only other distraction from herself and her affair with

Secchi was her brother. In 1901, Tullio created a new crisis with his father, influenced, apparently, by his friend Severo Dalla. *"Twenty-seven years of thought, care, continual planning, have brought me to this,"* old Murri fulminated to Linda. *"I have a son who challenges somebody to a duel, like some prince of Savoy, electing for his representatives a cretin and a worshiper of public women. He asks my opinion on such matters as his travel arrangements, but he puts me at a distance when it's a question of his honor or maybe his life."*[54] Dueling was more common than Professor Murri acknowledged—at parties, at the gambling tables, on the floor of parliament—everywhere that young men gathered, and men who were not young as well. In 1898, two years before Professor Murri's diatribe, the editor of Milan's *Il Secolo* died in his thirty-third duel, killed by a rival editor fighting his fifteenth. The year before that, the king's own nephew (a prince of Savoy) fought a duel with a French prince who insulted the Italian army. Tullio had impregnated a married woman whose husband found letters revealing the affair.[55] The husband, an army captain, demanded that his wife leave their home and challenged Tullio to a duel. The crisis was eventually resolved without violence, and both Tullio and his father rededicated themselves to making Linda happy. Professor Murri wrote to a friend, *"I will leave behind a son who is anything but the model I would choose and a poor daughter so unlucky as to meet two men who have made her suffer."*[56]

During the separation from Cesco, Linda developed intense relationships with several women who were later closely investigated. Vittoria Fancini was a maid in the Bonmartini household for two years until Cesco dismissed her in 1899. After Cesco and Linda parted, Linda rehired Fancini for another two years. Rosina Bonetti, the wardrobe woman, was Tullio's longtime mistress, a semiliterate four years older than he. These women, along with Secchi's nurse, Tisa Borghi, were the repository of Linda's secrets. Linda had always encouraged the maids to call her by her first name and to treat her more as a friend than an employer—she had left it to her husband to correct the servants when necessary or deny them requested favors. This in itself was extraordinary behavior by the lady of a well-to-do house. Now she began spending long hours closeted with Tisa or Rosina. No one outside the home was especially aware of these intimate friendships, but the other Bonmartini servants, jealous of the attention to Rosina, were readily conversant with Linda's odd habits. When the authorities asked Linda if Rosina were her confidante, Linda replied, "Rather, I was hers."[57] But the cook, maid, and seamstress protested with one voice that Rosina could not have had so many arresting and complicated secrets to fill the hours Linda spent closed up with her.

After Cesco's murder, many a newspaper in Italy claimed to have information concerning "inconfessable" and "unutterable" relations between Linda, Tullio, and the "base woman" Rosina, whom Linda and Tullio were rumored to be sharing. Since the gossip was printed in the newspapers, people were skeptical. Whereas a large American city of today might have only one or two local news sources, perhaps owned by a single company, Bologna had several newspapers, each one reporting from a different, clearly biased perspective. Those citizens who read at all usually scanned more than one gazette (they were not large) and read opinions from all extremes, since the extreme articles were the most entertaining. Thus they emerged with a kind of balance, even though most newspapers were not overly dedicated to truth. Arguing over the conflicting reports in the papers was a lively pastime of the middle class, which had little taste for straightforward fiction. The Murri case was better than a novel and promised to last longer. The Catholic press eagerly ascribed to the Murri brother and sister every kind of depravity, while the anticlerical papers professed shock at the prurience of the Catholics. A socialist paper trying to defend Tullio called *L'Avvenire d'Italia* "the pornographic Catholic journal of Bologna."[58] *L'Avvenire d'Italia* (The Future of Italy), though strongly Catholic, was in fact a new lay newspaper that launched itself with a relentless anti-Murri campaign. A postcard was circulated picturing *L'Avvenire*'s publisher, Rocca d'Adria, saying his prayers: "Give us this day our daily—scandal."[59] In truth, all the papers that identified themselves with the Church were shameless. Rome's *Il Messaggero,* for example, was known as "the official organ of the murdered, the throttled, and the suicides."[60] The newspaper paid a half lira to the first person who brought it news, which, if sufficiently sensational, would be reported with copious, lurid details. The windfall of rumors concerning Linda and the maids did not strike the newspapers until after the murder, however. While Bonmartini was still alive, the main topic of whispering was Linda's affair with Secchi, and it had not yet been mentioned in the press.

That affair had become steadily more fervent and exposed. Sometimes it seemed the only person in the Emilia region who didn't know about it was Bonmartini. Then suddenly, in March 1902, came the reconciliation. There were many speculations after the murder, when Linda's affair with Secchi was blazing from the newsstands, as to why she had been willing to live with her husband again after two years of freedom, while she and Secchi were more deeply involved than ever. For months she and her family had talked of nothing but divorce, and for the previous two years, she had categorically rejected Valvassori's urging of a reconciliation. Cesco himself was adjusting to the estrangement and no longer pleaded for a reunion.[61]

Professor Murri was against bringing Bonmartini back. He was optimistic that Linda could get complete legal control over the children; but even if she were compelled to put the children in a boarding school, he thought the sacrifice was worth it to get rid of Cesco. Tullio, however, favored the reunion, perhaps because he knew what Professor Murri did not: that if Linda's morals were scrutinized in a courtroom, Bonmartini would be in a stronger position. If Cesco himself did not realize Linda's vulnerability as a model of virtue, one of his friends would no doubt come forth to enlighten him about an affair that had been going on for four years. Two of his colleagues in fact debated whether they should warn Cesco away from this ostensible reconciliation by telling him about Linda and Secchi. In the end, they decided to keep quiet.[62]

And so the pretentious ceremony with Archbishop Svampa took place. Bonmartini moved into Via Mazzini in April 1902, to a bedroom he soon equipped with bolts, and resumed the narration of his grievances in a second bitter diary. According to their agreement, Linda and Cesco were supposed to dismiss their current servants and begin with a new staff. Linda thus fired Vittoria again, but she continued to correspond with her. In her letters, Vittoria called Bonmartini the favorite epithet that all the Murris and some of the servants applied to him: "that ruffian." She suggested that Linda write to her under a false name if she wanted to hide their communications.[63] Though Vittoria was gone from the house, Linda formally hired Rosina, not as a maid but as a wardrobe caretaker, on account of her chronically swollen leg. [64] And, so that Bonmartini would not object to Tullio's mistress—who would presumably be Linda's partisan and Cesco's antagonist on the domestic battlefield—Linda disguised Rosina's identity by giving her a false name: Maria Pirazzoli. Professor Murri had by this time moved his home and clinic alongside Giardini Margherita, to the street that is now Via Murri. He purchased a large, three-story building for 33,000 lire, the amount of his coachman's wages for 110 years.[65] On Via Mazzini, Linda was near both her parents and Secchi. In a fifteen-minute stroll under the arcades, Secchi could walk either to Linda's house or to the city gate, where he could look up from the Indian corn growing in the moat to the splendid windows of the Murri clinic. There was one more detail. Linda rented a small apartment next to the Bonmartini dwelling, in fact contiguous to it, for a fictitious salesman, Luigi Ferrari, the fictitious nephew of Carlo Secchi. When it came out much later that Linda had paid for the lease, people assumed that the apartment was a love nest. There was no linen on the bed, however, and the apartment seems never to have been used.[66] As a final precaution against any true reconciliation, Linda had Bonmartini state in writing that he would expect no sexual contact with her. Thus was the famous reunion effected.

In her memoir, Linda tried to answer accusations that she never intended to find a modus vivendi with Cesco. "They believe that I was tired of him [Bonmartini] because he was uncultivated and of mediocre intelligence. No, it's not true. I was always ready to lift him. I had hoped to make a man of him—noble, good, intelligent! My God!"[67] However, neither her campaign to lift Cesco nor their reconciliation had interfered with her affair with Secchi. Soon after Cesco moved into the Via Mazzini apartment, Linda left for a one-week trip to Salsomaggiore, near Piacenza, where Secchi joined her. It was after this trip that Cesco welcomed Linda home by filling her room with flowers. According to Linda, however, Cesco was more hectoring and narrow-minded after the reunion than before it—and more determined than ever to be her father's assistant.

The last summer of her husband's life, Linda traveled. The railroad was convenient but slow and expensive, though almost everybody qualified for some sort of discount. Trains panted out from Bologna to all the major cities—at twenty miles an hour, with signs posted to remind the patrons, "The polite person does not curse or spit on the floor."[68] Linda's first-class one-way ticket from Bologna to Salsomaggiore, a trip of five hilly hours, cost 15½ lire, whereas a first-class room in the resort (lights included) cost only 3½, or a little more, if the hoteliers were apprised that she was sharing the bed with Secchi.[69]

Meanwhile, Bonmartini, sick with a chronic stomach irritation, settled himself, the children, and the maids in Venice. The seaside was not as restful as we might suppose: Venice contained one and a half times as many residents as Bologna—148,000—even without visitors. Cesco rented the entire second floor of the Palazzo Paolucci on San Toma; the son of Robert Browning was his neighbor. He paid 25 lire a month for gondolas, not counting the tips to unsalaried "hookers" whose abstinent duty was to unfasten the boats from the walls and aid unsteady passengers on and off the water. Through one window, Cesco could see Guggenheim's antiquities shop and the traffic on the Grand Canal—"the most beautiful street in the world"—a block away; and through another window he could look down the labyrinth of lanes paved with stone, brick, and asphalt that led inevitably to the Piazza San Marco. However, like many residents, he may have kept the windows closed: mosquitoes and tourists owned Venice in July, and the narrow canal below the house received sewage from every bedroom window bordering it. Cesco went out infrequently, according to a servant charged with hailing a gondola whenever the family or their guests left home. He had no female visitors except the children's tutor, who glided over every day from the Rialto. Even Cesco's stomach was tranquil there on the bright, smelly water.[70]

Yet it was a summer full of evil portents. On July 14, 1902, the bell tower of Saint Mark's collapsed, all of its 300 feet and 1,000 years crashing to the pavement and destroying the church vestibule.[71] The event muted the festival that always came in the third week of July. Venetians went about crossing themselves whenever they came within sight of Saint Mark's and bought out the trinket campaniles carved by the youngsters at Venice's Industrial Home for Destitute Boys. Throughout all of July, Linda remained in Switzerland where she was to have a tattoo on her eye. Cesco did not know that Tisa Borghi accompanied her—he had been told that Maria Pirazzoli (alias Rosina Bonetti) was going to make the trip with her. Nor did he know that Carlo Secchi met them in Zurich. Linda explained to friends that she was living a life of sacrifice, both in reuniting with her husband and in seeking a cure for her illnesses, although her excursions with Secchi around the Swiss countryside were probably painless. At the end of the month, she came back to Venice without having had the tattoo procedure.

The justice investigating Bonmartini's murder—for in Italy, regular judges conducted murder inquiries—considered this trip to Switzerland an important element in unraveling the crime. Another

element, most critical, was a postcard that was never mailed. The
card was written by Linda around August 12, and it was intended for
Tullio:

> *I can almost imagine what you are telling me about the remarkable
> business: I'll bet it's got to do with A. and that the other actor is
> you. So I've guessed the winning three names! I am very curious to
> hear from you. Dear Nino, I don't hear anything more about S., did
> the medicine work? Write me a signal. Many, many kisses.*[72]

Linda had not seen Secchi for almost two weeks. Was he the "S." she
was referring to? At about the same time the card was written, Tullio
visited Bonmartini in Venice. He drew his brother-in-law into a
friendly wrestling match and affectionately took his leave two days
later, having said nothing about Cesco's becoming Murri's assistant.
Linda returned from Rimini. She and Cesco had the argument in
which he almost threw the chair. Linda then left again for Rimini,
taking Maria Pirazzoli (Rosina) with her. She detoured to Bologna to
see Secchi, but instead of staying at her own apartment there, or the
secret apartment next to it, she stayed at Tisa Borghi's. When Linda
got back to Venice, she told Cesco that the manager of the Bologna
house was asking for the quarterly rent.

Cesco by now had given orders to pack up the Bologna house,
since he intended to move the family—or at least the children, if
Linda refused to go—to Padua. Linda sent a telegram to Rosina, addressed to Tullio, instructing Rosina to pick up a dress in the Bologna
house that Linda wanted to have mended. It was that dress which
Rosina—the lady with the hat—went to fetch on the evening of the
murder, when the portinaia saw her go up the stairs in her hat to
knock on Bonmartini's door.

Secchi, meanwhile, had left Bologna for a vacation in the Apennines, even though he had just recently returned from Switzerland.
He sent Tullio a telegram on August 8, a message that he signed al-
lonymously:

I forgot to tell you I'm waiting for news. I am established at Castiglione dei Pepoli. Best regards. Borghi.

In the four days between August 24 and 28, the night of the murder, more than four letters, some cards, and a blizzard of telegrams were sent between Linda, her brother, Secchi, and Rosina/Maria, all under false names; but of this active correspondence, little survives except a record of the dispatches and a few cryptic messages:

> CONTESSA BORGHI (probably Rosina writing for Tullio) TO CONTESSA BONMARTINI: *Delay departure as long as possible.*
> UNSIGNED (Linda at Rimini) TO ROSINA BONETTI: *Do what you wanted to do.*
> X (Linda, in Venice) TO SECCHI: *Excuse previous desperate letter. Last news gave back life. Yours faithfully.*

Tullio even sent one card to Linda written entirely in a code of slashes, dashes, and dots. [73] Telephones were in use in 1902—the Vatican library had them—though they were not yet installed in the Murri habitats. But post offices all over northern Italy were open twelve hours a day, seven days a week, and telegrams cost one lira per fifteen words—a day's wages for a maid but a negligible sum for a countess. Linda and her cohorts were thus well served by technology.

The bustling communication among them was not limited to letters and telegrams. There was also a secret conference. After Tullio's visit to Bonmartini in the middle of August, Tullio and Rosina returned to Venice early on the morning of August 26; Rosina went to Linda's house and brought her to the Public Gardens where Tullio awaited them. The Giardini Pubblici was a green space of twenty acres laid out by Napoleon on the southern end of the island, at the opposite end from the train station and the two Jewish ghettos. While Rosina stood a little way off, Linda and Tullio had an animated discussion. According to Tullio, Linda unleashed all her anger against

Bonmartini and expressed her rage at being forced to make impossible choices. She could either move to Padua, stay in Bologna without her children, or sue for a separation and fight for custody in the courts. That, according to Tullio, was all they talked about and why they met in the park. According to Linda, the discussion concerned Rosina. Linda advised Tullio that the time had come for him to marry someone of his own class. A marriage was in fact being negotiated between Tullio and a dowry of 200,000.[74] According to Linda, sister and brother had then discussed the problem of how to detach the devoted, unfortunate Rosina, who sat on a bench just out of earshot. Afterward, Tullio and Rosina returned to Bologna without Bonmartini ever having been aware of their presence in Venice, since all the servants and the children were warned "not to tell Papa that 'Maria' [Bonetti] was here."[75]

Two days later, on August 28, Cesco left for Bologna after his name-day party. The very next morning, Linda began telegraphing friends with the news that her husband was missing and asking as to his whereabouts.[76] As soon as the body was discovered and Linda was notified, Tullio sent a telegram to the detective investigating the murder. He assured the authorities that Bonmartini had, as suspected, kept an appointment with a donna allegra who had then let in the killers; Tullio offered to share the details with the police.[77]

After Cesco's death but before Linda left Venice, she took care of one chore. She called Frieda Ringler to her, gave her 70 lire, and coldly instructed her to get out of Italy. "Tomorrow you must take Train Number 2 for Munich," Frieda quoted her. She accused Frieda of spreading gossip about her and insisted that Frieda was neither to stay in Venice nor return to Bologna. Linda warned her that if she went near the Murris, Giannina was likely to mistreat her. Frieda assumed that Linda was trying to keep her from telling the Murris what she knew about their daughter's relationship with Secchi. Unintimidated, and lacking sufficient money to get to Munich in any case, the plucky Frieda went directly to Professor Murri and related the whole interview. She then applied to her previous employers in Bologna, who took her in.[78]

Cesco meanwhile had one more trip to make in that summer of much travel—his remains were to be sent back to Padua, where he would finally be laid to rest in his newly purchased tomb. Linda was not there to receive the body. She had left for Switzerland, this time with Tullio, her father, her doctor Dagnini, and her uncle Riccardo. Linda and the others returned at once, though not in time for the funeral. Tullio remained in Switzerland.

When Bonmartini's body was found, public opinion was at first tender toward Linda, the sickly, genteel widow who had silently endured her husband's infidelities and abuse and would now be left alone to rear two young children. "Finally you are free of him," wrote one of the dozens of strangers who sent her supportive letters after the murder.[79] But by the middle of September, all the newspapers had found out about the apartment in the Palazzo Bisteghi rented for the use of Dr. Carlo Secchi and his paramour, Linda Murri. *L'Avvenire d'Italia* described concupiscent scenes that might have taken place in the infamous nest. Linda wrote to Cardinal Svampa requesting that he suppress information about her secret apartment, for the sake of her father. Svampa not only permitted the reports to be published; he also released Linda's letter to him, which was printed on September 12 in the respected Turin daily *La Stampa*.

The public then turned on Linda, vilifying her for her presumed atheism, perjury, adultery, lesbianism, incest, participation in murder, and, worst of all, her socialism and privileged upbringing. Svampa was an influential religious and political leader—in Catholic Italy, the two were intertwined, much as they are today in the theocracies of the Muslim world. He began his clerical career as a fundamentalist and extremist but had moderated somewhat by the turn of the century. Like many conservatives, he held the father responsible for the crimes of the son; that is, he believed the tendency to evil was to some degree an inherited condition. In attacking socialism and atheism, he gradually became an antagonist of rationalism and finally opposed even science, which he saw as antithetic to Church teachings. The Murri case became the occasion for his attacks on atheism, as well as the event that pushed him again to the extreme right.

Rosina Bonetti was arrested the day that Italians learned about Linda's and Secchi's apartment. The carabinieri seized nearly everything in her upstairs flat at 97 Via Santo Stefano, though at first little of it seemed important. In addition to a prayer book, there was her savings passbook, which held 35 lire, the last deposit of 15 lire having been made a month before. They decided not to sequester three vases of flowers but gave them instead to her elderly landlady "as they otherwise would have gone bad." Just as the two officers were finishing up their search, they came upon something that they both sat down to peruse: another savings passbook belonging not to Rosina or Tullio or even Linda, but to six-year-old Ninetto Bonmartini. The passbook contained only one lira; the rest of the account, 600 lire, had been withdrawn the previous month.[80] Who had cleaned out little Ninetto's savings, and for what? Had Rosina stolen the passbook and somehow gotten access to the money?

No details of Rosina's interrogation were released; therefore the starved newspapers invented testimony for her. Every day, headlines barked from the newsstands about her deposition—revelations she had supposedly made about life and lust in the bedrooms of the Bonmartini house. Every sort of rumor was printed, then retracted, then printed again with modifications: the count had walked in on Linda and Tullio in an "inconfessable"—the favorite adjective—embrace; then it was Rosina who had seen an inconfessable moment between Linda and Tullio; then Linda who had caught the count with Rosina, and so on. According to *Corriere della Sera,* nothing in Italy's recent history had elicited such an intense public reaction. "Its enormous notoriety has caused an unprecedented sensation."[81] The publicity was in fact just beginning.

The night Linda Murri was arrested, September 12, she was in bed at her parents' villa in Rimini.[82] Uncle Riccardo's wife was in the room with her. Two officers of Bologna's Public Security rang the bell and asked for Dr. Silvagni, Murri's assistant and colleague, who was residing at the villa. They courteously circumvented Silvagni's assertion that Linda was too ill to be moved to the prison. Brought to her room, they explained that the doctor would have to be present while she dressed. "What are you afraid of?" Linda asked. "If I had wanted to kill myself, I would have done it already."[83] Then, without any show of emotion, she slowly and carefully attired herself in a black mourning gown with a gold clock necklace and a crepe hat with a large veil. She did not speak of her children, who were still in Venice. She drank a small glass of liquor brought by her mother and then went down the steps on the doctor's arm, followed by Uncle Riccardo and the two functionaries. At first she had asked to speak to her father, but then decided to spare him the pain of parting. However, as the little party reached the first-floor landing, they heard Professor Murri's footsteps behind them. He ran to his daughter with a cry of "indescribable desolation," according to the arresting officer who tried to describe it.[84] Seizing her hands, he kissed her cheeks and hands again and again as he wept. Though her heart may have been breaking, Linda was outwardly impassive, dry-eyed and mute; every newspaper reporting the arrest repeated the officer's comment about her "feline" self-possession. After a few minutes, the professor released his embrace and Linda was escorted out.

Linda was "captured," according to the police terminology, with every conceivable courtesy. The police commissioner even sat up with the coachman on the drive to the prison so that Linda's doctor and uncle could accompany her. The prison of San Giovanni in Monte was a restored fifth-century monastery, as dark as the grave and attached to a church that was also disconcertingly dark inside. Even in 1902 it was a landmark that impressed tourists who could grope their way to the altar.[85] The Bonmartini apartment where Cesco died was just down the block from the prison and looked out on its imposing roof.

In the prison waiting room, Doctor Silvagni asked for an armchair for Linda but was told that only the director could authorize a chair. The director arrived, Silvagni was sent away, and Gotti, the prison doctor, was called to examine Linda. She was then taken to Cell 28 in the infirmary, a so-called paying room with fairly comfortable appurtenances for which the inmate was charged a fee. She brought 1,100 lire with her to prison. Eventually she was moved to a two-room cell where the nuns who supervised women prisoners made the beds and cleaned the accommodations. These nuns reported that Linda remained exceptionally taciturn and calm, even when signing over the care of her children to Valvassori. She did, however, say several times that she expected to be released within a few days.

The next day Linda was questioned for four hours by two magistrates, led by Justice Augusto Stanzani, the judge who was the head of the *istruttoria,* the fact-finding investigation. The interview was the first of nineteen such interrogations. She was quite composed, neither resentful nor cynical but rather, according to the information released to the press, "very intelligent, clear-headed, and reflective."[86] In the absence of any other information, the newspapers speculated that she was pregnant, a proof of infidelity that would have given Bonmartini a stronger case for getting custody of his children. Therefore, explained the papers, she had plotted his murder. But Linda was acquitted of pregnancy after the nun supervising her showed Dr. Gotti her exonerating rag with its "sparse spotting." Linda's periods were few and irregular, giving encouragement to the rumor.[87] Pregnancy was only the first of many "Linda" theories that had to be abandoned.

The suspects in the Bonmartini murder were arrested by either carabinieri or officers of the public security, and then turned over to the investigating judge. Carabinieri were the traditional policemen of Italy, brightly uniformed in red, white and blue with three-cornered Napoleonic hats appropriate to the Napoleonic law that governed the country. They were organized under the Ministry of War, received military training, and were considered the "first arm" of the Italian army, but they had the responsibilities of a normal national police force and functioned under the Ministry of Justice. They were popular among the people. The officers of the public security overlapped the carabinieri in their duties. Though armed, they were civilian guards responsible to the prefects and the minister of the interior, frequently called upon to investigate thefts, vandalism, "offenses against good customs," and the like. Generally underpaid and undermanned, they were not supposed to investigate ordinary crimes except at the request of an investigating magistrate.

When the police believed a crime had been committed—as when they discovered Bonmartini's body—they reported it to a "judge of instruction," a *giudice istruttore,* in this case, Justice Stanzani. His *istruttorie* records are called *Atti*—Acts—which provide the information for historians examining an event such as the Murri case.

The substance of Linda's interrogation was guarded closely. However, the press soon learned that Justice Stanzani, who was by now in possession of several telegrams using false names, asked her if she ever knew a "Contessa Borghi." Linda at first answered no, but then recalled that she received a telegram signed with that name. She had asked Bonetti about it and was told it was from Tullio, who did not want Bonmartini to learn of his arrival in Venice.[88] This telegram would be important in the investigation and trial.

The day after her interrogation, Linda requested crochet supplies and books; she spent the long prison hours reading and making baby clothes for the poor. She spoke little, either to the nuns or to the cellmates who were occasionally housed with her. But imprisonment failed to isolate her completely. Linda's experience with coded messages and dissimulation served her well in jail. Within three weeks of her arrest, she had begun smuggling out letters, the most interesting one to her lover, Secchi:

> *My Carlo,*
> *I can't tell you how in the middle of this misery, my tortured*
> *thoughts are constantly of you. When I think of what you have*

*suffered and will suffer because of me, it makes me not want
to live. . . .*

  *I am writing these few lines to tell you that as far as health,
I'm not worse, but rather better than when I came to this
horrendous place, so be reassured about that, Angel of my Life; and
to tell you again all the words of love that were ever in the heart of
a woman. Sad as my days are, as despairing as my thoughts are,
you remain always my adored dream. . . . Always, always, always I
will be faithful to you in body and spirit and with my life!*

Linda then wrote not few but many lines swearing her undying love,

  *Oh! my Carlo how many things I would like to tell you. . . . From my
cell I hear the little clock that chimes near your house. Ah! How this
brings me closer to you! At midday, send me a kiss. I will send you a
thousand and a thousand. And be calm because I am calm. I will
defend myself to the last breath, and only for you my dear one. . . .*

  *If the investigators ask me if we ever talked of marrying, I will
say that I didn't want to think about it because I was afraid you
would be severe with the children. And that you told me, "Eh! I pray
God that man lives a long time, because when you are with him,
you love me that much more." It's the truth. I am sending you this
flower given to me by good doctor Gotti, whom I see every morning.
Keep it in my memory and with it this card and eternal kisses.*[89]

Linda gave four letters to a nun who in turn asked a beggar being released from the prison to deliver them. Three of the four, including
the letter to Secchi, were seized by Stanzani. In one of them, Linda
had written to Uncle Riccardo, instructing him to send money to
Rosina Bonetti "so that she will not feel abandoned." Money was a
useful resource in Italian prisons, where inmates' families were expected to supply food and fresh laundry and to pay for the cells. In
another letter, Linda directed her family to let her know they had
received her communication by putting a pomegranate in the meal

they sent her. No pomegranate appeared, as this was one of the letters that was confiscated. The one missive that made it out was a card to Secchi in which she cryptically warned him, *"About the apartment, you should tell the truth."* The card was sent to Severo Dalla, who gave it to his brother Ernesto, who bicycled to Castiglione, where Secchi was still vacationing, and delivered it.

The letters of the prostitute sharing Linda's cell were seized along with Linda's. Poor Teresa Spinelli had tried to communicate with her children. She first informed them that she was sharing two rooms with a celebrity, meaning Linda, and remarked that Linda would not be detained long. She devoted the rest of the letter to pleading with her children's caretakers to dress them warmly so they would not get sick.[90]

A ruckus followed the discovery of Linda's contraband letters. The Belgian nuns supposedly supervising her were taken to task. The interior minister of Italy threatened to prosecute the mother superior, and the nun's own superiors threatened to transfer her to some unspecified discomfort. Doctor Gotti, the source of the flower Linda sent to Secchi, was asked why he was bringing bouquets to a prisoner, especially one who was the lover of his close friend, Secchi. He was obliged to explain that Linda had admired the flower in his lapel and, proud as all gardeners are of their products, he had kindly offered it to her. In an article headlined "Linda Punished," *Corriere della Sera* reported that she had been deprived of a cellmate. She was now spending many hours in prayer, encouraged by the sisters.[91] On October 12, she was interrogated again, and this time her sang-froid broke. The papers reported that she suffered a "violent nervous depression" but calmed down after some hours. Meanwhile, Secchi himself was being questioned by the justice, along with all the servants, relatives, and friends of Bonmartini and the Murris.

Linda's children had been told that both their parents were sick. When she had been in prison two months, Linda sent a letter to Signora Valvassori, asking if the children might write to her. She then received a wistful card from them that had been channeled through

Stanzani's office. Frieda Ringler meanwhile told the justice that when Linda was present, the children were restrained in their expressions of love. But when they were alone with their father, they showered him with hugs and kisses.[92]

Bonmartini himself was all but forgotten—except by his children— in the frantic publicity surrounding Linda and Secchi. Despite many visitors to his grave in Padua, the site was covered only with earth, adorned no longer with flowers—for who, after all, was there to tend the grave? A wreath that had marked the spot was now gone, leaving only a supporting post and a ribbon which in the intervening two months had lost the name of the sender.[93] Another large wreath sent by Tullio Murri had been placed over the coffin the day of the funeral. That, too, had disappeared and was not replaced by the Murris, to no one's surprise.

By this time, even Professor Murri knew that Linda and Secchi had been lovers, despite Linda's insistence to him that their relationship was purely spiritual.[94] With her sex life being daily described in the papers, Linda felt obliged to write to her father, apologizing for having lied to him: "*Perdonami, Papà, mio caro, perdonami*"—Forgive me! Papà, my dear, forgive me![95] It is not clear whether Professor Murri received the apology or whether it landed with other letters on the desk of Justice Stanzani.

Two weeks after the murder, Augusto Murri telegraphed the Italian authorities from Switzerland, requesting an interview. He asked Justice Stanzani to meet him at the Murri villa at the gate of Bologna, asserting that he had information of the most serious nature to impart: he was on his way back to Bologna with the name of Bonmartini's killer. Throughout the night of September 12, as the train skimmed the Italian borderlands, Professor Murri sat austerely in his compartment staring into the blackness, into "an emotional abyss" as the sympathetic Bianchi, reporter for *Corriere della Sera,* characterized the scientist's devastation. The next day Murri met for three hours with Stanzani and two other magistrates. He wept throughout the interview. No details of what Professor Murri said slipped out of Stanzani's closely guarded file. The newspapers could report neither the motive for the crime, the presence or absence of accomplices, nor the connection of Linda Murri to the homicide. They did report, falsely, as it turned out, that after the interrogation Professor Murri went upstairs and committed suicide.

The single fact confirmed by the police concerning the meeting was soon shouted on street corners all over the country. On September 13 the front page of every major newspaper in Italy announced that the man Professor Murri named as Bonmartini's murderer was none other than his own son, Tullio.

4. THE BROTHER

All his short life, Tullio Murri had been unusually caring toward his parents and sister. He was well spoken, intelligent, and courteous to everyone. Whereas Linda grew up in the stifling and turbulent pressures of the Murri home, without even cousins her own age to share her anxieties, Tullio was an extrovert, always out with fellow students, journalistic colleagues, girlfriends. Linda was outwardly reserved; Tullio was affable— a nice man, as he was characterized by everyone except his father, who distrusted congeniality and was attracted to distress. As newspapers did not yet print photographs as a matter of course, reporters covering the Murri case informed readers that Tullio was not handsome but had an aristocratic head and beautiful teeth.[1] It was in fact a bourgeois head; Linda was the only Murri with a title, acquired through her great sacrifice in marrying Bonmartini. Tullio held legitimate claim to his teeth, however, at a time when noteworthy teeth were not commonplace even among young people, and painless dentistry did not exist, except what was painless for the dentist.

People who knew Tullio were aware that he was excitable and temperamental. But outsiders found it hard to accept the idea that such a shockingly brutal murder could be committed by a man of Tullio's education. University attendance was high in Italy, but forty percent of the people one encountered from day to day could not write their names.[2] College graduates in any profession were considered quite simply a better class. Tullio had all the credentials of a sensitive youth. He had enrolled in the University of Bologna when he was sixteen and in 1894 received a degree in law, then part of the undergraduate curriculum, at the age of twenty. While still at university he had organized a student socialist organization that was noisy enough to irritate Cardinal Svampa, the righteous representative of Bolognese conservatives.[3] Tullio had won prizes for two verse dramas: "David Rizo," written at the age of nineteen, and "The Conspiracy of Milan," written at twenty-one.

In 1898, when Tullio was twenty-four, riots broke out in several major cities over the high cost of bread. Some of the demonstrators were shot by nervous policemen, an incident that led to more violent disorders. Eventually the army was called in and martial law was declared in four provinces. Newspapers were suppressed. Hundreds of people were shot during skirmishes and thousands more arrested. Socialist leaders were pulled into jail for no specific reason and given long prison terms by military tribunals—the socialist leader Filippo Turati was sentenced to twelve years.[4] The government cracked down on leftists of all stripes—prohibiting meetings, carefully monitoring publications, watching party functionaries. Tullio was sufficiently well known as a socialist writer that he had to go into hiding for several months to avoid arrest, until a new government was formed that lifted martial law and restrictions on the press. When he emerged from hiding, he had become a political activist almost by default.

Tullio never practiced law. This may not have been his own capricious choice. One prime minister called unemployed lawyers the truly "dangerous classes" in Italian society, and perhaps he was right, since they turned up as leaders of the socialist, anarchist, syndicalist, and later, the Communist parties.[5] A third of all Italian students read law. Each year, the universities were steadily producing 1,700 lawyers, an intellectual proletariat that was chronically in need of clients and, in desperation, sought posts in government and journalism. Tullio said that he became disillusioned with the Italian system of justice soon after obtaining his license—a system he probably never had a chance to enter. He therefore took a second degree in 1901 in the traditionally fallow field of literature, where unemployment after graduation surprises no one. He continued writing fiction and poetry, and contributed articles to socialist newspapers. In 1902 he was elected secretary of the provincial council of Bologna in a popular election, winning over the well-known writer Giosuè Carducci, a moderate. The same year, Tullio was named director of *La Squilla* (The Trumpet Call), the organ of the federation of Bolognese socialists.

Bologna was the party's fortress, braced by both industrial laborers and landless agricultural workers. In fact, in 1904, while the Murri case was still being investigated, Bologna would be paralyzed by a huge general strike incited by socialists. There was a socialist popular culture in the city—or rather, a counterculture—and a socialist morality. The party tried to rival the Catholic organizations in ritual fervor, charitable work, and initiatives for social reform— day nurseries for working mothers, breakfast programs, and the like. Socialism meant anticlericalism. The May Day processions competed with traditional religious festivals. "Socialist funerals" with bands and banners tried to give the worker a more promising send-off than he could hope to receive from the Church. There were even socialist baptisms, at which the infant was dedicated to suffering humanity: "You will struggle for the redemption of the class to which you were born; you will be a champion of socialism, the light of the future."[6] At twenty-eight, Tullio was in a position to exercise some influence in the socialist party, which was still a young party of young idealists who, it seems evident, had a lot to learn about entertaining crowds.

Like many middle-class intellectuals in the left and center, Tullio had never for a moment experienced the working class privation, anxiety, or grinding labor that he inveighed against so passionately in his articles.[7] In the caffès around the Two Towers, where he did his writing, he was not exactly a member of the idle rich but rather part of the jobless upper class that could be found reading newspapers at sidewalk tables all over Italy. When he fervently attacked the "ferocious bourgeoisie"—"ferocious" and "atrocious" being his favorite adjectives—he was attacking his own class, with no apparent awareness of hypocrisy. Regarding the "atrocious" Boer War that was raging in South Africa, he wrote, "Our voice will not have much effect from afar and not be of the least use to the poor victims of the ferocious bourgeoisie that is taking away their country, family, and life."[8]

Meanwhile, Tullio's country was the theaters and dance halls that ringed the university. Trams and horse drawn omnibuses heading for one or another of the city gates—Porta San Stefano, Porta d'Azeglio, Porta Mazzini—clattered back and forth all day and evening, as noisy as artillery on the cobblestones in front of his favorite haunts: the Caffè del Corso, Belletti's restaurant and *birreria,* the bar in the Hotel del Commercio. The year Bonmartini died, Eden Music Hall offered apprenticeships to young women in an effort to fill its chronic shortage of chorus girls.[9] In the gambling room of Club Rigosi advertisements had been thoughtfully posted by a German steamship company inviting losers at the tables to try for better luck as emigrants to America. Even the liveliest streets were riddled with poisonous, flowery canals breeding mosquitoes and water lilies with golden stamens. Farther away from the leaning towers and overlooking swampy waters, the shops and houses were more spread out. Vendors sold hares still in coats the color of chestnuts and bunches of two dozen birds still afeather. Tullio had no need to go to those markets; he had breakfast daily at the Caffè Ponzio, and always seemed to be able to gather sufficient resources for himself and Rosina to dine where there were tablecloths and evening editions of the newspapers spread among the booths.[10] However, though always comfortable, he was always broke. *"I am perceived as rich in an organization of poor people,"* he wrote to Linda by way of explaining his expenses.[11] Unlike some companions who sat with Tullio in the bistros discussing Marx and Mazzini, Tullio was not poor; he simply had no money.

But it was impossible to think that Tullio Murri had slaughtered poor Bonmartini in order to rob him. Other, more sordid motives must have caused the tragedy. During the days before the murder, Tullio had done nothing out of the ordinary, so far as anyone noticed. He was seen at the usual bars and coffeehouses, lately in the company of a doctor he had met long ago at the university, Pio Naldi. *Dottore* Naldi did not practice medicine any more than *Avvocato* Murri practiced law. He was "stricken with the gambling disease," as writers then described the addiction. Naldi appeared to be an innocuous and scruffy young man, not much different from some of Tullio's other friends, but he was regarded with special disdain by journalists investigating Tullio. Socialists might be disliked by most of the middle class, but they were respectable, with well-placed defenders. Gamblers were considered part of the underworld of vice. Unlike socialists, they had no high-minded newspapers explaining their views, no spokesmen addressing the government. Socialists were elected to the Chamber of Deputies; no gaming representatives stood up in parliament. The anti-Naldi attitude of the journalists mattered: all cases were tried in the court of public opinion before they opened in the Palace of Justice.

The evening of the murder, August 28, Tullio and Rosina looked for Naldi in his usual settings but failed to find him. They had dinner at the trattoria Palazzina until about eleven, one of the popular nightspots in a city that loved the night, and then they walked to the Caffè del Corso on San Stefano. Tullio wrote two postcards, to his mother and sister. They left quite late and went to the railroad station. They waited for about two hours for the train to Rimini, fifty miles and two hours from Bologna, where the Murri family had its villa. Tullio was later described as being extremely nervous. By this time, it was about three in the morning. They came back later that day and behaved quite normally. The afternoon after the murder, while Bonmartini still lay unseen in his bloody apartment, Tullio went to the library after wandering in a few of the surrounding shops. The investigative reporter for *Il Resto del Carlino* saw him in the Archiginnasio* between one and two o'clock. Tullio smiled his recognition as he passed the reporter on the stairs, then went to a table in the reading room and sat calmly absorbed in a volume of Hesiod. The reporter described the incident ten days later.

By that time, Bonmartini's corpse had been dissected and buried and the police were sternly looking for Tullio. The coffin was laid to rest in Padua on September 5 with none of the Murris in attendance, since they had all left the country the day before. The lawyer Riccardo Murri, Professor Murri's brother, notified Justice Stanzani that Dr. Dagnini had ordered Linda to Switzerland for immediate treatment to her eye. Her condition, Riccardo wrote, was considered by the doctor to be urgent. Furthermore, according to the letter, she needed to be accompanied by her brother.[12] Thus, Linda, Tullio, their father, their uncle Riccardo, Dr. Dagnini, and the Murris' cook all boarded the same night train for Zurich. Linda's children remained in Italy. Professor Murri got off the train in Milan, where he met his wife. In the lounge car, Tullio spoke privately with his uncle. Then, as soon as the train crossed the Italian border, Linda withdrew to the restroom and Tullio addressed Dr. Dagnini: "Now that we are on foreign territory and you are no longer obliged to report this information to the authorities, I am requesting that you treat the knife wound in my arm. I was stabbed while fighting with my brother-in-law, whom I killed." Tullio was hoping to escape from Switzerland to America or, failing that, to seek asylum in some European country that had no extradition treaty with Italy. Uncle Riccardo thought Serbia might be the place.

The dismayed doctor refused to rebandage Tullio's arm. They all got off the train at a Swiss station. Tullio went off to find another doctor and a hideout, and Linda and the others returned home. By now, the police had determined that Bonmartini had not been done

*The same municipal archive, then a public library as well, now keeps newspaper accounts of the Bonmartini murder; the Murri istruttoria, i.e., Stanzani's record, is nearby in the Archivio di Stato di Bologna, across the central piazza.

in by robbers or a mistress, but by killers who carefully decorated the crime scene with props they brought in beforehand. The investigators found Linda's and Secchi's secret apartment next door and in it they discovered bottles of champagne that matched the bottle found on the victim's table. Justice Stanzani wanted by all means to interrogate Tullio. The chances are that Tullio would have eventually slipped away to America among some shipload of Italians who were embarking from various European ports by the thousands every month. Despite the unwelcoming attitude of the receiving countries, Italian authorities viewed this exodus of its citizens with benign indifference.[13] With 240,000 surging out of Italy every year, the authorities might never have caught up with Tullio. Every day Italian newspapers speculated on his whereabouts and debated his intentions, while also informing readers of Professor Murri's distraught state of mind. *L'Avvenire d'Italia,* which was always colorful and occasionally correct, placed Tullio in Austria, Germany, Serbia, and Turkey.

But then, on September 12, the police climbed the two flights of stairs to Rosina Bonetti's apartment. The little dwelling consisted of a long bedroom that looked out over Via Santo Stefano and a dark living room that faced the cluttered courtyard and the outhouse downstairs. Rosina was about to flee to join Tullio when she was arrested; her luggage was by the door. In her apartment, which the detectives noted was "very clean," they found the note paper for the letter signed "B."—the one that had been placed near Bonmartini's body. An unsigned telegram from Rimini turned up, among many others, dated August 28, the day of the murder: *"Do what you want. Baggage ready. We'll all be together tomorrow."*[14] Rosina was in police custody. Three days later, it was Linda who was in prison.

That changed everything. Tullio may have been a butcher, but he was hardly the man to leave his sister and his lover to bear the consequences of the crime. He had written to his father. Now Professor Murri went to Switzerland to meet him and, after long discussion and deliberation, notified the authorities that his son was coming back to Italy to give himself up, as Tullio himself wrote, "to put things aright and free my sister, who is innocent."[15] Tullio was thus arrested on the Austro-Italian border and interrogated in a prison near Verona, where he gave his first deposition, a document he later elaborated into a memoriale for the justices. He hotly denied any incestuous relations with his sister and insisted that neither Linda, Rosina, nor Naldi had any part in the murder. He confessed to being the sole guilty party, without accomplices or instigators, describing minutely how he killed his brother-in-law and why.[16]

Tullio said that he waited for Cesco outside the Palazzo Bisteghi and even saw a carriage overturn just before the count's carriage pulled up. (The collision, the interrogators noted, actually occurred after the count was let down.) "Do you seriously intend to move to Padua, knowing the anguish it will cause my sister, sick as she is?" Tullio asked as he met Bonmartini.

"Linda doesn't have to come if she doesn't want to," Cesco answered. Their conversation continued as Tullio followed him in but was interrupted by Rosina inquiring after the dress; Cesco told Rosina to return the next day. Tullio protested that Linda would be separated from the children unless she followed Cesco to Padua. Cesco pointed out that Tullio was interfering in his business.

"My sister's life is not only your business," Tullio reported answering. "If Linda dies, I'll kill you."

"Instead of coming here to threaten me," Bonmartini was quoted as saying, "you'd do better to tell that scoundrel of a father to keep his promises!"

According to Tullio, he then "lost the light of reason" and punched Bonmartini in the face, knocking him against a wardrobe. Regretting the attack, he took a few steps toward Cesco to help him up. "In the shadows of that darkening room, in that instant of intense excitement, I saw him put his hand down, I don't know if toward his pants pocket or toward the chair next to him. Then the gleam of a knife blade!" Tullio described how, as they struggled over the knife, Bonmartini cut Tullio's arm.

"And here began an atrocious struggle," Tullio wrote, "body to body, I desperately holding on to his wrist and he trying to free himself and stab me again. . . . The blade that he still grasped wavered terribly between his face and mine." Tullio commented that it was probably during this struggle that he received four cuts on his arm. Finally, with both his hands on the knife handle, he was able to point the blade toward Bonmartini, and "in a flash" the blade "cut horribly into his chest." Enraged by the wound but still holding the knife, Bonmartini redoubled his aggression and the battle became even more fierce. They rolled on the floor, knocking over plants. Neither of them shouted, sensing that this was "a fight to the death" and that any interference from outside would come too late. With Cesco on top of him, Tullio was hemorrhaging and losing strength. "Life or death depended on my seizing the single weapon, a few centimeters away, that would kill either him or me." He finally was able to grasp the knife and bury the blade "two or three times" into Cesco's neck. Cesco tried to regain the knife, but his movements were ineffectual. "The fight was over." Fearing that his report of what had happened might not be believed, Tullio admitted setting up the champagne glasses and the note from "B." and leaving the bloomers, which he found in a dresser, to simulate a tryst. He took the money and jewels so that Bonmartini would appear to be the victim of a robbery. He washed his wounded arm and finally left the apartment, he said, late that night.[17]

Typically, in a murder investigation, the istruttore judges asked the accused to write down his description of what happened, without consulting lawyers or other defendants. This memoriale, the first of several by Tullio, ran to 10,000 words. On learning of the deposition, Linda wrote at once to Cardinal Svampa, confirming that Tullio's version of the murder was the truth. "As a fair man, I beg you not to try to find fault in this absolute confession, the holy truth given by my poor father."[18] Of course, it was her brother who had offered the version, but Linda apparently thought that associating her father with the deposition would influence Svampa, and for good measure, she added a smattering of Christian pieties. A year later, after seeing the autopsy report, Tullio amended his confession to declare that the first wound to Bonmartini had been not to the chest but rather to the neck.

Tullio's was a good story, well suited to the requirements of a twenty-eight-year-old still desperate to be regarded as a model son. Bonmartini had not merely affronted him. That could be borne. He had insulted his father, whose name was worth defending. More important, the story absolved Tullio of premeditation, the one element which, he knew, having been trained as a lawyer, was absolutely critical to his defense. Throughout all the subsequent months of the investigation, Tullio remained steadfast as a tick on two points: his sister had no part in Bonmartini's death; and he had not premeditated the killing.

Researchers who take up the Bonmartini murder usually feel constrained to explain the astonishing, sustained public interest that the case evoked. Each development in the investigation, such as Linda's arrest or Tullio's confession, swelled the newspapers and renewed the debate that had by now become nation-wide over the guilt or innocence of the Murris. In large measure, the continuing avalanche of publicity was the result of the subtle political situation in Italy in 1902, whereby the country enjoyed great national newspapers but not yet any great national parties. The main forum for political and ideological debate was the press.

The leading editors and journalists were politicians, for all practical purposes, who were using journalism as the first phase of a political career. Most newspapers could be clearly identified as radical, ministerial, socialist, clerical, business, positivist, and so on, and lined up accordingly on one side or the other of the Murri divide. Professor Murri represented a liberal, bourgeois, secular—even agnostic—challenge to the conservatives, to the nineteenth-century Italy of aristocrats, landlords, rural peasants, a structured and largely immobile class system. He was the enemy of a society which, if not a theocracy, was an oligarchy dominated by the Catholic Church and its powerful bureaucracy. The Church, allied with landowners, was on one side, with its long history of feudal domination over the lives and minds of Italian people. The Italian state was on the other side, with its secular authority, universities, intellectuals, and political parties, its army, its anticlerical king always surrounded by military pomp and nationalistic propaganda.

The Catholic press, and many right-leaning newspapers, entirely discounted Tullio's narration of events and placed Professor Murri behind the murder. The "tragedy of Bologna," as they called it, had been caused by luxury and liberal education. One writer counseled that the only weapon against evil and violence was a little book of catechism, the one book that "medical men and pedagogues" had no use for.[19] Bonmartini's murder delighted the conservatives. Here at last was proof that rationalism and relativism were dangerous ideas. Rationalism—implying science, as well—became a synonym for criminality, as it had long been a synonym for anticlericalism.

Each member of the Murri family was dissected. Giannina, who weighed ninety pounds, was described as "a small pallid creature," a "Xanthippe." Linda, who was repeatedly described as "not pretty," was, according to the conservatives, having sex with her maids, her brother, her father, and, last and least notable, her lover, Secchi. Rosina received the most cruel treatment. She was called "semiliterate"—never a term of compassion in a society ashamed of its illiterates—"low class," "an ugly figure of femininity, astute under her appearance of vulgar simplicity."[20]

The liberal and socialist press fought back as well as it could. *Il Socialismo* countered the blizzard of anti-Murri publicity with an account of all the crimes of the popes, which, though serious, were but quaint old felonies compared with the Murri scandal. *La Rana*, a satiric journal, offered a section of "letters" from purported readers giving their insights into the case. One "Artemis Idiot" reported that his mother had been a wet nurse for Tullio; she complained that he used to bite her hard enough to draw blood. This was evidence of his bloodthirstiness that showed itself even at a tender age. "Annibale

Fritter," a "waitress" in a hotel, observed that whenever Tullio ordered steak, he wanted it "rare and bloody," which was no doubt a reflection of his wayward nature. The journal remarked that the Bonmartini case at last gave Italy something to make the French envious. Parisians had no tragedy of Bologna to provide them with free drama.[21]

Tullio reminded his accusers that he had returned voluntarily to face them. He told a story not of an impulsive attack but of cumulative frustration that burst into unintended violence after watching his beloved sister tormented by a bumptious husband. "Bonmartini had a natural instinct for evil—the desire to see suffering. My sister was very ill with nephritis. . . . Knowing how the children gave the poor thing her one pleasure in life, he threatened to shut them up in a boarding school or take them away so that she couldn't see them." Linda's sojourn in Switzerland with Secchi was described by Tullio thus: "When she was forced to go to Zurich for the treatment of her eye (unfortunately lost), she implored her husband to bring them to Bologna for a day or two before she left. He answered that he would take the children to Cavarzere or to the sea, just so that she couldn't see them."[22] Tullio was shown the postcard Linda had addressed to him that included the remark "I don't hear anything more about S." Who was "S"? Secchi? Tullio couldn't say. He had not received the card and could not place it in any context, or so he replied.

Linda was called on to corroborate Tullio's account of her marriage, but her testimony was no help for him. Tullio had made an elaborate point of Bonmartini's violence, evident when he menaced Linda with a chair. Linda had described the scene to her parents and brother and wrote that if such turmoil continued, she was going to kill herself. That, he insisted, was the reason for his own overwrought state as he approached Bonmartini. When questioned, Linda seemed not to remember the incident. Moreover, she stated that her husband could not have been armed with a knife, since he never carried anything but a pistol.[23]

There was one other problem with Tullio's story—a big problem. Naldi had already told the inquisitors a much closer version of the truth.

At nine in the morning on September 13, Dr. Pio Naldi arrived unbidden at Bologna's police headquarters in a carriage, carrying a proud collection of documents to prove that he could not have taken part in the execution of Cesco Bonmartini. Naldi's interview with Justice Stanzani lasted several hours, during which the young doctor (he was twenty-eight, like his friend Tullio) thought he had acquitted himself well. His interrogator noticed that Naldi was wearing almost new yellow boots. When the ordeal of questioning was over, Justice Stanzani walked Naldi to the door and made an expressive gesture to two agents who were waiting just outside. To Naldi's utter amazement, one of the agents reached in his pocket and took out a warrant for Naldi's arrest. Deathly white and trembling violently, Naldi had to be helped to the police carriage that brought him to prison.[24] His arrest was a new and critical development in the Murri case; many newspapers issued an extra edition on September 14.

Naldi was a pitiful character, even when he was not in the stressful clutches of the police—the newspapers called him a *traviato*—a lost soul, from a tragic family. He was from Castel San Pietro, just outside Bologna. His father had tried several occupations—stationmaster, schoolteacher, grain merchant—and stayed poor through all of them. Neither of Naldi's brothers was studious. One was a mechanic employed by the railroad; the other, a sailor, had committed suicide. Naldi was able to attend the University of Bologna thanks to Professor Murri, who had obtained a scholarship for him because of his academic promise. Murri persuaded him to switch from literature to medicine. His meager stipend was supplemented by small contributions from an elderly aunt who lived on Via Pratello in Bologna. Neither his parents nor his brother ever once communicated with him or with the authorities during the years of the istruttoria and trial. He had last seen his father in 1901, a year before the murder. Naldi was tall and gentle, with a dulcimer speaking voice. He was blind in his left eye. The pupil lay hidden under the lower lid; it made people recoil the first time they saw it. But his appearance changed completely when, on rare occasions, his face broke into a radiant smile.

"Pio was not a criminal by nature," one of his old professors wrote. Given his talents and deficiencies, he should have had "a life rich in intellectual satisfactions and terribly poor in everything else."[25] Because of his "vice," as gambling was inevitably described, he never practiced medicine. At some point during his lifelong streak of bad luck, he had pawned his surgical instruments. Even the casehard-ened pawnbroker felt sorry for Naldi when, a few weeks before the murder, he brought in his last two shirts and a hand-knitted sweater. By the time of his arrest, he had lost the pawn ticket.[26]

Naldi first met Tullio at the university, where he recognized him as the son of his respected sponsor, and later saw him from time to time at the card or dice tables. The two were not close friends—people no-ticed that they used the formal *Lei* in addressing each other. Naldi was chronically in need of money, a starveling who dressed badly and lived in a dingy fourth floor room in Via Roma for which he paid twelve lire a month. At the time of the Bonmartini murder, he was five months behind in his rent. When the police searched his room, they listed his entire wardrobe: a nearly new suit. His only other possession was his diploma. The summer of 1902 had been especially hard for Naldi. An acquaintance—not a sympathizer—reported that he lost whole nights to gambling at the Buvette Ponzio or the Club Rigosi, where he played at the tables but could not afford any of the food that was all around him; when he was not gambling, he stayed in bed all day because of hunger. He cheated at cards, stole petty sums, and was often heard railing against God and society. The night before the murder, Naldi had been seen at the Rigosi with Tullio, where they had a drink. When Naldi left, to the astonishment of everyone who was used to seeing him penniless, he tipped the barmaid.[27]

Naldi told the justices that late in August Tullio asked his help in obtaining 5,000 lire, a very large sum for Naldi, who could barely scrounge a few lire here and there from his best sources. When, after a few days, Naldi reported that he had not been able to borrow the money, Tullio confided his plan to kill his brother-in-law. Naldi tried to talk him out of it, but Tullio was a man obsessed. He replied that delaying even another day would mean the death of his sister. Tullio offered Naldi a thousand lire for his assistance—more money than Naldi could hope to acquire in a year—assuring him that he could get the money because his father had deposited 60,000 lire in a bank in Tullio's name. Tullio promised Naldi "a secure alibi." Tullio himself had planned an escape; he expected to be out of the country before the murder was discovered. He mentioned that he had told his parents of his intentions and that his mother had made him promise he would stay away from Bonmartini; but he would have to break that promise, he told Naldi, in light of the urgency of Linda's situation.

It was entirely true and startling that Professor Murri deposited 60,000 lire in Tullio's account. Severo Dalla, Professor Murri's accountant and Tullio's friend, had made a number of deposits at the Banca Popolare on Via Carbonesi within a few months preceding the murder, ending with 5,267 lire placed in Tullio's name on August 13, 1902. Then, using an authorization from Professor Murri, Severo withdrew all the money and deposited it in his own name.[28] Professor Murri had always been penurious with Tullio. The most he had ever even promised his son was 5,000 lire a year, and in fact, usually gave him only 1,200. Why had he suddenly provided such a large sum? And had Tullio in fact discussed the murder plan with his parents? If so, was Professor Murri supplying the money for a hit man? Or money to escape abroad after the deed was accomplished? If the money was not provided for escape, why had it been removed from Tullio's account? Obviously, to avoid having it sequestered by the police after the body was discovered.

According to Naldi, on the day before the murder he was still trying to reason with Tullio. He and Tullio and a woman Naldi did not know—Rosina—were walking and arguing under the arcades until Naldi found himself at the very entrance of the Bisteghi Palace. Tullio produced a key, and the three of them entered the Bonmartini apartment. Naldi accompanied Tullio, he said, in the hope of dissuading him from his project. He felt he owed it to the Murri family to try to prevent Tullio from involving them all in a senseless tragedy. He was horrified when Rosina locked him and Tullio in the apartment and left. Tullio explained that after the ambush was over, Rosina would return to let them out. Seeing Naldi's agitation, Tullio told him there was another door through which he could leave, if he really wanted to. However, he took away Naldi's shoes to keep him from going. Tullio himself planned to wait overnight for the count, who was due the next day, and vowed he would carry out the assassination alone, if necessary. "You'll see if I'm a man of courage and a man of my word," Naldi remembered him saying. Tullio then went into the children's bedroom and stretched out.[29]

Though he later changed many elements of his narration, Naldi never modified his statement as to why he was in the Bonmartini house: to prevent Tullio from committing the murder. Throughout the next day, August 28, Tullio was intensely excited, red-faced and feverish. Moving a knife in and out of his belt, he kept repeating that if Bonmartini were allowed to live even one more day, it might mean the death of his sister. Tullio and Naldi ate ring cake that had been left by Bonetti; they drank champagne, while Tullio's agitation steadily mounted. It was by now 5:30 and nearing the time for Bonmartini's arrival. Naldi decided to make one last attempt to persuade Tullio to abandon his project. He thought he had succeeded when Tullio opened a back entrance and bade Naldi go out, saying that he would follow. Finding himself in the street alone, Naldi then thought of waiting for Bonmartini outside the house and warning him. But when Bonmartini did not appear, Naldi simply wanted to flee the whole situation. He went home, he said, quickly changed clothes, and reached the station in time to take the seven o'clock train for Florence with five minutes to spare. Between the time Bonmartini arrived at the Medaglie d'Oro station in Bologna at 6:07 and the time Naldi left from the same station at 7:00, exactly fifty-three minutes elapsed. He could not, he insisted, have accomplished a murder in such a brief space.

Naldi told the justices that on arriving in Florence, he took the first bus he saw. It happened to pass the Hotel de Russie, where he stayed in Room 39. When the investigators checked this part of the story, they found that the Hotel de Russie was rather difficult to get to by omnibus. It was not the sort of place usually patronized by the Naldis of the world. The desk clerk at the top of the marble stairs had taken a hard look at the frayed young man with the afflicted eye, observed that he carried no luggage, and, suspecting that he might be a dangerous anarchist, called the manager. An anarchist was not a good thing to be taken for in the Italy of 1902. Not only had anarchists assassinated the king of Italy in 1900; the president of France, the prime minister of Spain, and the empress of Austria had recently been dispatched by Italian anarchists. They and their confreres in Europe continued to blow up trains, public buildings, and public officials with disturbing frequency, especially targeting the hotels and habitats of the wealthy. While Naldi was presenting his travel-shabby self to the hotel clerk, an anarchist was being arrested elsewhere in Italy for setting off dynamite, and the owner of a newspaper was about to go to jail for four and a half years for writing three articles that "excited hatred between the classes."[30]

Naldi would have been thrown out, but he told the manager that he came to the hotel on the recommendation of a colleague at Bologna's Rizzoli Orthopedic Institute, an olive and tan former monastery he had no doubt seen on the edge of town but may never have entered. Only then was he allowed to rent a room; the hotel owner's son had once attended the prestigious institute. Naldi remained in Florence only one day. Carefully saving his hotel receipts, he went to Livorno, Pisa, and finally Genoa. In each port he tried to find a transatlantic steamer that would accept him as the ship's doctor. In Genoa he enlisted the help of his old mentor from the university who had become the director of *Il Giornale del Popolo*. The editor gave him a letter of introduction and suggested a vessel that plied the Mediterranean. He noted that Naldi seemed unusually confused, fearful, and glum. Naldi could not find a ship willing to take him on. He read in the newspapers that Bonmartini's body had been discovered on September 2, confirming for the first time, he said, his fear that Tullio had actually carried out the murder. Then, learning that the police in Bologna were looking for him and that Tullio had already confessed, Naldi gathered the proofs of his whereabouts on the night of the murder, immediately boarded the train to Bologna, and presented himself to Justice Stanzani. That was his story.[31]

Naldi had thus confessed that he knew what Tullio was planning but denied that he had a hand in the actual murder. Yet when he was arrested, Naldi had just returned from an expensive two-week trip and was carrying over a thousand lire. Where did he get the money? Had Tullio paid him for his participation? No, Naldi answered. He had won the money from Tullio some time before in a series of card and billiard games, and Tullio simply fulfilled his accumulated debt the day before the murder.

Tullio of course denied this version of a planned murder. He denigrated Naldi, calling him a thief and a chronic failure and saying that Naldi had confessed to cheating at cards on several occasions. He admitted to having disclosed to Naldi his disgust with his brother-in-law. But he vehemently denied enlisting Naldi in any sort of conspiracy or paying him. If he had been plotting a murder, he said, he certainly would have chosen a more competent collaborator than Naldi. Neither his sister, nor Rosina Bonetti, nor Naldi had had any part in Bonmartini's death, for which he, Tullio, was alone responsible.

But this account had problems. According to Tullio, after the fight with Bonmartini, he had planted the champagne glasses and letter from "B." The police knew the letter had been written before the murder because it was splashed with tiny drops of blood. Questioned again, Tullio changed some details and filled in others. He now gave the time when he left the apartment as 8:15. He went to Rosina's and left with her again at 11:00 to go to a caffè. There he wrote his cards, went looking for Naldi, and finally ended up at the railroad station. He and Rosina went to Rimini during the night, where he rented a boat in order to throw the murder knife, his own stained clothes, and even his sister's stolen jewels into the high tide. He returned to Bologna early in the morning, went out to breakfast and then to the library where he was seen by the reporter. After going out to dinner with Rosina, he went shopping for clothes to replace those that were bloodied during the fight—stores of course were still open deep into the night, though the clerks were no doubt wilting. Finally, Tullio went back to Rosina's so that he could have Secchi dress his wound, telling the doctor that Rosina had cut him with a pair of scissors during a jealous rage.[32]

Tullio reminded the justices that in the first part of his memoriale he had laid out the history of his own ungovernable temper, even listing incidents where he had started fistfights with men who offended him. He had come from a line of violent men. His grandfather had once chased his grandmother with a sword; another grandfather had been abandoned by his wife because of his tantrums. His father, Augusto, had earned the nickname of "Terrible Gus" in his youth; his uncle Alfredo was feared by his brothers because of his violent temper, and so on. The justices did not entirely discount these digressions, as they were completely within the resilient Italian conception that the family is and ought to be the most inescapable influence in a person's character. The idea that heredity determines everything is a monarchist conception, and Italy was a constitutional monarchy. According to Tullio, only his sister had escaped the deforming Murri heredity: she was "mild, melancholy, and resigned." Tullio declared that he had never given Naldi money, either for his assistance or to pay off some supposed gambling debt. He demanded a face-to-face confrontation with Naldi in front of the justices. Such confrontations were commonplace in Italian investigations—the normal procedure when suspects gave conflicting accounts.

And so Tullio and Naldi were placed at opposite ends of a table where the investigating judges, notebooks poised, settled in alongside them to watch. Before beginning, Tullio demanded that Naldi repeat what Tullio had told him about Linda——that she knew nothing of the plan. The entertainment then lasted less than half an hour. Tullio was alert and restless, Naldi as skinny as the Savior on Brunelleschi's Crucifix and scarcely more animated. Both men appeared embarrassed before each other at first, but as Tullio warmed to his task, he became lively and assertive, while Naldi began to stumble and contradict himself. Tullio insisted that he had not spent the night of August 27 in the Bonmartini apartment, much less with Naldi, who, he said, had never been there. According to Tullio, Naldi had made up the whole story of having been a murder accomplice in order to make himself seem important. At first Naldi replied, in his diffident way, "That's not true. I was there." Naldi, who had answered every question of the justices with a babble of information, had already described the apartment in detail and even mentioned the kinds of sandwiches and sweets they had eaten, the crumbs of which had been carefully swept up by the police and sequestered. There could be little doubt that he had spent considerable time there. But midway through the debate, Naldi began to think that Tullio was providing him an escape from the whole situation. He asked for another interrogation and told the justices that Tullio was telling the truth: he had not been in the house the night of the murder. He knew the apartment because once Bonmartini had invited him in before they went out together. Naldi of course was not aware that Bonmartini had moved to Via Mazzini only four months before his murder, long after he had stopped having any intercourse with Naldi. He had left Tullio for the last time on August 27, Naldi said; he had spent that night and the next day at home and had simply taken the seven o'clock train to Florence to pursue his plans for the future.[33]

Where, then, had he acquired the money he had when he was arrested? the justices asked. Tullio still denied having given it to him, saying that after his battle with Bonmartini, he had gone to look for

Naldi to give him some money so that he could leave Bologna and not be around to tell investigating judges that Tullio had been furious with his brother-in-law. But he had not found him. He had wanted to give Naldi 5,000 lire to get him far away. He had remarked to Rosina that money was missing from his wallet. Naldi now gave a new answer concerning the money. He said that at the train station he got into a card game with some men, the sort of cardsharps who were sometimes found in stations of the time. He won the money and of course did not know the names of the people he played with. Twelve hundred lire in Naldi's pocket was more money than he had ever possessed at one time in his life. It was the strongest material evidence tying him to the crime.

Naldi soon regretted changing his story. Tullio had not exonerated Naldi; in fact, he had enmeshed him further in the crime, because the justices did not believe Tullio and assumed that both men were lying. They thought some evidence had been destroyed which showed that Bonmartini had found out about Linda's and Secchi's affair. To protect his sister from exposure, they concluded, Tullio murdered her husband with the help of Naldi, Bonetti, and perhaps others.

By November 1, six weeks after his arrest, Naldi had either exhausted all the money he brought with him to jail, or it had been stolen from him. He was starving. Hunger was his old, old enemy, and he was accustomed to its stages; but this was extended famine such as he had not known before. Feeding the prisoners was supposed to be the responsibility of their families. The prison provided only enough bread and water to sustain life, however miserable a life it was. If the families could not bring meals, food could be purchased from the guards, who became independent businessmen within the jail—a system that naturally led to all sorts of wickedness. Naldi's aunt could bring him dinner only twice a week. As the winter cold set in, he was reported to be continually and frantically pacing his frigid cell in a febrile, loud, and incoherent dialogue with himself.[34]

* * *

That left Tullio's lover, Rosina Bonetti, to be broken down by interrogation. Although the investigating magistrates might have expected Rosina to be the easiest of the suspects to intimidate, she turned out to be the hardest. From the beginning, they regarded Rosina as one of the key perpetrators of the murder. She had been party to any conspiracy; it was she who was reported to have locked Tullio in the apartment, and had exposed herself to suspicion and danger by returning to inquire about Linda's dress and to let Tullio out. After the murder, Tullio was with her. When Naldi asked Tullio how he could confide murder plans to a woman, Tullio had answered that Rosina would gladly kill for his sake.[35] More that that, she would kill herself. Rosina had one thought as she faced her interrogators: to protect Tullio.

"Do you realize that you may go to prison for thirty years?" Stanzani asked her. "If you tell us the truth, you will be spared."

"What happens to me doesn't matter," she answered.

Once she gave any statement, she never felt obliged to explain or defend it. She denied, for example, that Tullio had destroyed bloody clothes, even after the questioners told her that Tullio had admitted the act. "He can say what he wants to," she answered indifferently. "I don't know anything about it." Or, having given an answer, she would be asked, "Is all that true?"

"Yes, all," she would affirm. But then they would tell her that Tullio had given a conflicting statement.

"That's also completely true," she would say simply. She made no attempt to be convincing in her statements, only to refrain from admitting anything that could damage Tullio's position. She denied that she had ever had any keys. At one point she even denied that Tullio's arm had been cut. That turned out to be a significant statement, as the justices were deliberating over whether Tullio might in fact have cut himself some time after the murder in order to bolster his claim of self-defense. In the confrontation that was arranged between her and Tullio, he finally had to warn her, "Don't say anything else."[36]

If ever a woman had a right to feel sorry for herself, it was Rosina

Bonetti. "La Cenerentola" the newspapers called her—Cinderella—but with Tullio instead of a prince at the end of her torments. Rosina was born into misery in 1867 near Fontanelice, twenty-five miles from Bologna. The investigators noted, in their conventional research into every suspect's family background, that her grandfather had been a notorious criminal, killed by the police while trying to escape capture. An uncle escaped from prison, was recaptured, and then died in a jailhouse fight. Her mother died of tuberculosis when Rosina was eleven. She and her four-year-old brother Leopoldo were then put out to beg on the roads of the area; everything they could get went to their father's drinking and to a prostitute who lived with them. The children were not so unusual in their wretchedness to merit anyone's particular notice. In every town, little beggars surrounded visitors, as they do today. Her father abandoned the family and went to France after he was convicted of theft. Tullio reported to Linda that Rosina had ten older brothers and a sister who all died of diseases brought on by malnutrition; only "Poldino" was left.[37]

At thirteen, Rosina found work as a maid for a kind couple who more or less adopted her. "Mamma Celestina" died when Rosina was seventeen, and she then had to make her own way, working as a maid in Imola, another community on the outskirts of Bologna. She and Poldino moved to Bologna in 1891 to work for a Count Rossi. The next year, she fell ill with a sort of paralysis that left her permanently lame; the doctors believed it was psychosomatic. Without X-rays, which were as yet still a novelty in magic shows, physicians were at a loss to diagnose malfunctions of the joints and limbs; one doctor ordered her to put her legs in hot sand.[38] She was kept successively by two men, and in her letters made references to a daughter who had died; the child does not seem to have been Tullio's. The justices, who would not have overlooked anything as censurable as an illegitimate child, did not connect him with the baby. Rosina met Tullio Murri around 1898 and, from then on, had no other men. The justices invented a poetic phrase to describe her. Her attachment to Tullio, they said, was "like ivy on elm."[39]

But Rosina was no parasite. "It's not true," she said in one of her interrogations, "that I didn't work. I couldn't do hard work because I couldn't stay on my feet, but I worked in clothes and laundry. And it's not true either that after I started up with Tullio I went with other men. He was giving me enough to eat, so I was always true to him." Tullio once wrote to his sister that he could not bear *"to see her suffering hunger and cold in order to remain honest and faithful to me,"* even though sexual fidelity, hers or anyone else's, *"doesn't matter a fig to me."*[40] Nor was she really maintained by Tullio, who helped her only now and then. *"When I first knew her,"* Tullio wrote to his sister early in the relationship,

> *I would see her in the evening and find out that she hadn't eaten all day. Now things are a little better because her brother gives her something. But what can I say after I tell you I have given her at the most twenty lire a month? Sometimes, when I leave her in the morning and see her cupboard is empty, I put a couple of lire there and the next day send over half a sack of coal. That's all. It's a little charity that I would give anybody. She always cries over having to accept it.*

In 1898, when the police were searching for Tullio and all leftist activists, Rosina had hidden him. Afterwards, his mother paid Rosina a visit to thank her. Rosina remained on affectionate terms with Signora Giannina, who had an inordinate fear of being alone. At 11:30 on the night of Bonmartini's murder, it was Rosina who telegraphed Giannina: "28 August 02. *Stay calm. Don't move. Tomorrow evening I'll be there.*"[41] The telegram was signed by Rosina, but she was probably writing for Tullio. Was it the prospect of being alone that interfered with Giannina's tranquillity or the anxiety over what Tullio might have done?

Rosina was not merely devoted to Tullio, she was also madly obsessed with him in a way that made their relationship a constant melodrama. Once Tullio called the police to subdue Rosina, who had attacked him in a jealous fury. From time to time he complained to friends of wanting to be rid of her. In a letter to Linda in 1899, Tullio described how, coming home from a ball, he and Rosina began arguing because he had not danced with her. The quarrel ended with Rosina swallowing a bottle of morphine. Unable to find a doctor, Tullio went out and bought several liters of coffee, which he forced down her by cursing and pounding the table until he broke it. Then, to Tullio's consternation, Rosina vomited copiously. According to the deposition of one of her women friends, Rosina attempted suicide on two other occasions: once when she tried to asphyxiate herself and another time when she tried to jump out of a window. "She was a good person," the friend said, "but her physical health and maybe her spirit were destroyed after her relationship with Murri."[42]

Around 1900 Tullio broke off with her, but he asked his sister to see to it that his mother hired Rosina as a servant. After each of Tullio's amorous adventures, he returned to her.

> *After four years, I feel—as I have felt with no other—that I could spend an endless honeymoon with her. . . . My love hasn't reached the point where I would say, "This one or nobody." But I can say that I prefer this one, even though she's ugly and four years older than I am, over the most beautiful and desirable women in the world."*[43]

In 1902 they were back together, closer than ever, when Linda, reorganizing her household after her reconciliation with Bonmartini, brought Rosina in under a false name. It could not have been arduous, taking care of the family's clothes. Washing machines were commonplace: bulbous tanks on legs with a lever sticking out that someone manually pushed back and forth to agitate the inside tub—in advertisements, a child was usually depicted performing the tedious task. Linda's wasp-waisted dresses could be run up on a new invention, the sewing machine, and a thin woman such as Linda could improve their fit by wearing "bust forms" that "won't be detected by sight or touch"—so long as she kept her dress buttoned.[44] Taking care of the wardrobe was a desirable position for a domestic servant.

It is not hard to see why Rosina was an enthusiastic conspirator in the murder. It was one way for her to become more deeply involved in Tullio's life, to supply something he needed that he could seek from no one else. She was not sentimental about death, having witnessed the slow death of nearly everyone she loved. As a lowborn servant, she was thrilled to be attached to a prominent family, to be privy to their secrets and their life, to be treated almost as an equal by a countess. Linda, always affectionate and friendly with the servants, was especially so with Rosina. Indeed, Rosina and Secchi's nurse, Tisa Borghi, were rivals for the ignoble office of participating in the murder.

With absolutely no cooperation from Rosina, the investigators established several pieces of information concerning her: Rosina was with Tullio before and after the murder and wanted to get into the apartment just after the count arrived on August 28. She had two keys, therefore she did not need to wait for Cesco's arrival to get the dress Linda ostensibly wanted. The justices supposed this was a pretext for finding out if the killing had been completed so she could then send a signal to Linda. Together with Tullio, Rosina left Bologna for Rimini the night of the assassination, arriving at around 5 A.M., carrying a little suitcase. At seven, she and Tullio left again by train for Cattolica, ten miles further down the Adriatic. They returned at once to Rimini and then went back to Bologna.[45]

After Rosina was arrested and denounced in all the papers as a party to a horrible murder, people were afraid to hire her brother Poldino. He seems to have been near starvation when Rosina wrote to Stanzani asking that a dress, a watch-necklace, and a savings passbook which the police had sequestered be turned over to her brother, presumably so that he could pawn the objects and use the money in the savings account. She assured Stanzani that these were her own property and not stolen merchandise. "The jeweler where I bought the chain can testify as to how long I have had it; regarding the dress, I can tell you who gave it to me, if you request." For a time, the authorities suspected that Poldino was an accomplice in the murder, but they could never prove any nefarious behavior on his part. Every few months he rode his bicycle to Fontanelice to see a cousin, stayed two hours, and pedaled back. That was all, until his sister's arrest. While Rosina was still awaiting trial, in January 1903, the brother, like his mother and siblings before him, died of malnourishment and tuberculosis. Rosina went into shock. She was moved to the prison hospital for a month. During the whole of that time, she could neither move nor speak.

Naldi's deposition, though it had been retracted, confirmed the investigators in their belief that Tullio had carefully planned to ambush Bonmartini. The wrestling match that had taken place on the beach in Venice, they surmised, had been an attempt to gauge Bonmartini's strength, to find out if Tullio would be able to subdue his brother-in-law unaided. When Tullio was overcome by Bonmartini, he realized that he would need an accomplice—Naldi—to complete the murder. But what could have been Tullio's motive? An incestuous relationship with his sister that Bonmartini perhaps discovered and threatened to expose? Then what were they to make of Linda's affair with Secchi?

It did not require a circumstance as sordid as incest to confirm that Tullio was, as Bonmartini asserted, "unbalanced" and in the grip of a peculiar morbidity. Early on, he had conceived the idea of being an orator and writer. However, he gave up speaking in public, he wrote his sister, because facing a crowd terrified him and he was incapable of improvising on his feet. As for writing, he lacked *the discipline to work and improve.* He was no longer able to study as he had done at the lyceum because studies fatigued and irritated him. Moreover, he had taken up gambling, since he was not able to live on his father's allowance of 100 lire a month. *How will all this end?* he wrote. *I don't know. I'm sure I need to get away from this corrupt Bolognese life where my troubles are getting worse every day.* Tullio was, as his father noted, keeping bad company. A police check of the regulars at the Club Rigosi and Buvette Ponzio, Tullio's favorite haunts, produced a catalogue of petty criminals who had been arrested for everything from pimping to larceny.[46] Under his lighthearted style, Tullio showed evidence of deep depression. *"The erotic drive, which is too strong in me, leaves me exhausted and weary most days,"* he wrote his sister. To his father, Tullio remarked that he wanted to write a tragedy based on ancient history. He felt, he said, that he had been born during the time of the pharaohs and could not adjust to modern life. Murri's response was that Tullio was a "mummy dressed in silk," a remark that clung to Tullio when the newspapers gleefully attached it to him.[47] *"Papà believes I don't know what love is,"* he wrote to Linda, *"and I even want to let him believe it. But it's not true. It's not true. My body is greased with a skepticism so terrible that love cannot take hold."*

"Skeptic" is a word that Tullio uses often in describing himself, but it hardly takes the measure of his broad and bitter misanthropy. Tullio's two verse dramas, written in 1896 and 1898, showed his promising talent for poetry——and his overweening propensity to violence. It cannot be denied that all popular Italian theater featured bloodcurdling murders—the average was seven or eight deaths per play, and any tragedy that did not involve gore was likely to be hooted off the stage. Tullio's plays provided plenty of gore. Along with mixing metaphors, he mixed lust and bloodlust in passages worthy of Sade.

"Davide Rizo" is an episode in the life of the Scottish queen, Mary Stuart. Rizo is an Italian poet at court, one of the queen's favorites but not her lover. Her husband Enrico Darnley kills Rizo in front of Mary Stuart. The homicide Darnley then tells another courtier, Douglas, that he can't find himself near the queen without feeling the need to kill her as well:

> Drunk with longing, I am aroused by her;
> But then I press my lips to her fair, eager face,

And see the white neck of soft marble.
Oh! When new love takes hold, the heart is consumed
With ferocious desire, the lips can hardly stop,
And under the secrecy of the blanket,
My hand closes around the handle of the deadly dagger.
Oh Douglas! How happily I would rip into that chest with my
*   steel,*
Down to the inmost fibers; and in a most gentle coitus
I would see rivulets of blood,
Of brown blood, flowing from her fair neck . . .

Oh, if but one time I could approach her, hold her in my arms
While she is in the anguish of death, and assuage this horrible
*   thirst*
In her torments!

Darnley was a nasty enough character in life; the Darnley of Tullio's drama, tempted by daggers and fantasizing about sex with a hemorrhaging woman, is ridiculously grotesque. The newspapers had characterized Naldi as a Dostoyevskian figure, the Gambler; but Tullio was himself Raskolnikov, the youth who murders to prove he has the nerve to do it.

If Tullio killed because he had a compulsion to butcher, why exactly did he butcher Bonmartini and not someone else, such as a political adversary? Did Tullio actually believe that Bonmartini was causing the death of his sister, or was this cynical hyperbole to justify a much colder nuttiness?

The answer is a Rosina answer: Tullio cynically defamed Bonmartini to justify murdering him; that is true. It is also true that he believed on some level that Bonmartini was killing Linda. All of the Murris and their allies pretended to believe it. There is, for example, a letter written on April 11, 1902, just before Linda and

Cesco's reconciliation. Husband and wife had agreed that they would move into a new residence. But Linda found moving inconvenient, though she was continuing her usual incessant migrations to vacation residences. Professor Murri wrote to Bonmartini's friend Cervesato, whom all the Murris constantly tried to win over to their side.

> *Home, 11.4.1902*
> *Dear Cervesato,*
> *Yesterday evening Linda was exhausted. The idea of moving out of a house is always serious for a woman, but for Linda, it's extremely serious. As I told you, I have to witness this suicide of my daughter while being powerless to stop it! What human or divine reasoning can justify that a gravely ill woman be continually exposed to emotional destruction? My feeling is that Linda must stay where she is. . . . Don't I have the right, as a father, to defend the life of my daughter?*[48]

Linda won. Cesco moved into the Palazzo Bisteghi on Via Mazzini where she had been residing during the separation.

Despite the opprobrium suffered by divorced women in European society, Professor Murri constantly badgered Linda to leave Bonmartini and take her chances on getting custody of the children in a foreign divorce court. *"I told you this before at San Remo: This can't go on."* Living with Cesco, he insisted, was *"an odious concession," "an immeasurable evil."* Regarding what he referred to as *"our cause,"* that is, winning a separation and custody, he consoled her, *"However it turns out, you'll be free of this life imprisonment that keeps you chained hand and foot."*[49] It was odd that Professor Murri had no dread of the odor that would cling to the whole family if Linda got the divorce he was instigating. He would lose patients. Linda would be the subject of gossip until the end of her days. The Bonmartini children would be stigmatized. Italy, and indeed most of Europe, did not really start the new century until after the Great War. The institution of marriage was intricately bound up with conceptions of class, religion, and comforting conventions; compromising it in any way—by crossing class boundaries or impugning the whole business—implied a threat to the social order and scorn for the traditions of decent people. Certain railroad cars were still reserved for ladies, so that their aloofness from men, and their image as gentlewomen, could be protected. Newspapers sniped for several days at a wealthy man who married his maid, and they sputtered for weeks because Franz Ferdinand, the Austrian archduke, planned to marry Sophie Chotek, a governess. Charles Schwab, the American vice president of Carnegie Steel Corporation, was criticized all the way across the Atlantic for seeking a divorce from his wife. In the Italy of 1902, there were fewer marital separations (831) than murders (2,000), even though separation was legal and murder, even in Sicily, was not.[50] And yet Professor Murri insisted that a divorce was not only preferable to separation or conciliation, it was an absolute necessity.

The rest of the family was no less obsessed with Linda's drama, an exciting saga of urgent sickness mixed with domestic strife. They all wanted to keep things stirred up. On August 29, 1902, crazy Giannina sent a card to her brother-in-law Riccardo. *"Received a card from Nino. There doesn't seem to be any new outrage, but I'm afraid he's not telling the truth. I've decided to go to Bologna myself because I'm not pacified about Linda's health, seeing that Nino has not come back."*[51] Even Dr. Dagnini, seeing the police who came to the Murri villa to arrest Linda, protested that Linda was too ill to be moved. The doctor was not embarrassed to make the statement, even though he had just accompanied Linda and Tullio on a trip and had seen her return to Bologna without even seeking treatment.[52]

In April 1901, Tullio wrote a family friend:

> *My poor sister, the unhappiest of women, has been in bed twenty-five days, atrociously suffering with her eye. Rarely happy as a child, my Linda became unhappy as a wife. Her health, formerly as robust as mine, rapidly declined. Recently, a colic caused by*

nephritis brought her to death's door. For some days, she lay inert
and waxen on the bed, almost without any sign of breathing. My
father thought of taking her to Sicily to breathe the salubrious air
of the eternal Spring down there.[53]

To Tullio, there was nothing unusual about taking an inert and
waxen, hardly breathing creature on a twenty-four-hour journey by
train and boat. "After nine years of marriage," Tullio said during one of
his interrogations, "my sister was weak, falling, old at thirty, very sick,
without blood, without energy, without color, without an eye, almost
without life. All this was her husband's fault, a man who was deprived
of any moral sense, selfish, who loved to put the most obscene pictures
before the eyes of his young wife, atrociously and systematically insult-
ing her family, a swindler who had an instinct for evil. That—hard to
believe, but true—was Francesco Bonmartini."[54] Tullio described how
Bonmartini, "the miser and swindler" had been given too much change
by a bank employee and went away "rubbing his hands together in
glee." Another time, he insisted on half fare when buying a railroad
ticket for his daughter, who was eight and too old to qualify, and made
a scene with the unfortunate employee who had correctly required the
full ticket price. Bonmartini was as "ferocious" with his peasants as
with his family. It was Bonmartini, Tullio insisted, who was the aggres-
sor. "Signor Justice," Tullio wrote earnestly, "I never premeditated anything; nothing in my conscience troubles me. I had no weapon, for I
had absolutely no hostile intentions."

"It is difficult to take love seriously," Tullio had once written to
Linda. *"Love doesn't exist. Why should the love of a rich woman or a*
virgin drive you crazy, while nobody is ever driven mad by the love of a
prostitute? Women for me are all the same."[55] But, like all the Murris,
he took himself and his love for his family all too seriously. If Professor Murri, a medical doctor, could assert that living with Cesco was
killing Linda, then it is not difficult to understand how Tullio—
volatile, confused, and immature—could work himself into a murderous rage over Linda's marital conflicts.

* * *

Meanwhile, the police were questioning everybody: the suspects, friends of the Bonmartini and Murri families, and especially servants, while newspapers were serializing Cesco's diaries, laying open to view a marriage where the main link between husband and wife was a chamber pot. No less than Tullio, Linda tried to paint Cesco as a domestic petty tyrant so that murdering him would not seem to be an important crime. Presented with the signs that Bonmartini had been with a prostitute at the time of the murder, Linda coolly observed:

> He never showed any fear of involvement with women. I have never been jealous. We had a period of disagreement, but we were reunited after friends, and especially Cardinal Svampa, intervened. Afterwards, we didn't question him; he had never cared very much about the family. He liked to stay out until all hours, not letting me know where he was, what relations he had, what he did.[56]

After first asking the justice not to compel her "to say anything bad about my husband," she confided that he refused to look at Maria for three days after she was born because he had wanted a son. She repeatedly referred to Cesco's *grossolanità*—his crudeness—quoting him as saying that if the next baby, Ninetto, had been a girl, he would have seized the newborn by the leg and thrown it into a pile of manure. Linda averred that Cesco was stingy, wanted the tutors to correct the children by hitting them, and planned to put them in a boarding school.

Physical violence? No, she conceded. But the instances of "emotional violence" were innumerable and continual. "Nevertheless, for the sake of the children I agreed to a reunion that was brought about by Cervesato and Cardinal Svampa." Linda hardly ever passed up an opportunity to drag Domenico Svampa into her testimony, as if she were close to the prelate and had been yielding to his wishes in reuniting with her husband, though it had been the Murris who requested Svampa's presence at the signing of the reconciliation. In a second interrogation, she asserted that Frieda Ringler had been dismissed on Bonmartini's orders, not hers.

The thoughtful reporter from *Corriere della Sera,* Augusto Bianchi, seeing only a summary of Linda's deposition, mused that it was possible she had told the truth about Bonmartini without much exaggeration, since she seemed to have had no awareness that his faults were not as heinous to others as she considered them and did not qualify him for execution.[57] As soon as Linda's lawyers saw her deposition—a year later, after the investigation was completed—they warned her to stop disparaging Bonmartini. At the trial, therefore, she once more rejected questions that required her to "say anything bad about my husband." Letters from Bonmartini's friends deluged Stanzani, all stating categorically that Bonmartini had been a gentle person, incapable of attacking Murri or anyone else.[58] Bonmartini's three closest friends gave repeated long depositions—Dante Cervesato, the pediatrician; Professor Giovanni Gallerani; and Cesco's cousin Batista Valvassori, the tutor of the children.[59]

Gallerani was a professor of experimental physiology at the University of Camerino. He had known Cesco for seventeen years, had stood in his wedding, and believed he could state with authority that his conduct was "absolutely irreproachable." Bonmartini was kind, reasonable, of a happy temperament, completely absorbed in music, photography, and his family. "I noticed that the Murris were intent that my friend Cesco should obtain a degree, an academic title, and he was planning to enroll in medical school." Bonmartini spent a period working in Gallerani's lab and was extremely studious. In those days, said Gallerani, Cesco carried around a photograph of his wife of which he was very proud. In showing it, he always mentioned that the dress she was wearing was one he had ordered for her from Paris. Cesco's taking pictures was a notable quirk to his friends because photography was a new-fashioned hobby. A very few touched-up photographs were beginning to appear in newspapers, and visitors to

Bologna were taken to see the fine cemetery Campo Santo, where photos of the dead were framed and put on tombstones. But in the country of millions of paintings, the realism of photography was considered, like Cesco himself, a little vulgar.

In 1899, Cesco told Gallerani of his separation. Gallerani offered to go to Linda in the hope that he could make peace between the couple. "I was received courteously enough. Serious accusations? None. Our very long discussion boiled down to this: Count Bonmartini was a little crude. Nothing more grave than that." When he read about the count's murder in the papers, he immediately suspected that the assassin was Tullio. On September 23, the pediatrician Dante Cervesato began a series of exhaustive depositions. The testimony was kept secret and was therefore assumed to be damaging to the Murris. The only information released to the press was that Cervesato affirmed, in the strongest terms possible, that Bonmartini had been an extraordinarily loving father.

Cervesato in fact deposed that Cesco changed during the years of his marriage. As a young man he had been negligent of his dress, parsimonious, and indifferent to society, caring only for music. But after marrying Linda, he became much more obliging and generous. He had conservative, almost medieval ideas about politics, but his authoritarianism was more in word than in fact, since he treated his peasant dependents well. His tenants were outraged by his murder, Cervesato said. Cesco's intelligence was only average, but his honesty and loyalty were extraordinary, traits that were never appreciated by the Murris, nor by the friends who succumbed to the Murri campaign to sully him. As the animosity between Cesco and Linda grew, Cervesato noticed that Bonmartini began to fear Tisa Borghi and various others attached to the Murris. "I told him that if his wife no longer loved him, he was still young and wealthy and should do things to take his mind off the situation. He answered me, 'You're not a father and can't understand what a father's love is like.'"

Cervesato described how the Murris tried to draw both himself and Valvassori to their side, alluding to some unspeakable moral lapse in Cesco but answering evasively when Cervesato asked them to explain. Finally, Cervesato took care to fulfill his promise to Bonmartini: he told the authorities that Cesco knew his brother-in-law was likely to murder him. About twenty other friends of Bonmartini were questioned, all of them professionals. The consensus of their opinions was that Cesco was "simple and ingenuous, but good," in the words of General Panizzardi, the man who warned him of Linda's infidelity.[60]

Cesco's cousin Battista Valvassori stated that Bonmartini was timid, unkempt during the early years of his marriage, and inordinately in love with his wife, though from time to time he wondered if she had an incestuous relationship with her father. Professor Murri refused to give Cesco even minimal assistance in entering medical school, and once his son-in-law was enrolled some distance away, old Murri and Linda did everything possible to keep him out of Bologna. From a young age, Cesco had always shown an extraordinary aptitude for managing his property. For the rest, Valvassori said, he was a good man. Alessandro Stoppato added to the growing compendium of arguments against Tullio. He addressed a long memorandum to the judges in which he made clear that he believed the Murris, abetted by the press, had conducted a campaign of lies to smear Bonmartini's reputation and dishonor his memory.

No deposition was awaited more breathlessly than that of "the German," Frieda Ringler. For several days, the governess's interrogation was kept secret—days during which the newspapers speculated on her remarks with prurient excitement. Frieda was said to have been aware of incestuous incidents between Linda and her father and Linda and her brother; she reportedly told the magistrates that Linda and Rosina slept together downstairs, while all the other servants slept upstairs. And she was alleged to have seen unspeakable acts between Linda and Secchi. *L'Avvenire d'Italia* reported that Frieda overheard Linda and Rosina plotting a cover-up for the planned murder.[61]

In fact, Frieda Ringler's deposition lasted several days. She described the quite noticeable affection Linda showed for Bonetti, whom she treated as a friend, but Frieda had no explanation for this partiality. She said she knew nothing whatever about the crime. Rosina was in Venice with Linda just before the murder, she said, but she slept on the second floor with the domestics, while Frieda and the family slept on the first floor. The children always slept with their mother. Regarding the chair incident, Frieda deposed that Bonmartini grabbed a chair and made a quick gesture as if to throw it, but let it drop to the floor.

Frieda knew a great many things regarding the contessa's relationship with Secchi, but she wasn't eager to inform anyone about it. Bonmartini knew little, she said, but had many suspicions. Frieda confirmed that Secchi stayed with the contessa on several out-of-town trips, even when the children accompanied her. Had Bonmartini learned of the affair from her? No. It was not her business to divulge such information. To the disappointment of everyone except the Murris, Frieda stated firmly that she knew nothing of incest between Linda and either her father or brother. She could attest that she saw Linda kneeling in front of Secchi, and she could verify that the servants generally gossiped about Secchi, and also about the long private hours Linda spent with Rosina.

What Frieda did know, and spoke about volubly, was Cesco's treatment at the hands of the Murris. Frequently, at the Murri dinner table, Linda and Tullio conversed in German, which the children spoke fluently. They mocked the count, even while he sat at the table and was aware that he was being discussed. The count, according to Frieda, had a reading knowledge of German but could not speak it. The Murris exchanged looks and signals and in various ways ridiculed him repeatedly in front of the children.[62]

While they were taking depositions, the investigators were also checking the information given by the witnesses, even to the smallest details. For example, to check Naldi's story of his trip to Florence, they interviewed train employees, the omnibus driver who took him to the Hotel de Russie, the hotel clerk, manager, porter, and maid. They followed the same diligent procedure in Livorno and Genoa. By now, the police had confirmed that Linda had given Ninetto's savings passbook to Rosina to pass to Tullio. She did it a few weeks before the murder. Uncle Nino (Tullio), with Linda's assent, had withdrawn his nephew's savings of 600 lire, in order, it appeared, to finance the murder of Ninetto's father.[63] The punctiliousness of the investigation must have surprised Tullio and Linda, who arrogantly assumed that false names and disguised handwriting, having sufficed to frustrate Giannina's inquiries, would mystify the police as well. In their confidence, it seems not to have occurred to them that bank and telegraph records could be summoned, and that even a less clever and hardworking detective than Stanzani would be able to identify "X" or "S" or the multifaceted "Contessa Borghi" flying through the hail of secret messages.

The autopsy report on Bonmartini was released in mid-September 1902. The examining doctors explained their conclusions with many particulars about Bonmartini's kidneys (brown), spleen (greenish), brain (almost liquefied and yielding little information), and penis (very slender, flaccid, and putrefied). Francesco Bonmartini had most likely died, they said, at about 6:30 on August 28. He was killed by a deep, violent stab in the chest that penetrated his heart as he fell backward. The knife was curved at the tip and was wielded by someone shorter than he. Bonmartini had been ambushed; no real battle had taken place. His clothes were all buttoned and in order. The most important conclusion given by the doctors was this: that there had been not one but at least two assassins. It was not the luckless, unarmed Bonmartini who inflicted the cut on Tullio's arm but Tullio's partner in the murder who struck him while trying to slash Bonmartini.[64]

Famishing in prison, Pio Naldi began to comprehend that he was not only charged with being an accessory to murder but would be tried as one of Bonmartini's two killers. He asked to be reinterrogated, writing that his most recent interrogation must be viewed "like the hallucinations of a sick person." He began a series of modifications to his story. In one interview, he said that he had spent about six months before the murder trying to find a third accomplice for the assassination. The investigators had already pursued the third accomplice idea for some time. They conjectured that another conspirator might have come from Imola, and investigated in turn Rosina's brother, the Dalla brothers, the servant Ettore Vacchi, and a medical graduate fond of the gaming tables, Alfredo Trolli, who had taken off for the Congo on October 15. They were interested for a while in a card player named "Eyes" Antonio, who had suspiciously left for New York in September 1902. The police located him working in a bicycle factory in Boston, but all they could ascertain was that his father had whisked him out of Italy as soon as the news of the murder broke, and that he rode a bicycle to and from work.[65]

Tullio, while insisting that he had not premeditated the killing, modified his statements, too. He had brought a knife and dagger to the meeting with Cesco, he finally admitted, but he intended only to threaten his brother-in-law; he thought that would be sufficient to make him change his mind about moving to Padua. On July 5, 1903, Tullio wrote a passionate letter to the justices:

> I declare and swear to God (in whom, it should be noted, I have always believed and still believe), on the life and honor of my parents, that the words and answers in my testimony, if found to be false in the slightest detail, let God destroy my father and my mother and any other person most dear to me so that I never see any of them again.[66]

After first asserting that Naldi was never present at the crime scene, he eventually said that Naldi had left before Bonmartini's arrival. Naldi was just as steadfast in holding that he was privy to a long conspiracy but had hoped all along to dissuade Tullio from the deed.

In June 1903, Naldi decided that he had left the Bonmartini

apartment by the back entrance, not the principal door. The two entrances were side by side in the upstairs apartment. One stairway led down to a long corridor that passed the portinaia's window toward the front of the house. The other stair led down to the side street, Pusterla. That was the exit Naldi now said he took. Then Naldi must have left after the murder, not before it, the judges concluded, since he would have had to get the keys to that door from Bonmartini's pocket. Naldi therefore amended his statements to say that Bonetti was not with him and Tullio when they went into the apartment— that they had locked themselves inside. The door could be opened only from the outside and with a key, the justices countered. Faced with that fact, Naldi reverted to his first story, that he had left from the principal entrance. This time, however, he confessed that he had stolen 1,100 lire from Tullio's wallet because he realized he could not get very far away from the murder scene in his destitute state. Tullio, however, was having none of it. "If he stole the money," said Tullio, "he certainly didn't steal it from me."[67] If he didn't steal it, then he was paid, Stanzani concluded. So Tullio had just broken off and smashed another piece of Naldi's alibi.

On August 26, 1903, nearly a year after his arrest, Naldi was visited by Justice Stanzani. The magistrate presented all the evidence showing that Naldi was one of Bonmartini's killers, a "hired killer," in Stanzani's words, who had no animosity toward the count. Naldi would be viewed by the court as a cold-blooded assassin who murdered a young father for money—a couple of thousand lire to squander at the gambling tables. Far from trying to talk Tullio out of his murderous plans, Naldi had encouraged him, kept him boiling, so that he could collect a reward for his assistance. If Naldi knew any detail—anything—about the murder that he had not disclosed, now was the time to speak about it, so as to mitigate the terrible guilt that the court would no doubt decide was his.

Naldi was ill before Stanzani's unexpected visit. When the prosecutor accused him of inciting Tullio, Naldi was seized with the terror of the damned. "How could I have done that when the whole plan for the murder had already been cooking for a long time? And what about the poison? They had thought about using the poison long before I was brought into it."

Poison? asked the justices. What story was Naldi inventing now? What poison?

"The poison," Naldi insisted. For months they had been planning to poison Bonmartini. For months. If the justices didn't believe him, they could ask Secchi. "Secchi will know something about it," he said. Stanzani stood in back of Naldi's infirmary bed with his assistants, pondering the words. Secchi. Poison. Naldi looked up at the small, worn glass under a crucifix on the wall in front of him. He saw Stanzani's face reflected back at him, his brows high, his gaze absent-mindedly fixed on himself. The judge's face was luminous.[68]

Two days later, Pio Naldi sliced open an artery in his arm.

5. THE LOVER

A stifling night was almost over on June 27, 1903, when Linda heard the news shouted by her daily source of information, the paperboys on the street below her prison window: "SECCHI ARRESTED! SECCHI ARRESTED! Dr. Secchi Finally Charged in the Bonmartini Murder."[1]

Of all the suspects in the Bonmartini case, no one had been questioned more closely than Carlo Secchi, and no one had caused the magistrates greater frustration. Before his arrest, Secchi was interrogated four times, as each new piece of information implicating him had emerged. Stanzani had interrogated Secchi's nurse, Tisa Borghi, not once but many times, hoping to hear some detail that would incriminate Secchi. Tisa, however, was loyal and careful. During the doctor's ten months of anxious freedom, Augusto Stanzani had circled around and around him, certain of Secchi's complicity but never able to gather evidence strong enough to spring an indictment. Naldi's mention of the poison at last showed Stanzani a track between the doctor and the murder. Now Secchi, too, marched past the school Rossini had attended and turned into the carriage drive to the angular fastness of San Giovanni in Monte, to disappear behind the guards at the great wooden doors.[2]

An *istruttoria* was supposed to be secret until the investigating magistrate, the *giudice istruttore,* finished his investigation, turned the evidence he had gathered over to a public prosecutor—the *pub-*

126

blico ministero—and declared the instruction phase closed. If the pubblico ministero decided that a criminal prosecution was warranted, he would then initiate the public trial before a tribunal and a jury, where the defendants would be represented by their own lawyers and expert witnesses.[3] Despite the zealous efforts of investigating magistrates to prove that everyone accused of a crime was in fact a criminal, juries were as independent then as now in assessing guilt; of the 885 Italians accused of serious crimes in 1902, more than half were acquitted.[4]

The secrecy of the first phase was intended to allow the magistrate to conduct a complete judicial inquiry, to discover the objective truth without defendants working together on a story or witnesses being influenced by publicity. However, there was always plenty of publicity surrounding an important investigation. People who were questioned by the judge or his assistants talked afterwards to the press, or their families did. When people were arrested, reporters appeared like genies at their homes to interview their agitated relatives and neighbors. Moreover, the istruttore judge himself routinely sprinkled benedictions of brief intelligence to the press. He released the information carefully, sometimes after holding it for months, in such a way as to raise public chatter against the future defendants or for the higher purpose of getting people who had not been questioned to come forward with information. So it was with Secchi. Extra editions of every major newspaper in Italy blazed with lies, half-truths, and truths concerning Secchi's testimony that could have been provided only by Stanzani. And as the justice hoped, Secchi's arrest produced magnificent revelations, though not from Secchi. The misinformation, adroitly placed, that he would be named as one of Bonmartini's butchers spurred a staunch, tight-lipped, essential witness to come before Stanzani's desk and, with no prodding at all, rattle out yet another murder plan with all its details.

Warned by Linda that the authorities knew about the apartment, Secchi admitted in his first interrogation that the rental next to the Bonmartini dwelling in Palazzo Bisteghi had been a meeting place for him and Linda. He had been there only twice, he said, in the nine months since Linda rented it, and not at all after the reconciliation of Linda and Bonmartini in April 1902. He began having intimate relations with Linda in the fall of 1898, not before. They stayed together in San Marcello Pistoiese in 1900 and again in 1901, while Linda was separated; Secchi rented a house for the vacations. Their sexual intimacy ended, he said, with the reconciliation. Later, Secchi was obliged to admit this was a lie. He and Linda were together in Zurich in July 1902, some weeks before the murder, while Bonmartini thought she was having her eye tattooed, and again in mid-August, when Bonmartini was wrestling with Tullio on the beach in Venice and trying to position himself as Professor Murri's assistant. Secchi said that his relations with Tullio were limited to greeting each other.

After Tullio killed Bonmartini on August 28, it was Secchi he summoned to treat his wounded arm. In a four-hour interrogation a month after the murder, his second questioning, Secchi told the prosecutors that he had been in Castiglione dei Pepoli, a resort in the Apennines, 2,000 feet up and twenty-seven miles away from the crime, from August 19 to September 1—this was his iron-solid alibi against their conjecture that he had been Tullio's and Naldi's "third accomplice." Pepoli was not far from Bologna; it was named after the most famous Bolognese family of the fourteenth century. But it was far enough for Secchi's purpose. On August 30, two days after the murder, but before the body had been discovered, he received a telegram asking him to come to Bologna for a consultation. He did not answer the summons, which was signed "Salviati." The next day he received another, this one signed "Borghi," warning that the sick person was in "serious condition." Thinking that Borghi was an agent he knew, he returned home to find that Tullio was asking him to come to Rosina's house. Secchi had believed Tullio's story that Rosina had attacked him, or so he maintained to the justices. He attended to the arm, he said, and returned to the chestnut forests clothing the mountainsides of Castiglione dei Pepoli. The examiners had of course found out that Borghi was the name of Secchi's nurse and one of the battle names he and Tullio used for their secret communications. Secchi then admitted that he knew the telegram had been sent by Tullio.

With Secchi's fourth interrogation, Stanzani thought he had him. The justice had discovered that a few weeks before the murder, Secchi gave Tullio 3,000 lire. Why would Tullio urgently need money just before his brother-in-law's death? And why would he go to Secchi for it? Three thousand lire was a large amount—Naldi's rent for twenty-one years, Tullio's allowance for two years, or the price of two visits to the Murri clinic. Secchi admitted lending the money, and he even admitted that Linda had arranged the loan. At first he characterized the money as a donation to La Squilla. Then he said he thought the money was needed to rescue Tullio from some financial embarrassment. Did he lend the money so that Tullio could escape after the crime? Or so that he could pay Naldi for assisting in it? Of course not, Secchi answered. He did not even know Naldi.[5]

Neither committing adultery, nor treating a murderer's wounds, nor lending money to a murderer, nor even lying about these actions was sufficient for the criminal indictment of Secchi that Justice Stanzani wanted, unless he could prove that Secchi had known a murder was taking shape. Naldi's exclamation concerning poison, however, was a new and wonderful magnet that could pull the doctor from the sidelines and drop him into the central ring of the conspiracy.

Secchi was visiting a friend, a doctor who lived near him, when two policemen knocked on the door. The public security officer, Francesco Christafulli, the man who had "captured" all the other defendants in the Murri case, wordlessly handed Secchi the arrest order. The doctor's face turned gray as he read it. He walked directly to the prison with the two officers. It was the last occasion in a very long while that Secchi would walk block after block unimpeded. He had 30 lire in his wallet when the police took it from him. He was led to a paying cell where he would have his meals brought from home.[6]

In the interrogation of his new prisoner, Stanzani did not go directly to the issue of poison. It had been twenty days since Secchi's last questioning. Stanzani first went over the damaging admissions Secchi had already made. Then he asked if Secchi ever made experiments with toxins in his laboratory and, if so, which ones. Secchi's answer was slow and desultory. He was interested in the physiology of the middle ear, he said. He had done a great deal of research in the laboratory of the University of Bologna, under Professor Albertoni, using various toxins in his experiments—chlorine, strychnine, curare, morphine, chloroform. In January 1902, he published his observations. He then stopped going to the laboratory but continued working at home in preparation for a medical convention in October at which he was to be a presenter. The poison most useful for his experiments was curare, since it paralyzed the nerve endings and muscles, causing immobility in the subject.

Curare had been used for centuries along the Amazon as the main ingredient in arrow poisons, though its other uses had not been much explored—except by tribal witch doctors—until the 1900s. The form known in Europe in 1902 was a dry, brownish mass. Contemporary writings describe curare as sometimes having teeth mixed in it—supposedly the teeth of the snakes from which it was procured. However, the poison is in fact derived from a plant. Depending on the quantity used, it was not always very toxic. The most powerful compounds were produced outside Italy, though some of the most advanced researchers were Italians. In a classic series of experiments, the French physiologist Claude Bernard gathered the urine of a poisoned animal and injected it under the skin of another animal, producing general paralysis. The animal's mucosa poured out liquid—tears, salivation—and one by one, its muscles stiffened, ending with the heart. With the paralysis of the chest, the animal suffered asphyxiation.[7] Secchi was repeating Bernard's work, giving more precise measurements and trying to learn more about curare's disabling properties. During his tests, he kept the animals alive by artificial respiration while the paralysis spread.

In a period when deafness was referred to as "paralysis of the ears" and inventors claimed to have machines that cured it, Secchi's experiments might have resulted in some contribution to science. Interestingly, his monograph, published in 1902, was dedicated to Professor Murri, with a frontispiece and long panegyric that began, "Dear Illustrious Teacher." Since relations between Secchi and Murri had been severed long before, this dedication coming out of the blue was a transparent attempt to flatter and win over his lover's father.[8]

Where did he get the curare, and what quantities did he use? He got it directly from Meerck manufacturers of Darmstadt, Secchi answered, having last ordered five grams in July 1902, of which he still possessed three. The invoice could be found in his desk at home. He could give an exact accounting of what he had done with the other two grams, which served him for experiments on five goats and four chickens. But a search of Secchi's house showed that he did not in fact possess the 3.80 grams of curare that should have remained from his accounting. Some was missing.[9] Could he explain, the judge asked, how Tullio came into possession of a certain quantity of dangerous poisons? No, Secchi answered. Stanzani would have to ask Tullio. (The interrogators here were shooting in the dark—they had not yet found proof of Tullio's having possessed any curare, only some other poisons that he took from his father's small store of medicaments.)

Finally the judges produced the note written by Linda, addressed to Tullio but never sent. The card had been one of hundreds the police had sequestered. When Stanzani first read it, he assigned no particular significance to it. But somehow, he could not forget the cryptic closing sentences. With each new arrest, he brought it out and asked his respondent for an explanation. When Naldi uttered the word "poison," a file opened in Stanzani's mind and a translation typed itself across the scribbled message. Now he daintily placed the card in front of Secchi and watched the doctor's eyes. *"I don't hear anything more about S. Did the medicine work? Write me a signal. Many kisses, Linda."* Did Secchi know what the card meant? No, he replied. He knew nothing about it. Wasn't the "medicine" curare? Hardly, answered Secchi. Curare is not a medicine.[10]

Naldi, meanwhile, was in another part of the prison in a frenzy of remorse. In relating his new version of how he entered and left the Bonmartini apartment, Naldi had added that Tullio was carrying a stick, a knife, and a dagger, as well as a sack of lead balls, a syringe, a vial with a solution of curare, and another vial with a mixture of atropine—an extremely strong poison—and morphine. It was as if Tullio had wanted to kill his victim six ways. In fact, atropine and morphine were found among the various chemicals in the Murri house, but not curare. Naldi reported that when he left, Tullio had not definitely decided to use any of the banes, although he had favored the curare because he believed it would leave no trace in the system and Bonmartini's death would be attributed to a stroke. Now alone with his regrets, Naldi cried out in anguish, "To think I've never before hurt anybody!" A guard overheard him punching his bed in the throes of contrition, sobbing that he was crazy when he confessed the information about the poison. Finally, he wrote a long letter to the judges insisting that everything he had said on June 20, his last interrogation, had been the fantasies of a sick person whom ten months of solitary confinement had rendered delusional. He put down his pencil and handed the letter to a guard, who took it away. He then picked up a drinking glass that had been accidentally left behind, smashed it against the stone wall of his cell, and used a shard to cut open his arm.[11] It was another failure in a life of failures: he survived.

But Naldi was not Stanzani's only informant concerning the curare. As soon as Secchi was arrested, a mystery witness came forward and laid in the lap of the judges the complete outline of the murder plan—or, rather, several plans, since the conspirators had devised backup strategies. Only one of these plans involved curare. From June to December, the newspapers gave daily reports about the depositions of the secret messenger—an article each day for six months on the revelations of one single informant.

Who were the conspirators? According to the voluble and knowledgeable person called "Witness X" by journalists, the conspirators were Tullio, Rosina, Naldi, Secchi, Severo Dalla and his brother, along with Professor Murri and his brother Riccardo. All these people had varying degrees of complicity in a homicidal mania excited by the woman at the center of it all, Linda Murri.[12]

Naldi had mentioned a sack of lead balls. Witness X corroborated the existence of the balls and explained their intended use. When Bonmartini was sick with abdominal pain, Rosina had come up with the idea of hitting him over the head with a sack of sand which, she thought, would leave no marks. Linda and Tullio rejected the sand as being an untried murder weapon. Then Rosina suggested that Linda entice the count into an embrace, positioning him so that Rosina could inject him with poison. The Murris rejected that plan on account of Bonmartini's repugnance for Rosina—he would never let her get so close to him, even if he had to disengage himself from his wife's arms and crawl out of his sickbed on his knees. Finally, Rosina suggested using a sack of *pallini* to stun Bonmartini so that someone—Linda, Tullio, or Rosina herself—could inject him with poison. The lead balls, about the size of a child's marbles, were normally used in the house to counterbalance window shutters and to clean bottles. Rosina had added the balls to their inventory of weapons after Tullio received a letter from Linda that made him and his family cry—the letter of August 15 in which Linda described Bonmartini's hurling a chair. Rosina carried the pallini in her purse during the weeks before the murder; they weighed 300 grams—less than a pound. The investigators found them now in another search of the Bonmartini apartment.

Witness X described how Tullio and Linda hit upon the idea of using curare and then asked Secchi about its properties. While Linda and Secchi were in Darmstadt, Linda saw to it that the doctor ordered a quantity sufficient for killing a man. Back in Bologna, Tullio and Secchi tested the poison on a goat. Witness X had held the creature still while Secchi injected it. The day following the goat experiment, Witness X had brought Tullio 1.20 grams of curare and the equipment he needed to use it. In a deal struck with the prosecutors, Witness X promised to bring them the leftover poison. What the prosecutors gave in return was clear enough: immunity from prosecution.[13]

Tisa Borghi had no intention of confirming Secchi's guilt by these disclosures. On the contrary, she was trying to show that Secchi, like Bonmartini, was the victim of Tullio's brutality and Linda's connivance and that he was drawn against his will into the murder conspiracy until he was helpless to extricate himself. Tisa was Secchi's Rosina. She was tough and coarse, happy to hold down animals while Secchi tortured them by cutting into their ear canals. The poison he used eventually immobilized them but did not lessen their hideous pain. Tisa was proud of her part in the hard-hearted experiments, proud that she had been a party to nearly every detail of the murder. She had hurried through the streets with messages, past the throbbing blue frescoes of Madonnas and Christs embedded in the arcades; she had sent telegrams from the Palazzo Comunale, arranged meetings for Secchi and Linda, cleaned up after the lovers, and covered Linda's tracks as she traveled around Italy, Switzerland, and Germany to her various rendezvous with Secchi. Even Naldi's alibi for the night of the murder seemed to involve her—it was Tisa who, before coming to Secchi, had worked as a nurse at the Rizzoli Institute in Bologna and knew that the owner of the Hotel de Russie had a slight connection to it. Tisa was less personally interested than Rosina in killing the count, since he had treated her well enough when she was a nurse in the Bonmartini household. Yet, like Rosina, she was an eager accomplice. Once the plot was exposed, she made no effort to dissociate herself from it and freely admitted her participation. Her only thought, apparently, was to protect the man who had involved her in it, Carlo Secchi.

Two days after his arrest, Secchi broke down in the face of the prosecutor's detailed information about the curare. He wrote a long interrogatory explaining his role in the murder, trying not to contradict his defender, Tisa, but putting things in such as way as to mitigate guilt for all of the accused, especially Linda.

"I have known Tullio Murri since he was a little boy," he narrated.[14] He described Tullio as generous, loving toward his sister and family, intelligent, courageous, but with an impulsive temperament incapable of thinking through his actions. (This was a striking understatement.) According to Secchi, when Tullio found out about Secchi's involvement with his sister, he approved of it. "You are perhaps her only joy," he wrote to Secchi. "Given my sister's ill health, I feel obligated . . . to remove her from possible danger from her husband and . . . to ask you with the promise of utmost secrecy to provide the means of freeing her from Bonmartini." That was the first time Secchi understood that Tullio meant to kill his brother-in-law. On meeting with Tullio, Secchi found that the young man had many plans for dispatching Bonmartini, but none of them was feasible. Tullio swore that Linda was ignorant of everything and would not become involved. "His behavior seemed uncertain and undecided," Secchi wrote. "In the hope of getting him to abandon his idea [of killing Bonmartini], I let him continue with his scheme." Tullio especially wanted Secchi to get him some curare. "I tried to explain the impossibility of using such a poison. It was to convince him of the difficulty that I carried out an experiment on a goat."

On the evening of August 10, in the lurid gaslight of Secchi's bare laboratory, Tisa pinned the goat's legs so that Secchi could make an injection near the heart. For more than ten minutes, the animal turned round and round the room as if nothing had happened. "Maybe the poison would work better on me," Tullio laughed. "It surely isn't bothering that goat." But finally, after fifteen minutes, the goat fell to its knees and then to its side, immobile. Secchi reached for a small knife and cut the animal's throat to kill it. Tullio, suddenly thoughtful, said, "I have to be able to do it alone."

"'Look,' I told him, 'what I just did is fine if you want to kill a poor goat that doesn't know what you are up to, but when we start talking about killing a man, that's a different story, especially if that man is young, strong, and a doctor to boot. He knows how to resist. You have to get him down, keep him from shouting for help, and keep him still while you get the injection into him. For the goat, a small amount suffices. For someone weighing a hundred twenty kilos, you would need an enormous dose.' I remember that to convince Tullio, who began making great claims for his own strength, I suggested he try to immobilize me. He seemed persuaded and didn't even want to try."

Following this emotional narrative, Stanzani asked only one question: What happened to the curare and syringe? "Tullio returned it the day I treated his arm," Secchi replied. "It had a strong odor, so I threw it away."

Tisa, meanwhile, had brought the missing curare to the justices in a long, thin, yellowish vessel with a large mouth and a stopper of frosted glass. It smelled only a little.

The next day, June 30, the judges interrogated Tullio about the poison.[15] Tullio at first maintained, by means of a letter to the judges, that he found some curare in his father's house and eventually threw it out on Via Pusterla as he left the crime scene. The judges then showed him first the bottle containing undiluted curare they had sequestered in Secchi's house and then the bottle with the diluted solution, stinking gently, that had been brought to them by Tisa Borghi. Tullio changed his story, saying that he was distraught over his sister's mistreatment by Bonmartini and even believed Bonmartini was planning to kill Linda. "I wrote to Dr. Secchi, asking him to help me save Linda." The discussions about poison, he said, were "always vague and half-joking." He described the experiment with the goat as the event that convinced him to abandon the idea of poison. Nevertheless, he had asked Secchi the following day to send him some curare and a syringe, "not knowing myself what I would do with it." Regarding the lead pellets, he said he discovered them in the Bonmartini house while he was waiting for the victim and thought to make use of them by hitting Bonmartini over the head while Naldi injected him. But Naldi put forth so many objections that he abandoned the idea and threw the sack into a trunk in the apartment. The only help he requested of Naldi, he said, was to prevent Bonmartini from fleeing during the expected confrontation. He flatly denied Naldi's claim that he, Tullio, had carried a knife and two daggers into the Bonmartini apartment.

"But Bonmartini was wounded with a double-edged dagger," the justices countered.

"He was wounded with a knife," Tullio corrected. "Only the curved point of it was double-edged."

Tisa Borghi was formally deposed on July 1. She was the first witness to state categorically that Linda was aware of everything Tullio did and planned and that she used every wile possible to involve Secchi. Linda reviled Secchi for not participating in their machinations, so that he was in continual turmoil over her reproaches. Linda made him believe that Bonmartini wanted to poison her. She said that her father had even stated that if it were not for the prospect of having a murderer for a son, he himself would provide the knife for Tullio to do away with Bonmartini. Murri said he would give half his fortune to anyone who would kill him, or so Linda had reported. In another version of the remark that Dr. Pacini said he heard from Tullio, Professor Murri had offered only 100,000.[16]

Tisa claimed she had overheard Linda and Rosina discussing their efforts, both past and future, to poison the count. The conversation took place while Tisa was in Linda's sitting room. Another time, Linda confided to Tisa that she had already tried killing her husband with arsenic, morphine, and cocaine, mixing them into his coffee, which she served him cold and bitter. Tisa cleared up any question as to why Linda had rented the apartment next to her own, which would have been a risky location for meeting Secchi. As the police had already guessed, since there had been only a bare mattress on the bed, the apartment was not intended for lovemaking but for storing supplies needed for the murder. The letter Tullio wrote to Secchi in which he confided that he wanted to kill Bonmartini had not been mailed; it had been brought to Secchi by none other than—Linda. The 3,000 lire that Secchi gave Tullio was not only requested by Linda; it was delivered by her from the doctor to the killer.

Tisa continued: Linda demanded that Secchi bring her with him to Darmstadt when he purchased the curare because she knew he was ordering the poison against his will and might abandon the whole idea as soon as he got two kilometers away from her. Meanwhile, Tullio had a plan when he went to Venice. He was going to get Bonmartini into a wrestling match and bring him down. Once Cesco was on the ground, one of the women, Linda or Rosina, would stuff a towel in his mouth to prevent him from shouting, while the other woman would inject him near the heart. Rosina brought along the lead balls when she and Tullio went to Venice just in case these, too, should be needed in the assault. Rosina welcomed the murder project because the crime would place Tullio "in her fist" according to Tisa, "and she would become a signora." Secchi, in contrast, wanting no part in the crime, thought constantly of breaking off with Linda. But Linda refused to part and threatened Secchi with a vendetta by her brother if he ended their relationship. That was the substance of Tisa Borghi's long deposition.[17]

The istruttoria had to start over, as if from the beginning. The next day, therefore, the justices began re-examining all the defendants. Tisa's deposition was first read to Secchi in its entirety. He said that it was substantially correct. Seeking perhaps to mitigate Linda's complicity, he suggested that the comments Tisa overheard in Linda's house may have been mere boasting by Rosina, who was proud of her fearless aggression against Bonmartini. Secchi said Tullio swore to him that Linda did not know the contents of the letter she brought inviting Secchi to participate in the assassination. For the rest, Secchi confirmed that it was true Linda told him she was afraid Bonmartini was poisoning her, true that she insisted on going with him to Darmstadt, true that she reported those declarations by her father.[18] The same day, Secchi was interrogated again. This time, he made a point of stating that the trip to Darmstadt had been made like all the others, for pleasure, and that Linda was merely accompanying him when he went to Meerck to order the curare, along with some medicines. Secchi obviously was trying to shield Linda in all his statements up to this point. However, the shield slipped when the justices asked him about a letter he wrote to Linda in which he warned her to watch her brother, to keep him from doing something stupid. He wrote it, Secchi said, after sending Tullio the curare. He was referring specifically to the poison (which Linda was not supposed to know about). And Secchi said still more. Shown again Linda's card, "I don't hear anything more about S," Secchi confirmed that the "medicine" probably referred to the curare experiment that he had promised to do for Tullio. Thus Secchi, perhaps made pliant by fatigue and despair, became the second accomplice to admit that Linda knew about the curare.

Another interrogation of Rosina, brief and fierce, was next. She said Tisa never heard anything in Linda's sitting room and she was ready to call Tisa a liar to her face. Asked if Tullio had expected to inject Bonmartini with the curare while visiting him in Venice, Rosina avoided answering with her usual method: "I'm not answering," she said.[19]

Tullio was next. He admitted that he might have had a conversation with Tisa about getting Bonmartini on the ground so he could inject him, but he insisted that such a discussion could not have been serious. He remarked again that his conversations were often jocular when he was around Secchi.

Linda had a long, minute interrogation on July 7. As with all the other interrogations, her answers were plausible and her position seemed stronger after the questioning than before it. The justices showed her the bottles of ether and morphine they found in the apartment next to her home—100 grams of morphine acetate, together with some of Rosina's handkerchiefs. Why were the poisons there? the justices asked. She put them there herself, she answered, on Secchi's advice, so they would be out of reach if, in a moment of despair, she were tempted to kill herself. She gave herself therapeutic arsenic injections and used the ether as a skin anesthetic. She was next questioned concerning the comments Tisa imputed to her. Had she upbraided Secchi for not helping her against Bonmartini? That was false, she answered. Also false were the remarks her father was supposed to have made about wanting Bonmartini dead. "My father, like me, only counseled against Tullio having it out with Cesco because Cesco would probably say something insolent and Tullio wouldn't be able to restrain himself."

Up to that point, Linda was subdued, almost languid. But when Stanzani described the conversation Tisa said she overheard between Linda and Rosina, Linda, still composed, raised her voice: "It's all absolutely a lie!" She vehemently denied having tried to poison Cesco with arsenic, morphine, or cocaine. She prepared his coffee herself and served it cold and bitter because that was the way he liked it. For the rest, the maids served his food, not her. He was sick before going to Venice, but she and Frieda and perhaps some others in the house were also sick. As for the trip to Darmstadt, she did not go to make sure Secchi ordered poison, she insisted, but to see the scenery. She did not know what exactly he ordered at the factory. Had they argued before the trip? They might or might not have, she answered. "Between Secchi and me there were many squabbles," she said. The justices finally confronted her with the plan that Tullio, visiting in Venice, would wrestle Bonmartini to the ground while the women silenced him and administered the fatal injection. Linda had perhaps reckoned on the question coming up, for her answer was remarkably quick, deliberate, and simple: "So why wasn't that done?" she asked.

The justices did not attempt to answer that excellent question, but they had many conjectures. In the first place, Linda was not on the scene to provide the help that might have been necessary. When the wrestling match took place, Bonmartini did not go down, Tullio did, and Cesco merely smiled a victor's gracious smile. The conspirators learned from the tussle that they could not count on overpowering Bonmartini physically. They no doubt considered injecting him while he was asleep, but that idea would have been discarded because of the elaborate precautions he took in locking himself in at night. Only when the justices asked if it were true that Secchi wanted to break off with her did Linda lose her poise. "That is a foul lie!" she shouted, her tight voice echoing against the stone all around her. "I would have suffered if Secchi had broken with me, but I would have resigned myself, and Secchi knew it. I told him I would never want to keep him by force."

The same day of her interrogation, a day that must have been one of the most exhausting of her imprisonment, Linda was confronted with Tisa. According to the usual procedure, the justice questioned the individuals whose stories conflicted, while he and his assistants weighed their responses; however, neither of the persons interrogated was under oath. According to the justices, who were the same men soliciting Tisa's testimony and were therefore hardly impartial observers, the nurse seemed frank and forthright, while Linda was agitated and uncertain. Linda denied again that she had pressured Secchi to help her dispose of Bonmartini; she had only asked him not to add to her troubles by insisting that she send the children away. In the middle of the questioning, Linda turned angrily on Tisa. "Why do you want to hurt me?"

"You!" Tisa spat out. "You drew everybody into a trap. You forced Secchi to get the curare. You remember that morning before leaving for Darmstadt? He asked you in the name of God to abandon the idea of the curare, but you insisted, saying you were going with him to be sure he ordered the medicine you wanted."

"None of that is true!" Linda retorted fiercely. "There were other reasons for the argument and the trip." It was from misunderstood conversations, Linda said, that Tisa formed the wild idea they were trying to poison Bonmartini. "I often said, for example, that so many people died, it would have been lucky if either I or Cesco had died. But I never said I wanted to kill him!

"I treated you like a sister," Linda continued in an outburst of grievance, "confided everything, but never, never did I say those things!"

"You told me yourself you were poisoning his coffee!"

"It's true you were there one morning when I made it because you came early," Linda protested. "It could be that I said the count took it bitter and cold. And I might have said, 'With a little morphine, I could send him to the other world.' Those were things said in irritation, not plans, and certainly not a discussion of things that had already happened." But Tisa did not back down.

The next confrontation, between Tisa and Rosina, was brief. The justices recorded that Tisa was again direct, whereas Rosina seemed worn out. Small wonder. Rosina and Naldi were the only defendants receiving no food except the prison allocation, sufficient only to keep them more or less alive. She was suffering from starvation. The Murris were sending their servants with meals for Tullio and Linda, but they did not trouble themselves to relieve Naldi or Rosina. When Rosina wrote to her brother complaining of her famine, Stanzani intercepted the letter and tried to bribe her with food to entice her cooperation. Rosina preferred hunger to helping Stanzani. Despite her weakened condition, she defiantly declared three times that everything Tisa said was a lie and everything she herself said was the sacrosanct truth. When the judges showed her the flacon of poison found in the "rendezvous" apartment and asked her to explain it, she answered, "I'm not answering."

Linda was interrogated again twenty days later, after she had been given time to think about Tisa's damaging information. On this occasion, the justices asked her about the famous card. In a previous questioning, Linda had said that the question about medicine having its effect referred to her mother's suspicion that a certain woman was romantically interested in Tullio. She didn't remember what the "S" referred to, probably something written by Tullio. Asked why she had disguised her handwriting, Linda responded that if her mother had recognized her script on the envelope, she wouldn't have hesitated to open it. The letter would have confirmed her suspicion that the woman was having a relationship with Tullio.[20]

Now, however, a month later, Linda definitively stated that the "S" in the letter referred to Sant'Elpidio, the home of some relatives to whom the Murris had lent money. On the subject of Tisa, Linda had organized many observations. Tisa was hallucinatory, she said, besides being crazy and malicious. She was suggestible and easily led by impressions, always ready to give things a pessimistic interpretation. When Tisa was with her, Linda said, the nurse spoke badly of Secchi; when she was with him, she spoke badly of Linda. After her previous interrogation, Linda must have known that Tisa and Secchi could destroy her. Asked what motive Tisa would have for lying, Linda replied hotly, as if blurting out a secret: "Tisa Borghi was Secchi's lover before me, and she's probably got back with him again, or has some hope that she might one day reinstate herself."

Secchi repeated in each questioning that he had always advised the Murri brother and sister against any violence. "I never counseled Linda to rebel against her husband," he said, "because that would have meant losing her children, which nothing could have made up for." Secchi, it turned out, had taken precautions to establish his innocence. After the murder, but long before the authorities knew anything about the curare, he had confided Tullio's requests for poison to a friend, a Dr. Enrico Pacini. That proved he had no criminal intentions, he said, since he would never have made such a dangerous revelation if he had seriously plotted to do Bonmartini in. In fact, Dr. Pacini was questioned by the magistrates and corroborated that Secchi was appalled and distressed by Tullio's attempt to involve him in murder.[21]

More seriously, Secchi had saved all of his and Linda's letters and entrusted them to Tisa, who in turn stored them at her aunt's house on Via dell' Unione, where she often stayed when she was not sleeping at Secchi's clinic. The letters were safe from prying eyes, even the prying eyes of the law; the aunt was completely illiterate, and it was not likely that the police would conduct a search there. Secchi thought the letters would show how unwilling he was to be involved in murder. But on September 11, 1902, the letters were destroyed, without Secchi's knowledge, on the orders of none other than Linda. Just before her arrest, Linda asked Severo Dalla to burn all the correspondence between her and Secchi being kept by Tisa. Severo, always careful to stay behind the scenes when conducting illegal activities, charged his brother Ernesto with destroying the evidence. Ernesto appeared unexpectedly at the aunt's house. He demanded that Tisa surrender the letters, and she, learning that Ernesto had been sent by Linda, watched him set fire to them.

"If you could but see the letters I wrote to Linda," Secchi said miserably, referring to the destroyed correspondence, "they would prove everything I am saying about the nobility of my relationship with Linda, the reasons why she and Bonmartini were incompatible." Most of all, Secchi told Stanzani, the letters would have given small, exculpating details of his own state of mind when he gave Linda advice. "If I had wanted to kill Bonmartini," Secchi concluded, "I didn't need recourse to anyone else. I am still a young man, fortunately quite vigorous, and I would have found a way by myself to do it prudently and successfully." Even people who viewed Linda's lover unfavorably—and there were many—had to concede that Secchi was not the man to collaborate with a hothead like Tullio in a project as fraught with danger as Bonmartini's execution. By describing Secchi's fascination with Linda and Tullio's pressure to have Secchi participate in the crime, Tisa had sought to save Secchi. Instead, she provided the strongest link between Secchi and the murder.

Indeed, it is not difficult to believe that Secchi, who at the time was preoccupied with the study of curare, was the one who suggested the poison that left no traces. It is easy to conjecture that Tullio asked him about the right poison and Secchi was not miserly with information, perhaps intending to be more flippant than serious. Somewhere between his first discussion with Tullio and the procuring of the poison, Secchi either began to understand that their conversations were actually plans and not just careless talk, or he realized the gravity of what they were discussing and got cold feet. He pleaded with them to think twice about the project because it would require both apparatus and some violence. The violence would leave marks, even if the curare did not. Like Naldi, Secchi appears never to have voiced any moral objections to killing Bonmartini. He merely thought the idea was reckless.

Though Secchi might not have minded if Bonmartini died, what would have been his motive for assisting in his death? By 1902 he had fairly easy access to Linda; they were in fact going away together several times a year. If the open secret of their affair caused Bonmartini to seek a separation and custody of his children, why then, Secchi had wanted the children out of the way anyhow. But the press was quick to point out that for both Tullio and Secchi, there was something else besides love in their calculations. Bonmartini was rich. If he died, Linda would come into substantial assets which Tullio could expect to share. Secchi, though already well off, could marry a rich widow. As long as she could hide Bonmartini's will, Linda would get control of everything, a fortune of one and a half million, not to mention the fortune she would inherit in her own right after her father's death.[22]

Like most people born poor, Secchi had a lively interest in money. His letters to Linda—those that were not destroyed—reflect the kinds of discussions about expenses that come up between all people on intimate terms. *"My poor little Linda,"* he writes when she is ill. *"Would you like me to get you a jar of chicken gelatin made especially for you? If you want it, even if it costs me a bundle, I'll get it for you gladly"*[23] (July 18, 1900). As they plan their idyll in San Marcello Pistoiese, he writes her, *"Tell me without ceremony what you want me to bring from here. For myself, I won't bring anything but boots and money, intending to live off my little Linda and the woods, but with*

you" (July 16, 1900). He sends her flowers and gifts without mentioning the cost, of course. When they are trying to find a house to
rent for a meeting place in San Marcello Pistoiese, three hours away
from Bologna, he advises her: *"Pledge whatever money, if you find
something, without thought to cost, and lease it for Signora Tisa
Borghi"* (July 8, 1900). She advances money for their excursions, but
he expects to reimburse her. *"You have told me that in money you are
rich, therefore I ask you to get the 200 lire that we need in one day, and
if for some reason that is not convenient, write me"* (July 18, 1900). His
most outright discussion of money is on July 31, 1900, when he begins to sound curiously like Bonmartini remonstrating about his expenses: *"Today they pressed me to make a decision about the hunting. I
don't know if I want to throw away a thousand lire a year on myself because I am gloomy about the future. If it were not for you, I wouldn't
think about it a minute, but I feel myself becoming a miser like I've
never been before. Then, too, because I don't know where the expenses
will end, I'm very much afraid of going into debt even for necessities;
you can imagine how reluctant I am to put anything out for luxuries."*
Perhaps the lost correspondence would have reflected a deeper concern with the state of his finances. The correspondence that remained indicated anxiety, but not the kind of frantic preoccupation
that would have led him to kill someone for money.

There were early letters that escaped the Dalla holocaust—
about fifteen, dating from 1900 and 1901, written as Linda began
the two-year separation from her husband. These letters vividly
show that, far from wanting to be rid of Linda, Secchi at that time
loved her sincerely, passionately, and with no reservations. *"I need
you body and soul,"* he wrote, or, as the Italians expressed it, "flesh
and bone." Augusto Bianchi, who for his daily reports on the Murri
case in *Corriere della Sera* read all the documents released by the
police, described Secchi's missives as "the letters of an old
bachelor."[24] "His love slides into degeneration," Bianchi pontificates,
"like a man accustomed to commercial love. He doesn't know what
to give Linda except things conventionally offered to prostitutes:

oysters, petits fours, champagne. He uses phrases, such as 'tricks to keep you happy,' that have pornographic double meanings. Such gross facetiousness from an old masher," wrote Bianchi, "throws a sad shadow on this guilty love that generated a crime."

But read from the distance of a century, the letters, penned by a fifty-year-old to a thirty-year-old, are very like the expressions of young, almost juvenile, love. He writes of passing under her window each Friday, a prearranged schedule so that she can at least see him when they cannot meet (June 22, 1900). They exchange letters every two or three days. *"Your brief letters leave me longing for more,"* he observes. *"Your long letters lighten the world and make me joyous"* (June 24, 1900). *"I want your mind to rest easy about me, to see you calm now and secure about the future. If you are afraid of losing this old thing of yours, keep getting closer, keep holding him tight, and remember that, as much devotion as he has to you, you deserve even more"* (July 6, 1900).

"It's worth an uncomfortable love," he declares, in one of his few references to her married state, *"worth the disapproving glare of public opinion, worth unlimited sacrifices, these are worth having your faith in me, your admiration, and the knowledge I keep in my heart that I will never lose you"* (July 24, 1900).[25]

He writes of having loved her years before, and of his life after parting from her. *"After I thought I had lost you forever, you became the paragon others were judged by. I never wanted to distance you, of course, but I was sure you deserved someone much better, and I was ready to sacrifice myself for your good"* (June 24, 1900). He expresses guilt for his past life and hopes that when he has made her happy for many years, he will live down liaisons that have left him *"filled with remorse."*

I love you with a youthful excitement, as I have never loved, and not only because of the sublime love you return to me—that would make me proud, if I felt worthy of it—but for your goodness, . . . your cleverness, because you are a good daughter, good thinker,

good mama, because you are beautiful. With you life would be
paradise. Believe it, my baby. It isn't possible to love more than I
love you. I would adore you on my knees if I could. I am looking
forward to the time when I can be there, near my little Linda, to
buck you up, to make you happy again and lovely as you were when
you were young and . . . loved me so much! (July 9, 1900)

He writes of thinking of her continually while he travels, recalling
their intimate talks that, happy or ugly, bring them closer together
and make their bonds stronger. *"Be jealous,"* he tells her in one letter,
"and let me be jealous, too, if it's a sign of love." He writes of wanting to
kneel before her. *"God knows how I love you!"* he exclaims (June 24,
1900).

His long letters touch on mundane topics: the discomfort of the
summer heat, people he has visited. *"I have ordered a nice blue suit*
that I like a lot. If it's well made, it may make me less ugly to my cza-
rina" (July 31, 1900). *"Take care of yourself, cure yourself. Your Carluc-*
cio wants it so much, because when you are well you love him . . . less
badly. Many kisses, but many, many of those . . . ours, our special ones,
that are like nothing else and leave an imprint on my heart."

He describes the torment of separation, of turning over and over
in his mind all day the things he turns over and over at night (undated, fall 1900). When separating from her, he is bothered for hours
by a lump in his throat (July 1900). After their thirteen-day idyll in
San Marcello Pistoiese, he re-enacts in memory *"the lovers' talk, the*
caresses, the reciprocal promises, the swearing of fidelity, your laughter,
your jokes, our life experienced so intensely in only 13 days" (undated).

On the second anniversary of their reuniting, September 27,
1900, he sends her flowers. As he is wont to do, he prescribes for his
beloved patient:

My poor Angel. Drink, drink a lot, but tepid and hot, not cold,
because hot is more quickly absorbed, coffee, tea, decoctions, wine,
diluted or not, lemon water, orangeade, even if you are not thirsty,

but drink a lot, and hot, not only water. I don't think of anything but you. The only comfort I can offer is love. (September 29, 1900).

If Secchi was not madly, selflessly, in love with Linda, he was certainly a skilled pretender. His letters imply that he is thinking about a future with her. *"I have spent an entire night thinking of you, of your health, of my love for you, of our future. My head is in flames, my heart grieving, and I don't live except for the desire to see you again or at least hear news of you. I love you more than it is possible to love"* (undated). He tells of wanting to write her long letters to describe *"my need for you,"* but his ideas *"crowd in,"* his words roil in his head, *"too confused to express."*

The letters show how dependent Secchi and Linda were on Tisa Borghi as their go-between, a dependence that became even more acute after Linda's and Cesco's short-lived reconciliation. Tisa had for years served as Secchi's assistant, errand girl, charwoman, and companion. She may not have loved him in any romantic way. She was in a sense his servant, his "woman," as he once offhandedly referred to her in a letter to Linda, paid a housekeeper's salary and with similar duties. Through their ten-year propinquity, they were used to each other and took their relationship for granted. Like 58 percent of Italian adults, they were both unmarried [26] If Secchi had brought Tisa to his bed, occasionally or regularly—though both he and Tisa denied it—that did not make them lovers. Such relationships were commonplace between professional men and their hired help. On the other hand, if Tisa was in love with Secchi, as Linda asserted, her life as his confidante must have been hateful.

Teresa Bonera was married when she met Secchi in 1893. He treated her for a grave and unnamed illness that lasted three years. They became fast friends; at some point, she separated from her husband and resumed her maiden name, Borghi. Nurses were not required to have formal training or to be licensed by the state. They acquired nursing skills by informal apprenticeships in clinics or doctors' offices. Eventually, Tisa became Secchi's full-time nurse, assisting him in his clinic of fifteen beds in Via Garibaldi for a salary of 20 lire a month. Her wages included room and board; but sometimes she stayed in her own quarters, that is, in her aunt's apartment several blocks from the clinic.

After Secchi was reunited with Linda in 1898, it was Tisa who carried their love letters and messages and arranged their meetings. *"My baby, how are you?"* Secchi writes to Linda in 1900. *"I am waiting only for the moment when Tisa will get here, since I am sure she must have seen you today."* In 1900, Tisa acted as Secchi's stand-in by renting a little villa near Linda's in San Marcello Pistoiese for the fictitious Engineer Borghi, who would be able to look down on the plains of Tuscany from his bedroom. She was sent to clean the villa before Linda's arrival and after her departure. When the vacation was over, Tisa was obliged to assist Secchi in his reminiscences. *"My heart,"* he wrote to Linda, *"after the last sad good-bye look that we exchanged I went into the house and did not come out except for one hour yesterday. For the rest of the time I was alone, thinking of you, or calling Tisa to talk of you or make her angry by talking ill of you, just to see her vexed and horrified, for she really loves you"* (July 8, 1900). Only once is there any recorded dissension between Secchi and Tisa. When he learned that she had allowed his letters to be burned, Secchi was beside himself with fury, she told the prosecutors. "You have broken me!" he cried in despair. "You have broken me!"

It is easy to understand why Tisa handed over the letters to Linda's messenger and watched them being destroyed. She was accustomed to following Linda's directions without question concerning communications between her and Secchi. Bonmartini's murder had been discovered, but when Dalla came for the letters, the investigators knew nothing as yet of the poison, Secchi's connection, or Linda's possible complicity. Linda claimed that she ordered the letters burned to save her dignity: she was afraid the intimate details of her love affair with Secchi would be exposed. Secchi knew what he had written in the 1902 letters. Why would he have desperately wanted the prosecutors to read them, unless they showed that he was trying to defuse the Murris' anger against Bonmartini? But would they have confirmed the case already developing against Linda? Was Secchi willing, then, to expose her? If Linda was worried about her dignity, why didn't she destroy Secchi's earlier letters to her, the ones that the police found? The letters from 1902 that Tisa was keeping might have saved her lover or at least mitigated his guilt; that seems clear. Secchi may have been the first person Linda thought of after her arrest, the first to whom she smuggled a love letter swearing her lifelong devotion. But two days before her imprisonment, when she was in imminent danger of arrest and Secchi was still only a secondary suspect, she tried to save herself by destroying his letters, even if it meant leaving him defenseless.

Dr. Secchi, the specialist, had long been well established in Bologna on a shady, prosperous street behind the city's central piazza. Patients coming for their two o'clock appointments would stop in the square in the dark cathedral of San Petronio when the noon sun, beaming through an astronomer's peephole in the roof, falls in an oval patch on the marble floor and moves in minute, stately pulses along a meridian, a particle of heavenly light traveling with the worshipers across the liturgical weeks. Fortified by the orderly little miracle, the patients would proceed to Piazza Garibaldi and climb the stairs to Secchi's office.[27] The stairs were well worn with the daily traffic of people bringing their suffering ears, noses, or throats for his examination, for no matter how many doctors established themselves in Bologna, there was sufficient misery to occupy them all. A quarter of Italian men drafted for the army each year were deemed too sick to serve, even according to the military's tolerant standards.[28] When Secchi's name was first connected to the murder, he stopped getting new patients for the first time in his practice, though his old patients for the most part continued their treatments.

But then Professor Murri learned from the newspapers that his daughter, the "pure spirit," had been sexually involved with Secchi. He began making public statements to the effect that Secchi was the evil influence, the "malignancy," that had infected Linda. Long before the magistrates charged Secchi with any crime, Murri let it be known that he thought Secchi was the murderer and went so far as to personally investigate Secchi's alibi. As a result of what Secchi called "jesuitical Murrian insinuations," many of Secchi's patients were scared off. "The great Augusto," as Secchi called him, was ruining his reputation, suggesting to people that their trusted doctor was a killer and persuading other doctors not to refer their patients to him. For eight months, Murri wrote anti-Secchi diatribes to their mutual colleagues, every few weeks sending out what Secchi described as "another of his stupid letters."[29] No wonder that after his arrest, Secchi was reported to be emaciated, very pale, and profoundly depressed.[30] Always a dandy in a country of exquisitely dressed professional men, he now let his beard and hair grow and appeared unkempt, or so the prison authorities reported to journalists, who of course were not permitted to see him.

Within three months, however, Secchi seemed sound again. Before his arrest, he had smoked Virginia cigars. Tobacco, along with stamps and salt, was a state monopoly that could be bought only at certain *tabaccherie* selling the three items; those resourceful merchants, the prison guards, could no doubt sell it underground, but prison rules forbade smoking. Like all prisoners awaiting trial, Secchi was permitted to write only one letter a week, one page long, which he invariably did write. His letters usually discussed neither Linda nor himself. Instead, having turned against his old mentor, he filled his allotted page by describing Professor Murri's general worthlessness as a human being. As he began to adjust to prison, Secchi asked one friend to send him the works of Gorky and Tolstoy. He asked another friend for a pipe, but the authorities seized it before it reached him. His letters calmed down. Nevertheless, he took up a little of his precious letter space to try to find out who else had been arrested.

What other names besides Linda, Tullio, Rosina, and Naldi were on the list of conspirators that Tisa gave to Stanzani? He hoped that old Murri was also constrained to writing only one page and that he, like Secchi, had lost a carefully built career. In short, he was encouraged by the thought that Professor Murri, too, might be anguishing in jail with nothing to smoke.

6. THE THIRD ACCOMPLICE

Of all the theories surrounding the Murri case, none fascinated the press more than the belief that there was a third, unindicted accomplice in the Bonmartini murder, that Tullio and Naldi were not the only ones waiting in the apartment. Every few weeks the newspapers stirred the crickets of rumor by suggesting a new suspect and examining his or her past life in searching detail. The third accomplice was a resilient idea that the public never gave up. Even today, a century after the trial, Venetian postcard vendors and Paduan shopkeepers will offer the information that Rosina or The Uncle or Linda—the most popular suspect—actually committed the murder that was blamed on Tullio. Nor is the notion of a third accomplice far-fetched: Justice Stanzani, not one susceptible to phantasms, believed it himself. It was information about a possible third accomplice that Stanzani was trying to wring out of Naldi when the wretch surprised him by spilling out the news of the curare. Stanzani considered Naldi a rabbit, not a killer; and besides, Naldi had an alibi, however problematic it might be. There was plenty of reason to doubt that he had actually wielded one of the murder knives. If Bonmartini was attacked by two killers, as the experts insisted, then who else besides Naldi had assisted Tullio?

Justice Stanzani maintained that the Murri family, Severo and Ernesto Dalla, and some of the servants all knew in advance that

Tullio was planning to kill Bonmartini and that they had either willfully ignored the conspiracy or actively participated in it. One of these people, he was convinced, was the third accomplice present at the crime scene. The most obvious suspects were the Dalla brothers, and Stanzani used the first opportunity to take them into custody and pressure them with interrogations. Whether or not they had any part in the attack or the conspiracy, they had tampered with evidence, according to Tisa's testimony, and that was reason enough for Stanzani to snatch them. Ernesto Dalla was thus arrested on July 4, 1903, and charged with *favoreggiamento*—interfering with the investigation of a crime, a charge that also could be used against someone who abetted a crime or helped a known suspect elude the authorities. Early in her affair with Secchi, Linda had warned Ernesto's brother Severo that she might one day ask him to burn some letters from her lover. On September 11, 1902, the day before her arrest, Linda judged that the time was at hand, and Ernesto was sent to carry out her order.[1]

By the time of Ernesto's arrest, Stanzani expected to hear arrant falsehoods from everyone connected to the Murri case; Ernesto Dalla did not disappoint him. At first, Ernesto said that he hardly knew Tullio Murri and denied destroying the letters. Confronted with Tisa Borghi, he claimed he did not recognize her; but eventually he admitted his part.[2] Could Dalla have been in the Bonmartini apartment the night of the murder? Apparently not. Ernesto worked as a clerk in an insane asylum in Imola, twenty miles from Bologna. Every two weeks he was allowed to go to Bologna for a day. He had requested special permission to be absent from the asylum from August 31 to September 8, 1902, that is, the period beginning two days after Bonmartini's murder, when the count lay dead but undiscovered in his living room. However, he was still in Imola on the night of the crime and could prove it.[3] The judge had him examined for traces of knife lesions that he might have acquired as Bonmartini struggled. No cuts were found.

There it was. Another glinting coincidence. Ernesto asks in advance for days off during precisely the time when Tullio will flee

Italy. Ernesto never offered the police an explanation as to what he was planning to do during this time off from work or why he chose those specific dates. If he were planning to help Tullio escape, that meant he knew about the intended murder. And if Ernesto, who was not a frequent companion of Tullio, knew about the project, then the Murri family must have known as well. But there was no proof to support Stanzani's suspicions, and he had to be content with detaining Ernesto on the feebler charge of destroying evidence.

The two brothers, Severo and Ernesto, had been more or less born into service to the Murris.[4] Their father had worked for the family and had always been treated well. At various times, both brothers had been entrusted with Murri money and secrets. Severo was as much a companion to Tullio as an employee. Accountant Severo Dalla, as he was known to the Office of Public Security, was shrewd, sly, and perhaps ruthless, since he used his brother as a shield whenever he was asked to carry out any task that qualified as a criminal act. Destroying evidence, delivering illegal messages—these were jobs for Ernesto. Employed as a bookkeeper, property manager, and general business manager for the family, Severo possessed the one skill necessary for all servants, servers, and representatives of the Murris: he was a cool-headed liar whose prevarications, though not believed, could not be proved false. Severo was the ghost whose blurred image appeared everywhere in the investigation without presenting a substantial presence that Stanzani could capture.[5] For example, he had keys to Linda's and Secchi's little apartment. He also possessed keys to the Bonmartini residence during August, but he said he returned those keys to Linda when he saw her in Rimini on August 22, six days before the murder. He was among the first people called to Via Mazzini to investigate the mephitis; but he did not come forth with any keys at that time, either because he had none or because he was too clever to admit that he had access to a room in which—did he know?—a man lay murdered.[6] Severo never tried to hide his dislike of Bonmartini. Why should he? Signora Giannina had told him that Bonmartini referred to him as "riffraff."

The details made Stanzani's tentacles twitch, but still he was not able to pounce on Severo as the third accomplice.

Severo was with Tullio on August 22, 25, and 27, the days before the assassination.[7] He had an alibi for the night of the murder: he was in the North, in Trent. But his alibi, too, went ringing into the loud bin of peculiar coincidences. The justice sat up straight and startled when he learned that Severo Dalla had traveled to Berlin and Munich a month before the assassination and in a separate trip had surveyed northern Italy, Switzerland, and southern Austria the week of the homicide. Considering that Tullio, fleeing the crime, had gone from Switzerland to Berlin to Munich, this was a notable, maybe incriminating concurrence. Severo explained it with a shrug. "I take a trip abroad every year," he said.[8]

Only once before the murder did Severo emerge from the brume to place his name on a traceable document. For several weeks prior to August 28, 1902, Professor Murri had been making large deposits in Tullio's account at the Banco Popolare in Bologna, amounting to 65,267 lire. On August 5, three weeks before the murder, Severo brought the bank a note from Professor Murri authorizing a transfer of all of Tullio's money to Severo's account.[9] When Tullio was asked by Stanzani for an explanation, he averred that his father never said anything to him about the large deposits, nor about the transfer—everything was done without his knowledge. Letters proved that Tullio was lying. Severo had no real explanation, either. He confirmed that usually Signora Giannina handled the Murri money and that usually Tullio received an allowance of 100 lire a month. The transfer had been made for the sake of "convenience," he said, not so that Tullio would have money during an anticipated flight. The authorities noted that, until Severo's arrest, they could not confiscate the funds, since these were no longer in Tullio's name.[10] With such fugitive evidence, Stanzani knew that it would be difficult to convict either of the Dallas of a serious crime. After many discussions, Stanzani and the prosecutors finally, reluctantly, released the brothers, after having held them as long as possible in the hope that they would say something to implicate Professor Murri.[11] But the suspicion never lifted that one of the Dallas, Severo especially, had a hand in the murder.

If Stanzani was doubtful about nailing the Dallas, he probably never expected to bring Riccardo Murri to trial for any charge more serious than being inept. It was incontestable that Uncle Riccardo arranged Tullio's escape; but the law was indulgent toward blood relatives who protected each other. Stanzani proceeded as if he really intended to prosecute Riccardo, again in the hope that the lawyer might blurt some information about the murder. But Riccardo did not appear much disturbed by being included among the defendants. He seemed confident that he would never face trial. He was formally accused of complicity in the homicide "by promising help that would be forthcoming after the deed"—a more serious charge than favoreggimento.[12] First in the bulging catalogue of marks against him was the long, deliberate meeting with Tullio and Linda that he convoked at Rimini six days before the crime (a meeting where Severo Dalla seems to have been present). Then there was the plethora of letters, cards, and especially telegrams going back and forth between Riccardo, Linda, and Tullio in the two weeks before the murder. Fifteen telegrams were sent from Rimini alone between August 15 and September 3, and many others from the various places where Linda, Tullio, or Uncle Riccardo lighted during that period. Some of these were quite strange communications: "Mariolina is sleeping" or "Minetta Mariolina are happy." Riccardo had no explanation for the mystifying messages, except to describe at length the family's various nicknames for Linda's daughter Maria.[13] Next came Riccardo's note to Stanzani explaining that Dr. Dagnini had ordered Linda to Switzerland. This was obviously a cover for Tullio's flight—a trip completely organized by Riccardo—since Dagnini protested that he had not even examined Linda, much less ordered any foreign treatment. He would have sent her to Switzerland if Professor Murri had asked him to, he said, but the request never came. Professor Murri responded by calling Dagnini a liar.[14]

In his interrogation, Riccardo described touching Tullio's arm and hearing his nephew emit something like a scream. "As I pondered that scream, I went to his room. Taking him by both arms, I pushed him against a wall and told him there was a great mystery going on, that his Papa was evidently tormented by doubts and that I wanted to know the truth."[15]

Tullio's story to Riccardo was that he had been wounded by Bonmartini and had killed in self-defense. Riccardo asked assistance from several fellow Masons in finding a sanctuary for his nephew outside Italy. Stanzani questioned each of the Masons. The grand master, Ernesto Nathan, after first categorically denying that Riccardo Murri ever confided anything to him about the crime, reversed his deposition a month later and admitted that he understood the reasons for Tullio's flight.[16] (The publicity surrounding Nathan's part in the melodrama apparently did not hurt him; he later became mayor of Rome.) The Masons had been no help to Tullio, but Uncle Riccardo did not give up. In the course of trying to procure a foreign passport for Tullio, Riccardo wrote to his brother, advising him to give a detailed description of Tullio's wound and to exaggerate its severity. "Help him prepare an apparently spontaneous explanation for what he did after [killing Bonmartini]. Meanwhile, I will try to throw off the judges in their investigation." Riccardo had blocked the wheels of justice in every way he could. But in the end, Stanzani concluded that none of his actions tied him firmly to the plotting of the murder or its execution. He had aided in the escape of a criminal, but since that criminal was his brother's son, Riccardo would never be convicted.[17]

If Riccardo had not plotted to assassinate the count, he diligently plotted to assassinate Bonmartini's character after his death. Professor Murri and Riccardo together hired a free-lance detective to inquire into Bonmartini's habits while he was a student in Rome, especially while he was hospitalized. In October 1903, a year after the murder, a certain Giuseppe Leti reported to Riccardo Murri that during Bonmartini's hospital stay of fifty days, the count had talked about nothing but "dirty things" and said he preferred any streetwalker to his wife. Most exciting was Leti's news that Bonmartini made a confession to the hospital attendants: he was a homosexual. Nevertheless, he was visited every day in his hospital room by "lady prostitutes," friends he had made while living in a boarding house that was also a bordello. According to Leti, Bonmartini had been diagnosed by the hospital as having a venereal disease and a cranky personality. Everything in the report was, however, denied by the hospital staff—everything. Leti's letter was never used by the Murri lawyers, since he had apparently invented the entire narrative.[18] Like the miscreants who jumped onto one's carriage in Via dell'Indipendenza, expecting to get a free ride, Leti was shooed away and not pursued for his outrage. In hiring the detective, Riccardo had succeeded only in wasting his brother's money.

As for Professor Murri, Stanzani finally, bitterly, gave up hope that he would ever be charged with anything, even a venial crime. When the family went to Switzerland immediately after the murder, Professor Murri gave Linda a roll of bills to pass to Tullio. He was without a doubt aiding a criminal's escape, but he was doing what every good Italian would do to protect his child. Tullio said he had discussed the murder plan with his parents and his mother had made him promise to stay away from Bonmartini. But even that admission was not strong enough proof that Professor Murri knew about the plot. Besides bank records, another document connected the father to the conspiracy, but it was an ambiguous document. On August 27, 1902, one day before Bonmartini's murder, Murri had sent a telegram to his friend Fabio Vitali from San Moritz, where he was vacationing: *"If you see Nino, talk to him privately at your first opportunity. I will let him do it."*[9] Do what? Professor Murri explained that he was giving permission for Tullio to talk to Bonmartini, despite the fear he had often expressed of Tullio's being provoked into a fight. Would he have telegraphed a colleague with a tiny detail—Tullio's talking to Bonmartini—concerning a marital conflict that had been going on for years? To anyone who knew Professor Murri's neurotic preoccupation with Linda's marriage, it seemed possible. No jury, however, would believe that he had telegraphed a colleague to say that he was letting Tullio kill Bonmartini.

On the other hand, there was that other, very public, very care-less record he had authored, leading directly from himself to the Banco Popolare to Tullio—a series of deposits, the last one for 40,000 lire on August 21.[20] This was Stanzani's searing evidence against Professor Murri. How could Murri have known, one week before the murder, that Tullio would need a great deal of money (to escape? to pay an accomplice?) unless he knew that Tullio was about to commit a crime? People conjectured that Professor Murri might not have fully realized that a murder plan was being hatched. But if he did not know a grave misdeed was in the making, if he thought he was providing an enormous sum for some other use, why did he transfer the money out of Tullio's name to an account that would not be sequestered if Tullio were indicted? Sixty-five thousand lire was a sum sixty-five times greater than Professor Murri had ever given Tullio at one time. The scholarship that Murri procured for Naldi for his full course of medical studies at the University of Bologna had only amounted to 3,000.

After the discovery of the bank deposits, Stanzani never doubted that Professor Murri, too, was part of the conspiracy. If the suspect had been anyone other than Augusto Murri, Stanzani would have or-dered him to San Giovanni in Monte, up the wooden staircase to the interrogation office, like the other suspects, and thence to a reasonably comfortable "luxury" cell.[21] The justice had caught Murri in a dozen apparent lies, both serious and silly.[22] But Stanzani was aware that the doctor still had many defenders who considered his integrity unassail-able. Probably Stanzani discussed the evidence of Professor Murri's guilt with the pubblico ministero, whose responsibility it was to decide whether to bring charges once the investigating magistrate turned over all his findings. Probably the prosecutor told Stanzani that he would not take a chance on allowing all the conspirators to escape conviction by placing in their midst a man who commanded international respect.

Possibly the public prosecutor consulted the minister of the interior, Giovanni Giolitti, who started the second of his five appointments as prime minister in November 1903, a tenure that would last until March 1905. Or maybe the prosecutor knew such consultation would be futile. Giolitti, along with Francesco Crispi, Agostino Depretis, and Giuseppe Zanardelli, had all been members of the center-left coalition that dominated Italian politics in *la bella epoca*. With each change of government they swapped ministries, including the post of prime minister. They had all known Murri—Crispi in fact had tried to get Murri to accept a Senate appointment after he himself withdrew from active politics, one of many invitations to the professor to enter government.[23] And of course, Professor Murri knew King Vittorio Emanuele III, whose mother had been his patient. For all those and maybe other reasons, Stanzani was finally discouraged from ordering Professor Murri's arrest.

Aside from trying to stay out of Stanzani's clutches, Riccardo and Augusto Murri were occupied with several lawsuits surrounding the Bonmartini case. In October 1904, the Murri brothers brought the most complicated and fierce of these libel suits against Dr. Aldo Massarenti. The trial lasted nine days and dominated the news for weeks.[24] Massarenti was a crime buff in Fermo, the Murris' native city, twenty-seven miles from Bologna, where the Murri Hospital was later raised. He carried a grudge against Professor Murri, who had once opposed the appointment of his father to the University of Bologna.

Professor Murri had been born in 1841, the second of five sons and a daughter. His father had fought with Garibaldi for Italian independence from Austria. After the father's arrest and exile to Corfu, his mother reared the family alone.[25] Augusto was at first self-taught and then was awarded scholarships that eventually allowed him to study in Paris and Berlin. The house where he was born in Fermo, like many houses in Italy, had a decorated entryway owned by the commune, a gilded portal dating from the sixth century with a painting of the Madonna del Pianto. In a prolix deposition, Massarenti claimed that Augusto and Riccardo were involved in stealing the Madonna from the portal in 1879.

Priceless Madonnas, then as now, cast their tranquil gazes all over Italy, looking down from the ancient doors of public buildings and the frescoed walls of shops where tectiform shelters shaded their dirty pink faces. Sometimes a gaslight burned before them all night, making their gilded frames shimmer in the dark. They were the objects of easygoing affection, like the middling Madonnas who also appeared on every street. Each carriage driver had his favorite lady and would tip his hat when he passed her, whether once or a dozen times a day. Mothers dedicated their infants to one of the Madonnas in their neighborhood—the Madonna della Guardia, the Madonna del Monte, dei Tre Fiumi, del Sasso—but would transfer the baby to a rival Madonna if the first one did not show sufficient interest in the child's welfare.[26] People in Fermo were outraged when the Madonna del Pianto first disappeared. By 1904, however, the crime of twenty-two years earlier had faded from the town's memory. Massarenti not only accused the Murri brothers of stealing the painting; he further revived an old suggestion that they had helped arrange the murder of a Dr. Pasini in 1893. One Ferdinando Tozzoli had been convicted of the murder and died in prison, but many considered him merely a hit man for the Murris. Massarenti had no proof for these allegations, although they had certainly been bruited in the 1890s, when the case was still fresh.

Hotels in Fermo were crowded with tourists coming to watch the Massarenti-Murri trial. It took several days to gather a jury, since only voters—property owners—could serve. For refusing to serve, or for abandoning a trial in the middle, a juror could be punished with only a modest fine. When the trial finally began, a hundred witnesses were listed. A peasant tenant farmer called to the witness box knelt before the president. Everyone in the courtroom laughed, and the poor fellow was cited for error. One witness repeated the rumor that Murri had tried to perform an abortion on a servant whom he had impregnated; the bungled operation was allegedly repaired by a Professor Loreta, who thereafter disliked Murri. Some of Massarenti's witnesses had been pulled out of nursing homes and sat quivering in the witness box, where they testified haltingly that they couldn't remember the Murris, the stolen Madonna, the Pasini murder, or the names of their own near relatives. A retired maid, fat and toothless, testified that she had relations with Augusto some thirty-five years before, but she couldn't recall anything about a pregnancy.

Professor Murri finally took the witness chair and stated that the bad feeling between him and Dr. Loreta had arisen in 1889 not because of an abortion but because Murri was promoting the use of antiseptics and chloroform in surgery. Joseph Lister had discovered antisepsis fourteen years before, and Murri was trying to get Lister's ideas accepted in surgical practice over Loreta's objections. After Professor Murri's testimony, Massarenti's lawyer withdrew his pleadings. If a plaintiff in a civil suit could prove that falsehoods about him were knowingly printed with malicious intent, the public prosecutor could call for criminal penalties against the publisher. The pubblico ministero thus demanded a criminal indictment of Massarenti. The president of the tribunal offered to simply close the case. Riccardo agreed and withdrew his libel complaint, but Professor Murri did not. Massarenti ended up paying a fine of 1,000 lire and going to jail for seven months.[27]

Meanwhile, having had no success in arresting a third accomplice to the murder, Stanzani had to declare that his work was complete. The istruttoria was published on September 20, 1903. With the investigation closed, defense attorneys for the first time were shown the formal accusations against their clients and were at last allowed to visit them, though only in a large, common room with a prison guard present.[28] The formal charges were: Tullio Murri, 30 years old and Pio Naldi, 28: murder. Rosina Bonetti, 34: accomplice to murder.

Teolinda Murri, 32, and Carlo Secchi, 50: complicity and conspiracy to incite others to murder. Severo Dalla, 31: abetting criminals after the crime and destroying evidence. Ernesto Dalla, 29: accomplice in the crimes of his brother. Riccardo Murri, 57: complicity in murder by promising assistance and help that would be forthcoming after the deed.[29] The charges against the Dallas and Riccardo Murri were withdrawn just as the trial was about to open.

Augusto Murri was not charged with any crime. But his name was further blackened by three stark happenings, coincidences of the sort denied to good fiction. On July 10, 1903, Dante Cervesato— the man who had steadfastly defended Bonmartini against all the opprobrium the Murris heaped on his name—died, having suffered from what the newspapers described as "a chronic intestinal illness." The very next day, Bonmartini's other close friend, his cousin Valvassori, who had likewise finally turned against the Murris, was reported gravely ill with intestinal inflammation. He died too.[30] That was not all. Secchi's letters had been destroyed, it was true; but Secchi's friend Dr. Enrico Pacini had given long depositions about Secchi's reluctance to get involved in the conspiracy and about the blistering antagonism that had developed between Secchi and Professor Murri. On November 10, 1903, it was reported that Pacini, Secchi's only defender against the Murris, had suddenly died. Professor Murri of course was suspected of arranging his untimely end.[31]

Though medical reports certified that all three men had succumbed to illness, their deaths became part of the larger mystery of the Murri case. Rumors throbbed until Cervesato's brother was obliged to state in the newspapers that his brother had not been murdered. But still the talk persisted: Wasn't the brother simply trying to placate the Murris because he was afraid of them? A year later, the insinuations resurged when it appeared from the Massarenti trial that the doctors in Fermo, Dr. Pasini and Professor Loreta, had suffered deaths remarkably similar to those of Cervesato, Valvassori, and Pacini. No one could believe in so many coincidences.

More dark information emerged concerning Professor Murri. In one of his letters to Linda written before Cervesato's death, Professor Murri warned her that the pediatrician would be against her in a separation suit. The president of the tribunal of Bologna was a friend of Cervesato. The judge, wrote Murri, was a "lowlife" and "a visible degenerate." The letter, written two days after Bonmartini's murder, was of course seized by Stanzani and cheerfully released to the newspapers.[32] The letter helped persuade the authorities to move the trial location to Turin, since prejudice against the Murris in Bologna was becoming quite impressive.

Professor Murri no longer had an impregnable reputation. But that was small comfort to Stanzani and the prosecutors. They despaired of ever being able to bring him to the defendants' bench unless someone came forth with such shocking evidence of guilt that all of his high-placed shelterers would be forced to eject him from the fortress of official protection.

7. THE LATEST NEWS

While Professor Murri remained immune from prosecution, the public watched each day's headlines, factory hands making wagers as to when he would be arrested and secretaries speculating about what new finding would emerge in the story of endless surprises. Between the discovery of Bonmartini's body and the opening of the trial, thirty months passed. For almost each day of that long period, the Murri case was on the front pages of every major newspaper in Italy. To keep alive the national obsession with the case, journalists were impelled to come up with wild theories about the murder that had been so senseless. The police were deposing hundreds of witnesses—425 before the istruttoria was closed—as they followed first one theory about the crime and then another. Even if the investigators had tried harder to keep the inquiry secret, many talkative insiders would have made confidentiality impossible.

It was illegal to write about an investigation while it was still going on or to publish its findings; nobody dreamed of obeying that injunction. The fine for violating the gag law was only 100 to 500 lire, which the larger papers could easily pay. Therefore, writers exploited all the details of the Murri case until the first day of court, after which developments in the trial itself were screamed by newsboys up and down the peninsula for an additional fifteen months. If Justice Stanzani decided to withhold information for a few weeks during the istruttoria, the press simply reprised what was already known and added some purported leaks—rumors and stories that journalists fashioned out of whole cloth. A paper would first report a stunning disclosure attributed to an anonymous source within the magistrate's office—for example, that somebody had revealed another "inconfessable relationship" within the Murri household. After three or four days of speculation about the thrilling intelligence, editorials then stated that the information was found to be untrue and took up several more days refuting the false story. Then the paper went back to interviewing prison authorities—who were forbidden to speak publicly—or reporting on the mental condition of various members of the Murri family, which was always attractive filler, until Stanzani resumed throwing out real bones for the journalists to gnaw. Foreign newspapers borrowed from the Italian press. Articles about the trial thus appeared around the world, more fiction than fact, usually, but all absorbing.

The real danger for Italian publishers was not from random police censorship but from private citizens bringing suits for libel, which in certain cases could result in a defendant such as Massarenti going to jail. Libel was a big business for the hungry lawyers of Italy, second only to "swindling" as the most common middle-class crime, though murder, of course, remained popular in all classes.[1] Some journals, especially the smaller ones, guarded against libel by finding an impoverished, preferably homeless person whose name could be placed at the bottom of the paper as the authority responsible for the publication. If anyone was brought to court, if anyone had to sit out a few months in jail because of a nefarious article, it was he. The "manager" was paid wages for each day that his name appeared on the paper when he was not in prison. At *Avanti!*, the socialist paper, the post was no sinecure; but the high-class papers were never punished with prison, thus the position of "responsible authority" was often sought after.[2] In the Murri case, Stanzani and the newspapers continually traded remonstrances, the magistrate asserting that no editor of probity would publish elements of a secret investigation, and *Corriere della Sera,* the country's most respected daily, replying that no civilized country should carry out investigations in secret.[3] The mutual complaints helped fill the long months until the trial.

Italy had 1,400 newspapers besides *L'Osservatore Romano,* the newspaper of the Vatican; 170 of these were dailies with morning and/or afternoon editions, plus another edition that came out between eight and ten at night, either regularly or only when there was salable news to report. Some were nationally distributed and fairly intellectual: Rome's *La Tribuna, Il Giornale d'Italia,* and *La Repubblica;* Turin's *La Stampa;* Milan's *Il Secolo* and *Corriere della Sera.* Though the crime reporter for *Corriere,* A. G. Bianchi, was a good friend of Professor Murri, the paper was independent of political bias and remarkably fair in reporting the Murri case. Local papers as well as the larger journals tried to keep up the Italian tradition of a literary press, with articles on science and the arts: *Il Resto del Carlino* in Bologna, *Il Giornale di Sicilia* in Palermo, *La Gazzetta di Venezia* in Venice, *Il Mattino* in Naples and Padua, and many others in Genoa, Florence, and other cities. Some modest provincial papers were printed on single sheets, like newsletters, but with well-written articles nonetheless. Each city also had a sensational paper, Rome's *Il Messaggero* being the exemplary national rag. Italians read the newspapers intensely. Travelers reported that people broke out their evening papers during intermissions at the theaters. On trains, passengers could be seen exchanging *La Perseveranza* of Milan for *Il Popolo* of Turin.[4] As the Murri case was the leading news in all of these papers, how could there not be enormous public interest in the drama?

Since half of Italy was still illiterate, we are prompted to wonder who was buying all the words about the crime?[5] Probably Italians in the North, where literacy was much higher than in the rest of the country, and where the Murri family lived. Upper class Italians, moreover, those who could afford theater and train tickets, were dedicated followers of the case, and they in turn spread information to their dependents. Servants saw the headlines in the newspapers of their employers and heard their patrons talking about the latest developments, and bureaucrats at least skimmed the newspaper that invariably came to most offices. Teachers discussed the case with their students; priests composed homilies around it. Shopkeepers relieved their mundane boredom by exchanging a few words about the Murris with their customers.

Newspapers were cheap—ten centesimi, even less for subscriptions—and whatever their circulation when Bonmartini was murdered, their readership soared as the istruttoria progressed. No issue, and certainly no criminal case, had generated such phenomenal national interest since the unification of the nation in 1861. Journalists could use all the space they wanted in writing about the crime. Unlike the British, Italians had no birth or marriage announcements in newspapers, only deaths and police reports. Comics were not yet part of the daily palliative, though readers could chuckle at the occasional political satire and revile the lottery results (some readers consulted witches before choosing their numbers). There were Italian movies in 1905 but no movie stars as yet. The most reliable celebrities, therefore, were accused malefactors and members of any royal family. The public was endlessly eager for secrets about European rulers and their relatives. However, most royal personages had no readable secrets and were not sufficiently eccentric to attract sustained attention. Criminals, on the other hand, were often rich in individual character and conscious personality. By 1905, journalists had turned the true-crime story into a popular art.

Only one serial drama weakly competed with the Murri case from 1902 to 1905: the recurring disgrace of a royal princess, Luisa of Tuscany, the princess of Saxony after her marriage and the sister of the scandal-haunted, fey Archduke Franz Ferdinand of Austria. Luisa delighted Italians by periodically running away to Italy—in 1902, 1903, and 1905—with ever younger lovers. In 1903, she fled to Florence with her newborn baby and its father. Her husband exhorted Italian authorities to seize the child, who was legally his property, if not his blood. He should have known that Tuscans were hardly the men to separate any bambina from its mother. He resorted to planting a maid in the lovers' house whose chores included kidnapping the baby. Luisa discovered the kidnap plan, locked the woman out, and threw her clothes out of a window after her. Luisa had still more escapades with more lovers, but after each affair, she returned to Saxony in order not to be separated from her other children.[6] Italian readers adored Luisa of Saxony as much as they abominated Linda Murri.

When titled aristocrats failed in their duty to be colorful, the press turned to untitled oligarchs—of government, industry, or finance. Wealthy businessmen, whose travels and appearances at the theater were noted, could attract a few new readers when they became involved in racy doings. Government officials were likewise acceptable as protagonists. During a lull in the Murri story, a member of the distant French parliament, Gabriel Syveton, drew the attention of the Italian press when he was found dead, killed by the novel means of an open gas spigot. Either he had killed himself because he was about to be exposed for having incestuous relations with his young stepdaughter, or he had been murdered by one of many interesting enemies, including his wife. Incest was a rather frequent element in murder and suicide cases of the turn of the century, much more than in later periods. Italians enjoyed the Syveton inquiry immensely—the killers and deviants were French, after all—though like most investigations and trials, the case was over in a few short weeks.[7]

More compelling than the breaches of any government figure or tycoon were the lives and loves of murderers whose otherwise respectable existence had been turned inside out by one impulsive act, an act such as Tullio said he committed. Italians loved all crime, but they loved verifiable crimes of passion best of all. Was the Bonmartini murder a crime of passion or a slow-bubbling, hateful conspiracy? No one could be sure until the curtain opened on the trial.

The journalists' attention to crime was not entirely sordid. In the absence of stable political parties, the press remained the main arena for political and moral discussion in Italy. Journalism was considered the proper background for a man who hoped to enter either government or politics—Turati, Nenni, Ferri, Gramsci, Giolitti,

Mussolini, and many others built their political careers on journalism. Many journalists were idealists seeking the social causes of crime. With few exceptions, all were intellectuals deeply concerned about the society of the new century.[8] The Murri trial was the great occasion for seeing the political center and left, the borghesia and the socialists, lined up together against the aristocratic and Catholic front. No longer did readers have to sort through boring discussions to place a public figure on the right or left. They could tell who was who simply by noting which side he took in the trial, the prosecution or the defense, Bonmartini or Murri. It is difficult for us to comprehend the importance of religion in dividing public opinion about the case, difficult to see the significance of Bonmartini's having been a Catholic and the Murris being agnostics. But if we compare the political-religious fractioning in the Muslim world today—the gulf between fundamentalists and secular Islamists—we can understand how the religious labels that were applied to both the victim and the defendants influenced the public for or against them.

Religion was only part of the reason the Murri case polarized the country. A society of the masses was about to emerge, formed by the growing middle class making common cause with the growing working class. Liberals were on the threshold of Modernism. The word, the concept, allowed them to join together behind one stirring abstraction and confront the still powerful, still living and breeding agrarian landowners—the Bonmartinis of Italy—who represented all the anti-modern forces. The friction between conservatives, liberals, socialists, and that most alarming element of all, anarchists, was not fenced behind clear factions, neither in Italy nor in most other places. The contadini and miners were the most revolutionary elements in society at the end of the century, especially in the South. Yet, though they might have been eager to shed the blood of landowners, they were, like their enemies, vehemently Catholic and completely alien to Marx and socialism. Both republicanism and anarchism were strongest in Bologna's Emilia region, but whereas republicanism—parliamentary democracy—was all-encompassing and weak, anarchists were few and effective.

Parliament unraveled with each minor crisis; sixty-seven ministries held office in the seventy-four years between the granting of a constitution and the accession of Mussolini. As one journalist commented, "A gust of wind, and these leaves that call themselves parliamentary deputies will be blown about and mixed up anew."[9] Anarchists, with their alarming political assassinations and indifference to the lives of innocent bystanders, terrified everyone, even the road brigands who were sometimes mistaken for them. Wedged between the liberals and anarchists were the socialists, who were also feared. Socialism was little understood and was often confused with anarchism. When Tullio changed clothes during a recess in his trial, journalists commented that his black outfit may have been a theatrical attempt to make himself look like an anarchist.[10] Unless he was as casual of his own life as he had been of Bonmartini's, such a thing could hardly have been in his mind.

The monarchy was supposed to be above political parties; it was liberal in some ways and conservative in others. On one hand, the king represented all the secular forces ranged against the Church; on the other hand, he exercised ponderable authority because of the chronic ineffectuality of parliament. The court of King Umberto and Queen Margherita tried to rival that of the Vatican in pomp. To leave a meeting with the king, everyone, even elderly ambassadors and frail ministers, made three deep bows and walked backward out of his presence. Their majesties sponsored fashionable fox-hunting parties in the English style, with red coats and sandwich lunches. The assassination of King Umberto in 1900 intensified the impression that the monarchy was a part of the conservative front. King Vittorio Emanuele III, his son and successor, followed the tradition of being constantly surrounded by army officers. Photographs of the king in civilian clothes were rare. Yet, though conservative, the king was a symbol for all the people, liberal and conservative alike.

Two worlds existed in Italy, with few bridges between them: the world of Sunday bathers at Rimini and the world of people who carried hand-washed rags to plague-infested, communal outhouses, if they brought hygienic material at all. A few segments of the upper borghesia, especially journalists and doctors, tried to bring the worlds closer together. Doctors were in the forefront of movements for social reform, education, and the enlightened relief of suffering. Professor Murri, wealthy and selfish as he was, belonged to the balcony of the country's humanitarians. The Bonmartini case, with its range of classes and types, was a mess of conflicting and overlapping symbols that evoked passion, agitation, and ambivalence in everybody who read about it.

The crowds carrying newspapers were not necessarily aware of all the social implications of the case. They felt compassion or disdain for Rosina because of her limp, and noted with disappointment or satisfaction the ordinariness of Linda's face and the banality of her dress. Like the public of any generation following a news story, reacting emotionally to the personalities, they didn't know why they found it so absorbing, but it was cheap entertainment, an excitement that cost them nothing. The imaginings conjured up by the rumors in the case could be dismissed without chagrin after the truth came out, unlike the fantasies connected to their own lives. The light of publicity falling on each detail of the murder made everybody think he had a stake in the trial. Not only were socialists, Catholics, and secularists involved. The public thought the Masons and chemists had a role, even though the Grand Mason testified that the Murris were no longer part of the organization and even though pharmacies could show that they had not supplied any of the defendants with curare. Doctors, lawyers, maids, professors, singers, accountants, aristocrats, hotel keepers, barroom owners, bankers, gamblers, contadini, landowners, and donne allegre all felt that the case somehow reflected on them. Whatever happened in the story was personally important.

If publicity was harmless to readers, it was considered damaging enough to those who were written about, especially Riccardo and Augusto Murri. Riccardo filed a defamation suit against the clerical paper *L'Avvenire d'Italia* for implying that he was one of the conspirators in the murder. Along with many other newspapers, *L'Avvenire's* circulation quadrupled during the Murri istruttoria, from three or four thousand to twelve or sixteen thousand; its director took the suit in stride.[11] Professor Murri sued *Il Giornale di Venezia,* a pro-Bonmartini paper, for writing that he had charged a colleague such an exorbitant fee to examine his wife that the colleague had to borrow money to get home from the clinic. He also sued Scipio Sighele and *La Gazzetta di Venezia* for slander because of an interview the prosecutor gave in which he basically outlined the pleadings he safely presented during the trial.[12] Libel suits surrounded the Murri trial like tornadoes accompanying a hurricane. Tisa, Frieda, and others also sued various newspapers.[13] And there was, of course, the Massarenti storm.[14]

By the beginning of the trial in February 1905, all of the defendants except Secchi had been in jail for two and a half years. During the istruttoria, they could receive letters that passed the inspection of the authorities, but they were not allowed to have visitors or personal contact with the outside. During the early months of waiting, Rosina prayed continually and was reported to be looking forward to the trial because it would give her a chance to see Tullio. But constant hunger and the death of her brother drained away her resistance. The nuns guarding her sometimes described her as a "vegetable."[15]

Since his suicide attempt, Naldi had been confined with two other prisoners and was under strict surveillance. His aunt still was not sending him much food, since it had to be ordered from a trattoria. Canned foods, less expensive than restaurant meals, were available—mock turtle soup, herring, and pineapple, for instance—but for some reason she was not able to supply them or to bring Naldi food from her house. He was obliged to watch his cellmates eat. Nevertheless, he had adapted well to prison life, perhaps because his life outside prison had been wracked by privation and envy. His aunt bought him clothes for the trial—even gloves. But he worried that, being a poor speaker, he would not make a good presentation. He had hoped to call seventy witnesses on his behalf. The trial judges refused to hear all but twelve.[16]

Secchi was dignified as always while he brooded in prison. At first he read about medical advances in the newspapers that were permitted to him: an electric medical battery that was supposed to aid poor vision; a gizmo that was being tested for the cure of headaches.[17] Perhaps the ear and eye specialist was able to read about Helen Keller's graduation from Radcliffe College in 1904. As the trial neared, he passed the anxious days reading about a new subject: agronomy. He expected the trial to set him free, according to newspaper reports, and planned to abandon medicine in favor of farming.

Linda spent her time in prison making baby clothes for the poor and writing letters imploring officials to release her. Her supplications to Stanzani having been ignored, she wrote early on to the vice-director of all the prisons—1,500 words—pleading that she was gravely ill. Stanzani, she asserted, did not care about her health. She needed better doctors than the prison could provide, and feared she would die. She had already been there three months, she complained. The vice-director had taken steps to alleviate the coldness of her cell, for which she was most grateful. Nevertheless, she was being subjected to "physical destruction" because of "all the darkness that has fallen on my poor life." She begged the official ("I beg you, I beg you, I beg you, in the name of humanity") to speed up the inquiry for the sake of her children.[18]

The famed criminologist Cesare Lombroso was called in before the trial to examine Linda. The public's fascination with murder was bound up with the scientific vogue for what was called "criminal anthropology," a field that had been invented by Lombroso. During his work as a physician in penal institutions, Lombroso decided that thinking and actions are conditioned by physical structure. Criminals were physically abnormal, atavistic, frequently epileptic—in short, victims of arrested development not fully responsible for their acts. Lombroso claimed to have discovered a new human subspecies: the born criminal, which he further separated into the habitual and occasional offender. Lombroso and his protégés Enrico Ferri, Enrico Morselli, Scipio Sighele, and Guglielmo Ferrero (all would have important parts in the Murri trial) swore by the scientific method, even though much of science itself was still out of their grasp.

Lombroso spent some hours feeling Linda's skull for cranial abnormalities, measuring her head, the length of her palate, and the distance from her nose to her ear. In order to make a judgment, he finally averred, he would need to study her and all the defendants for several weeks, with scientific procedures and instruments. He was serious about the instruments; among them was a huge contraption—a "craniograph"—that he used for measuring heads.[19] Of Linda, Lombroso wrote:

> It is known that her father adores her. If she is convicted, he will die . . . Murri is a scientist of genius, a clinical physician of the first order, and at the same time, a liberal, a socialist, who has emancipated his children from all traditions of the past. . . . But you know that often the children of superior people can be degenerates.

He did not, apparently, hold it against Linda that she had been tempted to tattoo her eye, tattoos being one of his designated markers for promiscuity and also one of the signs of women's inferiority to men, since the prosaic tattoos of women reflected their weaker imaginations.[20] He did not hesitate to cite "hairy moles" as a characteristic of moral degradation, since they occurred in forty-one percent of the prostitutes he examined.

Lombroso's writings are now cited mostly for entertainment, although the general idea of his work—attributing antisocial behavior to anatomical aberrance—finds expression in the current medical vogue for treating psychotic behavior by correcting chemical abnormalities in the body. Lombroso once published a finding that, of two thousand prostitutes, three quarters had taken up the trade because of impoverishment, the death of parents, or abandonment that had left them with no other means of survival. The others were selling themselves, with or without moles, to support families, orphaned siblings, and the like. None had turned to prostitution because of a strong sex drive. Nevertheless, Lombroso maintained that it was physique and not destitution that predicted whether girls would fall into habitual wrongdoing. In one of his studies of female offenders, Lombroso identified unusual nipples as a marker for "moral insanity": "Out of 130 cases, I myself found nipple atrophy in 12%," he wrote. "One swindler lacked nipples entirely."[21]

The so-called positivist thinkers dominated jurisprudence and ran the defense of the Murri trial, especially Tullio's defense, relying in general on Lombroso's notions that the criminal does not willfully choose to commit misdeeds but rather succumbs to overweening inborn tendencies. Lombroso himself declared Tullio "impulsive—a sick man."

> He can't settle into any life. In politics, he's almost an anarchist. In literature, he wrote a play in which all the protagonists kill each other in the last act. Tullio has a malformed and bizarre cranium, a narrow forehead, high and receding, and hesitant eyes. To me, Tullio seems affected by latent hysteria that shows itself in murderous anger . . . in the instinct for evil.[22]

Tullio—whom Lombroso never examined personally—was meanwhile behaving with great restraint, following all the prison rules except one. In Bologna, where he was not supposed to have any writing materials, it was discovered that he had written a comedy in the margins of a book and a magazine that were given to him.[23] For a pen, he used the point of a pencil that he hid in his mouth. Thenceforth he was not allowed any more books, and even letters from his family were taken back after he had read them.[24] As soon as the investigation was closed, when he was permitted to write again, he wrote an entire novel, a historical study, and a number of poems, all of which were confiscated by Stanzani.

In one of his last Memorie to the investigators, Tullio claimed that he did not plan the murder until the twenty-sixth of August, when he received Linda's letter describing the chair incident.

In my mind arose hidden terror . . . a burning heartful of affection and pity, full of the spirit of sacrifice. Oh! How true all this is! How true! This is the story of my life. My father was a rigid man of habit, severe and sober, who never went to a caffè nor to the theater. In 28 years of living in Bologna, he never set foot in a tram . . . began studying at three in the morning . . . dispraised any pleasure that wasn't intellectual and any discussion that wasn't scientific. . . . I remember once when I was eight or ten going into his study wearing a mask, and he was so infuriated, he kicked me. . . .

Mamma! My poor Mamma! I loved her intensely and she me. Though economical and modest, she was also more indulgent in understanding me and guiding me. In Mamma I always found a heart of limitless generosity.[25]

It was Tullio's mother and not his father who corresponded with him in prison. Neither parent attended the trial, and none of the Murri relatives were permitted to testify, in accordance with Italian criminal procedure.[26]

Finally came the day when the defendants were brought to Turin, a city of 277,000, to stand trial in the formidable Palace of Justice.[27] Linda rode in a second-class compartment, otherwise empty. She was dressed in dark blue and even on the train wore a hat with a veil that completely covered her face. Asked by the sisters guarding her if she wanted anything to drink, she requested coffee with a little cream, syllables that were carefully reported in the newspapers. She was moved from the train station to prison in a carriage. Each time she was taken out of a vehicle, a crowd invariably gathered and caused some commotion. Linda wrote to her mother that the ire of the crowd did not sadden her, except for the pain it must cause her father.[28]

Naldi arrived in a third-class car. He was described by journalists as gray-faced, although one writer commented that from time to time he exhibited the stammer of a scholar, coupled with an infantile blush.[29] He wore his only suit, dark blue, with a cloak, and he was handcuffed. When the guards tried to help him down, he shrugged them off, saying, "You're afraid I'll escape." Secchi also left Bologna in a third-class car with a marshal and police escort who carried his suitcase. He sat between the two, his head lowered. He was dressed in black with a deep blue raincoat, hat low, hands cuffed. His eyes remained fixed and he seemed quite depressed. As Rosina came out of the train, she was observed by a priest who wrote in a weekly newspaper that she carried a rosary and appeared unable to walk easily. A dressmaker in Turin was moved to send her some food and clothes. Only Tullio arrived in a reserved compartment. With him came 1,092 pages of testimony and 7,000 documents.[30]

When she first went to prison, Linda had seemed preoccupied with Secchi, reassuring him that separation would not dim her devotion. Secchi, in his first interrogations from inside prison, had unfailingly referred to "la Contessa," with lavish respect and noticeable efforts to surround her name with decorum. They were about to spend the next year in the same courtroom, parted by only a few feet. But the months in separate prison cells, and in the separate prisons of their thoughts, had changed everything. Longings that they thought would score their very souls had faded and disappeared. Feelings that they thought time would never change were now hardly remembered. It had been three years since their last meeting. Barely glancing at Secchi, Linda would walk into the courtroom in Turin no longer his lover, no longer remotely in love.

8. THE TRIAL BEGINS

The foreign correspondents stood apart from the rest of the crowd on the old concrete steps of Turin's Palace of Justice, shifting about resentfully as guards checked the names of the fifty journalists allowed inside the building—all Italian, since the authorities considered the case too sordid to expose to outside observers.[1] The other people gathered on the sidewalk and in the snow were lighthearted, though they could not get in either. They smoked and chatted while awaiting the arrival of the defendants, or rather, of Linda Murri, for it was she above all whom they had come to see.

A horse-drawn public carriage pulls up, escorted by two policeman on bicycles. A woman emerges—it's Linda, heavily veiled, accompanied by her lawyer Giuseppe Gottardi. The crowd closes in. She is tall, in a black silk dress with white edging, matched by a black and white hat. Within a month, the "Linda" look—severe black silk with lace collar—will be fashionable throughout Italy, and even magazines abroad will feature models who resemble her.[2] She climbs the steps uncertainly, her eyes fixed on the ground. Behind her trails the caravan of the others. Rosina, too, is wearing black, with a scarf covering nearly her entire face. She grasps the banister so as not to fall. Tullio goes nimbly up the steps despite handcuffs. He has grown a chestnut beard with two points and has gained weight. Like Linda and Secchi, Tullio has had his meals sent into prison. With his prominent eyes and full body, he looks, one reporter comments, like a German student.[3] Following the robust Tullio, Carlo Secchi seems small, squat, and haggard. He is handcuffed. His hat falls over his eyes as he gets down from the carriage, exposing the striking baldness of his head in back. His skin is yellow and finely wrinkled, like old paper. So this is the lover! Naldi is the one most changed by prison. Inside his black suit, made for him two years previously by his aunt, he is long and spidery. His cheeks are two high knobs holding up the rest of his face. A large soft hat, carefully tilted over his lifeless eye, seems to point down toward two thin ink strokes—his tiny, long mustaches. His collar is too high, and he is wearing matching yellow gloves and shoes. No one would imagine that he is a doctor; except for the manacles, he looks like an underfed street sweeper dressed up for an important funeral.[4]

Inside, the hall is dark in the February gloom, despite the electric lights. Guards stand at every door, their movements echoing across the empty benches as they verify the identities of people coming in. On the first row of press seats are representatives from Agenzia Stefani and the largest papers of Turin, Milan, Bologna, and Rome, all furiously scribbling as they take in everything about the room. The defendants are led to a cross wire cage set perpendicular and to the right of the tribunal. Inside the cage are two benches, one behind the other. "I thought I was dreaming," wrote Linda in a book published after the trial.

> I sat down in a corner. A moment later I heard near me one
> of my companions in misfortune. The person sat behind me and
> sighed. I recognized that breath! I knew it was he, the man I had
> loved so much. That sigh, in a flash, brought me out of that cursed
> cage into a heavenly room, near an adored face, near a mouth that
> said only words of love. I felt faint and leaned on the bars.[5]

However, the reporters, who were punctilious in noting such details, all observed that Secchi was in place before Linda finally yielded to the usher's pointing finger and took a seat next to Naldi and Rosina on the front bench.

The accused were not allowed to talk to each other, so at first they stared straight ahead, into the thinking eyes of the reporters whose section was directly opposite the cage. Watching Rosina on the bench in front of him, Tullio slowly began to weep, but the others eventually started looking around. Officials were entering in twos and threes—twenty-four barristers, irritated because they had been required to dismiss their assistants and carry their own voluminous documents in and out of the cramped courtroom; twenty-three expert witnesses; three magistrates; a pool of jurors from which fourteen would be picked. Witnesses were being kept out of sight in adjacent rooms. There was space for only thirty spectators. The authorities had deliberately chosen this room, forty feet by forty, to constrain the theater atmosphere. Instead, the narrow space made the trial even more of an exclusive show for society people. Each one gave his ticket to the usher, waved with cheerful surprise to acquaintances he spotted in the room, and settled in to watch the presentation. At 9:20, the campanile of the courthouse chimed; Secchi passed his hand over his face; and Italy's trial of the century began.

The first hours were taken up by jurors who sent their servants to request exemptions. The twelve jurors and two alternates who were finally chosen were landowners, retired teachers, government workers, a doctor, and a lawyer who satisfied the legal requirements of education and property. Italian criminal cases were decided by the jury and the judges together, the opinions of the lay people and the magistrates being theoretically equal. While the court addressed procedural matters for more than a week, the defendants sat in the cage like strangers on a tram, day after day. The ritual of arriving and leaving was repeated before a crowd that constantly increased. Without photographs in the newspapers, and with journalists having little to write about other than the appearance and mannerisms of the defendants, the descriptions incited curiosity; soon hundreds came in person to catch a glimpse of the not-pretty enchantress and the other interesting killers. As the days wore on, more and more observers turned up in beards groomed like Tullio's or, especially, black silk dresses with veils. The crowds gradually became surly. Derisive comments and whistles followed Linda; but more than once someone said sympathetically, "Coraggio, Signora," and Linda answered, "Grazie."

Finally, on February 23, 1905, the first witness is called: Rosina Bonetti. She gets up and limps forward, making echoes in the hall, but she stops at the door of the cage.

"Don't be afraid," says the president of the tribunal, Ernesto Dusio. "It's your turn to give your reasons. Say what you think the court and jurors should know when they weigh your case."

"Can't I say it from inside?" she asks.

"Nobody will be able to hear you from there. You know the accusation—that on August 28 you assisted in a murder carried out by Tullio Murri and Pio Naldi, who set a trap for Bonmartini. What do you say in your defense?"

By this time, the bailiff has urged her into the witness chair where she sits trembling and crying.

"Didn't you have relations with Tullio?"

"Yes."

"When did you first meet him?"

A long pause. "I don't know."

"Let's see, uh, how many years ago?"

"Five, six, seven."

"You loved only him?"

"Yes, only him."

There has been no swearing in, for this is not part of the legal procedure. The president will ask practically all questions, acting as both a prosecutor who presents the state's case and an arbitrator constrained to give the defense a fair hearing. There will be no formal cross-examination. Instead, it is up to the president to point out contradictions, if he so chooses, between the testimony in court and what was uncovered during the istruttoria. From time to time attorneys for one side or the other may ask for elaboration, and the other defendants may even put in a word or two unbidden. Based on the testimony the president elicits, lawyers for the two sides will call witnesses to corroborate or refute what the court has heard, and will finally present their own long and scouring interpretations of the facts and testimony.[6]

After the long months of the istruttoria, the magistrates might have expected Rosina's spoken testimony to be something of a formality. Yet, she surprised the court once she took the witness chair.

"What name did you take when you were hired to work in the Bonmartini household?" Rosina plucks up a bit. "I called myself Maria Pirazzoli."

"Who gave you the name Maria Pirazzoli?"

"It was the name of a girlfriend of my Poldino."

The president protests, "During the istruttoria, you said it was Linda Murri who suggested this name to you. And didn't changing your name seem like a strange idea?"

"Well, Tullio is not named Nino, but everybody calls him Nino."

"That's different," he responds. "Nino is a nickname. You always kept your address hidden from the count, didn't you?"

"I don't remember," Rosina answers finally, and resumes crying, hiding her face in her handkerchief. The examination continues, with Rosina sidestepping most questions, breaking down in tears, or sliding off the point of the inquiry. Determined, the president asks her to describe the incident in Venice when Bonmartini seemed to threaten Linda with a chair. Rosina shakes her head no. "The signora asked me not to talk about it."

"But you already told all about it in the istruttoria."

The president moves on. When she and Tullio went to Venice on the thirteenth of August, did she carry a sack of lead balls with which to bludgeon Bonmartini? No, comes Rosina's answer. Justice Stanzani had made her say whatever he wanted during the istruttoria. But later she remarks that the suitcase she brought to Venice was heavy because of the lead pallini it contained. Dusio's strategy with Rosina was to jump back and forth over time so as to catch her in such contradictions. Rosina's strategy with Dusio was to deny responsibility for any answers she gave during the istruttoria because her only thought then had been to avoid incriminating Tullio. She said that Tullio had planned to confront Bonmartini on Via Mazzini, but only to talk to him. She had begged her lover not to go.

Rosina was crying again. In the defendant's cage Tullio wept. Linda sobbed. After many questions, Rosina confirmed that she, Tullio, and Naldi went to the Bisteghi house together on August 27, the day before the murder, and that Tullio then ordered her to leave. When she protested, Naldi told her, "Don't worry. We'll be leaving, too, in a little while." The men did not follow her, however, and the next morning she got a card from Linda instructing her to go get the gray dress from the count, who would be at the house in Bologna around six. This card, according to the prosecution, was a signal to the killers that Bonmartini would soon be arriving.

In a speech that seemed to come out quite easily, Rosina recounted how the count, without opening the window, told her to return for the dress the next day. She went home and found Tullio there; they went out to a caffè where he wrote some postcards. As he started to pay for their meal, Tullio exclaimed that some of his money was missing, apparently stolen by Naldi. In vain, they looked for Naldi, and then took a train for Rimini. Before the president could ask why they had gone to Rimini, Rosina, Tullio, and Linda began a commotion of sobs and wailing that moved many in the audience to take out their handkerchiefs as well, although no one seemed to have the slightest idea what was so upsetting about taking a train for Rimini. "I don't want to stay here any longer!" Rosina shouted. But she remained in her chair as the keening subsided.

Rosina thus asserted that Tullio had remained in the Bonmartini house all night together with Naldi, who had stolen the money thought to be his payment for helping in the murder. Naldi had insisted on this point in one of his depositions. Comforted by the president and pressed to continue, Rosina said that Tullio left her in Rimini and went alone to the town of Cattolica, about ten miles farther down the coast, where he dumped his weapons in the sea; he then returned with her to Bologna. Tullio had thus divested himself of all weapons while Bonmartini remained in his apartment, safe and more or less sound. However, once back at the station in Bologna, Tullio left her, telling her to wait for him. When the wait stretched to two hours, she went home, and a little while later, Tullio came in. He was in a terrible state.

"He threw himself on the bed," Rosina said, "yelling, 'Poor Papà! Poor Mamma! Poor Linda!' He had a gash on his arm. He burned his shirt full of blood and changed his clothes, because he always kept clean clothes at my place."

"Why only the shirt?" asks the president.

"There wasn't time. We burned the other clothes later."

The courtroom was now in an uproar with Rosina's new version of the crime, a version that placed Bonmartini's murder around midnight between August 28 and 29. If the jury believed her, Naldi would be completely exonerated, since he had an alibi for every hour after seven o'clock. Rosina's story explained certain curious details: Tullio had not yet committed the crime when he dined with his usual good appetite on the evening of the twenty-eighth and then sat in the Caffè Corso casually addressing postcards. But were listeners to understand that Tullio, still innocent of any crime, felt a sudden impulse that evening to rid himself of weapons he had been carrying for some time? That he took a train to Rimini—a good two hours from Bologna—and then traveled to Cattolica–another half hour—in the middle of the night to find a means of disposing of them? Then, returning to Bologna, he went to talk to Bonmartini, who later turned up dead, having somehow been attacked with a knife or knives like those Tullio had just taken pains to drop into the sea? Why wasn't there time to burn all the clothes at once, since, according to Rosina, Tullio no longer had any trains to catch? The next days would reveal that it was not only Rosina who turned her back on much that she had said in her depositions. All of the defendants, after legal consultation, changed their stories when they entered the cold chancel and took the witness chair.

The questioning continued. Rosina stated that she had never seen Linda's and Secchi's apartment next to the Bonmartini dwelling, had never heard Naldi's name before the night of the crime, and had never seen the poison that was at the heart of the alleged conspiracy.

"But in the istruttoria, you said you saw the poison on August 22," protested the president.

"The justice told me that if I took all the blame, I would only get thirty years in jail and Nino would go free; so I was trying to look like the guilty one," answers Rosina. It was she who, while in Venice, had stolen the keys to the Bonmartini apartment without Linda's knowledge. Had she then mailed the keys back to Linda? She did not know. On August 29, the day after the murder, Tullio gave her a sealed package to send to Linda, using the name of a servant in the Murri household. She needed the help of the post office clerk to address the parcel. It was she who purchased the knife used to break into Linda's jewelry box so that it would appear that thieves had killed Bonmartini when he caught them in the apartment. She bought the knife in May or June, she thought.

A report was read from the Rimini police who, years earlier, had been called to prevent Rosina from stalking Tullio when he tried to break off with her. The audience laughed lustily at a second police deposition from her home town, asserting that she had the reputation of a prostitute in Fontanelice but that her conduct had always been good. Next, the president brought out the famous red underpants found in Bonmartini's bed. Rosina said she did not recognize them. The bloomers now had holes, the president told the court, because during the investigation, they "had a rough time." Everyone laughed except one of Rosina's lawyers, Bernasconi, who turned away in disgust.

"Is it because you are one of the youngest lawyers that you get mad so easily?" asked the president, pleased at the chance to provoke a defense lawyer. Tribunal magistrates did not enjoy the prestige or reverence accorded to American judges. They were regarded like the referees in an athletic contest, who must be obeyed but not necessarily respected. Judges were bureaucrats who had never practiced law and entered their professions straight from the university, satisfied with the security and power that accompanied an appointment to the bench. The president of the Corte d'Assise of Turin earned about 600 lire a year; each trial lawyer standing before him earned an enviable thirty or forty thousand.

The last questions to Rosina concerned the meeting between Tullio and Linda in the park in Venice, where Rosina had stood apart. "You said," the president began, "that the contessa approved of Tullio's marriage. That would have been in conflict with your interests—"

"Nino's marriage would not have put me out," Rosina interrupted firmly. "He would have come to me just the same."

"Just a little walk outside the pasture, eh?" remarked the president, as the audience, now in a jocular mood, laughed again. "Is it true that you told Tisa Borghi that by becoming Tullio's accomplice, you could keep him near you forever, that it was the way for you to become a signora?"

"That is not exactly true," Rosina answered with affecting candor. "I never expected to make like a lady because . . . there are things . . . well, I wouldn't know how."

"Those things are easily learned," the president quietly replied.

The courtroom remained lighted throughout the night, with a policeman guarding the evidence. Spectators and experts were ushered into the morning silence. The three magistrates took their places at the front of the hall, and with a nod to the guards, the president ordered a carabiniere to escort defendant Pio Naldi to the witness chair. Not that he was afraid of the witness escaping, he averred, but to be correct in every detail.

"We guarantee that he won't escape," the defense attorneys assured him.

"What about you? Are you afraid he will escape?" the president asked the carabiniere. Smiling, the guard shook his head but nevertheless stationed himself three feet from Naldi's remarkable yellow shoes and remained there throughout the questioning. Like some other witnesses, Naldi wore his hat, coat, and gloves as he testified.[7]

Yes, Naldi confirmed, he was thirty-two years old, born in Bologna, was a doctor and surgeon, and his father was living. Professor Murri had encouraged him to study medicine instead of literature and arranged a scholarship for him. As there were only 1,500 students at the University of Bologna, he had of course met Tullio. In later years, he often saw him in the Buvette Ponzio, a room behind the Club Rigosi, where they sometimes gambled together. Naldi knew Bonmartini, too. He had even tutored him to prepare him for his final examinations, although afterwards, they hardly acknowledged each other. The president observed that Naldi and Tullio became closer in April and May 1902, "which is amazing," the president added gratuitously, "considering your reputation as a cheater at cards."

"Many things are said about me," Naldi replied mildly. He then narrated how he confided to Tullio his desperate need for money and his desire to start another life away from Bologna. Tullio said that he would gladly help Naldi but that he himself needed 5,000 lire.

"On August 27 Tullio came looking for you?"

"He came late that night to the Club Rigosi." Tullio had decided to confront his brother-in-law, to take some action, even if it meant committing a crime. "I was dismayed," Naldi continued, "because Murri had a bright future ahead of him, a fine, comfortable life, and it seemed absurd to me that he would give it all up on a whim such as you'd expect from some good-for-nothing. I told Murri I thought it was a crazy idea. He insisted that even without me he was going by himself to the Bonmartini house—he had the keys—to wait for his brother-in-law and kill him."

The hall was hushed. "And then?" asked the president softly.

"I was upset when I left him, although I didn't give much credence to what he said. I thought it was just hot air. I decided to wait in Via Borgonuovo to see what he would do. In a little while he turned up. There was a woman dressed in black with him. So he really meant to go! I felt guilty letting him go alone to Bonmartini's; I remembered all of his family's benevolence toward me. I knew Bonmartini would not arrive until the next day, so I thought I would go with him and try to dissuade him. Without saying anything, I fell alongside him. We went to the Pusterla entrance. The woman went away.

"The door to Via Pusterla, was it locked?" interrupted Carlo Nasi, the attorney for the absent Bonmartini children, and thus one of the lawyers ranged against the defendants.

"It was open," said Naldi.

"You've gone in, you've climbed the stairs . . . who opened it?" asked the president.

"I don't know," answered Naldi.

"And then?"

"Then we made our way inside in the dark. I told Murri I wanted to go back outside. He told me not to be afraid, to stay, that I could leave later if I wanted to. He lit a candle, and we found ourselves in a room with two little beds."

"Up to then you hadn't said anything to Murri?"

"I don't think we talked," Naldi answered.

"What time was it?" asked Nasi.

"It must have been two in the morning."

Naldi then recounted that in a long discussion, Tullio said he planned to inject Bonmartini with some curare he had procured in order to kill him. "That idea," Naldi said, his voice rising, "seemed impossible, senseless, laughable. He also talked about a sack of lead balls." Tullio quieted down and fell asleep, according to Naldi. But the next morning, he awoke even more agitated than before. He paced through the apartment, telling Naldi that besides the curare, he was carrying a stick and a dagger.

"And a knife," added the president.

"A dagger," countered Naldi.

"No, a knife besides the dagger," insisted the magistrate.

"I don't think so," Naldi responded. Whether Tullio carried one or two blades was an important point in Naldi's defense. In order for there to have been two attackers, there had to be two knives.

Naldi described Tullio's increased excitement as the day wore on. They ate a ring-shaped cake and drank some champagne. Naldi was more convinced than ever that he had to leave, but he realized that in staying so long, he had already compromised himself. He hadn't a cent, and thought that Tullio must have with him the money he had promised him. With his polished speech and calm voice, Naldi no longer seemed a ridiculous figure and instead took on the forlorn look of starved gentility.

"What money had Murri promised you?" the president asked.

"Five or six thousand lire." Naldi related that he found Tullio's jacket on a chair and stole 1,500 lire from the wallet. "When I left, Murri was in much worse condition than before. I even thought he had a fever. He told me to go and he would leave, too. So I opened the main door and went out."

"This time you went out from the main door?"

"I've always said so."

"No," countered the president. "Five times you said so, but one time you said something else."

"That time was a mistake which I corrected."

"But it was even in one of your letters that we will read . . . it wasn't invented by the prosecutor," the president said with some vexation.

"I don't believe I implied that the prosecutor invented it," Naldi answered softly.

Naldi described going home, changing his clothes, and going to Florence, Livorno, and Genoa.

"Where did you stay in Livorno?" the president asked, apparently to amuse the audience, which laughed heartily at Naldi's answer: "On Prison Street."

The president then pointed out conflicts between Naldi's testimony and his earlier depositions. Had he been locked in the apartment, as he stated during the istruttoria? He wasn't sure, he replied. He had said so in order to justify his staying so long in the house. According to Naldi's deposition, Tullio had told him Rosina would return to unlock the door. Was that true? No, Naldi answered. Stanzani had constantly accused him of trying to protect the others; therefore, he had invented that detail to emphasize Rosina's complicity. Had he gone to wait for Bonmartini under the arcades across the street, to warn him? No. He had only considered it. Had Tullio taken away his shoes to prevent him from leaving? That, too, was invented to excuse his long presence in the house.

Naldi was an effective witness, speaking in a controlled, convincing tone and gesturing often. However, the president found many discrepancies in both his depositions and the testimony he had just given. Naldi explained that he once stated he had gone out of the side entrance because in the confrontation with Tullio, he discerned that Tullio wanted him to say it.

"You say now that Tullio had a dagger, but in the istruttorie you affirmed that he had a knife as well."

"The justice kept talking about a knife that I had not seen. I said he also had a dagger because I had seen it," Naldi responded.

"Was it a weapon that closed or not?"

"No, it was an open blade," said Naldi. "It was contained in a scabbard that was shown to me during the istruttoria."

"But in the istruttoria," protested the president, "you said you didn't recognize that scabbard."

"That was because I had already given a little different description from the one they showed," Naldi replied. "I was afraid to contradict myself, so I said that wasn't the scabbard."

"You are trying to pretend that you never had an agreement to help Tullio."

"Tullio might have assumed I would help him," Naldi answered, "but I never promised him."

"Before going to the Bonmartini house, did you discuss the price of murder?" asked the president.

"Before, no. I was in turmoil, confused."

"Wasn't there mention of 5,000 lire that Tullio was supposed to give you right away and 60,000 lire that he had on deposit?"

"He spoke to me about it after I was there."

"In the istruttoria you said he spoke to you about it first. So you went as a hired killer." This was another important point. If Naldi went with the intention of helping Tullio and being paid, it was much less likely that he would have left before the completion of the crime than if he simply found himself in a dangerous situation and decided at the last moment to extricate himself.

"I said it," Naldi answered, "but it wasn't true. Tullio talked to me about the money later on, to convince me not to leave." Tullio, he said, had even tried to show him how to point the dagger. The questioning then turned to Naldi's attempt at suicide. Why had he done it?

"I was in a state of complete nervous exhaustion. For three months I had been segregated like an animal, overwhelmed by interrogations. The istruttore judge became very familiar, treating me almost like a boy; he patted me on the arm affectionately, gave me cigarettes, told me he didn't believe I was guilty. He said I was sacrificing myself for the others, that I should confide in him, that he was the only one who cared what happened to me. It seemed as if he were waiting for some important revelation from me. He kept implying that I had not told the whole truth and that unless I did, he wouldn't be able to help me. I thought he was referring to the curare, so I came out with it. Stanzani was delighted. But as I thought about it, I realized that what I said hadn't been of any use to me and had hurt the others. So I wanted to kill myself." The courtroom was quiet. Suicide was frequent in Europe and almost a commonplace in Italy.[8]

"Talking to someone in a caffè," the president commented, "and letting him think that you wouldn't hesitate to knock a man on the head—didn't that indicate to Tullio that you were open to anything?"

"I had been able to talk about it, but only talking. I understand that when I am here under such a serious charge, things I said acquire a significance I didn't mean them to have; but everybody knows that there are things you think about doing and might even discuss, but you don't really go ahead with them."

Naldi was asked to describe Tullio's state of mind when he was inside the apartment.

"Anything but normal," Naldi confirmed. "You could see it in his face. He was pale, dazed, didn't know what he was saying or what he wanted to do. He said that Bonmartini's death was inevitable. Especially toward the end of the day, he was utterly prostrate."

At that instant Rosina stood up and told the carabiniere that she had to go out, so the noon recess was announced. So far, Naldi had acquitted himself well. But his self-possession, his odd composure, was almost like coolness. At times it seemed as if he were one of the experts, objective and disinterested, testifying on behalf of some accused person whom he did not know personally. He had not aroused any sympathy except among those who were already disposed to him.

While in prison, Naldi had written several letters to his aunt Cesira. All had been intercepted by Stanzani, including one penned just before the start of the trial, when he learned his aunt had hired a lawyer. *"Your caring stirs so much shame in me,"* Naldi wrote,

> *because I've done nothing to merit so much goodness. I'm a useless being, maybe even destructive. When for the first time I found myself in a dangerous situation, my behavior was so stupid and reckless that I might as well have been a child. When I think of it, I*

am utterly disgusted with myself; with all my heart I want to wipe out this burden of a life.

The lawyers protested Stanzani's conduct during Naldi's interrogations. Vincenzo Tazzari, one of Naldi's lawyers, expostulated, "When Naldi was lying in bed with his veins slashed—is this true or not?" he asked, turning to Naldi, "—even in that tragic hour, Justice Stanzani tried to wring a confession out of him!"[9]

"I had lost consciousness," Naldi answered, "but the nurses told me that's what happened." Stanzani had already been accused of interrogating Rosina while she was hospitalized. None of the judges appeared to doubt that his conduct had been improper, even scandalous, and none cared about it in the slightest.

Led to the circular space in front of the tribunal, Carlo Secchi inclined his head in a modest bow and took his seat. In the fashion of men of distinction, his formidable mustache was waxed into two cursive flourishes that swept across his cheeks like a confident signature. He wiped his hand over his face in his characteristic gesture of anxiety, but then he took on a look, an expression of impassive self-possession that rarely deserted him throughout his testimony.[10] So far, Linda's name had barely been mentioned in the trial, but that was about to change. Secchi described the early years of his relationship with Linda, his break with the Murris, and his reunion with her at the Rusconi house in 1898. "It was on September 27," he said, "a date that remained sacred for us. Nothing serious happened between us then," he averred. "Nothing serious." He described visiting her in San Marcello Pistoiese in July 1900, where he used the name "Borghi." In 1901, they had another tryst when he occupied the other side of her vacation house. Linda kept her eyes lowered through this recounting except for one single glance at her former lover.

"Bonmartini came once to San Marcello Pistoiese," said the president. "Did they give him something to eat?"

"No," Secchi replied. "he was sent to eat at a hotel with the excuse that it was inconvenient. He was there all that day, however."

In 1902 Secchi bought an expensive radiator for Linda, he admitted; she was separated then, he explained, and was receiving only 600 lire a month from her husband.

"There is a witness, one who feels affection for you, who says that Linda Murri was costing you a good deal," the president said.

Secchi spoke coldly. "If you are talking about Tisa Borghi, permit me to say that it's a curious sort of affection that comes from a woman who is trying to damage me." This, then, was to be Secchi's about-face. He would reject the door that Tisa had opened for him when she insisted that he had been drawn unwillingly into the conspiracy. He would return to his original story: that Linda had nothing to do with the murder plans. As in his early depositions, his references to Linda were brocaded with elaborate respect. And yet, if Secchi had not in fact been frightened by a murder conspiracy that he saw forming, frightened in exactly the way Tisa Borghi described, why had he taken the precaution of writing to his friend Dr. Pacini about Tullio's plans and his own refusal to participate in them?

Secchi repeated that he was appalled by Tullio's schemes. Aside from other objections, he said, was the inconvenient fact that curare does leave traces in the urine. "Finally," said Secchi, "I told him, 'If I could show you the effects of curare, you'd forget about using it.' 'Then show me,' Tullio said. He insisted that Linda knew nothing about any of it, and I had no reason to think otherwise." In July 1902, Secchi met Linda in Zurich and she accompanied him to the Meerck factory in Germany where he purchased the curare.

"Why don't you explain how you were planning to use the curare in more than a hundred clinical experiments?" his lawyer suggested.

"I had intended to study the inner ear," Secchi said. "No one has ever done a rigorous investigation of that organ with careful tests. . . . Now, of course, I won't be the one to do that study." Saying this, Secchi gripped his throat and fought back tears, but he pulled himself together.

"Tisa Borghi maintains that the contessa insisted on accompanying you to make sure you procured the curare and that you resisted, saying that killing Bonmartini was unnecessary. When Tisa Borghi's deposition was read to you by the justice, you said it was essentially the truth."

Secchi took his time answering. "Tisa Borghi told the justice certain things that were superimposed on what I had already said; when I heard it, I replied that in substance it was the truth, especially where she said I opposed the contessa's coming with me to Darmstadt. Naturally, in her fragile health, she shouldn't have undertaken a trip."

"This is not what you told the justice," the president objected. But Secchi disputed him.

"All this came out in the istruttoria. I don't want it to appear that I'm coming here with something new. What Tisa said certainly is not true."

The president moved next to the fateful month of August 1902. Secchi was asked to explain a number of strange telegrams. From Linda, August 4: *"Excuse first desperate letter. Latest news gives back life."* Linda, said Secchi, was explaining that she was happy he had decided not to travel that month. No one asked why a two-week vacation would make Linda desperate. Despite Secchi's controlled demeanor, he knew that the telegrams exchanged just before the murder between Linda, Tullio, and himself were critical. There had been so many of them, all signed with false names, all appearing to be coded communications.

The questioning continued. Secchi described the cautionary experiment with the goat and his own admonition to Tullio that it would be much harder to repeat the procedure on a man. "I told him," Secchi recounted, "that six persons were not enough to hold down a little boy in the clinic when we needed to operate on him. . . . I explained all this better in the istruttoria," Secchi added awkwardly, "when I wasn't overcome with emotion as I am now."

"Did you send him some curare?" asked the president.

"Yes, unfortunately. I did the wrong thing. But if I had refused, any pharmacy or laboratory could have provided it to him. I sent it to convince him that his plan was impossible, and as an extra precaution, I sent him a weakened solution."

"It was an amount sufficient to kill ten men!" the president said, almost shouting the last words. "You said so yourself."

Secchi passed his hand over his face. "Would you like a little water?" asked the president, his own composure having returned.

"No, no."

"Well, then," he resumed. "You sent him a quantity sufficient to kill ten people?"

"I had prepared a weakened solution to kill a goat." Secchi began. "Of that solution, I sent one part to him that was more potent, but with the warning to add an equal amount of water. I sent him a syringe difficult to use, calibrated, which he gave back to me just as I had given it to him. When I sent him the curare, I felt deep down that he would never use it, if only because the tools were just not feasible."

"Why didn't you reveal all that to the justice in the istruttorie?"

"In the deposition I was constrained by the feeling that I was keeping a sacred confidence for a poor youth who had already confessed. Mrs. Borghi told me that when she brought Tullio the curare, he said, 'I am convinced Secchi is right. The thing isn't possible.' So I was relieved and thought the discussion was closed."

"You didn't speak of it to Linda Murri?"

"I wrote to the contessa that she should be on guard."

"Regarding the curare?" asked the president.

"No, not regarding the curare—the contessa knew nothing about that—but in general, because Tullio was so worked up about Bonmartini. It was general advice."

"You put back the curare, you put back the syringe, and then you went to Castiglione dei Pepoli?"

"Yes, Sir."

The president asked why Secchi gave Tullio 3,000 lire, with Linda's knowledge, which was repaid exactly on August 28. He reviewed the telegrams sent by "Salviati" and "Borghi," asking Secchi for treatment. Secchi insisted to the court that he still did not realize that Tullio was the author of the missives. When he finally saw Tullio's infected arm, he pretended to believe the story that Rosina had cut him with a pair of scissors, but he suspected the truth. After the discovery of Bonmartini's corpse, he felt "a great deal of pity for the family."

"And for the dead man—nothing?" asked the president.

"I am not here to judge the dead man," Secchi responded. "I'm here to defend myself."

He wrote letters to Linda that would have proved his innocence, he insisted. He lamented out loud that Tisa had allowed them to be destroyed. "I don't know how it happened," he said. "The poor thing must have been alarmed. Suddenly a stranger appears one evening and insists that she burn all my letters in his presence." Secchi did not, however, mention Linda, who had ordered the annihilation.

Regarding Bonmartini, Secchi said, "I never knew him, except by sight, but I had the impression that there was a great difference in temperament between him and the contessa."

"Weren't specific things about him ever told to you?"

"Never."

"According to Tisa," said the president, "there had been attempts to poison Bonmartini even before the curare."

"I don't agree with that. Bonmartini was sick, but with a gastric illness." Secchi did not explain how he distinguished between gastric illness and poisoning.

The prosecutor asked Secchi to explain again why he gave Tullio the curare.

"I spoke to Tullio as a man of honor," he began. Another prosecutor snickered sarcastically so that everyone in the hall could hear. Secchi stopped suddenly and seemed about to rise. The color left his face and he wrung his hands nervously. But he lowered his head and slowly regained control of himself. He explained again that he lectured Tullio on the danger to which he was exposing himself, his sister, and his family.

"Then why did you give him the curare?" persisted the prosecutor.

"Curare such as I gave him could be had from all the laboratories, all the pharmacies, all the infirmaries, but no one, perhaps, would have had the forethought to give it to him diluted and with so many warnings."

Secchi's lawyer Morello watched his client closely while these critical questions were posed, but he did not intervene. Another prosecutor interjected: "In providing the curare, didn't it occur to Dr. Secchi that he was making it easy for Tullio to get his hands on poison? He was well aware of Tullio's violent projects, was he not?"

The courtroom was charged with the tension of this exchange. How indeed could Secchi justify giving poison to someone who had clearly stated he was planning a murder? Everyone was listening attentively. Secchi leaned forward. His face was earnest.

"I wanted to convince Tullio. I believed he would abandon the idea once he got hold of the medicine—" he began.

The prosecutors and the judges all raised their heads at once and looked at one another. Secchi's lawyer involuntarily clapped his hand to his mouth. All the jurors had heard it. An eerie silence fell on the hall.

"You called it medicine," the president said slowly.

Secchi's response was quick and nervous. "I have been calling it poison, but up until recently it was also medicine."

Two days—thirteen hours—of thoughtful, effective testimony had been wiped out with a few careless syllables. Probably Secchi would have paid anything to buy the word back, the expensive word that, once having fallen out of his mouth, might cost him years of his unassuming life. Secchi was sent back to sit in the defendants' cage, restless and miserable, while four of his letters and his long deposition were read by a clerk, inaudibly, so that the audience had time to muse on the possible code words for "poison."

The questioning ended with the only topic that could now hold the court's attention, the postcard written by Linda Murri: *"I don't hear anything more about S. Did the medicine work?"*

He was the person referred to as "S." And he was the person who gave "the medicine" to Tullio. Wasn't all that true? And who else was aware of the plan with "the medicine"?

One person in the courtroom already knew the answers to all those questions. The hall stirred with awakened interest as he was led to the witness chair, still in his tan overcoat with the velvet lapels.[11] If Secchi's demeanor had been self-possessed and calm, Tullio's agitation burst forth every few minutes, drenching him in sweat and tears as he was pricked by first one question and then another. If Secchi was careful not to denigrate either Bonmartini or other actors in the drama, Tullio dropped insults like a person carrying too many to hold. He cried as he related how Linda became more and more melancholy after marrying Bonmartini. "By the end of 1898, she was almost at the point of death."

The president interrupted. "But you knew Linda had a lover? You didn't think that could have contributed to her condition and her intolerance for her husband?"

"I didn't know it. And usually when women have lovers, they feign more affection for their husbands."

"It doesn't always happen that way," the president opined. "Often the marital chain weighs that much more heavily."

Tullio had, however, noticed that Linda developed an ardent friendship with the Marchesa Rusconi, "who everybody knew was Secchi's lover and not very intellectual." He wondered if Linda had been drawn to Rusconi because she talked about Secchi. During this disquisition, Linda kept her face in her handkerchief. When Tullio said that he eventually surmised the relationship between his sister and Secchi, Linda, still in her handkerchief, sobbed audibly. Secchi followed the discourse intently, as did Rosina, who wrung her hands in anguish each time Tullio broke into tears. Now and then, the reporters on the second tier of benches, who could not see the witnesses unless they stood up, got briefly to their feet to confirm that another outbreak of crying had caused the proceedings to pause.

"You knew that at some point there arose a quarrel within this trio? So you wrote a letter in which you said if Rusconi were a man you would smack her."

"Yes."

By that time, Bonmartini had made the marital separation necessary, said Tullio, because of "his violence toward my sister." And though he had badly wanted a reconciliation after the three-year parting, he was worse than ever when he moved back home, "marching around like a little dictator, threatening to take away the children."

"These scurrilous attacks on a dead man," objected the prosecutor Nasi, "are not true," and he slapped the table in front of him to accompany the last words. The defense attorneys beat their table, too, in counter-protest. Tullio resumed. Having counseled Linda to reunite with Bonmartini, he felt responsible for her woes. At this point, both Tullio and Linda cried copiously. The attorneys on both sides, now pacified, watched the outburst with placid indifference. Tullio said he became preoccupied with opposing Bonmartini's "physical violence" with his own "psychological violence." By the time he tried to involve Secchi in his plans, he was consumed by the idea that he must "save Linda at all costs." With that, Tullio sobbed convulsively, his hands covering his face.

During the whole demonstration with the goat, according to Tullio, Secchi was jocular and patronizing. Knowing Bonmartini's repugnance for Rosina, Secchi said, "You know how to do it? While Bonmartini is sitting down, Bonetti can just go up to him and offer to give him this little shot." Tullio thought Secchi was lying about the impracticality of curare. "I thought, 'If Secchi gives me the curare, it will mean that he is telling the truth and that it really is inadequate.'" When Tisa brought the poison, Tullio said, he jokingly asked if she didn't want to help him administer it to Bonmartini. Tisa answered him, "'You're an idiot to hesitate. Give him a good knock on the head, and then you'll see . . .' I went to give her a squeeze, and she said, 'Let me be. I'm a married woman.' I kidded with her and then made a date that she swore on her word of honor she would keep; but she didn't come. Still in that bantering way, I sent her a little il- lustrated postcard, and wrote on it, 'Word of Honor!'"

Tullio passed over the wrestling match in Venice. It was Cesco who suggested they arm wrestle, and succeeded in pushing down Tullio's arm. That was all there was to it. But no sooner had he left Venice than Linda's letter arrived in Rimini describing what Bonmar- tini did to her with the chair. At the same time, Linda wrote to Rosina asking her to go get a dress at the Bisteghi Palace on the twenty-eighth, when Bonmartini would be there. "I resolved to go there and confront him, to intimidate him," Tullio said, with another thunder of sobbing, so that the president declared a two-hour recess to let him collect himself.

When he returned to the witness box, Tullio had changed into black clothes. He confirmed borrowing money from Secchi just before the murder and then going to Rimini to talk to his parents. While there, he received a frantic letter from Linda reporting that Bonmartini was starting the move to Padua.[12] Tullio decided to go back to Venice that very day to confront Bonmartini and to make sure that Linda was not left alone with him. As he waited at the Rimini train station, Severo Dalla came with another letter from Linda in which she repeated that a separation was absolutely nec- essary in order to save herself from the "emotional violence" that was evidently her husband's program for her.[13] The prosecution would eventually point out that Tullio obviously did not go to Venice to confront Bonmartini or to protect Linda from being alone with him, since he met his sister in the park in order to avoid even seeing Bonmartini.

Tullio began making firm plans to murder Bonmartini, he said, only after his return from Venice. As his intentions took shape, he re- alized that he needed a doctor's help to carry them out. Naldi at first thought Tullio was joking and then tried to talk him out of his plan.

Here Tullio held his face between his hands and resumed his loud sobbing, drawing everyone in the witness cage into his bath of tears. Naldi and Secchi hung their heads. Linda and Rosina cried uncontrollably. "I was trying to save . . . my sister's life," Tullio finally choked out.

"Describe the discussion between you and Naldi," said the president.

"No discussion," Tullio answered. "I was obstinate, told him I would do it one way or the other by myself." By now Naldi had joined the chorus of loud wailing. Tullio described how Naldi walked with him to Via Mazzini. Once inside in the dark apartment, Tullio himself unlocked and relocked the door, allowing Naldi to believe that Rosina had locked them in. He described how, the next evening, he went through the rooms "like a madman," and walked on the bed. Naldi asked me, 'Do you think in this condition you can attack a man?' But I was under something—a big stone. I had carried morphine to kill myself. What more could I have done than sacrifice my own skin?" Tullio asked, as if expecting an answer.

"You didn't sacrifice your own," the president dryly observed. "You sacrificed Bonmartini's."

"Naldi insisted he was going to leave, and he finally did, by the main door. After a while, I gathered my weapons and went out by way of the balcony on Via Pusterla, where the portinaia could not see me. I went to Via San Stefano, to Bonetti's house," he said, and resumed wailing.

The courtroom was getting noisy. People were becoming surfeited with the lachrymose spectacle. However, as Tullio repeated the latest version of the murder, placing the time around midnight of August 28, the hall quieted down. According to the new story, which the newspapers labelled "the Turin story," Tullio left the apartment before Bonmartini's arrival, waited for Bonetti at home, and then the two of them had dinner at the Caffè del Corso, where he wrote cards to his mother and Linda. He went looking for Naldi and instead saw Bonmartini from afar in the Piazza of the Two Towers. "I

206 — INDECENT SECRETS

only wanted to talk to him. I was not far from the porticos of Via
Mazzini. When I was close enough, I called to him. He turned; he
was almost beside me. We greeted each other."

"What time was it?" asked the president.

Close to tears again, Tullio answered, "Midnight."

The audience was again as attentive as if they were watching a
play. Linda, bent over the railing, hid her head on the arm that was
holding on to a crossbar of the cage and sobbed steadily. Bonetti
cried, her face to the ceiling, from time to time emitting something
like a lament. Between the two of them sat Naldi, white as a ghost,
with his lifeless left eye and his drooping mustache, also apparently
quite moved. Secchi left his position in the corner, moved to Tullio's
place, and seemed to be leaning over Linda. The snow that had been
falling outside for several hours was the only noise.

"What did Bonmartini say when he saw you?" asked the president.

Tullio, halting and sobbing after each phrase, described how
Bonmartini remarked that he was planning to spend the night at the
Hotel d'Italia and was going to pay the rent on the Bisteghi apartment and pick up his luggage. As they entered the Pusterla door,
Bonmartini lit some candles and went to change jackets. "I went into
the hall toward his room, saying, 'Is it true that you are going to
move the family to Padua?' 'Yes,' he answered. 'Then,' I said, 'I have
to talk to you.'" Although at other times Tullio had said he couldn't
remember much about the fight with Bonmartini, he now narrated
the death scene with a novelist's attention to detail, mindful of the
sounds and setting of his story, building it carefully to its climax.

"My voice was quite changed," he began. "In an agitated tone I
said, 'Why don't you ever think of how unhappy you are making
poor, sick Linda?' I heard him move and mumble, but still he didn't
come out. Finally, he came almost to the door and moved toward
me, saying, 'So you came up here to give me orders?'

"'For pity's sake, don't do it! Don't do it!' I shouted at him, 'or
I'll go off the deep end. I'll skin you alive!'"

"'Instead of threatening me, you'd better go tell that traitor, your father, to keep his promises.'

"At this insult, I felt an internal spasm, lost the light of reason, and let go with a fist."

Tullio then described the life-or-death battle on the floor, a struggle that ended when he got control of Bonmartini's knife and turned it into his attacker's chest. Swept by remorse, he went through the apartment, trying to hide the crime by planting the letters and props he had prepared when he and Naldi were waiting for Bonmartini earlier that day.

"How was it that you left a letter you wrote that day, if you had decided to abandon the idea of committing the crime?" the president asked, knowing that the letter had been placed on the table before the stabbing.[14]

Tullio, unaware that the letter had been found lightly splashed with blood, replied that the note was in his wallet where he had put it earlier. After attending to these details, he went to Cattolica, "as if in a dream," to get rid of evidence. Rosina had testified that they went to Cattolica before the murder. How could she think they had taken a three-hour journey before the crime unless she had memorized a prepared fiction and gotten the sequence wrong under the pressure of testifying? Was this why Tullio and Linda had begun caterwauling during Rosina's testimony—because she had made a mistake and they wanted to signal her, or distract the listeners?

The prosecution brought out a telegram that Tullio sent to Linda three days after the murder: *Telegraphed Papà asking advice. . . . This morning I sent cascara sagrada. Nino.*[15]

How did the red underwear and blond hair get into the house? Why did Tullio claim he bought the pallini in Venice, "acting on Tisa's suggestion," whereas Rosina testified that she bought the pellets in Bologna three months before the murder? Why was it that Naldi admitted taking a 1,500-lire note, while Tullio said he was missing one note of 1,000 lire and one of 500? Tullio's answer to each of these questions was that he didn't know. The stolen money was the most damning contradiction. If Naldi insisted he took one note and Tullio said he took two, it would seem that they were both lying. Naldi had said at one point in the istruttoria that the money he had in his pocket when arrested had been won in a game at the train station; at another point that Tullio had given him the money to repay a debt; and finally that he had stolen it from Tullio's jacket.

Tullio was questioned about Rosina. She was selfless, he said, though so ignorant that she did not know the months of the year and so childlike that she sometimes amused herself with dolls.[16] He turned away from the president, his eyes watching her tenderly as he described her. Were Tullio and Linda lovers? the president asked, suddenly changing the topic. Dusio was a clever interrogator. Having fixed the court's and Tullio's attention to the engrossing question of incest, he shifted again and demanded that Tullio explain Linda's card asking if "the medicine" was effective. It did not refer to poison, Tullio answered, since curare is not medicine.

"Didn't you hear Secchi refer to it as medicine right here?" asked the president.

"I don't know that he did that," Tullio answered.

Secchi intervened. "Formerly curare was used as a medicine. Not now, however."

Tullio's wordy memoria was read. "Bonmartini," the reader droned, "was a pederast and a necrophiliac." No one in the court was listening.[17] Finally, the court reporter read the letter Tullio wrote to Linda at the time of the reconciliation—the time, according to the prosecution, when Tullio and Linda began seriously planning the murder: *"I believe the solution suggested by you is the only one possible. We will hardly find Papà favorable: I will try to talk to him about it."*[18]

Tullio had been in the witness chair three days when the president announced that the ordeal was finished. The audience stirred, waiting for the court's dismissal. The prosecution lawyers seemed uniformly downcast. Soon everyone understood why. Tapping his gavel, the president revealed that another of their star witnesses had died. Ermolao Barbaro, one of Bonmartini's intimate friends, had given two heated depositions disputing any notion that the count had sex with men and corpses. Barbaro was prepared to tell the jury that Bonmartini knew he was being stalked and that his life had been turned into a hell of anxiety. But now Tullio would not have to face him—or another of Bonmartini's confidants, his cousin Enrico Antico of Cavarzere, who had followed him to the grave. Secchi's confidant Pacini was gone. All of Bonmartini's closest friends, his cousin Valvassori, and the most knowledgeable of all his defenders, Cervesato, were, like Bonmartini himself, dead. Tullio, drained and dazed, his face swollen, his shoulders collapsed, his jacket tear-stained, and his hands bound—Tullio nevertheless walked out of the courtroom on March 4 an extraordinarily lucky man.

Outside the Hall of the Assize it was carnival time, with fireworks, torchlight parades, and candles shining from the windows of every house. All over the downtown section of Turin, streets bright with decorations were filled with musicians and lively young people. Even the horses pulling carriages wore hats and necklaces. Still, people left the gaiety outside to crowd into the bare, funereal courtroom. All binoculars were fixed on Linda in her black habit and heavy veil. Throughout the trial, she had been referred to as Linda Murri, and it was that name the president pronounced as he settled himself for the March 4 afternoon hearing.[19] She walked unsteadily to the witness box and stumbled slightly. No sooner had she sat down than she put her head on the table where evidence was to be exhibited and began sobbing, filling the room with wracking gasps that covered even the street noise. "Remember that the president is not here only for the prosecution, but for everybody. You can give your explanations. . . ." When Linda continued to cry, Dusio said, "Now, take a moment and calm down."

Linda raised her veil, wiped her cheeks, and remained with her hands holding on to the seat, watching the president with her taffeta eyes. He began with questions about how she met Bonmartini and their early years of marriage. Linda spoke carefully, stopping almost at every word. She had cried when she realized their incompatibility, she said, "because I had married above all to have a soul mate."

"And he wasn't it?" asked the president. "What did he do?"

"It wasn't him, poor thing. We saw life differently because we were brought up differently."

"But your letters were very loving. You said that without him, life was no good."

"In my family we all express ourselves very affectionately."

The president quoted several of her rapturous letters of 1897, which Linda explained in various ways. She talked of clinging to her father, whom she described as "my happiness."

"Did you have sexual relations in Bologna?" asked the president.

"I know what this is leading up to."

"Well, we do have to get to it."

"Yes, yes, I know. I am more convinced than you of my own guilt, and I will say so frankly." She gestured toward the jury. "None of them can judge me as I have judged myself. I alone know how many tears I have shed over my guilt." Linda resumed sobbing but added, "That's the only thing I'm guilty of. For the rest of it," she exclaimed, stopping a moment to wipe her tears, "I am innocent!" The audience was thoughtful. "My poor father knew how I was suffering; he was upset by that life of hell I was leading that threatened my health."

"At the end of 1898 your relations with Secchi became more intimate?" the president prodded.

"I was reduced to a very sad state, and Secchi more than all the others understood me; he was so sorry for the bad luck that I had had."

"He came to you at San Remo?" persisted the president.

"For one day only, because of the seriousness of my condition."

"Then came the separation?" the president asked pointedly.

"Secchi wasn't the cause. . . ."

"Was Bonmartini happy about the separation?"

"No, no."

"Then he loved you?" asked the president. "Secchi met you again at San Marcello Pistoiese," he continued. "How did that look to you," he lectured, "as a wife, a woman of social position who had two children and carried a name like yours?" As she was of course expected to do, Linda hid her face in her handkerchief and cried. "You wrote to your husband from San Marcello Pistoiese, 'Deception and scheming from Linda Murri—never!' You said that life had no smiles for you, except that it allowed you a pure conscience. And did you tell him that an 'engineer' was living there in your villa?"

Linda slowly raised her head and looked the magistrate in the eye. "It is understood that a woman who finds herself in this situation certainly cannot confide in her husband even though they are legally separated. I wrote him that because one time Bonmartini came home looking for me and I was gone, and he thought I was hiding somewhere so as not to see him. Since he told me openly what he had thought, in my letter I wrote him that he should never expect such deception from me. And then," she continued, lowering her voice, "that time in San Marcello I was so sick, so sick. Secchi's company was very welcome, not only because he overwhelmed me with attention, but because for me he was like a nurse."

No one recorded the jury's impressions of this exchange. Linda's explanation was so cogent and reasonable, so well constructed to slide the focus of the answer from her lying to Bonmartini to her sickness. Could she have thought of such an effective response there in the witness box and delivered it as she did with complete self-possession?

The president pressed on. "You wrote to Valvassori that your husband suspected you had taken up again with Secchi and that such a suspicion was an insult to you." Linda again responded with an account of her illness. She had been "a walking cadaver." The president admonished her for some letters between her and Secchi written during the separation, letters that he described as "not the most suitable" between a gentleman and a lady.[20]

"You are right, Signor President, you are right," Linda replied. "I reacted against those letters many times, and Dr. Secchi can confirm it." Saying that, Linda cried, and Secchi held his handkerchief to his eyes. Didn't Secchi sometimes send her flowers and sweets? the president wanted to know. Linda's answers invariably brought the discussion back to her health, to the doctors' fears that she would not survive, to her lack of appetite. Hadn't Secchi sometimes sent her oysters? Since oysters were considered an undisputed aphrodisiac, any mention of them enlivened the atmosphere. "I have confessed my guilt, Signor President," Linda replied. "Why are you tormenting me?"

She and Bonmartini suddenly, inexplicably, reconciled, and she rented the apartment next to her own, the president observed. Her father had agreed to the reunion, Linda explained, as if that were reason enough to accede to it. A lively correspondence started up between Tullio and Secchi in May, just after the reconciliation, and lasted until August, when the murder was committed. Linda knew nothing, she said, of any correspondence.

"Didn't you go away with Secchi in July 1902, specifically to plot the murder? Weren't you present when the curare was ordered? Isn't it true that you spoke of acquiring it for Bonmartini?"

"It is all false, all false," Linda insisted. "You need to realize," she said, "at that time I still loved Dr. Secchi so much. During the depositions I tried to defend myself without saying more than was strictly necessary."

The questioning turned to the single most damning piece of evidence against Linda, the famous twenty-cent postcard, undated, addressed in a disguised handwriting to Tullio Murri, Rimini:

> *I am almost imagining what you tell me of the extraordinary business. I'll bet it's got something to do with A and that the other actor is you. I had correctly guessed the list of three. I am very curious to hear from you.*
>
> *Dear Nino, I don't hear anything more about S. Did the medicine work? Write me a signal. Many, many kisses.*

In her depositions, Linda had said one time that the S referred to a married woman and another time that it stood for Sant' Elpidio, where some relatives lived. "Now I am explaining things as they really are because my attorneys have recommended that I not hold back anything." Linda then went forward with a completely new explanation of the card, having to do with Tullio's flirtation with a married woman. This time it was not the woman's name that began with "S," but a rival suitor whose behavior was the "medicine" that could drive the woman back to Tullio. If this new version was a lie, it was the lie of an expert, as subtle and tangled as truth. Linda expatiated on it for perhaps twenty minutes. Asked why she had lied about the card previously, her answer was temperate, considering that perhaps a decade of her life was at stake. "I didn't want to compromise that lady."

"You are writing to Tullio about somebody referred to as S. But doesn't Secchi often become S in your letters?" asked the president. Pressed to justify her previous story, Linda proceeded with a very long and involved explanation of the prior explanation, elaborating for perhaps thirty minutes on the necessity of shielding the relationship from her mother's curiosity and the intricate jokes between her and Tullio that were part of their communications.

The president suddenly switched back to the month of the murder. Asked to describe the scene with the chair, she gave a long account of the quarrel between her and Bonmartini, which she said the servants had watched while the children wailed. The president countered, "Bonetti confirmed that the count apologized, and a little while later you went out for a walk together."

"Rosina invented that," said Linda, "perhaps to lessen the importance of the quarrel, since I told her to keep quiet about it, out of duty and respect."

"But didn't you write to your mother about it? Why did you write her such a desperate letter?"

"I was letting off steam. Don't you understand? It was my mother."

"One of your frantic letters provoked two telegrams from Rimini on August 25, both from Tullio, signed Contessa Borghi and Maria Pirazzoli, and a visit from Tullio and Bonetti on the twenty-sixth."

Linda testified that she had never before heard the name 'Pirazzoli.'

"I knew only that Rosina had made us call her 'Maria,' but the last name was completely new to me."

The president wanted to know what she and her brother talked about in the public park in Venice. Her marriage? "You must understand," she answered, "I had an exceedingly sad and sensitive disposition. I was overwrought." Linda cried several moments before resuming. "My poor brother always loved me . . ." The fugue of crying began again, Tullio holding his head between his hands. She had been exasperated and excited, Linda said. She returned to her familiar theme: "My weakness, my state of illness, my tendency toward tears, my shortness of breath—I couldn't hold back." She did not imagine that her words would activate a plan Tullio was already mulling, she said.

"How is it possible," asked the president, "that peace and tranquillity could ever return to a home when a lover stands between the husband and wife?"

"Let's look at the facts. My husband's soul might have been one way, but in reality he was what he was. When we reunited I put in the pact that we would be together as friends, demanding complete freedom. This freedom certainly would not be invoked to go make visits. For my part, I intended it as a loyal affirmation of reciprocal rights . . ." Linda pulled off her glove in apparent agitation and, turning to the president, said, "You told me how could I speak of peace, having a lover. Between peace and love there is an infinite difference. Peace concerns the rapport necessary for common affection."

Who gave Tullio the keys to the apartment? Linda insisted that Rosina took them from their customary hanging place without her knowledge. "She says she took them; it must be that she did." Linda received a package labeled "cascara sagrada" after the murder. Did this package contain the keys? No, Linda responded. She opened the package in front of a maid.[21]

"When you left Bologna right after the murder," the president asked, "did you know the truth about the crime?"

"No," replied Linda. "In those days I was reduced to a rag, I was like a body without life, I didn't know myself what to think. I didn't know anything. . . . I was so worn out, so shattered, that my father wanted me to go to Switzerland to gain some strength. My father, my poor papa," exclaimed Linda with an inflection of tenderness in her muffled voice, "was afraid that I might lose the other eye and advised me to leave at once to finish the cure that Dr. Haab had started and told me to resume in September."

"In all the days that followed the crime, didn't you ever think of him?" the president asked.

"Who?"

"The poor dead man. In prison, you shouted a cry of love, but not for him, for someone else. There is a letter in the evidence . . . but we will let it rest for now."

"No!" insisted Linda. "I have to justify myself in front of the judges and I am doing it. If I had not felt this duty, I would not have had the courage to ask for the pictures of my adored children. I am their mother," she exclaimed in a rapture of sobbing, "innocent!" She stopped to cry a while before continuing. "I was thinking in prison that Secchi had suffered just as I was suffering. I thought of his remorse. I thought we wouldn't see each other anymore for the rest of our lives, but I didn't want his last memory of me to be one of regret fixed in his heart. It was a letter of comfort."

"I am finished," said the president.

A prosecutor spoke up. Who had opened the door when Secchi came to see her? She had, Linda answered. "No one was informed of our relationship except Secchi's servant," she said pointedly, indicating Tisa.

Linda was asked to describe her upbringing. Her lawyer Enrico Cavaglià interjected, "The mother has for many years been subject to profound melancholy, and everything makes her suspicious, even little things. Otherwise, she is a very good woman."

"Yes! Yes!" Linda added, "My poor saintly mother! She is so, so good."

"All mothers are saintly," the president commented, "when they're not here."

The session was finally over. Secchi, who had been more emotional during Linda's testimony than at any other time throughout the trial, remained several moments with his face hidden in his handkerchief. Linda, elegant but exceedingly thin, walked past him with her characteristic bent posture. The usual crowd awaited her outside. [22]

9. THE MYSTERY WITNESS

The defendants all having testified, the hapless jurors could not have imagined that the trial would last another five months. However, some two dozen experts still had something to say. Besides the living witnesses who were yet to testify, there were those who had died after being questioned in the istruttoria—their depositions had to be droned aloud. Minor voices would have their turns—a tailor who said Tullio moved his "wounded" arm freely while being fitted for a jacket the day after the violence; families going to the public bath or public latrine who had noticed shadows or odd sounds on Via Pusterla the night of the murder.[1] No information was considered too irrelevant for a hearing; and since the court paid the travel expenses of witnesses, many were willing to come forward in the cause of justice.[2] The unwilling sent their servants with excuses: they were "unreliable" or "semi-crazy" or planned to be sick for the coming months.

The material evidence in the case was treated as carefully as if it had been important. Linda Murri's books no longer aroused interest, even well-thumbed copies of *The Libertine* and *School of Caresses*. The newspapers had been given the long list of arresting titles when the books were seized and for two years had been filling every shallow of the istruttoria with editorials about the baleful influence of French novels on the morals of upper-class Italian women.[3] The empty champagne bottle and the rolls, now moldy, that were found in the apartment were solemnly presented, along with the shards of glass Naldi had used to slash his arteries and the scrap of pencil that served Tullio to outline a verse drama during the istruttoria. The bloody towels Tullio had used to wrap his arm were displayed as evidence, the clerk holding them at a distance, for they stank mightily. Bonmartini's briefcase was brought out and emptied onto a white oilcloth: an image of the Madonna came tumbling out, along with a revolver and a small clock that he had kept in its original box. Much was made of the simple black rosary found in Bonmartini's pocket when his body was examined, along with the cloth envelope containing a lock of hair and the first tooth lost by his little girl.

More was made of his pornography collection. The doors to the courtroom were closed while the judges performed their assiduous duty, inspecting each picture a long while before releasing it to the jury. The audience had to make do with the glimpses they could catch through binoculars. While everyone was still in the mood for the distasteful subject, the prosecutors read aloud Secchi's so-called obscene letter. When it was over and the courtroom doors were reopened, a nun refused to enter and give her testimony about Linda's behavior in prison. "Nothing will be said here that you can't hear," the president reassured her.

The portinaia of the Palazzo Bisteghi, Teresa Cicognani, confirmed the testimony she had given four times during the istruttoria. A perfect, small model of the town house appeared in the courtroom; the jury by now understood that there were two doors to the corner building: the front entrance, where Signora Cicognani was stationed at a window, watching the comings and goings of the street in the venerable pastime of old people, and the side entrance on Via Pusterla where, to reach the servants' staircase, one crossed through a gated and locked courtyard similar to the one protecting the front. The portinaia was dressed for her court appearance in a little black woolen hat and gloves, her dress enveloped in a big ash-colored shawl. Suddenly self-conscious as the president observed her over his eyeglasses, she turned before sitting down and made him a brief curtsy.[4] The downstairs gate to Via Pusterla had remained open the night Bonmartini died, she explained, since vandals were presumed to be on vacation, like everyone else in Bologna during the month of August. Though the defense lawyers peppered the old lady with tricky questions designed to show that her eighty-year-old memory was faulty, she was clearheaded in contending that Bonmartini did not leave again after he arrived. Her testimony was corroborated by a young companion who was with her at the window.

Others, however, came forward to say that they saw Bonmartini out and about, in the company of a blond woman, after he was supposed to be dead. Though Stanzani had tried to discourage them from making their statements, two neighbors insisted that they noticed Bonmartini walking under the portico near the apartment at the time when the autopsy report placed him in his apartment, already sliced up. A Dr. Tirelli testified that, at eight o'clock on the night of the murder, while enjoying his usual Friday night gathering of friends at Restaurant Belletti, he had seen Bonmartini at one of the tables. Belletti's was a pub with an open-air restaurant near the Piazza of the Two Towers, an unpretending, dignified retreat for men with modest manners and appetites.[5] During the investigation, the doctor had hesitated to make such a strong statement. "You have to understand the ambience in Bologna," he explained. "Only three days ago a clerk in the pharmacy said to me, 'Ah, you're going to Turin to defend the Murris. Well, we're not interested in waiting on you.'" Nobody imagined so much hatred existed against the Murri family.[6]

Rarely in a trial were the opinions of servants given such attention. One after another, maids and cooks were asked who loved the children more, Bonmartini or Linda, who spoke ill of whom, whether the count had ever carried a knife, and particularly, how often Linda bought oysters. Linda was generally favored, though the count certainly had admirers among his tenants. One of them called him "the very flower of a gentleman" and then, to the consternation

of the lawyers, sat down amidst them after his testimony and remained there, being too deaf to realize that their flailing arms were
directing him elsewhere.[7]

No fewer than seven thousand letters had been seized by the authorities, including those written by the defendants while in prison.
When Justice Stanzani intercepted the prisoners' letters, he released
them to the press without informing anyone. During the istruttoria,
the defense lawyers sputtered, Professor Murri and Naldi's aunt
were dismayed to open their newspapers and see for the first time
letters addressed to them. Every second or third witness complained
that Stanzani had tried to slant his deposition, and all of the defendants had grievances against him. Linda, for example, was not allowed to be alone for a half hour a day so that she could "attend to
her intimate necessities," prison apparently having cured her intestinal problems so that her necessities were reduced.[8] The president
shrugged. The trial already had too many defendants to add Stanzani
to the cage, he said, looking around at the audience to see if they appreciated the wisecrack.

The testimony was desultory, aimed at first one defendant and
then another. Marchesa Rusconi, the "caterpillar" whom Bonmartini had despised, took the witness chair at ten one night and surprised the tired jury by declaring that whenever she met
Bonmartini, he seemed such a perfect gentleman that she began to
doubt Linda's complaints.[9] The owners of the Club Rigosi and the
Caffè del Commercio testified that Pio Naldi gambled in their
clubs but could not afford to eat there.[10] The caffè was only a birreria in a moderate hotel, but still too fine for a man who was five
months behind in his rent. Had Naldi returned to his rooms to
change clothes on August 28 before leaving on the seven o'clock
train for Florence? According to his landlady, Lucca Pallido, he paid
12 lire to settle his back rent on August 27. She wasn't sure if he
had returned on the evening of the twenty-eighth. The president
challenged her: "In your deposition, you were quite explicit in stating that he did not return." Like other witnesses, Signora Pallido

was not afraid of the president; and like others, she readily confessed to lying in the deposition because she was influenced by
what she read about the defendants in the papers.[11]

Severo Dalla, who had been arrested for complicity and only recently released, appeared quite capable of defending himself before
the severe questioning of the president. Cool and well-spoken, he
blithely admitted sending his brother to destroy Secchi's letters, as
Linda ordered. "I did it," he said, "to protect the dignity of a woman I
considered and still consider innocent, and would do it again in the
same circumstances."[12] Linda had explained in a letter to Severo the
reasons why she would be exonerated: her father's reputation, her
brother's youth, and "my own, pure conscience."[13] Dr. Dagnini was
aware that Bonmartini's private nickname for him was "Dr. Dead-
head"—the servant Vacchi had kindly revealed it.[14] Nevertheless, he
and other doctors joined against the Murris by testifying that Professor
Murri was intoxicated with his daughter. "He wanted to make a doctor
out of her," one physician remarked tersely, "but she didn't want to go
to high school."[15]

Finally the bailiff called out the name the audience had been waiting
for. She was not a defendant but someone who walked in and out of
the courtroom unguarded, past her handcuffed collaborators, while
freely admitting that she knew everything about the conspiracy and
had participated in nearly every part of it. The press constantly referred to her as the "mystery witness," even though her identity had
long been known: Teresa Bonera Borghi—Tisa! The judges reposi-
tioned themselves on the bench. The defendants shifted in their cage.
The audience fell silent as the woman walked from the back of the
courtroom to make her accusations in person. She was tall, thirty-
four years old, neatly attired in black but not dressed up, and she approached the semicircle of the inner court with a manner one
reporter described as "nonchalant and a little vulgar."[16] She might
have once been comely. She wore a black scarf over her head that hid

the lower part of her face and muffled her first words. The defense attorneys (knowing exactly what they were doing) asked her to take away the scarf, and everyone saw at once the vulnerability beneath her sassiness: cheeks sunken into a face that, from the eyes down, was drawn and aged. Without teeth, her speech was sibilant, and even her voice sounded like that of an old woman.[17] Tisa had been interrogated no fewer than nine times, but only in June 1903, after the arrest of Secchi, had she raised her obstinate accusations against Linda. How had Tisa come to know Secchi? the president asked.

"Before he went with her, he went with me," she answered simply, without qualifying the meaning of "went."

"What happened when you all were in Switzerland?"

"The contessa wanted to go with Secchi to Darmstadt, but he didn't want it." She answered succinctly, as if she were summarizing her testimony instead of just beginning it.

"You said more during your written interrogatory," the president urged.

"And I will stand by it word for word," Tisa declared.

"What did Secchi say to the contessa?" asked the president.

"Secchi tried to discourage her from going," responded Tisa, "but the contessa told him, 'You don't love me anymore.'"

"Didn't Secchi say that there was a place in the world even for Bonmartini?"

"Many times," Tisa confirmed.

Linda jumped up from her seat. "It's all lies! Lies!"

"It's the truth! Truth!" Tisa answered, mimicking her. "I swore to it, and I'm still ready to swear to it."

"So then they went to Darmstadt, Secchi and the contessa?" asked the president.

"I don't know." Tisa answered. "But a little box from Darmstadt arrived in Bologna"—presumably the curare. Tisa described the experiment with the goat, after which she brought the poison to Tullio. She related the "ugly joke" Tullio made about wanting her to meet him. Did Secchi want Bonmartini out of the way? she was asked.

Secchi and Linda sometimes discussed her getting a divorce, she answered. Secchi's solution was to put the children in boarding school and let the separation stand, but Linda said that she could not renounce her children.

"Did you overhear discussions between the contessa and Bonetti?" asked the president.

"Yes. The contessa and Bonetti said they wanted to poison the count to get rid of him."

At the last words, Linda turned pale and, pressing her knuckles together, jumped again to her feet. "It's not true! It's not true! What is this?"

"Let her speak," the president chastised Linda.

Tisa continued unfazed. "Bonetti said, 'When I've done what Tullio wants, Tullio will be mine.' She used to consult witches to find out how to get closer to him." At this point, Bonetti, too, was on her feet in protest. But Tisa was unperturbed.

"What do you know about Professor Murri's comments?" asked the president.

"He said if it were not for the shame of having an assassin for a son, he would hand Tullio the knife to kill Bonmartini."

"It's not true! It's not true!" Linda shouted.

"Who told you this?" interrupted Linda's defense.

"The contessa," answered Tisa. Hearsay evidence was permitted in Italian courts, although it was not given as much weight as a witness's own knowledge.

By now, Tullio was pacing and turning to and fro in agitation in front of his bench. "Look at her!" Rosina shrieked. "She's the color of saffron because she knows what she's saying are lies."

"Be still," the president said to Rosina. "You have said in the deposition that what Tisa says isn't true. We will get to the confrontation and read it." Though the president ordered them all to sit down, Linda remained standing.

"What was Secchi's behavior during this time?" he asked.

"Secchi always tried to talk the Murris out of their plan," Tisa answered. "He said one time that if something happened, even if he wasn't guilty, he would be upset."

"Is it true that Secchi wanted to break off with Linda?" the president asked Tisa.

Secchi had even given Tisa the keys to the apartment to return to Linda, she answered. "The contessa said, 'So this is what he wants to do to me! If I tell my brother, he'll have a nasty fifteen minutes to go through.'"

"That's not true," Linda insisted. "I have always said that the worst thing Secchi could do was to stay with me if he no longer loved me. I made him promise he never would. And he can tell you I did." From his bench, Secchi nodded "yes," but Tisa talked over them.

"The contessa asked me to convince Secchi not to leave her. 'My brother and I,' she said, 'will rent two rooms for you, and you will be happy with us . . .'"

"It's not true, not true!" Linda railed.

"Was Secchi spending a lot on Linda?" asked the president, characteristically skipping from one topic to another.

"That's what he said," Tisa responded.

"My God! My God!" Linda cried out. She turned toward Secchi and, looking at him squarely for the first time in all the long weeks of the trial, sneered at him in disgust. Secchi was squirming visibly and twisting his handkerchief.

"But they were saying I was a kept man," he protested to Linda, thereby confirming that he had indeed complained about his expenditures.

"You, Secchi," the president looked at him. "What do you say to all this Tisa Borghi has described?"

"Not a bit of it is true," Secchi responded, but without heat. "About the trip to Darmstadt, there was an argument, it's true, but as I have said, it started because I didn't want her to come on a trip that I thought would be bad for her condition—"

"Was there or was there not a discussion about poison?"

"Not at all," answered Secchi, still temperate. "We spoke of medicine, but it was cascara sagrada deamarizzata, which in fact I did buy."

"When these very things were presented to you, you didn't make all those objections. In fact, you said that what Tisa said was 'substantially the truth.'"

"But right after that, I said that there was a pact between Tullio and me agreeing that Linda was not to know anything," responded Secchi.

"'Substantially,'" said the president, "means what she said was true."

A fiery debate followed, in which Secchi's attorney Fabri read Tisa's deposition out loud: "'I heard not once, but many times, Signora Linda insist that Secchi acquire a medicine—I don't know what name she called it—but it was what the justice found in a little bottle with the jar for preparing it.'" If Tisa didn't remember the name, Fabri argued, how could anyone be sure she was talking about curare?

"How did you come to say the name 'curare'?" the president asked Tisa.

"Because the investigating judge said it to me," Tisa answered.

"HA!" the defense attorneys shouted in unison.

"—because I no longer remembered the name," Tisa added.

"However, you witnessed the opening of the little box when it arrived from Darmstadt and saw it prepared for the experiment with the goat," the president added helpfully. It was not a minor point. "What reasons would Borghi have for saying these things if they were false?" the president asked Secchi.

"There are reasons why I think she's lying," Secchi answered.

"What reasons?" the president insisted. Secchi did not answer.

"You don't know, or you don't want to say?" the president asked.

"I don't want to say," answered Secchi.

Tullio decided it was time to register his outrage against Tisa's reference to his father. To Tisa, whose shoulders were turned away from him, he shouted, "You don't have the courage to look me in the face!"

"Oh, I'll look you in the face all you want!" Tisa replied, turning on Tullio "like a viper," according to the *Corriere della Sera* reporter. "I was told all of it by the contessa!"[18]

"That's not true!" Linda shouted.

"But did you ever hear Professor Murri say it?" asked Linda's lawyer.

"No, no," said Tisa. "I don't know the professor except by sight."

"I must have said," Linda intervened, "that to see me happy, my poor father would have given all he possessed."

"Nobody has incited you to say all this?" the president asked Tisa.

"Absolutely nobody. Not even Secchi," Tisa answered.

"Then why were you so late in coming forward with it?"

"I thought I would say it eventually," Tisa responded. "As long as things were going as they were, I kept quiet, but then when I got into a tight corner, I told everything."

"What tight corner?" asked one of Linda's lawyers.

"First, it was me the newspapers were against," said Tisa. "Still I kept quiet. But when I saw another person attacked—Dr. Secchi—put in prison for someone else's crime, then I spoke up."

"When they did the experiment, who held the goat?" asked Altobelli, lawyer for the Murris.

"I did," Tisa answered.

"And when you brought the curare and the syringe, did you know what it was for?"

"Yes. I knew it was to inject Bonmartini." Then, after a pause, Tisa added, "However, I knew that this poison, according to Professor Secchi, would not do the job."

"And how was it that after July you still wrote very affectionate letters to Linda Murri?" asked Cavaglià from the defense table.

"I was writing for Secchi," Tisa answered.

"No, no, no. The letters are yours. One from August 7, 1902 says, among other things, *'I don't know what to do to make you happy. I would give my life and everything in the world I hold most sacred. I want to see you happy and hope in the future some godsend arrives.'*"

"The last sentence," Tisa interrupted, "was written knowing the contessa had to get back together with her husband."

Cavaglià continued reading: " *'My heart aches not to be able to express what I feel. I can tell you that I want so much to see you.'* You end by sending her a kiss," Cavaglià concluded. "I ask you, were these letters written to the same person you are now denouncing as a poisoner?"

"Up to the last," Tisa explained, "I believed the contessa was really the victim. From what she said about him, I believed she was the victim. But when I saw her pulling to assassinate him, then I changed my thinking."

"Yes? Well, the letter was written after Darmstadt," Cavaglià retorted, "where Linda is supposed to have procured the poison."

"I was at a loss as to what to think," Tisa said. "I didn't believe the contessa could be so evil. When I saw what was happening, then I changed my opinion."

The president, amid rising tensions, wanted to know more about Tisa's overhearing the plan to poison Bonmartini. "It was in the contessa's house," Tisa affirmed. "I don't remember exactly when, but I know it was after San Lazzaro, that would be in June."

Cavaglià interrupted, "Nevertheless, after that you were most affectionate."

"Well, I believed that after that attempt, things would calm down," replied Tisa.

"When you wrote to Linda about Secchi, what name did you use?" asked the president.

"I referred to him as 'Carolina.'"

"And when did you leave Secchi's employ?"

"I'm still in his employ," she answered.

Tisa was finally dismissed, but she was not yet offstage. With great poise, she took her time walking past the defendants' cage, focusing a long, malevolent look on each one in turn. As her eyes reached Linda, Tisa's forehead suddenly relaxed and her toothless mouth formed a slow, wide smile that she held until she reached the aisle. She made her leisurely way out of the room, her head high. It was too much for the Murris' lawyer Berenini. "Go away laughing, venomous thing!" he sputtered after her. "You talk about poison, but you're the one bringing poison right here! And you, Signor President, you're a gentleman. You see it!" But, like Tisa, the president had left the room and did not hear the frustrated outburst.

Two of Secchi's colleagues corroborated Tisa's testimony the next day. They stated that soon after the crime, Tisa had unburdened herself to them, asserting essentially the same things about Linda and Secchi's role in the murder as she told the court.[19]

By April 1, 1905, the last snow had dripped off the trees outside the courtroom and damp, cold days had given way to damp, stuffy ones. The trial had been going on for two months. Nobody trusted just one newspaper's account of the trial on April Fool's Day, for even serious journalists liked to prepare pitfalls for their readers. But after Tisa's testimony, there was little new information to read about. Alessandro Stoppato's deposition had been chanted by a clerk in a hurry to get the ordeal finished.[20] Linda had deceived everyone, stated Stoppato. Bonmartini was, the clerk whined, *"il più buona pasta d'uomo che sia mai esistito"*—the most good, solid man who ever lived. The depositions of Bonmartini's deceased friends Cervesato, Valvassori, and Gallerani were read to the court—some of Cervesato's examinations had lasted five hours in Stanzani's office, and there were six of his depositions to get through. Though Cesco bragged of his conquests, Cervesato had said, Nini was the only one, and the count broke off with her immediately when she threatened to tell his wife about their affair. When the reunion occurred, Linda wrote to Cervesato of having given *"my sacred word before God and with all my heart—my mind is inflamed with my sacrifice."* Yet, he pointed out, it was only two months after that reconciliation, in June 1902, that Cesco began having serious intestinal suffering and started to fear for his safety.

According to the depositions, Linda tried to turn Bonmartini's friends against him by pretending that he had made some shocking confession. Valvassori said he didn't know what Linda was talking about when she kept mentioning Bonmartini's "grave misdeed." Valvassori's deposition ended with a reading of one of Bonmartini's letters: *"If you see Linda,"* Bonmartini wrote to his cousin, *"tell her that for all that she doesn't want it, the queen of this house is always her."*[21]

The reading of Bonmartini's heartfelt diary was one of the most boring days of the trial, according to reporters who slept through it, along with much of the jury, because the long document was read in a monotone by a barely audible lector. Nevertheless, there was laughter from the audience at the section where Bonmartini described "the humble service" of emptying his wife's chamber pot. Linda hid her face and cried. Finally she demanded to be recognized, though still sobbing fluently. "If I had written a diary at that time," she said, "it would have shown that I had no other thought but dying. It's not possible that any spirit in the world suffered more than I suffered in that period."[22] In a long, passionate speech, she said that she had always found the courage to cope with her husband's different upbringing and character, but that when she became ill, she could no longer hide her displeasure. She sat down and resumed crying into her handkerchief as the lector mumbled through the second part of the diary. By now the reading had turned into a hum, and Linda's interruptions were the only indication to the audience that something significant had been presented. Whenever Professor Murri's name was mentioned, Tullio or Linda could be counted on to rise to the challenge of defending "my poor Papà." Until the readings, interruptions by the defendants had been few and brief, as when Rosina blurted out to a friend testifying in her behalf, "You can't say you think this or that! You have to say it's true!"[23] But with the reading of the diary, Linda discharged her pent-up responses in madrigals of self-justification that the president did not suppress.

One of Bonmartini's letters evoked a storm. In it, he had

pleaded with Linda to live with him in friendship, if love had vanished forever, for the sake of the children. *"You know,"* he wrote, *"when I think of them, and I think of them often, I know that I would give my life for them. Since you are a good mother, you must feel the same. Have we truly done our duty towards them? Our little ones were put in the world by us; I believe they have the right to exact any sacrifice."*[24] The defense lawyers and Tullio loudly protested that the trial was making a pervert appear to be a saint. Linda as usual broke into the bickering to insist that she was the real martyr, constrained to protect both her brother and her husband's memory. "The jurors are men of good heart. I ask them if they have ever seen a defendant in a more tormented condition than I am."

Professor Alberto Rovighi of the University of Bologna was a friend of both Bonmartini and the Murris. He explained in the witness chair once and for all that the charge of necrophilia against Bonmartini was absurd, since the cadavers were not intact by the time they reached the anatomy students. Rovighi added that old Murri was endlessly loving toward Linda but cold and severe towards Tullio, complaining constantly of his son's trigger temper.[25] Tullio, flushed and quivering, instructed the court that he was not always impulsive. He was once playing pool, he said, with a *camorrista*—a gangster—who uttered an unpleasant remark; Tullio made him repeat it not once but three times before he threw the cue stick in his face.[26]

Everyone—probably even Linda—was curious to see Bonmartini's mistress, Clelia Castellani, whose letters to Bonmartini were variously signed "Nini," "Clelias," "Clesias," and "Sylvia." Clelia was twenty-four and lived in Rome. She met Bonmartini there when she was singing at a coffeehouse.[27] Her family was respectable—one brother was an engineer, another a businessman. Beautiful, buxom, and fashionable, she was a lively talker. "When I heard the count was murdered," she said, "I said right away it was no use investigating the society women, since the assassin was in the Murri family. They threatened the count; he was especially afraid of his brother-in-law, because he's somebody to be feared of!" Questioned about Cervesato, she said, "No, no. I loved him, but I never went with him. He loved me very much. He called me his 'little girl.'" Nini had been in the witness chair only five minutes before the audience, doped from the deposition readings, was alert again and laughing.[28]

"Did you speak of these things with Bonmartini?" asked the president.

"We spoke of our own love," she replied. "However, he talked a lot about his wife, and he was crazy for the children, especially Maria. She resembled him."

"Among the documents," noted the president, "there is a rather long correspondence between you and Bonmartini."

"Yes," she answered, with a single, slow nod and a tone full of dignified condescension. As the letters were read aloud, Nini chuckled from time to time. At one point the president noted her reference to a woman in the Padua train station. Had Bonmartini looked at the woman?

"No," she answered dismissively. "He loved only me." Nini justified her demands for money by explaining that Bonmartini was "tight."

"Tight?" asked Linda's lawyer with alacrity.

"Yes, but in every other way he was splendid!" she answered, to the delight of an audience that was ready to give every comment a risqué significance. Nini confirmed that the photographs found among Bonmartini's belongings were of her, "wearing very little." A friend in Livorno had taken them, but she refused to give his name, since that would be violating "professional secrecy." The Murri lawyer was going to question her again about her relationship with Cervesato, but Nini asked the court if she might be dismissed so that she could keep an appointment. When the audience erupted in laughter, she added, "It's about a contract." Leaving the witness circle, she murmured fretfully, "Nothing ever happened with

Cervesato. If there had been something with him, I would have said so—one more, one less," and she shrugged to herself as she took a seat in the hall, disregarding the appointment.

Cardinal Svampa elicited a little interest, but not as much as Nini, when he was ushered with some pomp into the witness chair.[29]

"Your Excellence," began the president warmly.

"Eminence," Svampa corrected him. Svampa had nothing new to add concerning the reunion. Linda appeared at the ceremony with her father and they both dispraised Bonmartini. The father, he recalled, told him that Linda "was incapable of lying." Only the president and the nearest observers discerned the prelate's dainty snicker as he pronounced the words.

Whenever the court turned its attention to Rosina, neither the experts nor the judges tried to hide their compassion.[30] According to a doctor who treated her, she had been paralyzed from the waist down for a five-month period in 1895. She contracted gangrene, and the operation resulting from it caused the limp that still afflicted her. In prison she was unable to sleep, so Gotti, the prison doctor, gave her "large doses of bromide and chloral." Both potassium bromide and chloral hydrate capsules were used as sedatives. The oily, liquid form of chloral hydrate was sometimes applied as a local anesthetic. A penetrating lung irritant, it was used in later years in the manufacture of DDT. Rosina reacted to the drugs with seizures and hallucinations. Throughout June 1903, according to Gotti, she could neither speak nor move. Her lawyer Abramo Levi asked if there were any questions Bonetti herself wanted to ask the doctors, and the president also encouraged her.

"It's no use," she shrugged. "Either they don't answer, or say they don't remember, or they just say, 'Yes, sir.'"

If Bonetti was not mentally capable of understanding the gravity of her crime, then Italian law had only one category that could have been applied to her—that of "conditional condemnation" for a minor woman of eighteen. Levi therefore gave a long disquisition on the inferiority of women to show that Rosina, being more inferior than most, qualified for the category, though she was not a minor. As for Tisa's attacks on Rosina, Levi insisted that the nurse hardly knew Bonetti, having seen her only two or three times, and could not have been the confidante she claimed to be. Tisa did not know Rosina's true name and misspelled her false one. She was jealous because Rosina was a servant like her, trying to protect her lover.

Bonetti's adoptive father, Antonio Ceroni, described her unhappy childhood, the death of her brothers, and her attachment to her younger sibling, Poldino. Ceroni said Rosina made several suicide attempts, but that she was a hard worker and a good girl—almost saintly. When Rosina was arrested, the family Poldino was working for not only dismissed him but saw to it that no one else in the area would hire him. Finding no work, he was starving when he contracted tuberculosis; he died while Rosina was in prison. It had been to help Poldino that Rosina had written in vain to Stanzani, asking him to release her meager belongings so that her brother could sell them for food.

"Was she pretty, Bonetti?" asked the president.

"Beautiful," answered Ceroni. "The most beautiful girl in the entire region."

Thirty-three physicians were eventually called to testify, but the one who knew the family best, Dr. Silvagni, refused to give his opinion of any of the Murris because he was afraid his family would be persecuted. "We'll never be left alone," he expostulated. "For two and a half years Bologna has been riveted to this crime. Everybody has his opinion. Many people say Tullio Murri is lying to protect someone, that he did not do the killing; that Giannina Murri is not the professor's wife; that Tullio and Linda are children of two different women. Some think this madness has taken hold because the major players are in a high social position, but I don't believe it; there have been other murder cases involving people in high places, and after twenty-four hours, no one spoke of them anymore." Professor Murri's supposed atheism was the real issue, he said. The Catholic press had turned the case into a battlefield of religion.[31]

Religion and social class were, indeed, relentless topics. Dr. Piccoli was called, the rightful owner of the name the count had borrowed for his correspondence with Nini. Like everyone in Padua, he had known Bonmartini's mother and testified that she was so excessively Catholic, she made the sign of the cross before performing the most mundane activities. In contrast, a comrade of Tullio was questioned about the socialist's dislike of the pious nobility and his preference for servant girls. "Doesn't the odor of dishwater bother you?" the friend had jokingly asked him. "No," Tullio had responded, "the odor of aristocracy does."

Just as the trial was becoming unbearably tedious, Tisa asked to be heard again. The courtroom filled up immediately. All the lawyers involved in the case were at their benches. Dressed in a cinnamon frock with a green velvet vest, she sat down comfortably.[32] When Linda returned from Venice in August 1902, Tisa said, she told Secchi that Tullio and Bonmartini had a wrestling match. Tullio managed to get Bonmartini down, but he couldn't keep him down, and so Linda was unable to give her husband an injection as she had planned. During the trial, it had never been established with certainty that Linda was in Venice at the time of the match.

"Linda had the curare with her?" the president asked.

"I think so," Tisa answered, "because there was a little bottle on the table during the conversation."

"And what did Secchi say?"

"He was very upset. He said, 'You are supposed to be intelligent people, but you act like imbeciles, insisting on trying something that can't be done.' I also want to say that when the signora had his letters burned, Secchi said, 'If you had left these alone, they would have proved my innocence and might even have led to the arrest of someone else.'" What happened to the little bottle? the president wanted to know. The contessa put it in her purse, said Tisa. The nurse added that, despite many insinuations, she was not Secchi's lover during the period under discussion. "During the period under discussion" left open a question, but the lawyers did not ask it. Instead, they tried to break down her assertions. The president ordered that Secchi be brought out of the cage.

"What do you say, Secchi, to these declarations by Tisa?"

"What she says regarding her honor is the truth. As for the rest, this is the first time I've heard about a bottle seen in her house on the seventeenth. If I had seen it, I would have been happy to take it back. Before my arrest, I always believed the contessa knew nothing. After my arrest, when I was doubting everything and everybody, I turned over and over all that had happened and all that was said between me and the contessa, but I found nothing remotely suspicious, and therefore I maintain what I have said, that the contessa was ignorant of everything."

"You never talked about a wrestling match?"

"No, absolutely not," responded Secchi.

Turning to Tisa, the president asked, "You heard what Professor Secchi said?"

"I told the truth," answered Tisa.

"Well, are all these things you said true or not true?"

"I am repeating," Tisa answered, "that everything I said is the truth. Why would I invent all this?" The president asked the question of Secchi, who only shook his head.

"Was it ever said that she was your lover?" asked the president.

"I don't know," Secchi answered.

"The contessa stated it pointedly in her interrogatory," said the president.

"If I had been Secchi's lover," Tisa put in sharply, "I would not have lent my house and my services to him and her, and of course I would have refused to go with her to San Marcello. If she thought I was his lover, it amazes me that she would have wanted me in her company."

"Do you know what period the burned letters covered?" asked the president. Tisa answered promptly that the letters dated from 1898 up to the murder. Secchi insisted that the letters had covered only up to 1901, no further. But if they dealt only with events up to

1901, why had Secchi always remonstrated that the letters could have absolved him of the murder? Linda rose to make a long declaration of innocence, followed by Tullio, who ended his furious response to Tisa by loudly pounding the bench.

It was becoming clear that on some points, Tisa seemed to be exposing the plain truth; concerning other issues, she was vaguely correct; and on still others, she lied, or embroidered information that may have been partially true or had merely been implied. The lawyers for the Murris demanded Tisa's arrest. How was it, they asked, that Secchi was in the defendant's cage but not the woman who held the goat for the experiment, carried the 3,000 lire for Tullio, and brought him the curare, knowing what it was for? Acts that sufficed to have others charged with complicity were somehow not sufficient for her. The pubblico ministero answered the defense attorneys with a sarcastic parody of Linda Murri: "In executing the duties of my office, I accept no guide except my conscience, which in this moment is not suggesting anything to me."

Tisa was not alone in wanting to add to her first testimony. Cervesato's housekeeper sent the authorities a long letter asking to be heard again. "What do you want to say?" the president asked.[33]

"Can't you just read aloud what I wrote?" asked Giuseppina Taormena. "Well, then just ask me some questions . . . I only wrote because I had to ease my conscience."

Taking a deep breath, she finally began in a Venetian dialect: It was Linda who wanted the reconciliation, but she persuaded Cervesato to act as if he had initiated it. Bonmartini, who was nervous about his safety anyway, found a new cause for anxiety when he read about a man whose wife cut off his *pene* while he slept. Giuseppina made a quick strike with an imaginary cleaver, looked wide-eyed at the president, who was looking with wide eyes at her, and snapped her head with finality. She continued. After the reconciliation, the count complained to Cervesato about stomach problems;

Cervesato, unsure of the cause, finally persuaded Bonmartini to get out of Bologna, with or without Linda. Giuseppina recalled advising the count to try a little glass of brandy for his stomach. The housekeeper wanted the court to understand above all that both she and Cervesato thought Bonmartini was being poisoned. "If others in the house had stomach sicknesses, it was for a day, while Bonmartini suffered for fifteen or twenty days." She had not said all this before, she explained, because even Cervesato had kept quiet about all that he knew. "He said that Bonmartini was dead, the Murris were still powerful, and he was afraid of them."

According to the housekeeper, Cervesato deliberately lied to Bonmartini about his wife's fidelity. Several people had already commented that Bonmartini questioned them in vain about the relationship between Linda and Secchi. "Naturally," remarked one, "nobody was going to tell the husband the truth."[34]

"You wrote this letter?" one of the defense attorneys asked Giuseppina.

"Yes, all of it," she answered.

"That's strange in view of the fact that you can't speak a word of Italian."

"When I talk, I express myself in dialect, but when I write, I can do it in Italian," she answered.

The defense attorneys glared at her sullenly as she left the witness chair. And though he knew he would be reprimanded, Linda's attorney Altobelli remarked unpleasantly, "Hope she doesn't come back a third time."

The variety show of witnesses was coming to a close. The testators took in the sights of Turin and, one by one, returned to Bologna. Following the 383 witnesses, the experts who filed into the courtroom seemed a manageable procession—three for the prosecution, eight for the defense. They came from all parts of Italy, full of words. Every point in the trial would be repeated many times by each side. All the attorneys and several of the experts now engage in a vigorous debate—one they will have again and again—over how much curare is needed to kill a man.[35] Bonmartini's autopsy had taken eleven hours. The experts need three times as long to describe it. One reads Tullio's narrative of the killing while the second points out discrepancies with the evidence. These prosecution doctors have surmised that, after stabbing Bonmartini in the heart, Tullio then grabbed his arms and the two fell to the floor while the victim struggled. A second assassin cut Bonmartini's throat while his arms were pinned.

No defense experts saw Bonmartini's body, either before or during the autopsy. Nevertheless, the defense doctors were able to raise some challenges to the prosecution's theory that Bonmartini had died by one violent blow.[36] The many superficial cuts on Bonmartini's body showed that there had indeed been a struggle, according to the defense's doctor, Lorenzo Borri. If the count had died after the first blow, a massive strike to the heart which caused him to fall backwards, then why would the assassin have continued flailing at him? If Bonmartini had been struck both in front and behind, he said, then one could believe in two assassins. But being cut on the right and left sides of his body proved only that there was a fight, not necessarily with two weapons, as the prosecution contended, but with one knife being twisted and turned as the combatants writhed. To produce the wound to Bonmartini's heart, a knife had to penetrate only four centimeters—less than two inches. A pocket knife would do it. The jurors were reminded that Bonmartini was timorous, Tullio courageous. "In a fight, it was those instincts that dominated," said Borri, "and that was why Tullio succeeded in defending himself."

Like the prosecution experts, the defense doctors referred to Tullio's memoriale. Turning the pages continually as he talked, Dr. Borri ranged over the prosecution's points, but in a disjointed way, jumping back and forth in time, so that the cumulative force of the prosecution's arguments was scattered and the sequence of events became confused. Finally, Tullio's expert reached the critical point in his client's defense. Dull as their testimony had been, the prosecution's doctors had evoked a vivid image: Bonmartini steps into his apartment, one hand holding a suitcase, the other holding his coat and briefcase, and is felled inside the doorway by a knife that an attacker plunges into his heart with all his might. The blow was ferocious, splitting his sternum, a flat bone that is the most compact and resilient human organism.

"But is it really so hard to perforate a sternum?" asks Borri. He places a strange instrument before the jury. It is a knife specially made by the Mathieux manufacturers of Paris with a gauge attached to it like that used to measure blood pressure. With it, he informs the jury, he has made eighty-four experiments on sternums, presumably removed from cadavers. The chest bones offered variable resistance to puncture. More than half broke with less than twenty pounds of pressure. In the bones of people who died between the ages of twenty and forty, the resistance averaged almost fifteen. Tullio Murri proved capable of exerting thirty-one pounds of pressure, double the force necessary to break the strongest sternum. The barrister was carefully eradicating the image of Tullio standing, waiting, then viciously sinking the knife into a surprised Bonmartini. He was replacing it with the image of Bonmartini lying on top of Tullio in a murderous embrace. "Twice the force necessary to break the sternum," repeated Borri. "How could Bonmartini have opposed it? The cuts to his left side show that it was exposed to Tullio's right side, there on the floor, exactly as Tullio described. And the fight was still going on even after the stab to Bonmartini's chest."

Tentative applause broke out when Borri finished his presentation. The audience had been impressed by his clever machine; Naldi's lawyer was elated. If the jurors could visualize a fight taking place between Bonmartini and Tullio, if they could conceive of Tullio winning without the help of a second attacker, then Naldi's alibi of being on the train at 6:55 would supply the rest of his defense.

The prosecutors renewed their argument that Bonmartini had been mortally injured and could not have offered any effective resistance. The wound in his heart was huge and produced an enormous hemorrhage. They pointed out again that Bonmartini's suitcase and briefcase were unstained except for a few drops of splashed blood. Bonmartini's hat was on the floor, the furniture was undisturbed, and it would appear to anyone of common sense that there had been no real struggle at the murder scene. In a long day of back-and-forth rebuttals, the prosecution rejected the whole idea that a sternum might be easily pierced like a sheet of paper. "Out of respect for the Murri family, I did not keep the chest pieces from Bonmartini's autopsy to show you how 'easy' it must have been," an autopsy surgeon remarked, as if the Murris would have held Bonmartini's chest in any particular reverence. In a final shouting match, the defense experts insisted that regardless of how Bonmartini died, the prosecution had not proved that two assassins killed him.

After the dry medical experts, the whole courtroom was ready for a bit of drama from the psychiatrists: two for the prosecution, four for the defense.[37] In 1905, as in our own time, judges and juries pretended to be outraged by behavior that they saw every day in their own families and among their friends. In this generation before Freud, doctors were beginning to see a connection between childhood experiences and adult delinquency; but the heavy weight of convention was still on physiognomy and a defendant's heredity—the deficiencies of his ancestors—which were discussed without fail in every criminal trial. It is easy to understand why Italians, for whom the family was the organizing unit of society, were willing to be told that heredity was destiny, though we can't be sure that jurors actually believed it. As for physiognomy, Cesare Lombroso's ideas predominated: the slightest deviation from what was considered normal was used by attorneys to add weight to an accusation or to give a defendant such as Tullio an excuse. As time went on, many people completely disregarded all notions of physiognomy or acknowledged the theories without letting them affect their decisions, as if they were acknowledging the influence of the zodiac. But lawyers anxious to present "scientific" forensic arguments kept Lombroso's ideas alive long after the general public had consigned them to the repository of old wives' tales.

Since Rosina would not let the doctors see or feel her body, the psychiatrists decided that her "hysteria"—her tendency toward psychogenic illness— showed up in her urine.[38] The prosecution's expert, Bellini, had no desire to condemn Rosina, judging from the description he gave of her miseries. She was descended from bandits and thieves; both her parents had been alcoholics. She never received so much as an hour of schooling. In childhood, she suffered typhoid and smallpox, and at sixteen was seduced by one of her father's friends. She was the only survivor of a nest of starvelings.[39] "She doesn't know how old she is and gets muddled when you try to get her to figure it out. She is weak-willed in everything except what concerns Tullio. Is she legally insane?" Bellini asked. "Hers is not a normal nervous system or a normal psyche; she is slightly retarded. But an insanity plea can hardly be justified in this case, where a cold crime was planned for so long." Rosina, he said, was "like ivy on elm"—completely in thrall to Tullio. "Her responsibility for Bonmartini's death," concluded the expert, "is therefore lessened but not erased."

With such a lenient analysis from the prosecution, the defense experts had only to convince the jury that Rosina was in fact legally insane. The doctors were aware that a jury in Milan had recently judged that a woman defendant was truly mad but nevertheless condemned her. Still, they asserted that Rosina's "hysteria"—paralysis brought on by an emotional state— was an inherited and definite form of insanity. Moreover, she had peculiar, fixed ideas that only a madwoman would entertain. "For example," one doctor offered, "she thinks she was assigned her place in the prisoners' cage, a place from which she can see Tullio, only because the president is partial to her. No one will ever be able to convince her otherwise." In her primitive religiosity, she once had Tullio's letters blessed by a priest. "Very simply, she is not responsible for her actions." While the doctors discussed her, Rosina—who might have been faking inattention—seemed lost in contemplation of Tullio.

The experts were reasonable in evaluating Rosina, taking into account her deforming childhood. However, when they talked about Tullio and the other defendants, the discussion reverted to superstition.[40] Professor Murri's rejection of his son was mentioned only occasionally; it was never suggested that Tullio might have killed Bonmartini in a frantic effort to win his father's esteem—a dramatic action undertaken "to protect Linda" and certify for all time his oneness with his family. The prosecution had one main objective: to make it impossible for Tullio to plead insanity. Their psychiatrist therefore maintained that Tullio's "gentle birth" militated against any form of mental weakness. "He descends from decent people," Lorenzo Ellero insisted, "despite his having had an epileptic grandfather." While in prison, Tullio had written more than a hundred sonnets. He had won many academic prizes (the doctor lengthily enumerated them), which showed that he was certainly capable of understanding the gravity of his actions. Ellero took some pains to establish that Tullio was not himself an epileptic, a condition that would have allowed him to claim diminished responsibility. "Good but impulsive—that is how we have heard Tullio described again and again by witnesses," said Ellero; but, the doctor argued, Tullio was not helpless against his impulses. "If he killed in self-defense, why the elaborate staging and props" to make the scene look as if a prostitute had set up Bonmartini? "The note, the glasses and champagne—these are not the actions of a man who has just been attacked and killed in self-defense, nor are they evidence of mental infirmity," said Ellero. Tullio emerged from the apartment apparently with no troubled conscience, no disorientation. The jurors could therefore judge for themselves whether he bore moral responsibility for Bonmartini's death.

The Lombroso protégé Enrico Morselli spoke for the defense psychiatrists. He had become director of an insane asylum in Turin when he was only twenty-eight. Now middle-aged, his reputation was secure. His major point was that Tullio could not escape the influence of heredity—the traditional defense, acceptable to jurists and taught by academicians in every law faculty in Italy. Morselli spent more than an hour proving that Professor Murri had suffered from headaches in his youth; thus he might have passed on some brain dysfunction to Tullio. The entire Murri family was disposed to "nervous illness." One uncle was "deranged and impetuous," another was "extravagant," and so forth. Having offered up these relatives as an insanity defense for Tullio, the doctor explained that the atmosphere in the Murri family was nevertheless "excellent." Giannina Murri set an example of conservative femininity and strong character. Apparently the doctor did not think that habitual, uncontrolled rage prevented one from having a strong character. Professor Murri never allowed his son to see either vanity or vulgarity. Tullio's affection for Linda, Linda's idolization of her father, the lawyer said, in a stirring understatement, "even seem excessive."

Just as he was getting to the true abnormality in the Murri dynamic—the unhealthy weld of Linda and her father—Morselli dropped the discussion of the family and instead began enumerating "anomalies" in Tullio's cranium, face, and ears. Tullio's teeth and palate were irregular. What the lawyer delicately referred to as his "paired organs" were asymmetrical. His digestion was "idiosyncratic and intermittent," as shown by his "stubborn antipathy" toward certain foods. "He doesn't use alcohol, but he abuses coffee," the psychiatrist thought it worthwhile to mention. Tullio's sexuality was "intense but normal," despite those physical "asymmetries" that indicated a "nervous constitution." To people of the Murri generation, nervousness was an upper-class condition. The implication was clear: a man of Tullio's station did not belong to the category of a common criminal.

Tullio was immature, said Morselli. His infantile character was demonstrated in his idolization of his father, the primitive way he adored his family, especially his sister, and a complex fantasy life that revolved around family situations. His impulsiveness and his craving for play and games were evidence of arrested development. Morselli did not discuss Professor Murri's insistence that for Linda, getting away from Bonmartini was "a matter of life and death" and the effect such statements might have had on Tullio. But he did say that Tullio had convinced himself Linda was dying. She kept him agitated with reports—of her albumin levels, her quarrels with her husband. Suggestible, Tullio immediately took up what all the defense attorneys called "Tisa's idea" of clobbering Bonmartini, as if Tisa, as much as Tullio, had conceived the murder plan. Tullio waited for Bonmartini trembling with anxiety. He was not in complete control of himself by the time Bonmartini arrived, and therefore, the doctor concluded after four hours, he bore diminished responsibility for his death. It was of course pointed out that if Tullio had been in the throes of a fanatical "morbid obsession," as the defense contended, he nevertheless calmed himself sufficiently before the murder to have a snooze while waiting for Bonmartini, and after the crime enjoyed a good dinner and made a carefully calculated trip to Cattolica.[41]

Regarding Linda, the defendant who was the most complicated psychologically, the psychiatrists noted only that her uvula was not centered.[42] Her brain, the prosecution experts were somehow certain, was larger than that of most women. The defense psychiatrists offered a good deal of vague praise for her "fine taste." She was, according to these doctors, "tactful, deep, sensitive, doleful, and utterly frigid." According to the defense expert Morselli, the only thing in life she could not do was to be calculating—this about a woman who corresponded under assumed names and disguised her handwriting so artfully that even her family failed to recognize it. She was not mentally unbalanced, both sides agreed. Though she talked frequently of suicide, her one attempt consisted of exposing her uncovered chest in an open window so as to invite pneumonia.

Tisa appeared one last time, a welcome presence amid the blur of doctors.[43] Called back to court by Senator Municchi, she was dressed in black, with the usual scarf covering her mouth. Having consistently denied having an affair with Dr. Secchi, why, Municchi wanted to know, was she willing to serve as his intermediary? Senators were not required to give up their law practices when they entered parliament. Municchi had defended the princess of Saxony, among other vestal martyrs, and was something of a celebrity lawyer.

"I have always enjoyed great kindness from Professor Secchi, even for my family," Tisa answered. "Fourteen years ago I was treated by him for three years for a throat disease. I began working for him. He was a very good person, and all his patients liked me. He had a great deal of respect for me, at least I think he did, and whatever he would have asked me, I would have done."

"What salary did he pay you?"

"Twenty lire a month."

"Including room and board?"

"Yes."

"And this payment continues even today?"

"Yes."

By the time the ordeal of the medical experts was over, all in the courtroom were numb with exhaustion. Linda's illnesses alone had taken up three days of talk. Naldi, as woozy as everyone else and weak as always, nearly fainted as the hall was emptying, though he finally walked out as if unshaken. Perhaps he was not as panic-stricken as the others at the prospect of a long jail term; once they passed out of the detention facility and were condemned, inmates in prison were regularly fed.

10. THE SUMMATIONS

It was time for summations to a jury that watched aghast as no fewer than five prosecutors and fourteen defense attorneys presented themselves before the tribunal, their proud, prosperous faces tense with concentration. By now the lawyers considered it their right to squander hours of the court's time on minor elements of the case.[1] No one placed a time limit on them or discouraged them from repeating each other and themselves. Each discourse was followed by long rebuttals and answers to the rebuttals. The summations in the Murri trial thus lasted not a few days or weeks but an entire summer, from June 7 to August 12, 1905, with court in session from 9:30 in the morning until, at times, midnight. Newspapers made a sardonic comment on the length of the trial by numbering the days on their front pages: "The Bonmartini Murder Trial, 94th Day. . . ."[2] The teachers on the jury learned that their pupils had graduated. Patients of the doctor had gotten well or died. Jurors who had been youthful and trim at the start of the trial in February were gray and doughy by the time it was over. Worst of all, the heat was insufferable in the courtroom because the windows were closed to keep curious faces from peering in.[3] During each session, the panes were covered on the outside with ears. Spectators on the lawn had turned their heads and were pressing against the glass to hear what was going on. As they hoped, more drama and farce were still to come.

* * *

The pleadings began first with Scipio Sighele addressing the court for the *parte civile,* representing the Bonmartini children who would have the right to demand civil damages from those condemned.[4] The parte civile were attorneys for future plaintiffs affected by the crime; in practice, they functioned as an extension of the prosecution. Sighele had made his name as a criminal anthropologist with his books *The Criminal Crowd* and *The Criminal Couple.*[5] He treated the audience to a vivid description of the cadaver and the campaign put in motion by the influential Murris to defame Bonmartini. "Two innocent voices are straining over the clamor of lies. 'Tell people that our daddy was good,' the children beg. 'Tell them that for our sake he overlooked insults and provocations.'" While Sighele read love letters from the marriage, Linda kept up an ostinato of sobbing.[6] "Bonmartini's nature was sincerely ingenuous and provincial." Sighele said. "The relationship with Nini De Clelias was a misdemeanor, something he could brag about to look like a lady-killer."

Sighele spun around to face Tullio. "I would understand you if you had the nerve to confront your brother-in-law in the street and kill him as you would kill an enemy, without accomplices." But Tullio, he said, had constructed "this architecture of deception, this cesspool of poison, planning, ambush," while pretending to be high-minded and idealistic. He waved aside Tullio's pretense that Bonmartini was violent and Linda's fiction that he was a poor father. Bonmartini had, said Sighele, a profound heart capable of the most tender feelings, and even with his mediocre intelligence, he surpassed his father-in-law in plain common sense. "His letters lacked the elegant style, the wit, the romantic quotations that adorn the letters of all the Murris. But which of their epistles comes close to his in integrity? And he foresaw, with frightening clearness, exactly what was about to happen to him." These were striking observations. Both Augusto and Tullio Murri could compose deceptively reasonable letters; but both of them wrote better than they lived. Sighele exhorted the jury not to perpetuate Italy's reputation as a country blind to crimes of passion and indulgent toward the powerful.[7] The crowd loudly applauded the six-hour address, during which Linda held her veiled face in her black-gloved hand. Tullio, having no veil to shield him, remained immobile, his head on his chest, evidently quite depressed. Only Secchi, agitated, and Naldi, indifferent, seemed attentive to the orator.

Carlo Nasi, already sweating abundantly in his advocate's heavy robes, continued for the parte civile by protesting against the encomiums heaped on Professor Murri.[8] "Only Riccardo Murri—I will still shake his hand because of it—he was the only one who cried at the hideous sight of the slaughtered man. Tullio Murri, who was at his uncle's side, for once did not cry. Bonmartini was painted by the Murris as a cheater, thief, boor, womanizer, and now an accusation that he had sex with dead bodies and boys.[9] Why this unending hatred? Because Bonmartini was an obstacle, that's all.

"Tullio the confessed killer, is supposed to be the classic man who acts on a fatal impulse, swept away by a primitive fraternal love." His crippled lover Bonetti, "the Negress of the group," Nasi says, "passes herself off as a dimwit. While the Bonmartini children are in her care, she is praying to Holy Mary that their father will die. The hired gun, Naldi, said to be an academic colleague, expects to be absolved," Nasi continued, "though he admitted stealing the money to make his escape. As for the adulterer, Secchi, who donated the poison, he's depicted as an experimenter, a scientific amateur who must now be allowed to return to his laboratory, as if the whole trial were somehow a publicity event. The dead man lies in his blood; his children will read bewildering lies about him; but the living will be given peace."

Nasi ridiculed the defense psychiatrists who portrayed Tullio as compassionate but impetuous. "Dr. Rubinato says he is incapable of seeing a goat, even a chicken, killed. Motivated by a noble obsession, says Professor Morselli, in the name of psychiatry."[10] Nasi paused and walked a few steps, his hand cupping his chin. "He sent his victim a telegram after the murder," Nasi reminded the jury, "telling Bonmartini his behavior was 'rude,' a telegram that the rude man never read, of course, because he was covered with maggots. Was all this noble obsession? Or impulsiveness? After committing the crime, what does Tullio Murri think of, this Knight of the Round Table? Why, of his own marriage, to tie a life stained with homicide to that of an unsuspecting young woman. And what of the woman whom he led into crime, Bonetti? What was he going to do with her? They come here, all these psychiatrists, all these Demosthenes, excusing him. But the facts are here, and the obdurate truth will not be destroyed by fancy terms."

Nasi had talked for an hour and a half, but his discourse was still building. "The date you must fix in your minds as you deliberate," he tells the jury, "is April 1902, the time of the reconciliation between Linda and Bonmartini. It was not a honeymoon, but nothing happened at that time to justify resentment. Nevertheless, at the end of April, Tullio writes to Secchi asking him for the means to kill his brother-in-law." It was clear, he said, that Linda, who had long refused to consider a reconciliation, changed her mind because she and Tullio decided it was easier to kill Bonmartini than to divorce him. "In August 1902, Tullio begins fraternizing with Naldi. On August 12, he receives the syringe and curare from Secchi. On the 13th, he goes to Venice, carrying these things with him, sleeps under Bonmartini's roof and sits at his table with the children. On that day there's a physical contest, but Bonmartini wins. On the 26th, Tullio and Bonetti are back in Venice, secretly. It is on that day, August 26, that the keys to the Bologna apartment are obtained—stolen or not stolen—and it is the next day, August 27, that Naldi announces to his landlady that he will be leaving for the country for several days. The 28th is the day of the assassination. Don't forget these dates."

The claim that Bonmartini, who never carried a knife, suddenly whipped out a blade and attacked Tullio was farcical. "Can you possibly believe," Nasi asked the jury, "that Tullio Murri, a lawyer, threw this supposed knife of Bonmartini into the river, the knife that could have proved the killing was self-defense?" Tullio's was an act of cold premeditation, Nasi declared. His planning was demonstrated by his writing the note supposedly from "B"—he changed his story three times regarding when he wrote it; by his carrying snacks and pallini into the apartment, along with a knife and a dagger; and finally by his bringing in a doctor to make sure things were done correctly. "Considering his supply of weapons, how can anyone deny premeditation?" asked Nasi. Tullio acquired 3,000 lire from Secchi. "What did he need the money for? He said he needed it to pay debts. But what single debt did he pay? He got the money in order to pay Naldi."

Tullio was in full control of his faculties after the crime, according to the lawyer. "He left Bonmartini's wallet, but took the money. He left a watch, because it was made of nickel, but took a gold chain. He planted the letter signed 'B,' placed the railroad schedule under the victim's arm, looked over everything, assessing it. He did not leave until he was sure of not being seen. And that's not all. He put a woman's long hair in the chamber pot. He went through the letters in Bonmartini's desk, keeping out one from his sister that he thought might prove useful." He was fully competent as he changed into clothes that were ready for him at Bonetti's, threw the bloody garments into the sea while the water was at high tide, and then sent disguised messages to Secchi and Linda. The lawyer followed Tullio after the murder as he went to the tailor, the library, the newspaper office, and dinner.

When the body was discovered on September 2, Tullio telegraphed the authorities: he had proof that Bonmartini was meeting a woman the day of his death. The campaign of defamation against Bonmartini had thus begun, but then Tullio suddenly made his confession to his uncle. "Good-bye, panties! Good-bye, donne allegre! The assassin is Tullio!" exclaimed the lawyer in mock surprise. "The evacuation takes place. Riccardo Murri writes to the justice that Dr. Dagnini has ordered the countess to leave at once for Zurich where she must have her eye treated, and she must travel at night for that injured eye! Dagnini, by the way, denies all that.

"Tullio flees, but since news of the murder has gotten out, he can't obtain a passport and comes back.[11] Finally we learn about the curare, when Naldi at last confirmed that, in addition to all the other weapons, Tullio brought curare and a solution of morphine and atropine into the apartment. Nevertheless," asserted Nasi, "they still speak of Tullio's having some mental infirmity!" The lawyer mimicked psychiatrists, "the so-called experts" who, he said, constitute "an aristocracy in criminal justice" even though they try to subvert the intention of the laws.

One by one, Nasi attacked the testimony of the four people who said they saw Bonmartini the night of August 28. Only one spoke up right after the murder; the others came forth seven months later. "Would Tullio have first entered the Bonmartini house," asked Nasi, "left there all the items he had prepared, and then gone out again, where he supposedly met Bonmartini? If he had left the house, he couldn't have re-locked the door from the outside. Even Naldi, who could have benefited from it, never said the time of the murder was midnight."

Nasi turned his malevolent attention to Rosina. The experts had suggested that she should bear diminished responsibility for the crime. But wasn't it Bonetti, Nasi asked, who assumed a false name and eagerly joined in the project of killing Bonmartini? Brought the pallini and the curare to Venice? Stole the keys necessary for the ambush? What about that comedy of going to fetch a dress, so that she could justify the secret messages that flew back and forth? "She is extraordinarily shrewd at the game of being a simpleton."[12]

The prosecutor's eyes scanned the defendants' cage and locked on Naldi, fixing him with a look of studied contempt. He was so cavalier about the murder, said Nasi, that when the audience in the hall laughed, he laughed too. "He thinks he's at the theater." Though the lawyers at the defense table flung the air and shouted protests, Nasi led the jury through a tightly constructed, persuasive attack on Naldi. The security lock on the Via Pusterla side door, by which Tullio and Naldi entered, would not close completely unless someone turned

252 — INDECENT SECRETS

the knob from the outside. Therefore, they must have been locked in by Bonetti; otherwise, Bonmartini would have been suspicious if he started to go in and saw that the lock was not engaged. "Naldi says he went out ahead of Tullio, before Bonmartini arrived. He could not have used the Via Mazzini main staircase because it was too public. If he tried to use the Pusterla stairs, he would have found the door locked; he could not escape until Bonmartini himself opened that door and met his death.

"Bonmartini arrived home at 6:20.[13] Even if he came at 6:30, Naldi would have had enough time, after a fight that took perhaps one or two minutes, to flee through the door that was opened by Bonmartini." Leaving at 6:40, could Naldi have had time to get to the station and take Train 19 for Florence? "Certainly!" the lawyer answered himself. "All those who tested the route reported that the walk required nineteen minutes. Naldi in fact had thirty minutes in which to carry out the murder and get to the station. He pretended at first that he left the apartment with the intention of warning Bonmartini—"

"But I said that in the first interrogation," Naldi broke in.

"Don't interrupt! You will talk afterward," admonished the president.

"But don't falsify the thing," Naldi protested.

Throughout the investigation, said Nasi, Naldi's landlady denied that he could have been in the house on the afternoon of August 28 and changed her mind only in the witness chair. Naldi evidently went directly from the apartment to the station.

It was Secchi's turn. "Did Secchi instigate the murder?" the lawyer asked. Probably not, he conceded. But did Secchi agree to the murder and prod Tullio on? "Secchi gave Tullio money to pay a hired killer; he provided the poison to kill and sent it to Tullio. He corresponded secretly, in code, with the killer before and after the deed. He treated the assassin's wound after the murder. Is it possible," Nasi asked, turning toward the jurors, "that a man who wasn't mentally ill could do all that without intending to?" A thunderclap made everyone look toward the window.

"That weather out there is getting ugly," remarked Secchi's lawyer.

"We have plenty of ugliness right in here," Nasi replied. He went over the plethora of communications between Tullio and Secchi. "First Secchi claims this correspondence concerned *La Squilla*. Then, when it turns out he provided 3,000 lire, he tries to pretend he gave a loan which the contessa merely carried. His project with the curare is exposed, thanks to Naldi, and Secchi is arrested. Still he continues trying to hide the truth and finally admits that Tullio wrote him, asking for some way to get rid of his brother-in-law. What would a gentleman have done in such a case? Surely not what Secchi says he did, that is, to give Tullio back the letter and calmly explain why the project was impossible. What was the result of this discussion? Why, that Tullio was impressed by the properties of curare and insisted on getting it! What does Secchi do at this point? Hide it from Tullio? No indeed! Not having any curare, he goes to considerable length to get some and complies with Tullio's request to see an experiment. The experiment is made on a goat, and from this, 'poor Tullio,' as Secchi always refers to him, was persuaded that even he would be able to use the curare. Secchi says he convinced Tullio that one man alone would not be capable of doing the job. So he even planted the idea of getting an accomplice."

"Secchi said," Morello interjected, "that it would take two men just to hold the victim down."

"The fact is that Secchi hastened to prepare a solution of alcohol and water with an enormous dose of curare, he gave Tullio a syringe, and all that on the day after the experiment with the goat. Secchi says he warned the contessa at that point, but he would have done better to—"

"Wait a minute! Wait a minute!" interrupted Cavaglià. "His warning to the contessa was not about the curare."

"I was going to say that I don't believe Secchi warned the contessa about anything. Are you happy now?" Nasi shot back.

Secchi listened closely, his head resting on his hand during the discourse. "Tullio brought the curare and syringe with him into the apartment, apparently with every intention of using them. Secchi provided Tullio with that curare," Nasi said, whereas, if he were really innocent, "the most logical thing was also the simplest: not to give it to him." After the crime, the prosecutor said, Secchi interrupted a long, expensive trip and claims he did not imagine that it was Tullio summoning him under a pseudonym they had used between them repeatedly.

"Tullio gives him back the curare and Secchi lets it go at that, apparently indifferent to the fate of Bonmartini. Secchi's number one excuse, that he gave Tullio a weak solution, is worthless," Nasi said. "The curare he provided was enough to kill ten men."

Nasi wound up his summary, which had lasted over sixteen hours, off and on. As admirers rushed forward to congratulate the lawyer, Secchi sat back on his bench, his hand still holding his chin with his fingers covering his mouth, his eyes unfocused and unreadable.

The pubblico ministero thoughtfully surveyed the restless assemblage that was to be his audience. Everyone knew the trial was about to take a nasty turn. Nasi had focused on the facts of the case. The job of the P.M., Giovanni Colli, was to stir up prejudice, to make the jury despise the defendants personally. His main target would be Linda Murri.[14]

Tullio's letters, Colli said, had tried to cheer up a sister "who had worn herself out with too much sentimentality." In those letters, Tullio revealed that he was revolted by life and numb to deep feeling, a man who preferred maids and cooks because his tastes were vulgar. Rosina was worse than vulgar, according to Colli. Descended from bastard thieves, she was a harlot before she attached herself to Tullio, who finished perverting her. "Now she mixes up vice with religion and prays to the saints to help kill off the victims her Tullio has designated. She offers a candle to the Madonna," said the lawyer, holding up an imaginary object, closing his eyes fervently, and letting his head shake, "praying for the Virgin's help so they can make a good hit. She's anything but a dummy. Even Tullio, as slippery as he is, couldn't get free of her when he tried."

Colli's eyes found Secchi on the second row of benches, and the jury's eyes followed. "He is a singularly repulsive figure," said the P.M., almost snarling, "who can't help being coarse even when he is trying to appear sensitive.[15] His love letters have obscene double meanings. He wants to be elevated, to fly, but every time, he winds up on his belly, flopping away in the mud."

Colli paused. "Pio Naldi!" he said so sharply that everyone in the courtroom shifted on the benches to look at the startled defendant in the cage. "To know what he's about, it's enough to look at him. Tullio recognized him for what he was the minute he laid eyes on him. He looks fishy, and he is. What good is it to argue about whether a knife can break a sternum when there were two vicious, lethal wounds in the neck inflicted by an expert hand, the hand of a doctor?" The apartment was covered with blood after the murder, the lawyer said, but Bonmartini's shoes were clean. He was obviously knocked down suddenly and finished off while on the floor. Colli ridiculed the demonstration by the defense's expert, "showing how to snap the sternum of—apparently some unlucky patient who had been under his meticulous care." The audience laughed gaily. "Bonmartini was dead at 6:30 when Bonetti went with the pretext of getting the dress. "She saw the count at the window? What did he say? 'Come back tomorrow. Today I'm busy getting killed'? It was Tullio's face she saw in the window, the trail of his own blood behind him as he went to signal her that it was all over."

Naldi had plenty of time to get to the station for 7:00, Colli said, because he didn't go home to change. He changed the day before, when he told his landlady he would be absent from Bologna for a while, and made all his preparations before going with Tullio to kill the count. "He was next seen arriving in Florence with a gloomy face. To tell the truth, his face was already repellant enough." According to the prosecutor, Naldi went to the authorities believing that he would be exonerated along with the powerful Murris. He had 1,500 lire in his pocket. He offered every lie imaginable to hide the true reason he was in possession of so much money: he had been paid for his services.

Colli, like Nasi, attacked the defense experts. "Psychiatrists are themselves people full of fixations. One of their fixations is that they think anybody is crazy if he has asymmetrical features, as if symmetry were some law of nature. They're trying to make lunatics out of people in that defendants' cage who have never been insane and never pretended to be." The laughter was loud and continual as the P.M. gave an imitation of an expert consultant. "The idea that Bonetti was not responsible is nonsense," he concluded, more seriously. "As for Tullio, his so-called obsession was premeditation, pure and simple, and it won't be cured by an asylum but by a prison." Rosina had conspired in the murder in order to secure Tullio, according to Colli; Naldi had wanted money; Tullio had hopes of getting his hands on Bonmartini's fortune. The prosecution did not, however, accuse Secchi of suggesting the crime.[16] For the P.M., there would be one sole instigator of Bonmartini's murder: Linda Murri. According to Colli, neither money nor the hope of marrying Linda could explain Secchi's involvement—he was "too comfortable in his armchair" to do anything criminal. It was only because of a powerful force that four bunglers were turned into assassins, according to Colli. That force was Linda, who functioned like a "malignant star," an evil center around which the others orbited, fixed in patterns they seemed helpless to escape.

Linda's ostentatious expressions of affection in the early years of her marriage were simulations, said Colli, the gaudy pretenses of a woman who was emotionally cold. Whatever sexuality she was capable of had been aroused by Secchi when she was young, corrupting her so that she could never then be satisfied with Bonmartini. Gradually, a system developed: to isolate her rich husband little by little from his circle, induce him to move to Bologna, and then throw down the mask and the pretense of loving him.

"This is infamy! These are inventions," cried the lawyer Cavaglià. "Cite where you're getting all this!"

"I don't need to," responded the P.M. When Secchi reappeared after ten years, he said, Linda used her sickness as the pretext for getting a separation and for whatever else she wanted to do. The P.M. created a lascivious image of Linda in a bedroom, enjoying oysters, champagne, and Secchi, while Bonmartini was in a hospital bed in Rome. "While Bonmartini's letters to the singer De Clelias are correct, those from Secchi to Linda have to be read behind closed doors." Colli went so far as to compare Nini and Linda. "Between the adventuress who hides nothing and the pure, intellectual contessa, I prefer the first one. If the count had pornographic drawings, the contessa had obscene books. In her case, what's more, it's her whole life that's dirty. On the same day that Frieda Ringler walked in on her and Secchi, she wrote to her husband, 'From Linda Murri, never lies or deceit.' "

Bonmartini loved his children and sacrificed his last breath for them, the lawyer said, whereas Linda never dreamed of giving up her affair. When she began to fear her doings with Secchi would be exposed in a legal separation, she pretended to reconcile. "Whom does she set up in the house as soon as they are back together?" asks Colli. "Rosina Bonetti, under a false name. And within a few days, Bonmartini has some crumbs analyzed because he fears he is being poisoned. He begins locking his door." The lawyer continues his retiary calendar of Linda's movements. In July, while Bonmartini was in Venice with the children, she gave Bonetti her child's passbook to give to Tullio. Then she went to Switzerland with Tisa, to be joined by Secchi. Linda and Secchi traveled together to get the curare. Here Colli mentions an inaccurate date and Linda's lawyer hastens to correct him. "I don't give a ————," the P.M. blurts out, annoyed at the interruption. Throughout the hall, voices are raised against the use of a word that is described as "hardly parliamentary language."[17] Recess comes and goes. Linda resumes her position with her head in her hand, her face somewhat hidden. Every free space in the hall is occupied, in the lively hope that the P.M. will again lose control of his vocabulary.

In the weeks before her husband's death, said Colli, Linda and the others exchanged incessant communications with false signatures, including the intriguing card by Linda to Tullio IN AN ALTERED HAND—the lawyer raised his voice momentarily—"I don't hear anything more about S." Pacing slowly but talking rapidly, Colli continued to lay out a sequence for the jury. "On the fourteenth of August, Tullio left Venice on good terms with Bonmartini, On the sixteenth, Linda went to spend two days with Secchi at Tisa Borghi's house. Bonmartini is making plans to move the family to Padua. He tells his wife this before she leaves Venice, incurring the scene where he grabs a chair. Linda takes advantage of the incident to stir up resentment against her husband, sending out pages of wrath against him. Once in Bologna with Secchi, she gets the three thousand lire to give to her brother, who will kill her husband ten days later. "Why did Secchi deny having given this money?" the lawyer asked. "Because he knew what it was going to be used for, and if he knew it, so did Linda." The money passed through Linda's hands, the prosecutor said, like a stripe connecting her to the murder. Tullio had a passbook carrying 65,000 lire. He didn't use his father's money in the bank because he didn't want it to be traced. That was why he turned to Secchi.

According to the P.M., Linda knew her affair was about to be uncovered. She therefore dispatched her frantic letters to her mother, and telegrams—even an express telegram—to Tullio and Bonetti, using false names. Linda was already up when Bonetti and Tullio came to Venice early in the morning of the 26th, Bonetti carrying lead pellets in her purse. Linda gave instructions that Bonmartini was not to know about the visit. Colli pointed out that Bonetti, Tullio, and Linda each had a different version of what was said when they gathered at the Public Gardens, showing that the true conversation could not be revealed. Tullio came back from Venice with the keys that enabled him to commit the crime. On August 27, Linda and Rosina are telegraphing back and forth, signaling Tullio to prepare the ambush because

Bonmartini was to arrive in Bologna the next day. "Thus," said Colli, "was Bonmartini sent to the butcher.

"On August 30, while they pretend to look for Bonmartini, Tullio telegraphs his sister that he is sending her cascara sagrada. The package is mailed by Bonetti not in her own name but in Secchi's. That package of 'solid medicine' was supposed to contain two bottles of liquid, but its weight was only about 400 grams, too small for two flacons, but just about right for keys. How could Linda need more sagrada when she had just purchased a liter of it in Darmstadt? She would give you gentlemen of the jury some of it, but you wouldn't drink it. That cascara sagrada was metal, and it was keys. Bonetti herself said in the istruttoria that she thought the package contained keys. Linda's taking back the keys," Colli insisted, "is equivalent to confessing that she was the author of the crime."[18]

After the murder, the P.M. continued, Linda helped circulate rumors about Bonmartini: that he had met a woman in the apartment; that a piece of jewelry stolen from the apartment was of great value. "She knew very well that the jewelry was cheap. Her solidarity with the killers could not have been clearer." Next was her flight to Switzerland, ostensibly because she was gravely ill—all so that Tullio could get away, with money provided by his father. Finally, Linda orders Secchi's letters destroyed, the act that sends him into a temper. Why? The lawyer asked. "Because the letters proved that Linda Murri put them up to the murder."

The day is over, and the pubblico ministero is almost finished. "They are relying on their father's prestige to get them off," Colli says, not needing to point out who was meant by "they." But soon the discussion narrows to "her." "Without her, the crime would never have been thought of because she was the only one with a true interest in having it done. Was Tisa telling the truth? Everything she said was borne out by the facts. She was trying to save Secchi, poor ignorant woman!" Colli held his palm open toward the angular figure in the cage. "Linda Murri. There she sits, an enchantress exerting her peculiar charm. Without her, the others would have continued on their way: one would have become a parliamentary deputy, the other would have inherited the clinical practice of Professor Murri. Rosina would have remained the faithful worshiper of a crackpot; Naldi perhaps would have wound up as a ship's doctor. If these pleasure seekers became murderers, it was because of her, the most guilty one of all." Colli pointed two fingers at the witness cage but remained facing the jury, his arm outstretched behind him. "Those two were born into wealth and education. For them, the road was very easy. They have no excuse. Strike them down!" The P.M. was done. It was many minutes before the well-wishers had finished pressing their congratulations and were induced to return to their seats.

The prosecutors had been careful, logical speakers schooled in stentorian and frightening eloquence. But Romoaldo Palberti, Tullio's defender, talked so much and so fast that the reporters in the hall were rarely able to quote him directly and had to summarize what they thought they had heard after the deluge of his words washed over them. Worst of all, his pastel voice never reached the corners, even in that hall that was only the size of a classroom. Usually the reporters in the front row could follow his oration, but the jury off to one side could not hear a syllable.[19]

He described how the prosecutors had tried to strike at Professor Murri, subjecting him to ridicule as they read out loud the letters of "a poor old man venting his anger over his family's bitter problems." Palberti spoke for an hour about Professor Murri and worked himself up to such a pitch that almost half the attendants could hear him. Suddenly he burst into tears, which greatly puzzled the half who had not been able to make out his words.[20] "Go to him! Go to him, O jurors, so that he understands we have the most profound tenderness, sympathy, respect for him, regardless of how this case goes." The defendants sat still, mildly astonished, as Palberti blew his nose and moved on to other matters.

The P.M. had stated that specific plans for the murder began in

April 1902, at the time of the reconciliation. Palberti tried to refute that contention.[21] The idea of homicide formed in Tullio's tortured mind only on August 25 and 26, he said, after Bonnmartini had "so brutally violated the terms of the reconciliation" by planning to move the family to Padua. "In the face of this sudden event, in the face of these driving psychological forces," Palberti asked the court, "how can we credit the prosecution's notion of premeditation?" Bonmartini was a man full of grandiose illusions about his wealth, his noble title, and the light shed on him by his marriage to the Murri name. "The true cause of the catastrophe," said Palberti, "was that Bonmartini insisted on being Murri's assistant. That was the true cause of the murder!"

Palberti insisted that Tullio's last version of the killing was the correct one. He listed the nine witnesses who saw Bonmartini go out between seven and eleven. All their testimony was attacked, he said, because they connected having seen Bonmartini with the publicized arrival in Bologna of the count of Turin, on August 28. "In the instuttoria," Palberti argued, "Stanzani told them, 'You're wrong, The count of Turin was not in Bologna on the twenty-eighth.' Who among us, confronted with that statement, wouldn't have said, 'Oh, then I must be mistaken!'" Regarding the keys Tullio used to enter the apartment, Palberti suggested that they might simply have been copies. "No blacksmith has come forth to say he made a set of keys," Palberti admitted, "but that is not proof that keys were not copied. When we see Bolognese doctors who risk losing patients if they give a deposition favorable to the Murris, we can certainly understand why a blacksmith would shrink from admitting that he furnished keys that are today a piece of material evidence." By the time he left the subject of the keys, Palberti was insisting adamantly that they had been copied and returned to their place without Linda's knowledge.

Regarding the money Tullio needed for a hired killer, the prosecution had maintained that Tullio did not use the 65,000 lire in his bank account because he didn't want it to be traced. "But see here," said Palberti, holding up a bankbook. "On August 27 Tullio deposited 40,000 lire. If he had wanted 3,000 without having any record of a

262 — INDECENT SECRETS

withdrawal, why didn't he just deposit 37,000?"[22] It was an impressive point, but it left the jury wondering exactly why it was that Tullio, with so much in the bank, had in fact borrowed 3,000 from Secchi.

In his final exhortation, Palberti attacked Tisa, who, he said, was astute and too well coached to be easily tricked. She had kept quiet until Secchi's arrest and came forward only in order to save him and herself. Their salvation, said Palberti, lay in accusing Linda, since Tisa was unquestionably a co-conspirator who would have been charged along with the others. Wasn't it Tisa who participated in the experiment with the goat, alongside Secchi? Carried the poison and instructions to Tullio? Advised him on how to use the sack of pallini? "As God is our witness, is this all true or not?" asked the lawyer. Those audience members who could hear him stirred appreciatively. Tisa was not particularly well liked in the hall.

Palberti attacked the P.M. for insinuating that Secchi had debauched Linda's girlhood. "That infamy that will torment you in your last hours."

"You're killing me off before my time," replied Colli languidly.

"Yours was an atrocity for which you will have to answer to God!" Palberti had again moved himself to tears. "But against you came a plebiscite of gentlewomen who filed in here, these ladies not familiar with the Corte d'Assise, to tell you that the adulteress you want to accuse of being a murderess is, in fact, an honest woman." The reporters shut their notebooks with relief when Palberti concluded, "with faith in the justice of my country." The lawyer had hurtled through his discourse, they complained, inaudible even when he had made himself semihysterical.

The press box found room for two notable visitors, the writers Edmondo De Amicis and Guglielmo Ferrero. Today, travelers to Turin are greeted by an enormous De Amicis, resplendent in bronze in front of the train station, perhaps still a socialist as he watches the traffic of the decades through his city. Ferrero was a historian, sociologist, and the protégé and son-in-law of Lombroso. He was somewhat more misogynistic than his mentor, insisting that prostitutes must be included in the category of female criminals. He conceded, however, that women's crimes were more insipid than men's on account of their defective biology. Since females were inferior to males, it naturally followed that they were less effective as criminals.[23]

The hall was now not as suffocating, thanks to the electric fans that the Municipality of Turin had specially installed. The defense continued through the day, though the festival of San Giovanni was about to disrupt the summations. Each city had its own celestial patron, honored by a week of festivities. The justice system was closed down while lawyers and thieves danced at the parties given by every family in Turin. Despite the anticipated interruption, Enrico Ferri began his summation for Tullio.[24] Ferri at the time was probably the pre-eminent personality in the socialist party, as well as a member, like Ferrero, of Lombroso's coterie. Editor of *Avanti!*, he held the chair of penal law at the University of Bologna, was a deputy to parliament, and had authored a book on homicide in which he presented the positivist argument that punishment should fit the criminal rather than the crime (particularly if the malefactor was an "occasional criminal"). In 1921, sixteen years after the Murri trial, Ferri drafted a new criminal code that would have made positivist theories the basis for Italian justice. However, Mussolini came to power the year after Ferri presented the draft to the legislature; all theory and justice except fascist ideology then went crashing under the trains.[25] By that time, the youthful socialist was turning into a fickle, aging fascist, and the trial that had made him the most famous advocate in Italy had eased into the catacombs of legal history.

Ferri glared at the jury with his usual air of righteous intensity. The newspapers, he said, were having a festival of their own around the theme of Murri incest, yet, through all the opprobrium, Tullio had emerged seeming quite human. He was excitable, a dreamer and lover of fiction, a good-natured fellow whose one fault was impulsiveness.

"In three years," the lawyer said, "Tullio made a hundred and ten bank transactions to lend money to friends: a hundred and ten!" He had a good heart, incapable of hatred. "The P.M. called Bonetti a 'bitch dog,'" Ferri said, which only demonstrated the P.M.'s callousness and Tullio's goodness. "Tullio was not in love," said Ferri, as Rosina looked straight ahead and tried to cover her pain with an impassive face, "but he wouldn't leave her when she became ugly and sick, because of his sense of right. The man in that cage," Ferri said, turning to look at Tullio at last, "sprang up two times, not for himself but to defend his father against Tisa's accusations. To find in him the things they are saying about him, you'd have to fabricate another Tullio, a depraved, damaged man."

Ferri described Tullio as a youth trapped in fixed ideas that overwhelmed his judgment. Only psychological fixation could explain how Tullio could be so good, yet kill a man without remorse. Ferri dismissed the prosecution's contention that Linda was never as sick as the Murris pretended. Her existence, he said, was one of constant suffering, holding on to life by a thread. Everything Tullio did, therefore—accepting money from his sister's lover, not confronting Bonmartini openly—was to avoid upsetting Linda or staining the family's honor.

Tullio was not the lunatic that the P.M. would have for a classic insanity defense. "No. He is something less and more," said the lawyer, clasping his palms as if he were shaking hands with himself. "He's irresponsible, a type that psychiatrists describe as being in an intermediate zone between crazy and sane. The crime was not a momentary aberration," according to Ferri, whose imagery became more specific as his explanation became more abstract, "but an insidious poison that bit by bit dominated and intoxicated him, a terror that his sister would die because of Bonmartini. On August 25, when Linda's desperate letter arrived in Rimini, he was jolted into action."

As Ferri completed his portrait of Tullio as a man out of control, he seemed to discount the self-defense plea altogether. "It doesn't matter to me if what happened on August 28 occurred at 6:30 or at midnight," he said. "The way Tullio set out to kill demonstrates that the deed was pathological—he arrives in a fever, bringing an arsenal of weapons, and then stays closed up for fourteen hours. He attacks in a paroxysm of fury—thirteen wounds." What he did after the crime was further proof of mental unbalance, according to Ferri, who claimed that Tullio covered up the crime to avoid any damage to his sister. "To say a crime is premeditated, it is not enough that it was preordained. Tullio Murri sacrificed himself to an intense affection, carried away by extraordinary love, without premeditation." Ferri had come close to saying that Tullio had been driven mad by his adoration of Linda. The lawyer ended his talk with a strenuous plea for mercy. His kinky hair and beard vibrated slightly as he invoked images of protective mothers, humble laborers, and the Passion of Jesus.[26] The handsome Ferri was a great favorite with the audience. Murmurs of approval followed him as he walked briskly to the door. Outside, the crowd, still held back by a phalanx of guards, applauded the speech they had not been able to hear.

Guido Bernasconi searched the eyes of the jurors.[27] "Many years ago, a barefoot little girl, dragging her younger brother behind her, went from door to door in a country town, holding out her hand for the charity of poor tenant farmers. The little one did not go begging because of her squalid poverty or even because of her hunger. She begged so that when she went home in the evening, the miserable prostitute who had taken over the house would not look at the empty hands and hit her and her little brother. But after many months of privation and beatings, the little beggar fled with her brother and sought refuge with a gentlewoman who accepted her. Not on her, this poor outcast, had life showered its blessings," Bernasconi continued, perhaps intentionally contrasting his client to Linda Murri, "nor had her young head ever felt the protective hand of a father. Today, after so many years, the wretched child of Fontanelice has become the famous criminal. The little beggar is seated in the shameful cage of the Corte d'Assise, with a face aged and withered by sadness and suffering, a defendant in the great Murri trial."

The judiciary of 1905 equated promiscuity with criminality, except in society women. Other women who disregarded the usual sexual restraints were classed as creatures of the underworld. Therefore, Bernasconi went to some lengths to show that for many years, Rosina had been devoted exclusively to Tullio. Her work in the Bonmartini house was not to plan a murder but to please her Nino, the lawyer said. The prosecution had invented a woman—vicious, lying, bigoted—in place of a girl who was so anxious to protect Tullio that she made herself guilty of imaginary wrongs to save him. Only a perverse mind such as Tisa's could suppose that Rosina cooperated in a murder to have Tullio "in her fist," to make him marry her; her love reached far beyond such simplistic explanations. And only people with "foul mouths," he said, would ridicule her piety, "her simple, ardent faith that makes her life less bitter." In one of his youthful letters full of sophisms, said Bernasconi, Tullio wrote that he didn't believe in love, that it was a passing illusion and certainly not eternal. "The man who wrote that now sees sitting there—her eyes only on him, caring nothing about herself—the poor, good Rosina. Prison has not changed her. Dead the woman who protected her. Dead the brother whom she protected. Dead for her, maybe forever, her Nino." Only the jurors, he said, acting out of either kindness or pity, could hold out some hope for her in life.

Vincenzo Tazzari, like most of the lawyers assigned to impoverished defendants, was young, but he was to prove an able representative for Naldi.[28] "He is the most humble of all the defendants," Tazzari began, "so obscure that nobody has even made a real case against him. They have dismissed him as a typical hired killer; but that picture doesn't remotely resemble Naldi."[29] The prosecution had emphasized changes Naldi made in his testimony to bolster his alibi. "We don't have to be concerned with such changes," the lawyer said, "because his alibi holds up in any version. The prosecution declares that if he had gone out the main door before the murder, he would have been seen by the portinaia and her friend." The young lawyer took a long pause and looked around the small courtroom before he made his next point, one that apparently had not occurred to anyone.

"Then they would have had to see Naldi if he went out right after the murder, too. Naldi was on the 7:00 train to Florence," he said. "If he left the way the prosecution says he did, by the Pusterla exit, he would certainly have been noticed by the portinaia, since the servants' stairs were rarely used by tenants." Naldi said that he left around 5:30 by the main stairway in front. The portinaia did not see him then. However, she did not see him at 6:30 or at 6:40. "She never saw him go out; yet we know that he was not in the room when Bonmartini's body was discovered a week later. Many people entered and left from the front entrance at that time of day without notifying the portinaia," the lawyer said, "because they could open the entrance gate as well as she could; it was unlocked. Even strangers went in and out that afternoon without her noticing it," he insisted, "people such as the witness Tanteri, who visited his fiancée, and servants of the Bisteghi family."

Naldi maintained in four out of five interrogations that he left by the Via Mazzini entrance, the lawyer said, and gave many details of the passageway; only once, when confronted with Tullio, did he say he left by the back door, and only because he is naturally easygoing and yielded to Tullio. By that time, Tullio himself had admitted that Naldi left by the front. Naldi's landlady testified that she did not hear him come in on August 28, but she reported that her elderly tenant did hear him. Naldi said that when he was changing clothes, around 5:30 or 6:00, he heard the landlady talking with someone in another part of the house. "That is perfectly true," said Tazzari. "It was a someone named Signora Monte who had come to visit, and Naldi could not have fabricated that detail."

The most compelling argument for Naldi's innocence, according to Tazzari, was that his apartment keys were found in his cabinet. He could not have left them on the twenty-seventh because he would have needed them to get in if, as the P.M. insisted, he changed clothes during the night. He had to leave them, as he said, on August 28. "If Naldi were planning on August 27 to commit a murder the next day, he would hardly lock himself out of the place where he could change out of his bloody garments. As a matter of fact," the lawyer pointed out, "no stained clothes of Naldi's were ever found, yet he was supposed to have committed a bloody atrocity. To insist that Bonmartini's wounds were inflicted by a doctor—as if one needed special courses in a university to know that a dagger in a carotid artery is lethal—is ridiculous," Tazzari continued. "The wounds in the neck were called 'expert cuts' because they measured 83 and 85 millimeters, as if the result would have been different if the knife had cut a little longer or shorter."[30]

Tazzari traced Naldi's movements after he fled Bologna. He went to Florence, to the first hotel he knew, and asked for some soup, but was told none was available at that hour. He declined an offer of hot water. "Surely someone who had just taken part in a murder would need water. But he needed no water, and had no blood on his things. Between the killing and the discovery of the cadaver, five days passed. Anyone wanting to flee needed only one. Naldi went from Florence to Livorno, and on August 30 to Genoa. He spent the thirty-first alone and inactive. Only on the first of September did he go to an old colleague to ask for a recommendation in the hope of being hired as a ship's doctor, and he didn't even pick up the recommendation until the third. Is this the conduct of a fugitive?" the barrister asked. "From September 2 until he gave himself up, Naldi appears to have had the untroubled conscience of someone who knows he is not responsible for the crime. He told friends he intended to go back to Bologna, since it would require two months to qualify as a ship's doctor. He wasn't fleeing; he was returning. The prosecutor says he had to go back because he was abandoned by the Murris who had promised him an escape. But how does he act during those days in Genoa? He finds the cheapest hotel and sleeps until noon, instead of getting himself out and finding the ship that could be his only salvation. He does find a ship, but without haste, without anxiety." Tazzari pointed out that Tullio's confession excluded Naldi from the murder. Naldi went to the authorities nonetheless and confessed the part he did have in the crime lest he be accused of a larger one. There was a big difference, he said, between Tullio, stabbing Bonmartini in the savagery of anonymity, and Naldi, whose actions were public and explainable.

The lawyer was hoarse as he began his last important point, that Naldi could not have participated in the crime if it occurred at 6:30. No one could go on foot from the murder scene to the train station in less than nineteen minutes. According to the prosecution, Naldi had fifty-three minutes to get home, change, and get to the station, where he caught the train for Florence. "All witnesses said Bonmartini arrived no earlier than 6:30," said Tazzari. "It is unlikely that the count, who was heavy and liked to travel with all his comforts, was the first one out of the train. When he did arrive, he was in no hurry. He paid the carriage driver, watched the carriage get into a wreck, opened the portinaia's gate, went up the stairs, put down his valise in front of the door to find his keys—all that must have taken him some four minutes, so now 6:30 becomes 6:34, the hour of his arrival." The prosecutors remained quiet at their table, though they knew that Bonmartini was already upstairs when the wreck occurred, and that the carriage driver had in fact equivocated about the exact time he delivered the count.

"Ten minutes would be necessary for two assassins to complete the crime, wash up, compose themselves, get dressed, as they must have done, since Naldi had no blood on him, and leave. Now that comes to 6:44, only eleven minutes until the 6:55. He needed at least nineteen." The lawyer stopped and walked silently back and forth before the jury for several seconds, shaking his head. "No, no, no," he said finally. "Naldi certainly committed a serious mistake, and he punished himself by opening up a vein. But you can't punish him for the murder of Bonmartini, because he didn't do it." The lawyer resumed his factual tone. "Naldi got his train ticket at the window.

He would have had to wait some minutes for his turn. The witness Marescaldi said there was a long line that evening. These are all small details, but each movement takes up time. Naturally, the investigators were not concerned with these points that could have exculpated Naldi." The jury in Turin may not have taken the full weight of the lawyer's remark. The Stazione Medaglie d'Oro in Bologna was notorious for lines of twenty or more purchasers at any hour of the day or night, a reputation it retains even today.[31]

Tazzari had spoken without flourishes or showy rhetoric. "It is the pride of my life to have argued this case before you. Naldi committed a minor crime in accompanying Tullio to the apartment. That's all."

Secchi's lawyer stood at his place and waved his notepad carelessly in the direction of the jurors. The case against his client, he said, was made of "shadows and dust," centering on a myth that Secchi was some sort of debauched opportunist.[32] According to Vincente Morello, Secchi was protective and unselfish with Linda, calling himself her "old thing," almost like a father. He had an affair with a married woman, but that did not make him the libertine the prosecution tried to portray. "Adultery wasn't invented by Secchi," said Morello. It's everywhere, cherished by society, celebrated in art, pardoned by religion that absolves it in the confessional." The prosecution made a great fuss about Secchi's letters, "as if they had been full of filth," but, as the lawyer observed, certain language is permissible between lovers and no one except a hypocrite pretends to be horrified by it. Secchi was not troubled by the proposed move from Bologna to Padua, according to Morello, and would not have been drawn into a murder because of it. "The move could have caused the separation of Linda and Bonmartini, that's all—a result that would have pleased him."

Morello went to the key issue against Secchi: the curare. "They claim," he said, nodding toward the semicircle of prosecutors, "that

Secchi sent Tullio an enormous dose. Enormous dose? Enough for ten men?" Morello walked a few steps, stopped before the jurors, and scribbled the air in front of their faces. "The prosecution was unscrupulous," he exclaimed, "in not making clear how many injections were necessary to kill a man. They realized if they said 'ten injections' out loud, that would destroy their case against Secchi. Ten injections! That number is his best defense. Fifty to 100 grams of curare could make at most a solution of two percent. Then the killer would need to give only five shots," said the lawyer with a sarcastic smirk. "Besides all that, Secchi warned Tullio that curare would leave traces. If Tullio was not convinced, it was because he was in the grip of an obsession. Secchi erred in giving Tullio the curare; it was unwise and showed perhaps that he is a little weak. Tullio was unshakable in his determination to kill Bonmartini. Nothing of the sort can be said of Secchi, whose only fault was not being able to keep Tullio from acting on his impulses."

The prosecutors naturally hoped to destroy Linda for the hypocritical pleasure of exposing a woman previously thought to be respectable. But the obvious and sincere venom they directed against Secchi was, as his defenders noted, a little perplexing.[33] When he was young and attending university, said his lawyer Fabri, he lived on 28 lire a month. "The pubblico ministero, who makes thirty or forty thousand, can't possibly understand his privation—or his character. When he started earning money, he paid off the debts of his brother. He treated the poor for free. For Secchi to be an accomplice," Fabri lectured, it must be shown that he was intentionally active and helped in some factual way. "From the standpoint of material assistance in the murder," said the lawyer, "what did Secchi give Tullio that was worth anything to him? Was the curare used? No. Thirteen knife wounds killed Bonmartini, not curare." The lawyer read part of a legal treatise to the jury: "'No intention or wrongdoing can be interpreted as complicity if it does not affect the action that is the main crime.' Therefore," he told the jury, "Carlo Secchi has nothing to fear from you."

* * *

The audience was excited and noisy as Giuseppe Gottardi of Bologna began his defense of Linda.[34] Her champions—and she had some—had waited three years for this moment, when all the outrages against her would be answered, the truth separated from rumors. Everyone else was simply looking forward with open prurience to a review of her alleged sins. The room was full and sweltering.

Gottardi addressed Tullio: "I have watched the relentless suffering of your father during this affair, and I know the relief you will feel when Linda is absolved." Having set the proper atmosphere by causing Tullio to cry, the easiest part of his presentation, and having introduced Professor Murri's name, Gottardi now expatiated for several minutes on the doctor's honors and his blameless life. He pointed out that many people close to Linda, even Bonmartini's manservant Picchi, never had the slightest suspicion that she wanted to kill her husband. From the beginning, the lawyer said, the contessa had been the target of brutal sensationalism. Here Gottardi had the high ground and he made the most of it, enumerating the insults that had been heaped upon Linda. In prison, she had been subjected to a physical examination to see if she were "in an interesting condition." The press then reported that the examination had turned up proof—as if such proof were possible—of incest and "other turpitude." One journal wrote that she had forced her children to witness what the writer called "'her base perversions: her obscene erotic fascination with Secchi, her filthy lewdness with Bonetti, all practiced before the children with utter shamelessness.'"[35] By now, many in the audience had stopped fanning themselves to listen more closely. The treatment Linda had suffered was worse than the American lynching of Negroes, the lawyer asserted. The press created a lascivious female out of someone who was actually emaciated and frigid. Even Linda's enemies in the hall nodded involuntarily: any honest observer of the trial had to admit that Linda did not have the air of a woman gifted with lechery.

Francesco (Cesco)
Bonmartini, 1902.

Linda Murri Bonmartini
at the time of her
marriage to Bonmartini.

Giovanni (Ninetto)
and Maria Bonmartini,
ages 6 and 8, in a photo
taken by their father.

Linda Murri and Cesco
Bonmartini during their
brief engagement.

Bonmartini's palazzo on
his estate in Cavarzere,
near Padua.

Linda signs reconciliation agreement with Cardinal Svampa, Bonmartini, and a notary (from an artist's sketch made for newspapers in 1903).

Linda Murri, with her characteristic somber expression. Photos made before 1903, gathered by police investigators.

Tullio (Nino) Murri, 1902.

"Devoted servant, Rosina Bonetti." Police attached the closing of one of her letters to Rosina's photograph, taken around 1902.

Augusto Murri.

Giannina Murri.

Palazzo Bisteghi,
39 Via Mazzini, in 1902.
Bonmartini was murdered
upstairs on the left.

San Toma, Venice, location
of Bonmartini's summer
residence.

The search of Bonmartini's
bedroom. An investigator
finds a woman's red
bloomers in the count's bed.

Dr. Carlo Secchi and Tisa Borghi.

Dr. Pio Naldi at the time of his arrest. "I am more stupid than guilty," he wrote to his aunt; "What happens to me is of no importance."

Interior courtyard of prison of San Giovanni in Monte.

Justice Augusto Stanzani, *giudice istruttore,* or chief investigator, of the Murri case.

Via Mazzini (now Strada Maggiore). The Bonmartini apartment is at the extreme right, looking down toward the prison of San Giovanni in Monte (with spire).

Naldi divulges the plans regarding poison to Stanzani from his prison hospital bed.

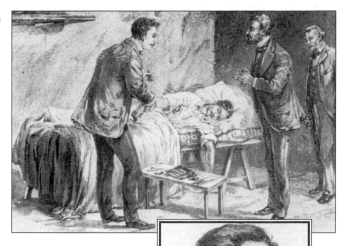

The "base woman" Rosina Bonetti, as she was consistently described in the newspapers, sketched while she testified.

Linda leaves prison to attend trial.

Giuseppe Gottardi, Linda's lawyer, during the trial. (From *L'illustrazione Italiana*, 1905)

Frieda Ringler, the German maid whose deposition was said to expose a labyrinth of "inconfessable" relationships within the Bonmartini household.

The defendants watch the trial from their cage in the court-room. Lawyers are ranged on the left tables.

Corte d'Assise in Turin. Tullio testifies before Ernesto Dusio, president of the tribunal of magistrates.

Linda Murri in the courtroom, from a contemporary photo.

 Tisa Borghi outside the Corte d'Assise. (From *L'illustrazione Italiana*, 1905)

The crowd in front of the Palace of Justice awaits the emergence of the defendants on an ordinary trial day.

Tullio Murri, with his beloved daughter Gianna Rosa, c. 1924. (Courtesy of Gianna Murri)

The former Murri Clinic as it appears today, still alongside Bologna's large park, Giardini Margherita, on a street renamed Via Murri.

The former Palazzo Bisteghi, scene of the murder.

Via Mazzini (now Strada Maggiore), just across the street from the Palazzo Bisteghi. Bonmartini was especially fearful of being attacked under these dark arches.

Augusto Murri in old age. (Courtesy of University of Bologna)

Augusto Murri at age 90, surrounded by colleagues. Tullio's daughter Gianna Rosa sits at his feet. Dr. Silvagni is standing in left rear, with white forked beard.

Giannina Murri at 80.
(Courtesy of Gianna
Murri)

Linda and Tullio Murri in a
photo taken by Bonmartini.
(Courtesy of Gianna Murri)

Gottardi elaborately described the minor accusations made against her—that she had tried to ruin Bonmartini's reputation among his friends, for example. He argued these side issues with the same emphasis as he disputed the charges that she fomented the murder. It was a canny strategy involving long and poetic oratory. Innocuous telegrams had been presented as evidence of criminal plans, he said, and to prove it, Gottardi dragged the jury through each of Linda's coded communications, providing multiple explanations and deranging the men's impression of a welter of intrigue.[36] Finally, he turned to the card, *'I don't hear anything more about S.'* "This message was the only time in the istruttoria when Linda Murri did not tell the truth, in order not to compromise the woman who was really meant by 'S.' To this day," Gottardi continued, "the defense is constrained not to expose a married woman." If anyone in the courtroom believed that Linda Murri would go to prison rather than embarrass an acquaintance, the defense lawyers had brilliantly succeeded. But what people in the courtroom, especially the jurors, thought about Linda was still a mystery.

Gottardi finished his peroration with a letter written by Linda to Justice Stanzani in 1902:

> *The Justice will enjoy this Christmas evening with his family, have his children around him . . . I hope he will reflect on the confinement that I am enduring, closed up, pulled away from my adored family. . . . Signore, I am innocent, innocent, innocent!*

Linda's letter continued for five long paragraphs, each ending with *"I am innocent, I am innocent, I repeat it a thousand times, endless times."* The missive was sent on December 25, the day on which a most unhappy Bonmartini had begun his diary three years before.

Defense attorney Arturo Vecchini of Ancona brought the jury's attention back to Linda's father.[37] "I see a modest house," he said, looking out of the courthouse window toward the spectators transfixed on the sidewalk, "where there is not yet celebrity, not yet

wealth, but children growing up in the light of Augusto Murri."
Giannina Murri had been painted as a despot, he said, but she was
actually devoted to her home and children. As proof of her motherly
affection, Vecchini offered one of Giannina's odder letters, written to
Linda in 1900: *"I may be excessive, perhaps eccentric. But I would will-
ingly be treated like a filthy dog if it would mean you could be happy
again."*[38] "What maternal cry could exceed that?" the lawyer asked;
and in truth, it was an apt question.

When Cesco "took it into his head" to become a doctor, Linda,
who had begun to see that he was "crude, parsimonious, and authori-
tarian," gave him what the lawyer termed good advice. Vecchini
quotes her: " *'Be prudent, don't disgust anybody. Don't put things off
as you tend to do. Don't act self-centered and mean.'"*[39] But Cesco does
not attend classes regularly and continues to be disgusting. He tells
Valvassori that he thinks Linda had incestuous relations with her father. "True, it was in a fleeting moment of anger," the lawyer con-
cedes, "but it is an idea that burns the brain, a word that dries up the
tongue, and exposes the sort of mind capable of imagining such
atrocious things." Bonmartini, Vecchini remarked, "was the product
of a late and sparse education. He was an unfortunate who spread
misfortune."

The lawyer then revisited the charge that Bonmartini had engaged in necrophilia. The aspersion had been roundly discredited by
the professors who supervised Bonmartini's autopsies. Linda's
lawyer might have preferred that the jury forget about the traduce-
ment. Instead, he talked about it in detail, with conviction, as if the
unspeakable deed were a fact of Bonmartini's past. In March 1898,
Linda confided to a doctor—Fabio Vitali, a good friend of Augusto
Murri—that Cesco had told her of an incident while he was an
anatomy student in Bologna. "Cesco and a companion were curious
as to whether a young girl lying on the anatomy table had kept her
purity. And so they proceeded," the lawyer said, raising his voice and
pausing for a sigh of lament, "not respecting what the poor girl had
respected all her life." In the same year, Linda met Secchi again, and

thus began, according to Vecchini, Linda's terrible battle with herself, a battle that echoed with cries of "anguish and desperation." Here the lawyer's voice broke in a single, resonant sob.

Medical training in 1905 relied on the dissection of cadavers that were not treated with any particular respect. In every medical school, there were stories of students playing practical jokes with dissected genitalia or using intestines to jump rope. Such pranks were viewed with stern disapproval, but not with the horror they would elicit today, when some medical schools hold burial services for the body parts after the students have finished studying them.

By afternoon, not a single additional body could be crushed into the hall. The courtyard outside the building was choked with people listening intently, piecing together what they could hear of the entertainment within. "Bonmartini never recognized his defects," said Vecchini, who did not neglect to discuss Cesco's all too evident fascination with Linda's chamber pot. "What he did is not important. Each of us, perhaps near the bed of someone dear who is ill, has done or would do the same. But he recorded everything scrupulously in the diary. He kept count." It is in Bonmartini's compulsive recording of the act, Vecchini averred, where he congratulated himself on emptying his wife's 'dung,' that he documented his own grossness. Having made this unassailable point about Bonmartini's indelicacy, the lawyer continued with a concatenation of truth and falsehood. He described clearly factual situations but then linked them to fictional incidents, as if these had not already been disproved in court. His tactic was to confuse the jury, to cause them to forget what had been proven as false; his talk was artful and effective. While Linda was "battling her attraction to Secchi with all her strength," Cesco shockingly demanded a separation—Vecchini thus characterized the marital breakup as Cesco's initiative.[40] He asserted, as if it had not been refuted by Cesco's doctors, that Bonmartini's illness in 1900 was not an intestinal sickness but rather a "secret malady."

The brief period when she "fell into sin" with Secchi was marked by incessant sickness. The lawyer went through Linda's medical history, organ by organ and year by year to 1900, when, in a trip to restore her health, she suffered the injury to her eye. From August to September, her eye was getting worse and was, in the lawyer's words, "horrible to see." Linda's one beauty had been her lively black eyes, Vecchini noted. Now that one beauty was gone. In November, he continued, it was her urine that was horrible—bloody, indicating a resurgence of kidney problems. "Here is the Messalina glittering with her pleasures," said Vecchini, alluding to the emperor Claudius's notoriously unfaithful wife. "Here is the woman," he said, "whom all the gallant men in Italy have spat upon with their scorn. Oh! The lover—wasn't he really more like her nurse?" Linda, motionless, accepted the court's attention with a low accompaniment of conservative sobbing, befitting a veiled martyr. Secchi, however, could not resist nodding: yes, yes!

"They create an entire fantasy around her," said Vecchini. "Signals are given nefarious meanings, and a package of cascara sagrada turns into a box of keys. Why? Why would Linda have needed to kill? For hatred? Of a man she couldn't love but to whom she conceded every indulgence? To be free? Wasn't she free already? For money? Isn't she the daughter of a rich man? For fear? Nobody knew of her guilt with Secchi, and whatever was suspected had not been proved.

"She is good to the depths of her soul," he said, looking at his client, a "divine example" of maternal love. The audience lisped its approval at first, and then spontaneous applause broke out. Turning his back on Linda, Vecchini faced the jury. "Defend her!" he exhorted. "Defend her, you who still have the good fortune to have mothers. Now, right now, I am surrounded by an image of sanctity. I am thinking of a humble woman far from here who is not beautiful, who is no longer young, who no longer hopes the dreams under her white hair will come true. But at this very moment, she is thinking of me, of her faraway son who received from her the first sweet words of her profound heart." The lawyer looked away from the fascinated jurors, into a neutral space. "I am seeing . . . I am seeing . . . Maria Bonmartini, who has gathered flowers and is calling, 'Mamma, Mamma, these are for you.' I see Ninetto," the lawyer continued, "and I hear him: 'Come, Mamma, come and get us. We are tired of this life of misery.' Ninetto and Maria are alone," the lawyer reminded his hearers, "left alone between a pool of blood and a prison. Give them back their innocent, sorrowing mother. Return her to them; return their life; return their future!"[41]

The orator closed his robes around himself and sat down. The entire hall was overwhelmed. Tears spilled down the faces of both men and women; all of the defendants were openly weeping. Linda, who had been sobbing during the entire delivery, was now shaking with uncontrollable spasms. Vecchini's reputation as one of the greatest orators of Italy had been reaffirmed. His colleagues fervently embraced him. Even the normally dispassionate correspondent from *La Stampa* exclaimed, "His address was truly magnificent!" Neither he nor the other journalists noted whether the jury, too, was weeping, only that the president was helpless to control the courtroom clamor.

11. THE CLOSING

As the trial moved toward its conclusion, all the newspapers noted that Linda left off the dress she had been wearing since October for another of black silk. The ideal of womanly beauty in 1905 was a full body, stout rather than slender, with fabric gathered to blossom out in front and behind. Linda's new dress emphasized that she was strikingly underweight, a condition looked upon with general distaste. The other late development was that Linda began interrupting the proceedings; her lawyers finally gave up trying to manage her. When Callegari of the parte civile asserted that it was her duty to refute Tullio's calumnies against Bonmartini, Linda jumped up. "I felt my duty. It was to defend him with my silence." Her voice rising hysterically, she shrieked, "I cannot act against my brother. He sacrificed himself for me. I am defending my children better than you. By defending myself, I defend them, you understand? I am innocent!"[1]

"All right, all right," said the president soothingly. "Now sit down . . ."

"I have been suffering torture in that corner," Linda cried, "but now I'm tired and I want to go away!" She turned toward the door of the cage, while Tullio began trembling violently and the defense attorneys put up a commotion. The lawyers' shouts were drowned out by the tumult in the courtroom. The president had to dismiss the session, but the drama was not over. Just as Linda was brought out of

the cage, she fainted. She was put on a bench and attended by a doctor from the audience. In the afternoon, she apologized to the court
but then launched into another interminable discourse.

Callegari finally reclaimed the floor and reminded the jurors that
the accusation of Bonmartini's necrophilia was false, whereas Tullio
Murri was truly a dissolute good-for-nothing. But then Callegari surprised the court by declaring that it was Naldi who had actually committed the murder with Tullio's help and not the other way around,
an argument he expounded for six hours. He next attacked the "sa-
tanic" Dr. Secchi and stretched his closing comments to three and a
half days.

When Carlo Municchi, the second lawyer for the parte civile, insisted that the amount of curare needed to kill a man was not 100
centigrams but 15, all the lawyers participated in a roaring match in
which Levi and Nasi, at the top of their lungs, invited each other to
shut up. Many were the prosecution's attacks against all of the defendants. Many were the interruptions of the other lawyers and of Linda,
who intervened at will.[2] The lawyers mimicked one another. "'Between a pool of blood and a prison,'" the P.M. Colli quoted Vecchini,
"'these children will be all alone.' . . . Oh, sure! Give authority over
the children back to the one who had their father killed. She will administer the estate of the dead man and will use it to soften the troubles of that dear Nino, who sacrificed their father."

As they repeated every argument, the lawyers became actors,
offering the same lines with ever more histrionics. Linda's lawyer
Altobelli leaned over the jurors as if to subsume them in his robes
and once even grabbed a juror and shook him.[3] The defense read
letter after letter written by Linda, Tullio, and Bonmartini, bom-
barding the jury with dates and quotations in the hope that they
would become too disoriented to remember any letters at all and
would forget the calendar of villainy that was drummed into them
by the prosecution. Municchi joked about a reference to his "senile
impotence" which, he vowed, he was trying hard to correct. The
president chortled, and the entire room giddily took up his laugh-

ter. But a moment later, Municchi described the Murri household as "saturated with morbid affections," and Linda's tirades resumed.

Finally, the lawyers were finished, except for one last plangent battery that each defender had planned for his finale. "Tullio never once accused Naldi of being his partner," said Carlo Felice Roggieri, as he ended Naldi's defense. "Naldi was never afraid of making Tullio angry. Not even when Naldi gave the crucial information about the curare did Tullio accuse him of anything more serious than being a cheater at cards." The law offered some mitigation of punishment if a killer did not want to participate in a murder or if a killer showed true penitence. Naldi fit both categories, according to his lawyer. He was not a murderer but a penniless, pitiful gambling addict. He could still turn his life around if given another chance. For one of the few times in the long, emotional trial, Naldi, surrounded by his indifferent companions in the cage, openly wept—and wept alone.

By now Tullio's lawyers had abandoned the self-defense pleading and were concentrating on trying to get a lighter sentence for him. Taking out his beacon handkerchief, Enrico Cavaglià read aloud a letter from Tullio's mother: *Tell the jurors that Tullio Murri has always been good, good, good. Don't let them forget in the hour of making their verdict what was the great heart, the great mind, of my boy.* Tullio was in a rhapsody of tears at the first mention of his mother and continued weeping louder than the applause that ended Cavaglià's talk.[4]

The seats were filled mainly with women when Berenini, the socialist deputy from Borgo San Donnino, gave the last defense of Linda.[5] While everyone in the audience and the lawyer himself yielded one by one to tears they could not restrain, Berenini read two letters from the children to their mother, whom they believed was ill. The letters were written ten days previously, on the occasion of their First Communion. *"In that sublime moment,"* Maria wrote,

> *I prayed for you, dearest Mamma, that God gives you the health that you need so badly. And if he hears my prayers, I will certainly*

be happy. How are you? I hope you will write me, and I send so
many kisses to our dear grandparents and so many to you that the
mouth cannot give them and the pen cannot write them.

And Ninetto wrote, *"In that supreme moment I thought of you,*
darling Mamma, and I asked God's grace to make you recover and re-
unite us as soon as possible." According to Venetian custom, the children could ask God a favor which on this occasion He would never
refuse. They asked God to save their mother.

The endless trial was ending. As if it were a portent of something unusual, a swift had flown in from its nest under the eaves of the old
building and was frantically trying to escape the courtroom. Italians,
rich and poor alike, thought the slaughter of small birds was an exquisite sport, and netted thousands as they migrated across the country. Travelers liked to say that no Italian could look at a bird without
longing to crush its skull. But now the bird produced no excitement
in the numbed crowd that watched it without interest.

The president asked the lawyers on both sides if they had anything to add. "For a moment, everyone looked toward the attorneys
with a wide-eyed expression not devoid of terror. But nobody said
anything," reported Bianchi of *Corriere della Sera.*[6] The procedure for
winding up the trial was that the president first went over all the
possible verdicts the jury might decide for each defendant. These
were termed *quesiti,* questions to be deliberated. Finally, each defendant's case was reviewed, first according to the interpretation of the
prosecution, then according to the defense. Tullio had several quesiti
that might mitigate or aggravate the charges against him: the jury
could find him insane or judge that he bore diminished responsibility
for the crime on account of his mental state; that he had acted in
self-defense; that he had responded to a threat with excessive force;
that he had acted in response to intense provocation; that he had premeditated the crime; that he had stolen some of Bonmartini's

money. For Naldi, the jury had to decide: whether he had participated directly in the murder; his degree of complicity in reinforcing
Tullio's plans; whether his complicity was necessary for the crime;
and his degree of premeditation.

August came in hot, humid, and sluggish, turning the airless hall
into a fetid oven. Hundreds of letters arrived each day in the Palace of
Justice mail room, most of them anonymous, addressed to the judges,
lawyers, defendants, or to no one in particular. Alessandro Stoppato
and Giuseppe Mainardi, the legal guardians of the Bonmartini children, appeared in court for the end of the trial to report that the children knew that their uncle had killed their father. Though both
children had adored Tullio, they had now turned against him. Ninetto
insisted on being called Giovanni. They did not know their mother
was on trial but were told instead that she was suffering an illness
brought on by the death of their father.

The defendants were invited to make their last declarations. Tullio's first attempts to speak were thwarted by his rising emotion, but
eventually he talked through his crying. He referred several times to
destiny and fate. He insisted that there was no rancor between him
and Bonmartini, but that as he saw his sister slowly dying, he knew
no other way of saving her but to remove Bonmartini. His mistake
was a mistake in thinking. "Is it my fault," he asked, "if Mother Nature
has given me this head? None of my accusers would be capable of
throwing away their lives for the life and happiness of a sister." He
never hoped to get away with it. Instead, he brought the poison with
him to the apartment to kill himself. He talked about the pain he had
caused his parents, Linda's children, and above all, Linda herself,
who, he stressed, was completely innocent. He apologized again and
again to her. "My one excuse regarding her is that I loved her so
much." He leaned toward her as if to kiss her but instead dropped
onto the bench with blaring sobs, his face hidden in his hands. Many
in the courtroom were crying. He had not said a word about Rosina.

"In this state of mind," said Carlo Secchi, white-faced and shaking,
"it is not easy for me to speak. I feel I bear none of the responsibility

with which I am charged, and I am sure that you, too, will be persuaded of that. I calmly entrust myself to your consciences."

"And you, Bonetti, do you have something to say?" asked the president.

Rosina, who had not ceased crying from the opening of the session, stood up, hiding her face with her hands, but then sat down quickly. One of her defenders spoke up. "Bonetti wanted to say that she had accused herself only because the investigating judge had promised that if she would, Tullio could go free. She wanted to beg the jurors to force the judge to keep his promise, but we defense attorneys advised her to keep silent."

The president turned to Pio Naldi. With the unwavering, almost scornful composure he had maintained throughout the trial, he said, "I have nothing to add to what my lawyers have said."

Linda Murri stood up as if exhausted, curving over the bar in front of her. She interrupted her long speech with long intermissions of sobbing. Like Tullio, she talked of fate, of the terrible misfortune that had befallen her. "I still want to tell you one more time, to protest with all my heart against this horrible accusation striking me." She described the pain her parents and her children were enduring and begged the jurors not to inflict more suffering on a mother. Finally, she, too, sat down, unable to control her crying.

"You don't have anything else to say?" asked the president. Linda shook her head. She had not asked for mercy for her brother or Rosina.

The president began his instructions to the jury, a summing up that required several days.[7] The first question, he said, was whether the crime took place at 6:30 or midnight, as Tullio had lately asserted. The president reviewed all the reasons why it could not have occurred at midnight, including the detail that those who claimed to have seen the count during the evening saw him in a frock coat, whereas he arrived at the house and was found dead in a gray suit.

He reminded the jurors that Tullio could not have left the apartment without killing Bonmartini, once Rosina locked him inside, since the door had to be relocked from the outside and he had no external key. Tullio had every reason to place the murder at midnight, since that allowed him to escape the full guilt of premeditating the crime. He could insist that he had abandoned the idea of killing Bonmartini, left the apartment, and only killed him later in self-defense.

On the other hand, Tullio's behavior on the evening of the 28th, as he placidly dined with Bonetti and wrote postcards, was not that of a man who had just committed murder. The autopsy on Bonmartini was useless for determining the time of death. Useless, too, were the opinions of the experts on whether one weapon or two had been used, since the experts were in direct contradiction on almost every point of the trial. Did Bonmartini make the cut in Tullio's arm during a fierce hand-to-hand battle, or did Naldi make it while trying to strike at Bonmartini, or indeed, did Tullio wound himself to support his story of self-defense? "As usual," complained the president, "science sheds little light and you may consider yourselves the experts." Bonmartini's keys were found a few feet from his body; they gave every appearance of having fallen almost as soon as he crossed the threshold of the room.

It was difficult to trace Naldi's part in the crime, the president said, since both he and Tullio gave several explanations as to why Naldi was carrying money when he was arrested. Naldi's defense essentially rested on whether the jury believed he could have left the apartment before Bonmartini's arrival without the portinaia's seeing him, and whether they thought he could have gone to his apartment, changed clothes, and made it to the train station if he left only after the murder. The prosecution claimed he had time after the murder; the defense said he did not. Naldi's attempt at suicide was evidence for the prosecution that he felt overwhelmed by the proof of his guilt; for the defense, it was the desperate act of an innocent man.

Turning to Bonetti, the president remarked that she clung to Tullio "like an oyster on a rock." Although she was the most audacious and cunning of the participants, her self-destructive passion for Tullio lent credence to the argument that she did not act with complete free will. Her behavior during the trial demonstrated that she had neither conscience nor a normal instinct for survival.

Dusio considered Linda and Secchi almost together. He noted that the letter in which Tullio asked Secchi for help in getting rid of Bonmartini was carried to Secchi by Linda. Did Tisa tell the truth about Linda's knowledge of the plot? Tisa was correct about Secchi's acquiring the curare on a trip he made with Linda—Secchi admitted that. She was right about the conspirators using the curare on an experiment with a goat. Linda rejected Tisa's accusations adamantly and charged that Tisa accused her out of jealousy, because Tisa was in love with Secchi. Moreover, the defense pointed out that in defending Secchi and accusing Linda, Tisa was finding a way out for herself, since she was just as involved in the conspiracy as he was.

How much curare would have been necessary to kill Bonmartini? Since it would have to be diluted in order to pass through the injecting needle, the killers would have had to make five injections of the solution Secchi provided. To plan a murder requiring five injections was crazy, everyone admitted, and the judge agreed. However, on the two occasions when they were contemplating murder, Tullio or Rosina always carried a sack of pallini intended to stun Bonmartini. Therefore, it was both true and not true that Secchi gave Tullio the means to kill Bonmartini. In his defense, Secchi used his own name and address when he ordered the curare, showing that he may not have had any criminal project in mind. He gave Tullio 3,000 lire which Tullio didn't need unless he intended to hide the expenditure from the police. But the fact that the money seems to have wound up in Naldi's pocket does not prove that Linda or Secchi knew why Tullio wanted it. Adding to the suspicion of Linda and Secchi were the dozens of letters that went back and forth among Tullio, Linda, Bonetti, and Secchi, in false names and disguised handwriting, in the two weeks prior to the crime. Never before had they written so many letters.

At this point, Linda, brushing aside the efforts of her lawyers to make her sit down, said, "I want to say that my brother and I always wrote to each other every day, every day."

"I would like to reopen the debate," asserted her lawyer, Altobelli, "because the president is introducing new arguments in favor of the prosecutors that they themselves have never raised. Only in Italy could this happen."

"That's right. Only in Italy would attorneys try to intimidate the president," answered the president.

"Intimidate my foot! We've been sitting here through this whole thing without a word!"

The president went on to the matter of the postcard, *'I don't hear anything more about S,'* pointing out that Linda had disguised her handwriting. Cavaglià spoke up: "Mention at least that only the envelope bore a false hand—inside there was no counterfeiting of any sort."

"You didn't give me a chance," protested the president. The summary unraveled as the attorneys and the president now began quarreling over every detail. After an hour, Dusio's lecture to the jury resumed and he pointed out that, without Linda's forewarning, Tullio would not have known that Bonmartini was going to be in Bologna on August 28. Did she provide the keys to Tullio that allowed him to lie in wait in the apartment? The defendants changed their stories as to how they acquired the keys. "The prosecution charges that the best proof of Linda's complicity is the package she received from Rosina on August 31. The maid Adele Calzoni testified that she opened the package and it did not contain keys. If you believe her, then there is no certain proof that Linda gave Tullio the keys. If you believe her testimony is false and that the keys were returned to Linda in the package, then that is strong proof of Linda's complicity.

"The cause of the crime, according to the prosecution, was none other than Linda Murri." Her meeting Secchi anew caused her to exaggerate Bonmartini's little defects and to invent a plan to get rid of him, a plan that Tullio would never have thought of on his own. Although a foreign divorce might have been an option, Linda was afraid of seeking one because her affair with Secchi was bound to be uncovered. If she did not fear losing custody of her children, she did want to keep her mask of being superior and pure. "Either you believe that Linda was the fulcrum of the crime," said the president, "or you believe that she knew nothing. There is nothing in between.

"The defense, however, holds that Secchi was attracted to her not out of lust but out of pity, that she is a good, moral, and tender person who would never sacrifice her brother for her own ends. The idea for the murder began in Tullio's confused mind, and he was propelled by fate and his own obsession. Of that obsession, the defense maintains that it was not true insanity but a single-minded morbid preoccupation with his sister that blocked out all moral sense and all fear of consequences in the overwhelming impulse to protect her, a state of mind that the defense believes justifies a finding of semi-responsibility."

Not only the Corte d'Assise but the entire area of Via Sant'Agostino was crowded with elegantly dressed people, mostly women, on the day when the verdict was promised in the Murri trial. The tribunal had ordered that no announcement should come either during the lunch hours nor the evening, for then the crowd might be so large with people freed from work that it would be uncontrollable. Linda had spent the night quite sick, according to her jailors. When her carriage approached the courthouse at 10:30, the crowd pressed in so insistently that the police decided to retreat and return with several carriages to confuse the observers and draw away some of the crowd to the carriages of the false Lindas. She emerged "pale as death," according to one reporter, supported by a carabiniere and the lawyer Gottardi. "Have courage, Signora!" a few called to her.

Rosina had spent the night on her knees, praying for Tullio. The assassin himself had gone through the night hours in a state of nervous agitation, nearly manic, from which he had not recovered when he arrived at court, twitching, with his eyes darting to and fro. Both Secchi and Naldi appeared calm. Secchi almost smiled while talking quietly to his lawyer. The president called the session to order and gave to the jury closing instructions that lasted for two hours. Despite Tullio's defamation of Bonmartini's memory, neither the charge of necrophilia nor pederasty was true, the judge said. His children could be proud of bearing his name, and his soul could rest in peace. At this point, Tullio insisted on speaking. "When I wrote those things about Bonmartini," Tullio said, "I knew that my father was being accused of incest and that my sister was very ill. There were even rumors that we had intended to kill the children. I was in an exceptional state of mind, and I ask pardon." He then proceeded to express regret for his deed and to ask forgiveness of the ghost of Bonmartini, his parents, and, most and always, of Linda.

Linda then wanted to speak and began without waiting for permission, despite the president's gesture of profound impatience. "I commend myself to you one more time, for the sake of my children. The poor juror who has a sick mother and may lose her . . ." (here Linda was referring to a juror who had been briefly called away because of his mother's illness) "Think! There are two children with a mother here. Her condemnation will be a dishonor for them all their lives. I commend myself to all of you who have had a mother. I have been sustained all these three years by my faith in my innocence. Don't let this hope have been in vain!" With several more such exhortations, she fell again onto the bench.

The judge then ordered the defendants removed to a room next to the court, ordering them sequestered until the jurors reached a verdict. "I have done my duty," he pronounced. At precisely 12:35 the jurors, having already had lunch, went to the deliberation room. The press repaired to the trattoria Marmi, but the people in the hall remained, lest they lose their seats. A large tub was placed outside the jury room for the purpose of burning the cards left from any straw votes; people closely watched the windows for signs of smoke. At one o'clock, the first burning occurred.

Three of the twelve jurors were teachers from the vicinity of Turin, including their foreman, a smiling man of about forty. The teachers took copious notes on everything from the heat of the room to the expressions on the faces of the defendants as the trial progressed. Also in the jury were a military man, a lawyer, a doctor, a railroad clerk, a postal inspector, and an innkeeper. Ten of the twelve were married, and one was engaged. After two hours with no word from the jury room, police reinforcements began circling the Palace of Justice on their bicycles, accompanied by journalists who had suddenly procured bikes, once they realized how far the courtroom was from the telegraph office and how crowded the telegraph facilities were likely to be.

Professor Murri and Giannina had not appeared in the courtroom, nor had they visited their children. Murri never wavered in his belief that Linda would be absolved. The consensus among the lawyers was that Tullio would be found semi-responsible and would not be given a heavy sentence. Now, as they all awaited the verdict, the defense lawyers received a a letter from Professor Murri that was to be given to Tullio after the verdict. *"My dear,"* he wrote to his son:

> *An impulse like fate compels me to write to you, even though I feel that if I possessed all the tongues of the world, I would not be able to find the right words. I can't hope to see you here this evening with Linda, and that makes my thoughts of you even more piercing. But if my body is here, my mind will be in your cell, embracing you, always more amazed at the depth of human pain.*
>
> *And with me will be the others, for it seems if one of us is missing, no one is here. To get used to living without a father is a natural thing; to live without a child is unnatural. It isn't human to accustom oneself to that. Think, if you can, about the imaginary ideas of the Stoics that you have adhered to so many times, think of their power. But I cannot believe that their power*

is real. Fate has put you to the test, it is true, and I can do no more than send you a kiss, the saddest of all kisses.[8]

At four o'clock, the carabinieri looked to their places at the great door of the Palace of Justice. Journalists were seen throwing their bikes outside and scurrying into the courtroom. Officials, too, began briskly coming into the hall. Despite the tense crowd, no sound was heard except the creaking of electric fans above the benches.

12. TUTTI

As a precaution against a possible riot, the authorities canceled all existing passes into the Palace of Justice on August 11. At the moment of the verdict, no journalists were in the courtroom, only officials and a few well-dressed women who had somehow procured the new special-admittance tickets. The audience that had faithfully attended the trial for months was left outside, milling about disappointedly under gathering storm clouds.[1] At 4:05 in the afternoon, the jurors returned to the dull air of the courtroom and the tense eyes of the lawyers. The five people whose lives would be shattered or restored this hour remained shut away in a waiting room down the hall while the verdicts were read to the judges.

The jury foreman, his hand on his heart, pronounced the formulaic preamble: "On my honor and my conscience, this is the declaration of the jurors." The president then asked specific legal questions to elicit a verdict on each count and for each defendant, regarding all aspects of the charges—premeditation, self-defense, mental abnormality, and the rest. The foreman was asked to respond to four or five questions for each of the accused. To these questions, he answered a simple "*Sì*," or "*No*," to indicate the jury's decision; the questioning took a good fifteen minutes in all.[2]

Tullio Murri, charged with theft and the premeditated murder of Bonmartini, was found guilty, with no mental abnormality to mitigate his responsibility.

Pio Naldi, charged with premeditated murder: guilty.

Rosina Bonetti, charged with premeditated conspiracy to commit murder: guilty, but also found to have sufficient mental infirmity to lessen her responsibility.

Carlo Secchi, charged with conspiracy to commit murder: guilty.

Linda Murri was found guilty of facilitating the murder and of exciting and reinforcing the intention of the murderer.

It had taken the jury three and a half hours to find them all guilty, an astonishingly quick verdict considering that for Tullio alone the jurors had to make a judgment on sixteen separate clauses.[3] There was rarely a unanimous verdict on the charges, which were detailed and legalistic. The jury was most divided on the charges against Linda and Secchi. It was most in agreement regarding the guilt of Tullio and Naldi. "*TUTTI CONDANNATI*"—All Convicted—would be the gigantic headline in newspapers throughout the country.

The president summoned the defendants. They had apparently been told the verdicts. Secchi entered first, so drained and bluish that he almost looked like a different person. He walked unsteadily to his usual post and seemed to collapse into his seat. The usher announced that Bonetti refused to come back, but before the president could react to the statement, she appeared, her face swollen as usual from crying, and wobbled to her seat. Naldi came in and walked to the cage exactly as he had during all the previous months, although instead of sitting in his assigned place near the women, he went to sit next to Secchi. Tullio walked like an automaton, his face frozen and vacant. The usher announced that Linda Murri did not want to come back.

"You go with two authorities and summon her. If she persists in refusing, tell her the verdict," the president said. Tullio, meanwhile, remained stupefied. Two carabinieri shook him, but he sat as if unconscious, his eyes wide. "If Tullio Murri is sick, they can give him a little liqueur," the president said. Though it was the last alcohol he would be offered for many years, Tullio did not respond. Occasionally he murmured, "Poor Linda! Poor Linda!" but otherwise seemed insensible to his surroundings. The president ordered the carabinieri to take him out, which caused Rosina to rush to the door of the cage, crying hysterically. Finally, the president sent doctors to attend to the three who could not remain in the courtroom and he dispatched an usher to formally read them the verdicts. Though the audience was noisy, everyone heard the piercing shriek from Rosina's cell, which was the nearest to the courtroom. Bernasconi ran out to see what had happened, while Levi asked the president to send Bonetti to a mental institution. The president ordered the formal reading of the verdicts to the remaining prisoners. Naldi listened without emotion. Secchi, his head between his hands, wiped his handkerchief over his face repeatedly.[4]

There was to be no delay in sentencing. The pubblico ministero announced his requests: the maximum sentences allowed by law for all. The defense lawyers made final pleas for leniency. Altobelli argued that to find premeditation on the part of Tullio, but not Linda or Secchi, was a contradiction. Borciani reminded the president that since Secchi was found guilty with a bare majority, the law allowed the tribunal to annul the verdict. Berenini, in a voice quavering with emotion, insisted on the innocence of Linda Murri and, despite the annoyance of the president, denounced the verdict at length as "incomprehensible" and "absurd." Voices in the audience encouraged him from time to time: "*Bene,*" they said, and "*Bravo.*" Secchi and Naldi, being the only defendants in the courtroom, were invited to make a last statement. Secchi declined. Naldi rose and in a firm voice declared, "For three years I have suffered, saying nothing, but now I can do no less than state to those who have condemned me that I am innocent and that I bear no guilt for the killing of Bonmartini."

One hour later, at 6:10, the sentences were announced. For Tullio and Naldi, thirty years in prison, including ten in solitary confinement. For Linda and Secchi, ten years each. For Rosina, seven years, six months, including three and a half in solitary.[5] None of the defendants received the maximum sentence allowed by law. Before thanking the jurors and closing the trial, the president reminded the lawyers that they had three days to appeal the verdicts to the Court of Cassation, the highest court in the country.

Outside the Palace of Justice, the promised storm had finally broken, soaking the triple cordon of armed police who surrounded the door. The jurors escaped through a side door. Despite the thunder and lightning, an enormous crowd awaited the departure of the prisoners. During the seven months of the trial, the trattorie near the courthouse had profited richly from the daily invasion of customers. But on this occasion, the people standing shoulder to shoulder on the street had gone without eating all day so as not to lose their places at the spectacle that was more compelling than any theater. Having been excluded from the courtroom, reporters had pleaded with pass holders to act as surrogates and take notes while they positioned themselves outside to see the protagonists emerge. At the front of the building, the crowd gasped expectantly each time the great doors opened for an anonymous individual. Everyone who stepped out on the walkway was immediately drenched.[6] Finally, the actors appeared. Secchi's lawyers, the first to emerge, relayed their client's message to a reporter: "If society feels it has a duty to condemn me, I will serve the sentence, but my conscience is that of an innocent man." Behind that lawyer came Secchi himself, apparently unable to walk without support. Naldi appeared calm and ignored requests for comment.

During the reading of the sentence, Rosina had re-entered the room and had been lying on the bench, her left side stiffening into paralysis. It required her lawyer, a doctor, and several carabinieri to carry her out. As soon as she reached the stairs outside the building, Rosina uttered a wild scream, began foaming at the mouth, and struggled to free herself. Not being able to speak at all, her talking hands described a beard, indicating that she wanted to see Tullio. At that moment, Tullio, still staring fixedly, appeared between two carabinieri who were almost carrying him down the stairs. Rosina threw herself on him, embracing and kissing him and shouting ferociously each time the carabinieri almost succeeded in disengaging her. The crowd, enlarged by people indoors who rushed out to see the commotion, began pushing to get a better view. The carabinieri had to struggle mightily to get Rosina out, all of them slipping on the wet sidewalk and roadway. She tore their clothes and beat her head violently against the carriage door after they had finally wrestled her inside. Police reinforcements were meanwhile called in to control the crowd which was rapidly massing despite the downpour.

Linda, still in a holding room inside the Palace of Justice, had seen the look on the face of the attorney Cavaglià when he came to tell her the verdict, but she insisted on hearing the words. "Tell me it's not true! Tell me it's not true!" she shouted, and fell unconscious into Berenini's arms. During the endless hour between the verdict and the sentencing, Linda fainted again and, when revived, beat the wall with her fist, calling for Ninetto and Maria. One of the attending doctors finally gave her ether. Four of her lawyers carried her unconscious to the carriage that took her to prison. To fool the crowds that waited along the way, a decoy carriage was sent out ahead, surrounded by a showy phalanx of carabinieri on bicycles.

The Murri lawyers spent a good deal of time summoning the courage to bring the bad news to the Murri villa. Finally, Guglielmo Ferrero and the Murri's friend Fabio Vitali went to the villa and gave the hateful verdict to Professor Murri, Giannina, and the professor's sister, Tullia. There followed a scene of desperate crying, which was begun afresh an hour later when the defender Teobaldo Calissano arrived with news of the sentences and of the stunned condition of Linda and Tullio. "A curse has fallen on my house!" the professor was quoted as saying.[7] Others reported only uncontrollable crying, followed by deep torpor and stupified silence. Even the prosecutors and anti-Murri journalists had believed that Linda and Secchi, possibly even Rosina, would be absolved, and that Tullio's guilt would be mitigated by a finding of mental abnormality. None had cared enough about Naldi to speculate on his fate. However, although few had expected the full severity of the law to fall upon the Murris, many felt that they deserved exactly the verdict they received. "Public opinion, in Turin as in Piedmont as in all of Italy, was and is, for the overwhelming majority, against the defendants, including Linda Murri, in fact, especially Linda Murri," wrote Bianchi in *Corriere della Sera*.[8] The press joined the people in reacting to the judgment with approval.[9] In Bologna, all the major newspapers ran special editions. *L'Avvenire d'Italia,* always anti-Murri, wrote, "The door that closes behind Linda Murri and her accomplices shows to all the civilized world that in Italy there is still justice." The director of *La Gazzetta dell'Emilia,* Ettore Gentile, intensified the publicity about a reputed third accomplice—he asserted that the trial had produced even more indications that Tullio and Naldi were not the sole killers. Gentile readily shared his private opinion that there had been incestuous relations within the Murri family.[10]

Like the other defendants, Linda had written a memoriale while in prison, a narrative to the istruttore judge giving her version of conditions or events that she felt had a bearing on the murder. Linda's memoriale filled five hundred pages. She had somehow managed to give it to a professional romance writer who polished the story. Her *Memorie di Linda Murri* was published less than two weeks after the trial, in thirty chapters, and was, of course, aimed at procuring a sentence reversal in the still-to-come appeals trial. The book described Linda's physical mistreatment by her mother, her disappointment on first seeing her husband's deteriorating "palace" in Cavarzere, and her affair with Secchi. She claimed to believe that after he was arrested, Secchi betrayed her by agreeing with Tisa's testimony. It would appear to any observer of the trial that Secchi insisted on Linda's innocence to the end, to the detriment of his own case. The only possible way he might have betrayed Linda was in directing the authorities to read her letters—the ones she had the forethought to destroy—which might have shown her guilt. Nevertheless, in the memoriale, Linda cast herself as the victim of Secchi, whose "incredible behavior" before the justices finished the breaking of her frangible heart. "When I cry, cry, cry, it is not because I still love him. Oh no! I don't love him. But I will weep into eternity for my shattered dream, so vilely betrayed. I touched heaven with my illusions and hell with the reality."[11] As might be expected, Linda wrote page after page of lyrical effusions about her father—his infinite rectitude, his exquisite nobility. She revealed her preference for Ninetto, "small, sickly, all finesse and sensitivity like the Murris" and her bias against little Maria, who "resembles her father in her aristocratic imperiousness." Bonmartini had noted her favoritism in his diary.

Linda was not alone in publishing her memoirs. Several of the lawyers on one side or the other published their summations to the jury—a common practice by lawyers, who sometimes sent a printed version of their pleadings to the newspapers to avoid journalistic errors in the reporting. People connected to the case in some way also wrote books explaining why one or more of the defendants should have been absolved. Even the clerk of court Ettore Landuzzi wrote a book about the istruttoria and trial.[12]

Appeals could be made only against legal and procedural error. In April 1906, eight months after the first judgment, the Court of Cassation in Rome heard the collective appeal of the five defendants. For once, the fate of the famous misdoers was not closely attended, for all over Italy people were riveted by news of the eruption of Mount Vesuvius. At just the time of the appellate trial, five hundred deaths were confirmed in southern Italy, followed at once by bulletins of the San Francisco earthquake that killed a thousand.[13] With less fanfare than usual, then, the defense lawyers gathered at the Palace of Justice, where clerks were making the transition to fountain pens and the defendants were making the transition from celebrity to obscurity.

The defense argument, that the lower court had made seventeen errors, was for the most part dismissed outright.[14] All the verdicts and sentences of the assize court were confirmed except for Bonetti's, whose sentence would be reviewed.[15] However, Rosina did not long remain in regular prison. Visited by Ugo Lombroso, son of the famous criminologist Cesare, Rosina attacked him, shouting "Nino! Nino!" She was taken almost at once to a prison mental institution, San Salvario, in Turin. When her case was reviewed, she refused to appear; the sentence of seven and a half years was allowed to stand.[16] The involvement of the Lombrosos in the Murri trial was not coincidental; Cesare Lombroso's daughter Gina was married to the Murri consultant Guglielmo Ferrero.[17]

The others were of course bitterly disappointed in the appellate ruling.[18] The ordeal was repeated of bringing the news to the Murri villa. Professor Murri faced the press with grim self-control, while Giannina sat white and mute. The doctor expressed thanks for the many letters of condolence he was receiving and complained that the authorities would not allow his wife to visit their children. His voice did not tremble; but the veins pulsated in his haggard face. The drama, wrote the newspapers, was finished.[19]

Secchi embraced one of his lawyers before being taken off to Conversano prison near Bari, in southern Italy. "Who knows if we will ever see each other again?" he said with tears in his eyes.[20] Tullio was sent to the Italian Riviera near Genoa, to the prison of Oneglia. His cell, number 112, was over a courtyard where an armed guard was stationed night and day. Tullio could not see the courtyard, as the cell had only a tiny window near the ceiling. The cells on either side of him were occupied by rotating live-in guards, since Tullio was to spend ten years in *segregazione cellulare,* without contact with other prisoners. He asked to be allowed to work. An instructor, himself a prisoner, was allowed into the cell for five minutes to leave materials and demonstrate the handling of a needle. Tullio was set to patching *berretti,* for which the prison pay was twenty-five centesimi a day. Prisons received contracts for such work, a great many from the fashion industry. The inmates typically made buttons, clasps, collars, and cuffs.[21] In addition to working, Tullio was allowed to read the doctrinal books in the prison library, which apparently had the hoped-for corrective effect. He became religious.[22]

As for Linda, she was never taken off to prison. Her prayers were answered immediately, since they were addressed not only to heaven but to the highest officials of government. One month after the appeals trial, Linda Murri was free, having been granted a commutation of her sentence on the grounds of her poor health. Professor Murri had appealed to Sidney Sonnino during the statesman's first, brief tenure as prime minister (February to May 1906); Sonnino asked his own appointee, the minister of justice, to allow the commutation. The king, remembering Murri's solicitude toward the queen mother, of course approved the action. Linda left the detention facility and was taken by carriage through the spacious streets of Turin, able for the first time to notice the modern glass buildings so different from the quaint warrens of Bologna, the beggars, the promenades, the Parisian loveliness of a place she had learned to dread and revile. At the train station she was met by members of the Lombroso family, some of her lawyers, her mother, and reporters from all over Italy who jostled one another on the station platform. Linda kissed her mother again and again, repeating, "Poor Mamma! Tonight you will sleep, poor Mamma!" perhaps forgetting that Giannina still had another cause for anxiety that would keep her awake for many more years. A newspaper in Rome reported that the most Professor Murri could do for Tullio was to have him transferred to the prison in Bologna, an event that was noted in the Bologna papers; however, the proceedings of the court do not show any such transfer out of Oneglia's distant hell.[23]

Linda Murri's release was bitterly denounced by most newspapers, but it at least gave them an opportunity to revisit the possibility of there having been a third accomplice in the Bonmartini murder.[24] Throughout the months following the final judgment, interviews would appear, supposedly sent from abroad, with individuals who had been approached by Naldi but who, instead of participating in the crime, fled the country. One of Naldi's attorneys, Bernasconi, was repeatedly questioned by journalists and stated each time that he was convinced Naldi knew nothing of a third accomplice.[25]

Naldi went off to prison in Volterra with the same air of indifference he had shown throughout the trial; but after eight months of seclusion, he suddenly demanded to see the director of the prison, saying he had important revelations to present.[26] "Linda receives a commutation, and the Murris have completely abandoned me," he is reported to have said. "I am more disgraced than the guilty ones; therefore I see no other way except to tell the complete truth."[27] According to newspapers, Naldi now claimed that he was originally hired by the Murris not to kill Bonmartini but merely to help dispose of the body by cutting it up. The assassination was carried out by Tullio and two other accomplices, including a blond man called "Eyes" Antonio, who had long ago fled to America. According to *La Tribuna* of Rome, Naldi further stated that he had not gone to Florence the night of the murder but in fact remained in Bologna, leaving directly for Livorno. A "false Naldi" had registered at Florence's Hotel de Russie, a man made up to look like him.[28] Given Naldi's injured eye, the makeup would have had to be remarkable.

Whether Naldi made all these assertions is doubtful, since exactly what he said in his new deposition was kept secret; but in April 1908, nearly three years after the murder trial in Turin, Naldi was again brought into court to make his accusations in public regarding the unindicted accomplices. The family of Antonio Occhi—"Eyes" Antonio—had brought defamation suits against *Corriere d'Italia* and *La Tribuna,* two Roman newspapers that named Occhi in their reports of Naldi's purported deposition. Naldi was transported to Rome from Volterra. Before he entered the courtroom, the racket of irons was heard on the stone floor outside the door, loud as artillery. Naldi was led to the bar in chains, past the suited lawyers and the comfortably seated ladies in their hats who had come to watch the never-ending show.

Convicts were given discarded clothes in place of a prison uni-
form. Naldi was wearing his torn prison shirt with the number 2192
printed on the back. He had been summoned by the defense lawyers
representing the newspaper owners; but when he came in, he had no
idea what the trial concerned or why he was being called. It is dis-
maying to see a man led by a chain leash shuffle across a room, the
dragging iron making its unmistakable shrill clatter. Even though the
chains were soon removed, people continued to stare at the convicted murderer in the smelly, misshapen shoes. Naldi was dirty,
unshaven, and a little weak from hunger; since he was being transported, he had not received even the minimum ration doled out to
indigent prisoners and had not eaten since the morning of the previous day. While he stood in the aisle, compulsively biting his lip, a
collection plate was passed to provide him with a meal. Meanwhile,
the president had begun the questioning.

In a strong voice, Naldi confirmed his statements that Occhi had
been present in the Bonmartini apartment at the time of the murder,
but in another room. Naldi was coming forward with this accusation
now, he said, because he felt it was unfair that Tullio bore the blame
for the crime, "though I know that he is innocent." At this statement,
the courtroom stirred. "My conviction was just," Naldi continued. "I
was guilty of helping to plan the murder. But people who were even
more involved in the killing than I was were allowed to escape disgrace."[29] In his latest memoriale, the president pointed out, Naldi
said that Professor Murri had provided the money for Occhi to emi-
grate to America, while Naldi himself had been abandoned. Naldi
now admitted that this part of the memoriale was false—he did not
know how Occhi received the money that allowed him to escape. He
repeated that Occhi had not actually attacked Bonmartini physically.
But he stuck to his claim that Occhi had been enlisted to help in the
ambush in return for a share of whatever the killers could steal in the
Bonmartini house.

At this point, to Naldi's utter astonishment, Occhi's lawyer called
in his client, whom everyone had assumed was still in America.

Antonio Occhi, his collar high and his hair keenly parted in the center, walked in from the double doors behind Naldi, his gleaming shoes cracking smartly against the floor that had been scraped by Naldi's chains a few minutes earlier. Like many of those who lived in America and then came back, Occhi could be easily identified as a returned emigrant by the gold teeth scattered across his smile. Unsmiling now and staring down at Naldi, he folded his arms across his chest and cocked his head to one side. Naldi looked up from the witness chair as if confronted by an apparition.

"You heard what Naldi said about you?" asked the president.

"Unfortunately, yes," replied Occhi, without turning around. "You're accusing me of killing somebody for the Murris' money?" he shouted at Naldi. "I'll take a crap on the Murris' money!"

"Watch your language and show some respect for this tribunal or I'll put you out of here!" said the president. "You think you're in a gambling den?"

"You don't know anything about the murder?" Naldi asked him earnestly.

"Nothing!"

"Really nothing?"

"Nothing!" repeated Occhi.

"You never spoke to me about Count Bonmartini?" Occhi swept his shiny head slowly and resolutely from side to side.

"Well then," said Naldi, "I take back everything I said. It's all lies."

"Explain, then, why you accused Occhi in the first place?" demanded the president. Naldi hung his head, shrugged his shoulders, and was silent. Some questions followed as to whether Occhi had ever talked of participating in the crime or whether he even knew Bonmartini. When the plaintiff's attorney persisted in linking him to the conspirators, Occhi threatened the lawyer: "Listen, you, I'm not Bonmartini! I've got two strong fists, and I know how to use them when anybody fools with me!"

In the course of the defamation trial, it came out that Occhi's father had long intended to send his son to America to get him away from the bad company he was keeping at the Caffè del Corso, and that his leaving right after the murder of Bonmartini was no more than a coincidence. In fact, Occhi had returned to Bologna while the trial in Turin was taking place. The only thing that could be proved against Occhi was that he thought a great deal of himself and had bad courtroom manners. *Corriere d'Italia* was found guilty of libel, its director sentenced to ten months of prison and a fine.[30] So pleased was Occhi with the outcome of the trial that, like the journalists and lawyers on both sides, he made a donation toward Naldi's dinner, remarking with a snicker, "He doesn't deserve it, but here you are . . ."

Naldi, meanwhile, had been taken to a side room where he slumped on a table and gave in to a paroxysm of crying. Between sobs that almost choked him, he lamented that even after creating so much commotion, he still had not been able to tell the truth. The guards tried to comfort him, but only slowly did he calm down. Finally, he ate the sandwich they had fetched for him from a nearby tavern.

"Those of us who have some experience with inmates see this sort of thing," the pubblico ministero told a reporter.[31] "In solitary confinement, segregated from other prisoners, they become obsessive. Some of them will even commit a crime in order to get back into court, if only for a few minutes, to be in the middle of life." The new development in the case had Naldi again spread over the front page of every major newspaper in the country. Naldi's penitentiary was a Renaissance fortress that stood, stone and stark, at the edge of towering cliffs on Volterra Hill southeast of Pisa, built at a time when inaccessibility was an advantage. Two other inmates in Volterra confessed to imaginary crimes so as to interrupt the insufferable pain of isolation, even if only to be brought out for interrogation.[32] Nonetheless, one of the attorneys for the publishers gave credence to Naldi's charges. It was clear, he said in an interview, that Naldi wasn't sure exactly what part Occhi had in the crime, but his statements had been made with great conviction, whereas in his retraction, he seemed to be merely giving up, despairing because he could not prove his suspicions.[33]

Naldi's testimony continued to occupy the newspapers long after Naldi himself had re-vanished into prison. According to the press, he wrote four more letters to the director of the penitentiary giving new versions of the crime, accusing first one accomplice, then another, including a blond man—the noted *biondino* who had occupied the police during the investigation—and one whom the newspapers carefully identified only as "an intimate of the Murri house." In one letter, Naldi averred that Rosina had been his lover, not Tullio's, and that they had carried out the murder together. Some people dismissed reports of these bizarre letters, saying that they had been invented by reporters to keep the story alive. By this time, Naldi had been isolated from other prisoners for three years in a cell as cold as Lapland, not permitted to work or exercise, although the head of the prison had provided him with some edifying reading. His letters to investigating officials, according to the prison authorities, were written with such reasonableness and fine form that the officials felt constrained at first to take them seriously.[34] Eventually, the authorities decided that Naldi had either become unhinged or was faking insanity in order to be transferred to the penal insane asylum, where inmates supposed that conditions were better.

Naldi had eaten well, for a change, the April day in 1908 when he received news of his father's death, since the prison distributed an Easter meal to the inmates. Only a week had passed since the debacle of the Occhi trial. Naldi's father Silvio had worked for the railroad, then had been the prefect of a commune, and then a teacher for the Collegio Ungarelli. He resigned that post and taught elementary school. Apparently he was an educated man who alternated between professional positions, laborer's work, and joblessness. He had three sons by his first wife: Naldi, a son who committed suicide, and another who followed his father into railroad work. By his second wife he had three daughters, all grown or nearly so by the time of Naldi's tragedy. None of the family would have anything to do with Naldi, either before or after the crime; his aunt, a seamstress who had once worked for the Murris, was his sole connection to the world. How Naldi received the news of his father's death was not reported.[35] After his last court appearance in 1908, his only contact with the world outside of prison was occasioned by a terrible catastrophe—an earthquake followed by a tidal wave that struck southern Italy and Sicily at the end of that year, killing 150,000 and causing Naldi's prison to take in injured refugees.

According to many reports, Naldi died in prison. In fact, he died only as a public figure. Both he and Tullio were let go in 1919, after each had served seventeen years of their thirty-year sentences.[36] Naldi was released in Civitavecchia, near Rome, lived a while in Benevento, and finally settled in the mountainous San Bartolomeo in Galdo, near Foggia. In that poorest of poor southern regions, he practiced medicine at last for several decades, asking little of his patients and giving much. Naldi died in 1958 at the age of eighty-four. According to a writer visiting the area in the 1970s, people remembered him with respect. Even citizens for whom the past was a vague, undifferentiated view from the mountaintop of old age could still clearly recall the generosity and kindness of *Dottore* Pio Naldi.[37]

Rosina completed her term in the prison insane asylum. Staffed by nuns, the mental hospital enveloped the patients in an atmosphere of want and benevolence. In general, women were treated leniently in the Italian criminal process; they were much more likely than men to receive light sentences, and the institutions housing them were less cruel. A compassionate woman who insisted on remaining anonymous provided money to the Turin institution so that Rosina would be adequately fed. Rosina was released on October 17, 1908, after a total imprisonment of six years. She embraced the nuns and thanked them for their care. Then, carrying all her belongings in a cardboard box, she left with her cousin for Bologna, where she happily and noisily changed trains for Fontanelice.[38] At some point, however, she was returned to Turin, to the civil insane asylum where she died in 1919, at age fifty-two.[39] The same writer who dramatized Linda Murri's memorie also wrote a book about Rosina Bonetti, purportedly based on interviews she gave in prison.[40] Rosina was the model for the protagonist in Tullio's novel *Romagnola* (Roman Girl), written while he was still incarcerated and published at his own expense. She died just as Tullio was released. Grieving, he wrote to a friend:

> *The more time passes, the more my heart is full of that poor thing, who was loved by no one on this earth except me. I would have to tell you a thousand intimate incidents to convey the real measure of the poor girl's infinite gentleness. Nothing ever made her give up on me—neither my young escapades during eight years of flirting, nor the unfolding of the trial and its hazards, which she willingly and courageously bore so as not to betray me—nor the seventeen years of not seeing me, which she could have endured if it had been thirty years, and still it wouldn't have weakened her feeling for me.*[41]

Secchi did not survive prison. For the first years, his cellular segregation appears not to have been strict. Isolation was a most expensive way of holding prisoners, and many institutions simply could not afford to execute the court's order. One inmate reported having learned a little German from the doctor.[42] Secchi spent many hours reading and writing. According to the newspapers, he once received permission from the inspector general of prisons to have, at his own expense, a liter of milk each day as part of a dietary experiment, but that report is hardly credible, considering the regime of filth and privation that prevailed in all the prisons.[43] In the memoir that Tullio left unpublished for his daughter, he accused Secchi of being the instigator of the murder. Secchi's own last words about the trial, carried out of the prison by an inmate who was released, were that he had been the victim of Tisa's furious jealousy and his own involvement in a hellish drama that had destroyed him. Sentenced to ten years, he died after four in the Conversano penitentiary, in 1910, at the age of fifty-eight, of pneumonia. To the Conversano hospital he left his many surgical instruments and money to set up a room in his memory.[44]

* * *

For a time after her release, Linda withdrew to the family's villa in Porto San Giorgio, the town that connects her father's hometown of Fermo to the sea—seventeen kilometers from Bologna. There she followed her lifelong interest in spiritualism, holding seances to conjure up the spirit of Bonmartini, who was invited, for once, to appear before her friends and give a true account of how he happened to be in the afterworld.[45] Eventually, Linda moved to Rome with the children and her second husband, the children's tutor, Professor Francesco Egidi, a man somewhat younger than she. Egidi was interested in government and was one of those who tried to induce his father-in-law to get into politics.[46] The marriage, however, did not last. Since Linda insisted on being called "the widow Bonmartini" for the rest of her life, she became separated from Cesco the Second while retaining the name of Cesco the First.

Linda's parents did not move with her to Rome. For a long time relations remained warm between Linda and her father, but the mutual obsession between them broke down in the years following the trial. In 1919, he wrote her a long letter describing a trip to Fiume. His acquaintance Gabriele D'Annunzio, the famous poet and arch-adventurer, had just seized the port in defiance of the Allies, who had awarded it to the new state of Yugoslavia. Murri went at the invitation of a colonel to one of the incessant celebrations D'Annunzio held during the year when he remained dictator of the city. *"Though I was reluctant on account of my youth and girlish timidity, I went,"* wrote Professor Murri. D'Annunzio was by this time bald, one-eyed, and nearly ridiculous. Murri had a long chat with him about their mutual friend, the actress Eleonora Duse, whom both had lost track of. Murri saw Linda's son Ninetto, a flyer who had fought in the Great War. Though Professor Murri disdained war, he was proud of his "heroic" grandson. There is no mention in the extant letters of his granddaughter Maria.[47] A few years later, Murri congratulates Linda heartily on her new work, writing articles on parapsychology for a Rome newspaper, *Il Giornale d'Italia,* under the pseudonym "Anhelus." *"I don't know how to express the happiness you have given me,"* he writes of this latest accomplishment. But the old, frantic edge is gone, and the letter is that of a normal father with a fond interest in his grown daughter. In another letter, he seems happy enough to let her have her faith in "the other world," though he cannot share it. *"Why don't I, too, fear the hereafter?"* he asks rhetorically. *"Because my conscience, that internal witness, tells me that in life I haven't done anything that deserves punishment."*

Not anything? Not a single instance of medical negligence? Not one patient overcharged? What about his mess of a family? Who was responsible for that? What was his guilt in Bonmartini's murder? Did he actively foment it, help to plan it, or merely allow the plan to proceed by intentionally ignoring it? His conscience was a cooperative witness that could be counted on to forget all sins the longer he lived, and to erase any troublesome smudges before it was time to submit a final accounting.

Murri remarks on the penetrating thought exhibited in Linda's writing. She is, he informs her, *"a real miracle in a feminine body, which is so malajusted to scientific meditation."* But this is only an afterthought, for he has already shifted the discussion to Tullio, who has become outspokenly religious, hates science, and also believes in spirits. *"He exceeds everyone in faith,"* he writes, almost admiringly.[48] Unlike the old days, when he would have fulminated against his son's superstitions, he now finds Nino's faith in man's goodness something of a wonder and discusses him at length. Tullio has replaced Linda as the focus of his thoughts. He no longer discerns illnesses in his daughter that must be treated with homeopathic excesses of praise.

Linda, whose frail health had been the excuse for a murder and a commutation, lived to be eighty-six. Starting in 1938, she wrote four parapsychology books under her pseudonym.[49] If she had been "always clinging to life by a thread," as her lawyer described her chronic condition, the thread proved nearly indestructible. She died December 4, 1957, in Rome's Via Sistina. According to one writer, she was paralyzed the last seven years of her life.[50] Survivor of two marriages, a prison sentence, two world wars, and the never-ending battles she reported with her conscience, perhaps she expected through spiritualism to survive death; but as far as anyone could tell, she did not. One of the houses she built in San Giorgio served the Germans as an antiaircraft emplacement and was later donated by her son to the commune for use as an asylum. Ninetto, who loved aviation, designed a plane that could take off in snow. He put it at the service of Mussolini. Known as Count Giovanni Bonmartini, a valued flyer in the Italian air war, he participated in the last campaign against the Russians in World War II. Maria Augusta Bonmartini married Professor Sabato Visco; both she and her brother lived in Rome.

As early as 1908, rumors emerged that Tullio had gone mad in his solitary cell in Oneglia. Two years later, the rumors were being reported almost daily in the newspapers. Tullio had by then spent three years in solitary confinement, in a ten- by four-foot cell designed to remove him from even the echo of a human voice. Once a day a transom in the door opened and a guard left his daily ration of bread. Tullio placed his waste vessel in an open hole in the wall, where it was removed from the other side. He was never allowed in the open air. Though it was reported that his father appealed to an ex–cabinet minister, he was unable to find out anything about Tullio's condition. Professor Murri, according to Tullio, then wrote to his son:

> I can do nothing for you, my poor Nino, nothing! But if you
> have not lost your mind, as they say you have, if you still have
> your reason, know that your father, not being able to see you, came
> to Oneglia to at least see the wall that shuts you in; and I kissed it
> as if the stone held something of you within it—and for love of
> you, I managed to resist the desperate impulse to bash my head
> against it.[51]

Prisoners were allowed to receive letters from their families only three times a year. The size of the paper and number of lines were strictly limited, so that even one excess word could result in a letter being withheld, without notice to either the inmate or the family. The contents of the letters were also censored. Did Professor Murri write this letter, or was it composed by Tullio after his release, a kind of daydream of what he would have liked his father to write? Since when was Professor Murri unable to get help from his highly placed friends when it was a matter of a small favor—getting information about Tullio's condition? The letter emerged only after Tullio came out of prison: he read it aloud to audiences who came to hear him speak on prison reform. Professor Murri never sent the letter to the newspapers, as was his wont whenever he sought to publicize what he considered unjust treatment by the authorities.

Professor Murri visited Tullio in Oneglia once every six months, as allowed by law. The visits of family members to prisoners were supposed to last no longer than one-half hour. The inmate was separated from his loved one by an iron grate. According to Tullio, if the conversation referred in any way to the conditions under which the inmate lived, the visit was terminated at once by the guard assigned to listen in, for even the prisoner's confessions to a priest were heard in the presence of the head guard. Whether or not all of these restrictions were regularly applied, or were ever applied in Tullio's case—a famous man visited by a famous father—is impossible to know.

Petitions asking for clemency for Tullio poured into the Ministry of Grace and Justice for years after his trial. Thousands of signatures were collected, including many from foreign dignitaries.[52] Polls taken by La Stampa, a generally anti-Murri paper, formed a kind of national plebiscite on Tullio's fate, a plebiscite that was repeated again and again. He was considered by prison authorities to be an ideal—almost saintly—prisoner. Finally, in 1919, Tullio was released. Perhaps out of a sense of fairness, Naldi was also included in the commutation, though not because of petitions for his sake. Tullio

thus emerged from prison at the age of forty-five, bald, his splen
teeth rotted by neglect and bad diet, but again a public figure.

He dedicated his free years to the cause of prison reform.[53] Lecturing in public, he could demonstrate a quite balanced perspective
about prison life. When men on a jury send someone off to twenty,
thirty years in prison, said Tullio, they imagine that living conditions
will be regulated by carefully applied, humane laws, so that a prison
term will be like an unpleasant but necessary medicine that cures the
delinquent. "However," he said, "everyone knows that prisons are
universities of crime." In truth, the convicted person disappears into
a tomb where no one knows what happens to him after the end of his
trial. He is abandoned to the caprice of a prison director who may be
well meaning and progressive or a brutal monster; either way, there
is no appeal against the director's absolute and secret power. The
guards are not degenerates who torture inmates for entertainment;
they are men like any others—some good, some bad. The horrors of
prison are often real and verifiable, Tullio said. But suffering cold and
chronic hunger or being covered with insects is nothing compared to
what he called, with his characteristic vocabulary, the "moral torture," "the violence" committed against the prisoner's will by forcing
him to depend on the whim of someone else to sleep, wake up, or
have a breath of fresh air.[54]

According to his autobiographical novel *Galera* (Prison), Tullio's
incarceration constituted seventeen years of ghastly misery, not only
because of his own privations but because of the sufferings of other
inmates that he witnessed. It was very easy for a prison authority to
torture a prisoner, if he had a mind to, by the smallest increase in the
severity of the rules. "To take away a privilege from someone who
has many disturbs him very little," wrote Tullio, "but to take away a
little thing from someone who has very little to start with means
everything." To take away a prisoner's shoes, for example, or his
jacket, to delay his letters, order that his window remain open in
winter, cut by two thirds the normal daily food ration of a pound of
bread and a cup of thin soup or chickpeas, deprive him of hygienic

paper (or the rags that were often used before toilets or toilet paper were considered necessities)—these were bitter dispossessions. If a prisoner dared to complain about verminous bread or bugs in his soup, he might be accused of planting the insects; then he could be punished by not being fed for two days of each week for several weeks. Or he might be punished for any real or imputed transgression without any declaration of punitive measures—by having his toilet vessel vanish, coincidentally, at the same time that a laxative was put into his food, forcing the miserable wretch to use his soup bowl for a chamber pot, to clean it as well as he could with spit, and to use it again for his soup or go without.[55] Such cruelties were more easily inflicted on those in solitary confinement. When the guards occasionally beat up a recalcitrant prisoner so that he needed treatment, there was no hope of a doctor intervening and complaining to higher authorities: the prison doctor held his position by the sufferance of local administrators and might be on the side of the prison director.

Being released from solitary also held dangers. The guards in Italian prisons were recruited largely from military veterans, but fellow inmates were more hardened veterans of ruffian squads—the hosts of garbage-strewn alleys throughout the peninsula. Living with them meant being side by side with feral animals day after day and night after night. Aside from the torments of the communal life of strangers, there were scurvy and typhus, the plagues of prisons. Impetigo, trench mouth, tuberculosis, influenza, and a hundred other mephitic contagions were epidemic in the overcrowded dormitories. A prison infirmary was no place for a sick person. There the foul mattresses made of corn shucks were never changed, though they had received the purulence, incontinence, and retching of hundreds of diseased men. The beds stank, Tullio wrote, a thousand times worse than dung.

In the general prison population, an inmate might be bullied by the *camorriste* who ran the day-to-day operations of every Italian prison. He had to watch out for the prisoner-spies who had been promised parole in return for information. He could suffer homo-sexual rape which, then and now, was not at all unusual in jails and, if his sentence was long, he was almost certain to be drawn into volun-tary liaisons. Among the prison thug gangs, the Neopolitans hated men from the north; Sicilians fought with Puglians; the murderers despised thieves who, being the most numerous of the prison popu-lation, found furtive, vicious ways to protect themselves. According to Tullio, murderers like himself caused the least trouble to the guards and fellow inmates: they had killed only once, usually, and were not career criminals who came from the underworld and went back to it in between jail sentences. For all convicts, murderers in-cluded, Tullio advocated time off for good behavior for, like the posi-tivists who had defended him, he thought punishment should be adjusted to the worth or worthlessness of the criminal and not the heinousness of the crime. If, in the inhuman conditions of a prison, a man could keep his sanity and control his rage for even a few years, that was proof that he had mastered his impulses and could be trusted to return to society. Tullio thought the guillotine was more merciful than life imprisonment with no possibility of release. Cer-tainly the guillotine was a correctional method that had never been known to fail in preventing a return to criminal habits; but Italy had outlawed capital punishment in 1878, except for treason.[56]

Tullio was careful in all his writings to point out that not all guards or prison directors, not all the ministers of justice, were bad people, but that the occasional sadist could cause untold suffering. There seemed to be little difference in civility between the keepers and the kept, except that the keepers were not as hardened. He was annoyed that the Sacco-Vanzetti case in the United States had gar-nered publicity and aroused so much sympathy in Italy for men who, for all anyone knew, might actually be guilty, whereas the cases he described in *Galera* had not resulted in one single investigation or re-trial, even when prison authorities confirmed that the subjects had been victimized or wrongly convicted and were suffering terribly.[57] Tullio had an idealized conception of prisons in the United States, where he thought an enlightened, more compassionate penal system was in force. In truth, American prisons were clement in theory; but, as in Italian jails, rules were applied arbitrarily. Conditions varied from state to state, but nowhere were they likely to be as forbearing as Tullio believed.

Tullio put his greatest efforts toward the abolition of cellular segregation. Total isolation originated in the United States as a humane practice and was then taken up by French prisons. Both countries had abandoned the practice by the twentieth century because an alarming number of prisoners receiving the humane special treatment seemed prompted to kill themselves. But in Italy, isolating new offenders at the beginning of their terms was still the general rule. The policy had been instituted in 1889 to spare them the gang rape and homosexual promiscuity that seemed to be the inevitable lot of incoming convicts, especially the youngest ones. Though the authorities rarely admitted it publicly, the seclusion of prisoners was also intended to thwart the crime organizations that had established de facto control of the prisons and easily recruited new inmates desperate for protection.

For many men, strict isolation, especially if it was imposed year after year, gradually removed the membrane of consciousness between thoughts and external reality. The cloistered prisoner would hallucinate, occasionally at first, then perhaps more frequently. He might harmlessly retreat to a dream world, but more likely he would become enraged, reacting to imaginary attackers or otherwise behaving in some way that called for restraint. Then, according to Tullio, he might be chained hands and feet to an iron bed especially constructed with a hole in the bottom, so that he could be forced to remain immobile every hour of the day. The confinement could last for months, until his back turned into a festering ulcer swarming with vermin.

Galera received in excess of 150 favorable reviews in the Italian press within four years of its first printing. This was enormous public attention, more notice than any Italian book received during the period. Every major newspaper in Italy discussed the book, along with journals abroad. Twenty thousand copies of *Galera* were printed within a year of its publication in 1920—a very large number, considering the size of the country and the paucity of book readers. *Galera* was in the windows of all the bookstores in Italy for months. It was translated at once into French, Portuguese, and English and was to have many reprintings in subsequent years. Tullio became famous in Italy as a writer (though not as famous as he had been a generation before as a killer), and the Italian penal system became infamous. *Galera* described a prison worse than France's notorious Devil's Island.[58] How could that be in the country that had produced the greatest names in penal reform and humanism—Cesare Beccaria, Cesare Lombroso, and Benedetto Croce—the country that was among the first to abolish capital punishment?

A thundering controversy erupted in the newspapers over the conditions portrayed in the novel. Reporters interviewed justice officials and prison authorities and made their own investigations.[59] One could not help questioning whether the man who had insisted in a courtroom on Bonmartini's "brutality" had also magnified the brutality of a prison where for the first time in his life he had encountered true violence and privation. Tullio was a gifted dramatizer; of all his talents, none was more impressive than his ability to deliver wild exaggeration with the outrage, seriousness, and heartfelt dedication usually reserved for truth. His incessant lying, in fact, was mixed up with his irresistible urge to turn life into fiction. He, of course, steadfastly maintained that the misery described in *Galera* was only a tenth of the true horror; on occasion, he provided his critics with the names of inmates whose mistreatment had inspired the novel.

Did Tullio exaggerate in *Galera*? Unquestionably. But perhaps not with the virtuosity he demonstrated at his trial, which had been a mythomaniac's *tour de force*. Prison authorities argued that some of the conditions Tullio described were found only in very rare instances, and the minister of justice sued Tullio for defamation.[60] But nobody stated categorically that what Tullio described could never,

ever be found in an Italian jail. Beginning in 1903, a landmark year of penal reform, Italian penitentiaries were not supposed to punish refractory prisoners by keeping them in dark cells, straitjackets, or cellular segregation for long periods (unless the isolation had been specified in their court sentences, as was Tullio's). However, it was left up to individual prison directors to decide what was or was not a long period. In 1908, many years before the publication of *Galera, Corriere della Sera* investigated the penitentiaries and found that in some places inmates were being held in irons, despite the banning of such punishment by the director general of prisons.[61] Long before, Italy had officially prohibited the use of the chain gang, the club, whip, shackles, cat-o'-nine-tails, lash with knotted cords, and all the other instruments of corporal punishment that were still being used in 1903 in France, England, Scotland, Ireland, Hungary, the Netherlands, Denmark, and Norway.

Holding prisoners in solitary confinement for the first years of their sentence was, however, a practice written into the penal code which could be changed only by parliamentary legislation. Common sense indicated that being shut up for years hurt prisoners both physically and psychologically. Still, the authorities insisted that madness and suicide in the solitary cells were just as commonplace in the prison population at large. It was not until the publication of *Galera,* with its attendant publicity, that Italian law was changed in 1922 to outlaw routine solitary confinement. Mussolini, who had ignored Tullio's requests for commutation of his sentence, now praised him in a telegram for his humanitarian work. After Mussolini's March on Rome in October 1922, prisons, along with many other institutions, fell under the random and uneven authority of the fascists. In some prisons, the inmates were under the official control of fascist-appointed wardens and staff, and in addition were unofficially subjected to warring gangs, many of them anti-fascist, that now swelled the prison population and infused their own sort of mundane violence.[62]

In 1902, Tullio Murri left a world largely at peace; in 1919, he returned to a world of maimed veterans and war-shocked civilians, where the sweeping affliction of a Great War had passed, but chancres of revolution, uprisings, street battles, and localized barbarity were erupting everywhere in its wake. If he had sympathized with the hungry beggars in Italy when he went into prison, when he emerged, he discovered that whole populations were starving across the world: Viennese, Poles, Hungarians, Chinese, and Indians. In Russia, all along the length of the Volga, great companies of famished men, women, and children were photographed eating grass and dry weeds.[63] Just as Tullio was getting a chance to take a good look at the twentieth century, Winston Churchill was declaring it already a bitter disappointment, and anyone coming out of his prison sleep might have been inclined to agree.[64] The Europe Tullio kept in his memory when he went to prison had been mapped with great empires, bright with decorative rulers and titled courtiers; he came back to truculent republics with difficult names, to presidents, commissars, and first secretaries in khakis and caps.

In one decade, a decade in which Tullio never saw a single city street, the carriages and horses that had been part of civilization since the beginning of history had vanished, supplanted by automobiles. Water had been the principal means of transportation everywhere in the world, more important even than horses. That was all changed by the despotic hand of time. Icemen and water carriers were replaced by refrigeration and indoor plumbing; "runners" and scriveners by telephones and typewriters; charcoal shops by gas furnaces; and traders with dogcarts had been swept away by department stores with elevators and blond Germanic mannequins. Canals that had limmed Bologna and made the city a fetid swamp had been dredged; where ditches had held waving sedges, there were now gasoline stations and tall, commercial banks, although mosquitoes still owned Italy at night. Tullio's way to prison had taken him through streets where goatherds wandered through the arches with their flocks, stopping at each door to ask if any milk was wanted. The way back home was resplendent with electric signs and movie marquees on streets cramped by lumbering, horseless buses. Around Rimini, the railway banks had once blossomed with dwarf acacias, wild thyme, and poppies, with ponds all over. Now roads had been cut alongside the rail beds to accommodate the cars. Over larch forests powdered with hoarfrost, airplanes broke into the quiet, cold sky.

Dismayed and disoriented, Tullio moved in with his parents in the Murri villa and was cherished. His father, who in the bad old times had given Tullio an allowance of a thousand lire a year so that he could stay away from him, now financed a real estate project for his son and resented a separation of even one night.

Tullio's socialism, the sentimental politics of "a dilletante lawyer" with "a haphazard education," as he described his younger self, was all but dead in Italy. The weak-willed and disorganized parliamentary system was being trampled by fascism on the march. Professor Murri appears not to have been molested during the fascist years, though he had connections to both the political left and freemasonry, two of Il Duce's prime targets. In general, intellectuals like Professor Murri were tolerated and flattered, bought off rather than persecuted, with university chairs and government prizes. Abroad, the fascist regime was endorsed by Freud and George Bernard Shaw; at home, by Pirandello, Marconi, and—passively and mildly—Murri.

With his father's capital, Tullio purchased a large tract for a housing development in a suburb of Bologna, Castel San Pietro, an area that was now accessible by automobile and therefore suitable for building. He bought the land from a Signora Bonetti whom he married in 1920, the year after his release.[65] The surname written large on the marriage contract is startling. Could it be that Tullio married Rosina Bonetti after their release from prison? But no, this is Contessa Cornelia Bonetti, a well-off widow who bore Tullio a daughter he named Gianna Rosa, after two of the three women in his younger life. Notably, the baby was not Gianna Linda or Rosalinda. The little girl was the idol of both Professor Murri and Tullio, who fretted over her health and in letters to friends described her every indisposition, from teething to head colds. When she was sick, Tullio thought of taking her to the Riviera, just as his father had taken Linda on trips to restore her health.[66] Gianna Rosa became the Linda of their later days.

Tullio wrote constantly in the eleven years of his literary life, even while attending to his building project—two collections of stories, a drama in 10,000 verses (*L'Incantesimo*), and a comedy for the stage (*In Vandea*), three very long poems, including "Bononi," many articles on both literature and penal reform, and six novels: *Galera, Romagnola, Anna Korrova, La Vincitrice, Dopo la morte, Una pagina di follia e di lagrime.* The era of verse dramas was well past; the public was now smitten with free verse. Nevertheless, Tullio's plays were produced in thirty theaters in Italy. His books received lavish praise but, aside from his influence in bringing about prison reforms, his work left no lasting mark on Italian literature.[67] His style is polished and his novels are well written overall but sentimental, like characteristic European fiction of the late nineteenth century. His heroes are saintly and pathetic, his villains zealously vile. *Galera* and *Romagnola* were written in prison and published immediately upon his release in 1919. The latter story describes the travails of an orphan (Rosina Bonetti with another name) forced to live on the street and saved from a life of vice by a young man who falls in love with her. *Anna Korrova* provides a more interesting and ambivalent character, a woman who takes a lover because her good, scientist husband is not as intelligent or strong as she is. *Dopo la morte* was Tullio's second autobiographical novel, in which he expressed his recurring fantasy of vanishing into the countryside: in the book, a convict released after seventeen years goes to live in a distant community with a poor family and falls in love with a local woman.

The best assessment of Tullio's work was given by a very sympathetic critic who wrote that, artistically, Tullio was old-fashioned. While in prison, he had missed twenty years of his country's literary development, so that his writing oscillated between the neoromanticism of a Manzoni and the naturalism of a Zola (whom Tullio greatly admired.)[68] To be twenty years behind the times is hardly noticeable—

in most times. But Tullio was writing during the literary tidal wave of the 1920s. He was a contemporary not of Gustave Flaubert, Antonio Fogazzaro, and Edmondo De Amicis, whose writing had shaped his taste, but of T. S. Eliot, James Joyce, Franz Kafka, Luigi Pirandello, and most notably, Sigmund Freud—all those whose thinking marked a sharp divide between modernism and the old order.[69] The national preoccupation with war and its aftermath was yielding among intellectuals to an infatuation with futurism. His work had the bad luck to be washed away in a cultural revolution in which traditional idealism, rigid notions of good and bad, and melodramatic extremes of character were rejected and despised.

According to his letters—all beautifully written—Tullio had regular bouts of severe depression when "everything irritates me, fatigues me, and seems like hard work."[70] At such times, his wife wondered if he still loved her. Even his fervid passion for women, which prison had not extinguished, was finally gone. At such times, he was maudlin about the past that "burned still in the bitter embers of remorse." He became superstitious and laughed at himself, confessing in a letter to a friend that he avoided the numbers two and eleven and that he conversed with spirits—"I see you smiling," he added.[71] Moreover, he had become outspokenly religious. He played with his little daughter, collected stamps, and gained weight—he was 228 pounds when he died.

To the end, Tullio continued to play sly games with writers who were interested in revisiting the Bonmartini murder. For example, in an interview with *Il Piccolo della Sera* he said, "Few people care about finding out the truth when it contradicts the traditional version, especially when it involves a trial in which nobody told the truth and in which a man accused himself."[72] Young journalists, meeting the courteous and sincere advocate of prison reform, insisted that Tullio had been innocent and was condemned through a tangle of juridical error and poor legal representation. Some votaries said that Tullio had told them the name of the true killer but had sworn them to silence.[73] He developed a large correspondence with the families of prisoners who sought his help; they were never refused, and every letter was answered. He fantasized about leaving Bologna, often stating that he wanted "nothing more than peace;" but for the most part, he enjoyed his role as returned martyr.[74]

He had long ago been released from his terrifying obsession with Linda. In his writing he even inveighed against the granting of royal clemency to convicts because this forgiveness was selective. The king granted freedom to a few, he wrote, while many others who were more deserving of mercy were ignored. It was just this power of royal clemency, granted to the daughter of a prominent man, that had set his sister free.[75] After his release, neither he nor his parents ever considered moving to Rome to be with Linda, and he never mentioned her in his letters. The version of the crime that Tullio passed down to his daughter was that Bonmartini's murder was Linda's project; she instigated and sponsored it; he took the blame—despite being completely innocent—for the sake of his parents. Gianna Rosa, Tullio's daughter, knew of only one occasion when Tullio saw Linda after his release from prison. Linda was received coolly at the Villa Murri. Only her mother, the maligned Giannina, was affectionate toward her daughter, who by then—around 1928—was gray and withered. Gianna Rosa vividly remembered Linda having a sickly sweet voice that mewed and miaowed through the tense visit. She was like the witch in a fairy tale, trying to lure her hearers into captivity. However, Gianna Rosa paid Linda one bitter compliment: "As a mother," she wrote, "she was a thousand times better than mine."[76]

As Tullio's distance from prison increased, his depression worsened, and he began having a serious intestinal illness with unremitting pain and vomiting.[77] He died of cancer in 1930, at the age of fifty-six. He was by then wealthy in his own right, with a large suburban tract of houses and bank assets amounting to 400,000 lire. He had moved himself and his parents into a three-story villa with thirteen rooms, Costa Bruna, at his development in Castel San Pietro.[78] His parents had begun to get on his nerves, as in the old days, especially when they knew he was sick. "I am incapable of any work, and

I can't even show myself at home because of the pity I feel for the two old people who keep their eyes fixed on me, only on me." On the other hand, he wrote of sending his wife and daughter to the sea while staying home himself, "happy like San Lorenzo to keep company with my two old ones."[79] Aside from Gianna Rosa, no one grieved for Tullio more deeply than his father, who, having been separated from him by the granite walls of the prison and his own psychological partitions, had finally learned to love him.

Gianna Rosa Murri became a writer, a good writer, with a frank engaging style. In 2003, when she was past eighty, she published a memoir of the father whose death had shattered her childhood.[80] In the Murri villa she described, the entire family had lived on the first floor after Tullio returned from prison because his parents wanted him as near as possible every hour of the day. At 3:30 in the morning, Tullio rose, made coffee, and brought it to his father, whom he then shaved and helped to dress. He prepared a large breakfast for his father. At seven, he brought caffelatte to his mother, Giannina, who slept in a separate room with a maid, and then to his wife, Nelia, and finally to his daughter, Gianna Rosa, who slept with a nurse. Professor Murri saw patients in his upstairs office from ten to twelve, followed by a nap until three. Tullio then accompanied him on a long walk of several hours.

Remembering mealtimes, Gianna Rosa declared that it would be impossible to spend so much on food and yet eat worse than the Murris, unless one starved altogether. Every evening the same boiled meat and vegetables cooked to a gelatinous mass, followed by boiled eggs and fruit. After dinner, the professor received his old colleague Silvagni, white and wizened as Moses, along with young disciples who came to pay homage and entertain Murri with reports of interesting cases that had come to their attention. Severo Dalla was frequently in the house and enjoyed the prerogatives of a family member: he once spanked Gianna Rosa for drenching him with water. At night, Tullio helped his father get ready for bed. Only after everyone in the house was asleep did Tullio spread his papers on the dining room table and turn his prolific mind to his writing.

The household revolved around Professor Murri. According to Gianna Rosa, her grandmother Giannina was a bystander; no one took much account of her. Professor Murri even forbade his wife to exhibit a picture of her father, whom he disliked. Nonna Giannina was a good person, her granddaughter recalled, but superstitious and stubborn in the way of people who are not intelligent, clever, or worldly. Gianna Rosa held a grudge against both her grandparents for what she described as their cruelty to her father, Tullio, who in childhood was blamed for all of Linda's many misdeeds. When the sister and brother were growing up, the family held it as incontestable truth that Linda was perfect and Tullio was evil. According to Gianna Rosa, Professor Murri kept a photograph in his desk of his own mother in her funeral coffin. Believing that this first Teolinda Murri had been a saint, he apparently tried to recreate her through his daughter; he would never hear any criticism of the younger Teolinda. Gianna Rosa thus interprets the killing of Bonmartini as the climax in a lifelong series of events in which a blameless Tullio accepted Linda's punishment in order to appease his father.

In a letter addressed to his daughter, Tullio asserted that Linda and Secchi instigated the murder, which was carried out by someone named LaBella, Tisa's lover. Anyone who studied the exhaustive investigation of the trial would be compelled to dismiss this version of a crime that took place almost a generation before Gianna Rosa was born. Tullio Murri loved his wife although, according to their daughter, Nelia was shallow and egotistical. Professor Murri left Gianna Rosa an enormous inheritance, but during her minority it was squandered by Nelia, whose bulimic extravagance exceeded even the Murri riches. That charge is borne out by at least one incontrovertible document. In a notarial act of 1940, when Gianna Rosa was nineteen years old, Nelia borrowed 300,000 lire in her daughter's name, to be repaid by Gianna Rosa in three years with interest, using the girl's property as collateral.[81] Perhaps the most remarkable detail of the document is Nelia's attorney. She is represented in the contract by, of all people, Giuseppe Gottardi, Linda's old lawyer!

At Tullio's death, Professor Murri rewrote his own will, carefully dividing all his assets—including a great deal of property— between his daughter Linda and his granddaughter Gianna Rosa, also making generous provision for "good Nelia," Tullio's widow, and his "good friend, Severo Dalla," his executor. Besides having a free hand in the administration of Gianna Rosa's fortune during her minority, Nelia was to have an allowance of 3,000 lire monthly for the rest of her life. (Unharmed by her daughter's sturdy hatred, she inconsiderately lived to be ninety-seven.) For carrying out his duties as executor and "special mandatory" for Professor Murri, Dalla was given a pension of 8,000 lire a year, beginning in 1916. Professor Murri expressly stated that if either Linda or Gianna Rosa contested his will, the malcontent would forfeit her part to the other one.[82] Since Gianna Rosa was still a child, the warning would seem intended for Linda.

Professor Murri recovered his respected position. Beginning in 1908 there were movements to induce him to run for parliament, the last one in 1923, presumably by Giolittian liberals trying to offer their ineffectual alternative to Mussolini's government bloc. Five times Murri rejected their blandishments to enter government. He said he did not believe in joining any association—religious, social, or political—because he thought such organizations interfered with the dictates of one's own conscience.[83] In truth, it was no time for a socialist or a liberal careful of his pleasant life to get into politics: opposition candidates in the 1924 elections were attacked and tortured by fascist *squadristi,* and the socialist leader who denounced the fraudulent elections on the floor of parliament was murdered by Mussolini's henchmen.[84] Though Professor Murri's daughter and grandson were supporters of Il Duce, the old man kept his distance from the new government and from the corporate state. "The individual," he wrote, "is always the victim of what are called 'common interests.'" He seemed to remain a tacit social democrat even while social democracy retreated before the fascist surge. Mussolini was the New Man of Italy, new because he was turning the masses into the reactionary masses, in the socialist Togliatti's noted phrase. Enrico Ferri, leader of the socialist party since 1904 and Tullio's lawyer during the trial, became more and more disaffected as the socialist tide ebbed. He ended up in fascism, like many other unlikely adherents, as the Second World War drew closer. Professor Murri had supported Italy's intervention in World War I. But now he returned to his position against strident nationalism. He didn't care that his ideas were unpopular, since he had no use for public opinion—it could only interfere with his hearing the voice of "this internal witness," his ever-friendly conscience.[85]

There is a telling picture of Professor Murri, great with honors, sitting amid sixteen of his colleagues during some honorary celebration held for him the year after Tullio's death and the year before his own. In the center of the gray eminences, between the professor's knees, sits a smiling Gianna Rosa in ribbons and a party dress. It was no place for a child, but wherever the professor was, a place was found for her. He adored her as he had adored Linda, but he didn't live long enough to ruin her. At fifty he had been convinced that his prime was over. At sixty he was waiting for death. At eighty-three, he was surprised that people still invited him to speak at public functions—that they were not afraid that during his talk he would "fall over from advanced age."[86] He had a long time to enjoy being old. He died in 1932 at the age of ninety-one.

During the two years after Tullio's death, Murri's declining relations with Linda became bitter. Some cattle originally left to her were now reassigned to Gianna Rosa. But that was not all. In 1940, eight years after old Murri's death, Severo Dalla came forth with an even later will, handwritten by Professor Murri on March 13, 1932, three months after his codocil transferring the cattle to Gianna Rosa. In this will, Murri left Linda only the portion of his estate that he was required by law to assign to her. All the rest was to go to little Gianna Rosa, including the family villa in Bologna where Linda grew up and where she first met Secchi.[87] Professor Murri had loved Linda insanely. Yet when he died, he wanted her to have only the part of him that the law compelled him to give her. Severo, no longer blond but still slippery, had the last will and testament in his possession for eight years but allowed Linda to enjoy her more generous inheritance until something happened—a falling out? Linda's refusal to yield something he demanded?—after which he finally decided to enforce Professor Murri's surprising last wishes. Severo gained nothing by bringing the later will to light—or so it appears from the documents—except Linda's animosity.

By then, both Severo and Linda were themselves old people whose other enemies were dead or unremembered. Everything that could have been said about the Murri-Bonmartini case had been said; even the family's Alpine collection of newspaper clippings was yellowed and tiresome to peruse. Perhaps both Linda and Severo were ready for a fresh hatred, one that would not wear out for the rest of their long lives.

13. CODA

Knowing the unreliability of juries, people could not believe that twelve ordinary, exhausted men had remained clear-headed through a trial that was as long as a war and almost as incoherent. Some people wanted to see the death penalty reinstated so that Tullio and Naldi could qualify for it; others chewed at minor details of the complicated charges or argued that this or that defendant should have been exonerated.[1] Except for their lawyers, few were conflicted over the fate of Carlo Secchi and Pio Naldi, and Rosina Bonetti seemed almost as well off in the women's prison as out of it, once the Murris washed their fickle hands of her. But the cases of Tullio and Linda were examined and re-examined, as if the fascinating Murris had been condemned because the jury and the newspapers hated them, while the true culprits had somehow escaped. The public could not let them go.

But when all was said and unsaid, the jurors were right about everything. They had seen through the magma of lies and courtroom strategies in reaching the verdicts. They were not responsible for the sentences; the magistrates determined those. And they had nothing to do with Linda's commutation. By their verdicts, they showed that they thought all the defendants should be sent to hell, and in that, they were entirely correct.

* * *

Though the evidence against Linda was circumstantial, it was powerful taken all together. The case against Naldi was debatable, but given his long presence at the murder scene, he could not have been absolved. Objectively, all of the defendants were guilty, and others as well, who were never indicted. The question, therefore, that was really behind the weary debate was not whether the defendants had done what they were accused of, but why. Why had no fewer than five people yielded to such a drastic idea as homicide merely to get rid of an inconvenient husband and then carried it out with such clumsiness? The murder was reckless; that was the only word for it. Though Tullio's escape was not well planned, he might have gotten away if his father had not talked him into coming back to exculpate his sister. But even then, what sort of life in exile could he have hoped for? Rosina would have been without her Tullio. Naldi, we can be pretty sure, would not have received the five or six thousand lire Tullio promised him—the exact amount had not even been established between them. Secchi could have married a widowed Linda, it is true, but he would have lived under a cloud of suspicion from his colleagues—a cloud that covered Italy far beyond Bologna. Moreover, he was the one culprit whose conscience might have muttered piacular reproaches when he looked at the miserable Bonmartini children. Linda is the only conspirator who could have enjoyed life after the murder—as in fact she did. The killing was a weird act that could not be explained rationally. There must have been some information that never came to light, people reasoned, some key to the whole situation that the trial, with all its redundancy, had not exposed.

Rosina's involvement was simple to understand. As the jury acknowledged, she was a woman too damaged by life and too warped by her contact with the Murris to understand common morality. Early in their relationship, Tullio remarked in a letter that he hoped she was enjoying the good weather. She wrote back, *"I am in the house of a woman with five children, two who can't walk and a sick girl*

who does nothing but cry day and night. That's my diversion."[2] She was
the poor servant of poor people who had nothing to share with her
but a little food. The Murris were her first experience with what she
assumed was normal life, just as Rosina was Tullio's first encounter
with want. The Murris were unquestionable. They were the doctor
describing how to stay well, the lawyer explaining what was legal
and what was not, the countess showing the difference between acceptable and unacceptable conduct. Rosina wouldn't have minded if
the supercilious aristocrat Bonmartini died in any circumstances; he
and the children detested her. But more important, Tullio wanted
him dead. Whatever Tullio and the other Murris did was right.
Everything else might be disliked and distrusted.

Carlo Secchi, decent and passive, was too much of a spaniel to stand
up to the Murris or assert himself against Linda's manipulation. After
being separated from Linda when she was sixteen, he did not attempt to see her, as a stronger individual might have. He continued
to grovel at the shrine of Professor Murri, dedicating works to him
with panegyrics long after he had been dismissed as the great man's
favorite. By the time the crime was suggested to him, Secchi had
reached the point where weakness is as despicable as evil because it
allows evil to go forward. A man of character would have threatened
to warn Bonmartini about what was being planned for him, or, if all
threats failed, he would have gone to the police while Bonmartini
was still unharmed. Secchi did not stop the frightful plan at its incep-
tion because he could not bear Linda's scorn. His love for her was an
addiction from which he was helpless to free himself even after he
saw its deadly effects. Though Linda destroyed what he thought was
proof of his innocence and refused to look his way in court, he protected her to the last and remained enthralled even as they swept
him into the dirty kennel of prison. He deserved his years in jail.

* * *

Tisa may well have been in love with Secchi and, seeing his fascination with Linda, sought his approval and attention in the only way possible, by participating in the affair as a necessary go-between. When Tisa met Secchi, Linda was not in his life. After he saw Linda again and became obsessed with her, Tisa may have tried to bury her heartache while remaining close to him as his confidante. But if what Tisa said about Linda's involvement were lies, she could have had no hope of winning Secchi's gratitude and love. True, the fear of her own arrest motivated her to come forward with new information. But though at the trial Tullio tried to place her in the planning of the murder by saying that she had suggested the pallini, Tisa was always peripheral to the crime; she fetched and carried, but her help had not been essential, and Justice Stanzani knew it. She could have elicited the same exemption from prosecution if she had offered to testify against all the others, cementing the evidence against Tullio and Rosina, describing the experiment with the curare and Secchi's dissuasive warnings, yet assuring the authorities that she knew nothing of Linda's participation. She accused Linda because she saw that Linda had positioned them all on a falling cliff, while she herself was walking away to safety on the arm of one of her doctor trainbearers. Tisa had a reason to lie about Linda: jealousy. But her accusations, rather detailed and yet imprecise, as events often are when they are recalled, did not appear to be lies. Secchi repudiated Tisa in order to protect his lover, but he misspoke in court by calling poison "medicine." That was the accident of an overly restrained tongue. In one electric instant it validated everything Tisa had said—and everything Stanzani suspected about Linda.

Pio Naldi is the most difficult of the defendants to condemn, yet at the same time, he is the only one with something palpable to gain by killing Bonmartini. It is hard to resist the fantasy of poor, weedy Naldi fleeing in a panic down the stairs of the Palazzo Bisteghi before Bonmartini arrived. His entire defense echoes through the prison corridors each time we remember his sturdy alibi: he was on the train to Florence at 7:00. Naldi's nature was that of a man who would run when the time came to perform a violent act. It was not the temperament of a killer, even a momentary killer. No one who has walked the distance from the Via Mazzini apartment to the Stazione Medaglie d'Oro, purchased a ticket at the window, and gone to the track to meet a train would imagine that it could be done in forty minutes, with time to spare for committing a murder. There was blood everywhere in the apartment after the murder, but none on Naldi. And so forth.

But Tullio was wounded in the apartment, not by Bonmartini, it is reasonable to assume. If Tullio purposely cut himself, he had to do it there, tracking his own blood to the bathroom where he drained some of it into a basin, and to the window where he signaled Rosina. However, in the moments after Bonmartini's murder, Tullio was pre-occupied with setting up a scene that pointed to other killers. He had not yet conceived of the claim that Bonmartini attacked him; if he had, he would not have gone to the considerable trouble just a few hours later of dumping all the weapons into the sea. He might have cut himself accidentally while attacking Bonmartini. This is a defense for Naldi that cannot be ruled out, but then, it does not answer the question of Naldi's money at the time of his arrest; if he truly stole it, why did his and Tullio's accounts differ regarding the denomination of the bills? The most logical explanation for Tullio's wound is that he was cut by an accomplice lunging at Bonmartini, an accomplice whom he paid. Was that accomplice Naldi? What other accomplice could have entered the apartment in the few minutes after Naldi says he left? Stanzani fanatically searched to find evidence that someone else participated in the actual execution of Bonmartini; Naldi himself apparently believed that others, especially the un-named blond man, were involved in planning the attack, but he could never convincingly place any one individual in the apartment. The accomplice who stood across the doorway from Tullio as the hapless Bonmartini stepped between them was Naldi. The doctor may not have landed a blow on Bonmartini, but he wielded a knife. Probably the attack happened almost as the autopsy surgeons described it: after Bonmartini was struck in the heart, Naldi held his arms so that Tullio could fulfill his fantasy, breathlessly described in his poem, of sinking a knife into a soft neck.

Naldi is the only defendant who had a reason to get involved in the conspiracy, even though he may have been horror-stricken by the time he was called on to perform. Days of shambling through back-alley clubs and lying in bed, incapacitated from hunger and self-loathing, had made him bitter and desperately frightened. To a man who could not afford twelve lire a month for his room, the resplendent promise of five or six thousand must have been blinding. If Tullio were going to kill Bonmartini anyway, why shouldn't he participate—a quick, distasteful act that would enable him to leave behind his wretched life in Bologna and make a new start abroad. Tullio even promised that an escape for both of them had already been planned. No doubt, as time went on, Naldi became disillusioned about the project. Perhaps he went along with Tullio to Via Mazzini uncertain as to what he would do and half intending to talk Tullio out of it. Or perhaps by the time the two arrived at the murder scene, he had come to his senses and wanted to get out of the whole mess, but Tullio, aggressive and emotional, pressured him to stay. In any case, he was pulled into the slue. The money in his pocket when he was arrested, however he acquired it, was a fraction of what Tullio had offered, and no escape was provided him.

Three years after the trial, his lawyer Roggiero gave a thoughtful assessment of gentle Naldi. Like any close observer, he was baffled and troubled by his case:

> Naldi was an enigma to me, then and still now. He was extremely intelligent, and that adds to the strangeness. Even in Rome [at the appeal] I didn't believe he was telling the truth. I am convinced that Naldi is absolutely incapable of killing a man. He was hiding the truth, from the jury and from me, always, obstinately, even when

eye to eye I begged him to confess everything, to confide in me.
I would not have hesitated to defend him with everything I had,
fearlessly, without worrying about coming up against anyone else's
defense or conflicting with some other version. Naldi answered me
in his cell: 'From the day I entered this place, I was convinced that
I can't tell the truth.'[3]

If Naldi had told his final version of the crime as soon as he arrived
at Stanzani's office and stuck to his story about when and how he left,
he might have been exonerated by the jury, *even though he was guilty,*
simply because the case against him was scratched with unexplained
details. Or if he had made a deal with Stanzani such as Tisa made, bar-
gaining his information about the curare in exchange for a lesser
charge than murder, the next seventeen years of his life might have
been different. If anything was unfair about the outcome of Naldi's
trial, it was the sentence imposed by the tribunal, a sentence that was
too harsh for someone who after the trial would be more of a danger
to himself than to society. Naldi did not instigate the murder and
would not have participated in it except for Tullio's insistence. He
did not deserve the same sentence as the man who trapped him in
the vicious helix.

Tullio was a writer whose fictions always ended in death. He wrote
the Bonmartini marriage, always with dialogue, making a fragile
woman the victim of a pervert; and he wrote the ending, with a
saintly brother sacrificing his life in order to save her by a violent act.
Tullio was overflowing with scalding but cursory emotions. For a
man whom everyone believed was compassionate, he proved ap-
pallingly cruel, not only toward Bonmartini but toward his niece and
nephew, whose lives he devastated without a second thought. He
turned on Secchi, who had done his best not to damage him. He had
always written about the plight of the suffering poor, but he made
Naldi earn his relief by dark labor, and was untroubled during the

confrontations when he saw his friend before him, starved and broken. The jurors saw, without the conventions of modern diagnosis
and terminology, the polar extremes in Tullio's moods. They discerned his chronic need to lie, whether by playing games with coded
messages or by making up charges against his brother-in-law.

Why would a man who disdained hunting stalk Bonmartini and
slaughter him? Aside from his congenital distempers, Tullio was de-
formed by his father's rejection of him. Older children, hungrily
watching a parent lavish attention on the baby, may take up the adoration of the younger child in order to share a little in the love celebration. That was what transpired when Tullio grew up watching his
father's delirious fascination with Linda. He may have told his daughter that he saw through Linda's viciousness even when they were
children; but his letters to his sister show that as a young adult, he
was drunk with her even through the last moment of the trial.
Killing Bonmartini was his way of being taken seriously, proving his
value in the family, earning love and a place in the inner sanctum. If
his planning of the crime was puerile, it was partly because he expected to escape and partly because, being a Murri and superior, he
thought he could outsmart anyone who was not a Murri with a few
false names and phony props.

According to officials involved in the trial, the jury was divided on
some of the charges against Linda, not because the men doubted her
guilt but because they were reluctant to deprive her children of their
mother by exposing her to a long prison term.[4] Few people reading
about the conspiracy doubted Linda's involvement when they looked
at the Mount Etna of her proven lies.[5] Seventy years after the murder, a movie gave a better explanation of the case, one that made
more sense than the truth. In that version, Tullio accepted the blame
for the murder that Linda carried out.[6] The case then came back to
life, resuscitated like one of St. Anthony's miracles, with a new generation discussing and debating it. But of course, Linda did not thrust

the knife into Bonmartini, nor did she directly hire anyone else. She was too artful to commit felonies that she could get vassals to commit for her.

Why had she conceived such a risky project as murder? First because, like Tullio, Linda was a compulsive liar who enjoyed the recreation of hoodwinking others, proving herself more intelligent than the milder minds around her. Linda tried never to tell the truth, even as a last resort; she enjoyed lying and intrigue as much as normal people hate it. Sometimes her lies were excellent, sometimes patently flimsy, as when she cast about to find an explanation for the initial "S."[7] It didn't matter. Being caught in a lie did not embarrass Linda, no more than it embarrassed Tullio or her father.

She was not afraid of the consequences of murder because very little in life made a deep impression on her. What her family interpreted as depression was the somberness of a numb creature. Everything was equally serious to her: Bonmartini's little faults and Tullio's act of homicide; her disappointment in Bonmartini and her children's loss at his death. She seemed not to understand the scale by which suffering is ranked, since both tragedy and inconvenience affected her the same. Like many people devoid of feeling, Linda knew how to simulate emotion. Joined by Tullio, she could cry threnodies, all the while speaking the idiom of love or outrage, but in fact she was, as the prosecutor correctly noted, cold. Her conscience was a serviceable abstraction. She mentioned it compulsively in writing and paid homage to it every time she stood up in court. But the word was merely part of the propaganda about herself that she and her father and her brother assiduously manufactured. She never once indicated that she had suffered self-hatred, regret, guilt, a desire to make amends, a realization that she had been wrong, or any of the other notions that a hardworking conscience stimulates. Like a performer improvising Hedda Gabler, she learned a vocabulary and a set of expected mannerisms and held the characterization without really living the life she was creating for her audience. The only trait that was not in her repertoire was a sense of humor. It is doubtful that she cared deeply for her children, since she did not hesitate to drown their young souls in grief by taking away the person who loved them best in the world. Then she used them, as she used everyone, to draw sympathy to herself. In every way she represented the end of an epoch rather than the beginning of one. As writers pointed out, she was a character of the fin de siècle who found everything within the family—even her lover—and made widow's weeds stylish for women never married.

The jury members watched the theatrics of Linda and Tullio until they were utterly sick of both of them. Even then, Linda might have been able to elicit some mercy for her brother if she had admitted to manipulating him, keeping him upset, spurring him on by lying about what was happening between her and Bonmartini. She might have been able to save Secchi altogether if she had expostulated about his efforts to calm the situation. Instead, she pretended to believe that Secchi was in league with Tisa against her and that she was, as always, a victim. The jury did not believe her.

Prosecutors everywhere have a bad press, and Augusto Stanzani—the villain, for anyone contending the innocence of one of the defendants— is generally reviled whenever the case is revisited. Yet, despite his prodigious chicanery, his irritating piety, his heartlessness, it is difficult to see how he could have conducted a more thorough investigation, one that was even fair occasionally. Examining the thirty volumes of the instruttoria—thousands of letters, including dozens of false confessions sent to the authorities; hundreds of depositions; uncounted interviews made by his small staff—seeing his meticulous care with the testimony and evidence and his attention to the legality of each procedure, it is hard to find fault with him. He questioned every single individual in Fontanelice who knew Rosina in order to find out whether, following the murder, she had asked anyone to hold evidence for her. He pored over the records of two dozen banks to determine whether the Murris had paid anyone to participate in the crime. He had a detective interview the clerks in Darmstadt who sold the curare to Secchi. He canvassed what must have been every carriage driver in Bologna—a city of 150,000 inhabitants at the time—to find out whether Naldi had taken a carriage to the station to escape the murder scene.[8] His researches were made for the purpose of confirming the guilt of certain suspects, but along the way, he also excluded many individuals. It was Stanzani, for example, not Vacchi, who proved that the servant injured his arm during a bicycle accident and not a murder. Stanzani deposed Tisa Borghi nine times for many hours each time before finally hearing the story that she gave in court. To trace the coded messages that the Murris thought the authorities would not take the trouble to find, Stanzani sequestered records from telegraph offices all over northern and central Italy. His istruttoria was obsessively detailed and reflected surprising resourcefulness. As a police detective, Stanzani was a prosecutor's dream.

Moreover, he was right about what he could not prove. He believed that all the Murri family and some of the servants and friends had varying degrees of awareness that a plan was afoot to kill Bonmartini.[9] The family talked and the servants were either taken into confidence or overheard remarks, and they in turn talked. Perhaps that was how Bonmartini himself came to understand that Tullio was after him. They all had a general idea that Tullio was working himself up to a violent attack; Riccardo Murri, for one, seemed to know specific details, formulated during his long colloquies with Linda and Tullio six days before the murder—conferences that Tullio, Professor Murri, and Severo went to Rimini to attend. As Stanzani noted in his communications to the pubblico ministero, the shadows of Riccardo Murri and Severo Dalla loomed at every point in the conspiracy and cover-up of the murder. It went without saying that Riccardo had no special regard for the truth. But although he had been stupid enough to get involved in planning a murder, he was probably too sane and timid to carry one out.

As for Severo Dalla, he presents one of the niggling puzzles in the case. When Severo took his exploratory trip to various foreign places a month before the murder, was it Tullio's escape he was rehearsing or his own? When Professor Murri transferred large sums from Tullio's account to Severo's, was he trying to protect money intended for Tullio from being confiscated, or was he in fact paying off Severo for some priceless favor? The money, incidentally, remained in Severo's account after Tullio's arrest. Stanzani badly wanted to charge Severo with murder, yet he could never find definite evidence of his participation in the act. Severo avoided the charge of conspiracy by his cleverness, though he undoubtedly knew about the plot— as he knew about every iniquitous activity of the Murris. He was even at the dinner table when Giannina expressed her fear that Tullio was about to do "something" dangerous.[10] However, given Stanzani's probing, it is difficult to see how Severo could have eluded detection if he had a hand in the actual killing. The chances are that he was too cunning to let himself be drawn in that far.

Stanzani was right in his conclusions about Professor Murri. Tullio confessed in his memoriale that he discussed killing Bonmartini with both his parents. His mother made him promise to stay away from his brother-in-law, a promise that Tullio did not hesitate to ignore. Professor Murri's foreknowledge was both more haphazard and more certain. On one hand, Murri gives the appearance of not being privy to the long-standing and complicated plan to get rid of Bonmartini, though he knew that Tullio had a physical attack in mind. In a letter to Linda at the end of August, Murri wrote that he understood Nino was going to Venice to threaten "a colleague"— meaning Bonmartini.[11] To his friend and fellow doctor Fabio Vitali, he telegraphed that cryptic, urgent message for Tullio, three days before the murder: *"Please tell him secretly at a suitable occasion: I will let him do it."*[12] In the last two weeks before the murder, he constantly mentioned his aversion to violence in the same breath with which he commiserated about Linda's terrible situation, writing on the day before the murder that he wanted her to proceed with a separation *"because I hate violence,"* as if that were the alternative plan.[13]

Those were murmurs of possible awareness. What screamed Professor Murri's complicity were the bank deposits—the large sums he placed in Tullio's account in the three months before the murder, half of the money within two weeks of the fatal deed, at which time he moved almost everything out of Tullio's name and into Severo's account. The money, 65,000 lire, was sufficient to pay off more than one killer and finance more than one escape. It was more than enough, in fact, considering that Professor Murri handed Linda another wad of cash to give to Tullio while they were on the train that took Tullio over the border, following an itinerary mapped out by Severo.

Professor Murri may not have realized that Linda was poisoning Bonmartini, although as a doctor, he might have connected Cesco's symptoms with his visits home. Murri's vagueness, his deliberate inattention to what was going on, was his protection against what he knew was a dangerous business. As to why he would condone the insane and apparently unnecessary killing of Bonmartini, the answer could be as straightforward as the one reached by Stanzani: Murri and his daughter were incestuous. Bonmartini had begun to suspect as much and was discussing it with his friends, and Bonmartini was apparently never wrong about his suspicions. In 1899, when Professor Murri was writing the most fervid of his surviving love letters to Linda, his congested desire was still a matter of words: *"I embrace you with the passion of a lover. . . ."*"*Since we don't make love, there is no love unless I tell you that I love you, dearest Linda, and that even if you were not my daughter I would love you just the same."* He merely seems regretful that his fusion with his daughter is only emotional. But by 1902, the relationship might well have crossed a line. Linda had then been separated from her husband for two years. Though old Murri would have nothing to do with his son-in-law, he hated him more than ever, with less apparent reason. Bonmartini would have aired all of his suspicions about his wife if he were faced with permanent separation from his children. Perhaps Murri's colleagues would have come forth to testify to old Murri's obsession with his daughter's body. Proof there probably would never be, unless a careless letter were discovered. But observers could no doubt have been found if Bonmartini had looked for them, observers willing to provide material for a sordid scandal.

But Stanzani's short explanation is not the only one. If he wanted to hide a dreadful secret, Professor Murri might have simply counseled his daughter to put up with her husband and avoid the whole unpleasantness. Yet it was Murri above all who insisted to Linda that her health was in danger if she remained married, and it was Murri who persuaded Tullio that getting rid of Bonmartini was a matter of Linda's life or death. He, as much as Tullio, was fanning out of control. More frightening to Professor Murri than the threat of exposure—assuming there was a sin to expose—was the possibility that he would be dispossessed of Linda. If he felt the rapture of a lover when he was near her, he felt the jealousy and desolation of a lover when he was not. He hated both Bonmartini and Secchi, murderously, because they interfered with his exclusive communion with Linda. In only a few years, a Viennese colleague would be explaining why a father's pathological attachment to his daughter was sufficient to produce rage and irrational actions, with or without the presence of overt incest and shame.

People who knew Murri resisted the rumors of incest because they had heard him talk—sensibly, moderately, objectively—about his private morality, and they believed what he said about his diligent self-examination. According to his letters, Professor Murri was completely dependent on his "constant internal witness," his vaunted conscience. In daily practice, that conscience was his servant, not his supervisor. It did not harass him about his systematic rejection of his son; it was silent when he tried to smear Secchi's reputation; and it did not question him during his long, odious treatment of his father-less son-in-law. Murri never acknowledged that he had made Linda into a semi-invalid whose health improved when she went to prison. He was not disturbed by Rosina and Poldino's starvation that had been brought about by their involvement with his family. Rosina's condition moved unwealthy strangers to help her, but it didn't move old Murri or, for that matter, Linda or Tullio. Professor Murri had known Naldi well and had once employed his aunt. He knew that Naldi, too, was virtually an orphan and that Tullio had drawn him into the scheme that led to his destruction. Yet while he was sending Linda delicacies to ease the discomfort of prison, both he and Tullio were content to let Naldi famish. Like Linda, Professor Murri talked about examining his mind and cleaving to right conduct. But no single act of either goodness or conscience can be assigned to him.

Giannina was the excuse for a palisade of forgeries and codes. She seems to have been the one Murri whose craziness was acknowledged. Today, she might be diagnosed with any number of personality disorders, official names for what everyone knew about her even without the benefit of psychology: she was a difficult woman. She was the daughter of a wealthy grain merchant who had fallen on hard times by the time she married Murri. Her education stopped after she learned to read and write. Aside from her Vesuvian eruptions of anger, she was subject to chronic, simple misery. She once wrote to Linda of having cried all night and all day, of attending Mass at San Petronio and leaving at once to hide her uncontrollable crying. *"Papà will say I am crazy, and you will repeat that I am nervous."* She only wants her family's happiness, she avers, and knowing that she causes them upset makes her wish for death.[14] Far from being the tyrant Linda depicted in her memoriale, Giannina was terrified of being alone and incapable of imposing any discipline on the children or servants. Her tirades were an irritation to be circumvented where possible, but they did not keep anyone from doing as he pleased. Giannina always referred to herself as "we" in her letters to the children, always associating herself with her husband, the only authority figure in the house, such that he was. She could not force Linda to go to school, though school would have gotten the girl out of the house and away from her mother's putative cruelty. Linda did not hesitate to move back to her mother in 1898, bringing her own child, after a brief attempt at living in a separate household. Though Linda had criticized her husband's management, she did not for a moment consider running the Cavarzere estate herself while Cesco was in medical school. Living with her mother was preferable.

Giannina was bitterly hurt by Linda's damning portrait of her in her memoriale and the book that was adapted from it. She nevertheless forgave her daughter quickly for what many would have considered unforgivable; her strongest rebuttal was *"You described us as if we were two ferocious beasts,"*—in truth, Linda had exempted her father from all criticism—*"but this character of yours certainly was not our ideal."*[15] *"If we corrected you harshly when you were little, it was because you had some tendencies that were not so good."*[16] The mother objected that Linda always found fault with others, but never with herself. But as always, she ended with maternal solicitude. *"Be assured,"* she wrote to Linda, *"that I loved you always, even when I was severe and demanding, and I will love you to the end of my life. I understood your sadness more than anyone else in the world."* Giannina became the Xanthippe of the trial and of all those who took Linda's description of her mother at face value. In contrast, Tullio, fifteen months younger than Linda and writing his memoriale in another part of the prison, described Giannina as the gentlest and most understanding of mothers. Her husband gave up trying to relieve her "melancholy," being too preoccupied with what he called Linda's "exquisite sadness." Her relentless depression was exacerbated by Tullio's long imprisonment. She was thus the most sorrowful member of a disconsolate nest.

Like her husband, Giannina was aware of what Tullio was up to in the days before the murder, but Stanzani never came close to suggesting that she be charged with any crime. He knew better than to persecute an aging mamma in Italy.

The most enduring mystery of the Murri case is how Linda managed to hold her husband, brother, father, and lover in thrall, directing three of them to kill the fourth and then join forces to erase her part in it. If Tullio's telegram to her can be held as an indication, the idea for the murder originated with her: *"Have decided your plan is the best. We will hardly find Papà in favor of it."*[17] Linda was not particularly fetching. She was not one of those sparkling girls who makes magic out of mundane life. Yet four intelligent men shared in the delirium of exalting her. Part of the explanation lies in her shallow character. Because Linda was a blank screen with no sincere values or deeply held ideas, people could project onto her whatever qualities they wanted her to have. Another element of her fascination lay in what they all believed was her sadness. Faced with her persistent glumness, all the men and many of the women around her became more and more engaged in trying to penetrate the wall that kept her turned inward towards herself. Even Tisa, tough and flippant, wrote that she would give everything she had to see Linda happy. Linda's melancholy seemed to confirm that Bonmartini was mistreating her. As each one tried harder to pull her out of her supposed depression, he became dependent on her to give meaning to his own life. They all ended up stuck to a tar baby, unable to free themselves, while she remained more or less oblivious to their exertions and sacrifices. Another of her addictive qualities was simply her lunacy. When people who are somewhat unstable themselves are confronted with fully developed madness, it takes them a long time to sort out the concatenated abnormalities and reject what is outside their own crackpot standards. As nearsighted and flawed as they were, Professor Murri, Tullio, and possibly Secchi eventually realized that Linda was pernicious, but they would have recognized her insane schemes much earlier if they had themselves been solidly planted. We can describe

344 — INDECENT SECRETS

Linda as sick, but more important, she was a sickness that infected others. She was the only one who emerged from the tragedy undamaged. Naldi fasted in a godforsaken fortress; Tullio froze in a solitary cell; and Secchi's life ebbed away with the tides that splashed against his prison walls. But Linda, her sentence commuted, enjoyed a long life of unearned ennui, pleasant with comforts purchased with money from her father and her obscenely dead husband.

The trial continued to occupy the press and the public for another generation, until fascism came to set a higher threshold for judicial outrage. Altogether, the conspirators served forty-four years which, if added to the thirty-three years Bonmartini lived, would have amounted to a normal life span. Bonmartini, for all that he was countrified, stubborn as stone, crude, odd, sometimes childish, and overly attentive to chamber pots—Bonmartini's life in its plaintive brevity was worth more than all their prison years combined.

NOTES

⁂

Chapter 1: The Murder

The *istruttorie* or records of the investigation into Bonmartini's death, containing all the material turned over to the public prosecutor, are located in *Causa Penale contro Tullio Murri ed Altri,* in ten volumes of *Atti* (generally, evidence and police reports) and ten volumes of *Testimoni* (generally, interrogations, depositions, and written narratives addressed to the investigating magistrate), Archivio di Stato di Bologna.

1.   Volume I *Atti,* 1 settembre 1902, Rapporto Questura; Verbale di visita di località; Verbale di visita del cadavere; Orma di scarpa; Volume I *Testimoni,* 5, 30 settembre 1902, Esami di Cenacci Faustino.

     First the manager tried to get into the apartment. Then one of the owners of the building sent a message to Severo Dalla, the manager of properties belonging to Linda Bonmartini's family; the Murri family itself was scattered at various vacation spas. Dalla said he had no key; the owner then called the police to break the lock. A detective, Giordani, was sent along with several functionaries and filed a long report.

2.   Ibid., Rapporto Questura. Via *Pusterla* is now *Posterla.*

3.   V. I *Atti,* 3 sett. 02, Verbale di autopsia del cadavere dell'assassinato; V. III *Atti,* 23 sett. 02, Verbale presentazione perizia necroscopia; Risposte dei periti.

4.   V. I *Testimoni,* Esami di Cenacci Faustino, ibid. In his deposition, Cenacci described his thoughts as he confronted the cadaver.

5.   V. I *Atti,* 4, 5 sett. 02, Rapporto Questura; Verbale di visita domiciliare in casa Bonmartini in Bologna; Informazioni P.S.; Verbale descrizione oggetti rinvenuti nella valigia del conte Bonmartini. V. I. *Testimoni,* 5, 6 sett. 02, Esame di Iguzzi Raffaele, Picchi Ferdinando.

6.   V. V *Testimoni,* 5, 12 sett. 02, Esami di Cicognani Teresa e Romagnoli Domenico.

7. V. I *Atti,* 7 sett. 02, Verbale di sequestre lettere nello studio Bonmartini a Padova. A license was required for carrying firearms.

8. V. II *Testimoni,* Esame di Agostino Gasperini [publisher of *Il Giornale di Bologna*].

9. V. I *Testimoni,* 22, 23, 25 sett. 02, Esami di Cervesato, prof. Dante; 14, 24, 25, 26 sett. 02, Esami di Valvassori n. G. Battista; 19 sett. 02, Esami di Brillo Antonio; prostitute quoted in [Enzo Rossi] Ròiss, *Il Delitto Murri: Documenti foto e testimonianze originali con 53 lettere di Augusto Murri* (Bologna, 1974), p. 137.

10. *L'Avvenire d'Italia,* 1 settembre 1902.

Chapter 2: The Marriage

1. Donatello's statue of Gattemelata on his horse is in front of the Basilica di Sant'Antonio.

2. One-half lira for entrance to the saint's chapel; three and a half lire to see the vocal chords, which arrived at the church a few years later; Karl Baedeker, *Italy: Handbook for Travellers, Part I, Northern Italy* (New York, 1903), p. 24ff.

3. *Causa Penale contro Murri, Naldi, Bonetti, e Secchi,* V. I *Testimoni,* 23 sett. 02, Esame di Cervesato Dante, Archivio di Stato di Bologna.

4. Ibid., 25–27 sett. 02, Esame di Valvassori n. G. Battista; 23 sett. 02, aprile 05, Esami di Cervesato Dante; Bonmartini's manuscript musical compositions are kept in music libraries in Padua and Milan.

5. Luigi di San Giusto, *Memorie di Linda* Murri (Torino, 1905), prima parte.

6. Letters reprinted in *Corriere della Sera* (Milano), 4–30 ott. 1902. Quoted letters throughout this work are abridged without the distracting use of ellipses; the deletions in no case distort the intended meaning of the document.

7. A. G. Bianchi, *Autopsia di un delitto: Processo Murri-Bonmartini* (Milano, 1904), pp. 252–253; 263–269.

8. In 1905, meat consumption was estimated at 14 or 15 kilograms per person per year for the total population of about 34 million; Massimo Livi Bacci, *The Population of Europe* (Oxford, 2000), p. 52; the salt tax made that commodity more precious than sugar, according to B. King and T. Okey, *Italy Today* (New York, 1901), p. 130.

9. Steel pens were commonplace, but the letter writers preferred the old-fashioned quills. By the late 1890s, illiteracy on northern farms was rapidly decreasing. Education through the sixth year was made compulsory in 1904. Literacy estimates are variable and unreliable. Martin Clark, *Modern Italy, 1871–1982* (New York, 1984), p. 36, quoting *Annuario*

Statistico Italiano and *Annali di Statistica,* gives the illiteracy rate in Emilia-Romagna as 46.3 percent in 1901; but the census of 1899 showed that only 5 percent were illiterate in the province of Turin, according to *Encyclopaedia Britannica,* 11th ed., V. 15 (New York, 1910–1911), p. 16. Emigration statistics are more reliable, since they can be compared with immigration figures of the countries that received the exodus. Italy had some 32.5 million inhabitants in 1901; some 4 million to 5 million Italians were living abroad. The number of emigrants would increase in the coming years.

10. In 1903, there were 333,731 deaths from malaria and 76,507 from all other causes; Corrado Stajano, *La cultura italiana del Novecento* (Roma-Bari, 1996), p. 445. About one million people suffered from malaria in 1898, but after 1900, when mosquitos were found to be the cause and drainage was undertaken, the incidence of the disease fell drastically; Clark, *Modern Italy,* p. 162.

11. Pellagra continued to be the scourge of Italy long after the cause of malaria was discovered in 1900. Pellagra was chronic and progressive, characterized by terrible skin rash, digestive and nervous disturbances, and eventually mental deterioration. It was more prevalent in the maize-growing regions of northern Italy than in the South, where wheat was the dietary staple. The disease was disappearing by 1914, as nutrition came to be better understood, and was almost wiped out after World War I.

12. William Dean Howells, *Italian Journeys* (New York, 1907), p. 178.

13. Linda a Cesco, Bologna, dicembre, 1894, quoted in *Corriere della Sera,* 3, 5, 8 ott. 1903.

14. Figures for 1902: The total number of students enrolled in medicine and surgery, 9,055; in law, 8,385. The University of Bologna had 1,711 students; that of Padua, 1,364. The prisons and penal colonies had 65,000; *Encyclopaedia Britannica,* 11th ed., V. 15 (New York), 1910–1911, pp. 16–17. It was conventionally held that Italy had more university graduates and more illiterates than most countries in Europe. The University of Padua and the University of Bologna were each reputed to have had a student body of around 10,000 during the Middle Ages.

15. V. I *Testimoni,* 22–25 sett. 02, esami di Cervesato prof. Dante; 26 sett. 02, esame di Gallerani, cav. Giovanni. Gallerani, Professor of Experimental Physiology at the University of Camerino and a friend of the Murris, said Prof. Murri made it clear that he wanted Cesco to get a medical degree. Mother's letter: Karl Federn, *Un Crime judiciaire: L'Affaire Murri-Bonmartini* (tr. from the German) (Paris, 1906), p. 25. For the chronology that follows, see *Corriere della Sera,* 24–25 sett. 1903.

16. The first letter was written when he departed for his first year in Camerino, in July 1895; the second example reached him in Cavarzere, where he was collecting rents; *Corriere della Sera,* 8 ott. 1903.

17. V. I *Testimoni,* 22–25 sett. 02, Esame di Cervesato, prof. Dante.

18. Federn, *Un Crime judiciaire,* p. 27.

19. Gynecologists of the time, wary of offending the Church establishment, pointedly refrained from commenting in surveys or in their articles as to whether condoms were much used; G. Mortara, *La Popolazione delle Grandi Città Italiane* (Torino, 1908), p. 146. Mussolini tried to reverse Italy's low birthrate when he came to power, but without success.

20. *Corriere della Sera,* 8 ott. 1903. She reported that Professor Murri played games with his grandchild to induce her to eat. He calls her a risqué name. "She laughs and laughs as if to make him understand that she knows very well that she is not a c———. Papa has so much fun with her" [undated].

21. *Corriere della Sera,* ibid.; Federn, *Un Crime judiciaire,* p. 27.

22. Linda a Cesco, Rimini, luglio 1898, *Corriere della Sera,* 3 ott. 1903.

23. The civil code firmly stated that marriage "is dissolved only by the death of one of the spouses," although the courts did annul marriages where the husband discovered, too late, that his new wife was not a virgin. Prime Minister Zanardelli brought one of many divorce bills before parliament in 1902. The clerical party gathered 3.5 million signatures on a petition opposing it. Even those politicians who favored divorce were cautious about antagonizing the Church by supporting it. For the debates on the 1902 bill, see *Corriere della Sera,* 14 dic. 1902. Divorce became legal in France only in 1884. The least complicated legal ground for divorce in all countries was adultery, but in Switzerland, the adulterous party was prohibited from marrying his or her lover.

24. V. III *Atti,* 17 sett. 02, Fotografia e lettera al dottore Negri nel portafoglio del C. Bonmartini.

25. This staple of 1900 sexology was even on sale in the Sears Roebuck catalogue (Chicago, 1969 reprint of 1908 edition), p. 87.

26. Linda to Cesco, Bologna, 26 nov. 1898, quoted in Bianchi, *Autopsia,* p. 271.

27. Karl Federn, *Ein Justizverbrechen in Italien der Prozess Murri-Bonmartini* (Berlin, 1925), pp. 26–27. This is the original version of the monograph cited above; the translated versions (French, Italian) include certain letters that are not in the original.

28. "I have my faults," Cesco wrote to Valvassori, "but who doesn't? Maybe she harbors some other ideal in her mind, but when bitter disillusion knocks at her door, maybe then she'll remember this poor Cesco who truly loved her and served her like a queen."

29. The letters between Cesco, Linda, and Valvassori are quoted in *Corriere della Sera*, 3, 5 ott. 1903. Federn, *Un Crime judiciaire* p. 34; and [Enzo Rossi] Ròiss, *Il Delitto Murri: Documenti foto e testimonianze originali con 53 lettere di Augusto Murri* (Bologna, 1974), p. 34. See also V. III *Atti,* 27 sett. 02, Trasmissione 3 cartoline e 5 lettere prodotto dal teste Valvassori, 29 sett. 02, N. 2 lettere esibite da G. B. Valvassori.

30. Excerpts of the diary appear in Bianchi's *Autopsia,* p. 250ff., and Ròiss, *Il Delitto Murri,* p. 33. For an unedited reprint of the diary see *Corriere della Sera,* 29 sett. 1903ff. The diary here is excerpted. Ellipses indicating missing material have been omitted, as these would be numerous and distracting.

31. 1901 census, quoted by Martin Clark, *Modern Italy,* p. 163.

32. Podophyllin (Podofillina) is a bitter-tasting resin used as a laxative; belladonna is derived from a poisonous berry, "deadly nightshade." Atropine powder, derived from belladonna and also quite poisonous, was used as an anesthetic and antispasmodic, as well as being used to treat asthma, colic, and hyperacidity.

33. Piazza Maggiore was also the name of the square before the accession of Vittorio Emanuele II. One can still walk everywhere within the city on foot, though the population now is almost 500,000.

34. Cesco records in his diary sending out to the Caffè dei Servi when the children ask for ice cream. The caffè is still in Bologna, still dispensing many flavors.

35. Cesco's Will: 29 dicembre 1898, in *L'Avvenire d'Italia,* 30 nov. 1902.

36. Only 831 judicial separations were granted in all of Italy in 1902, the year their separation ended; *Encyclopaedia Britannica,* V. 15, p. 7.

37. Cesco successfully resisted Linda's demand for a lump sum deposit of 20,000 lire. At the last moment before the separation was formalized, Linda insisted on a written statement from Cesco renouncing all of his conjugal rights, a detail that Cesco interpreted, correctly, as an effort to add to his public embarrassment; V. II *Atti,* 20 sett. 02, Verbale separazione coniugi. The judicial separation was granted by the Tribunal of Padua.

38. For contrasting opinions, see Karl Baedeker, *Italy: Handbook for Travellers,* and William Dean Howells, *Italian Journeys,* p. 5.

39. Gallerani quoted in *Corriere della Sera,* 5 ott. 1903; Cesco quoted in Federn, *Ein Justizverbrechen,* p. 41.

40. Quoted in Ròiss, *Il Delitto Murri,* p. 257.

41. "Dear Cesco: I told you that it was not possible for you to become my assistant. Instead, you reported [to the university officials] that you had no doubt of my support. I see that we are not meant to understand each

other, and therefore it is useless to talk and write. I believe that I was reasonable, but you have demonstrated that reason is not sufficient to stop you; ibid.

42. V. IV *Testimoni,* 17, 29 marzo 03, Esame di Stoppato prof. Alessandro; V. I *Testimoni,* 19 sett. 02, Esami di Morandi Bonaccorsi Prof., Brillo, Antonio, e Memoriale presentato dall'avvocato Morandi.

43. V. 1 *Testimoni,* 29 sett. 02, Esame di Pigozzi avv. Giuseppe; 19 sett. 02, Esame di Barbaro Ermolao. The lawyers advised him to find a courageous Bolognese attorney and to have his wife watched. When he had gathered convincing proof, he should confront her and ask her to surrender the children or face an onslaught of ugly publicity.

44. Bonmartini wrote to Valvassori saying he was against the idea of getting back together with his wife, but that for love of Valvassori, who urged a reunion, and for love of his children, he had resolved to agree to a reconciliation.

45. Svampa's deposition to the *giudice istruttore* is quoted in Ròiss, *Il Delitto Murri,* p. 68–69.

46. V. 1 *Testimoni,* 19 sett. 02, Esame di Morandi Prof. Bonaccorsi (Piero), Memoriale presentato dall'avvocato Morandi.

47. For the second part of the diary, see *Corriere della Sera,* ottobre 1903.

48. Outbreaks of plague and other contagions were a continuing danger, especially in port cities.

49. The University of Bologna even had an agrarian faculty to train the sons of aristocrats in up-to-date farming techniques and tenant management. Statistics for 1900 are from Denis Mack Smith, *Italy* (Ann Arbor, Mich., 1959), p. 218; percentages for 1906 are from *Encyclopaedia Britannica,* V. 15, p. 17.

50. Guido Baccelli, the doctor whose innovations included intravenous injections.

51. Population figures vary widely. A conservative estimate for 1906 is as follows: Milan: 560,613; Naples: 491,613; Rome: 403,282; Bologna: 105,153; *Encyclopaedia Britannica,* V. 15, p. 7.

52. V. I *Atti,* 8 sett. 02, Verbale di presentazione documenti. Tattooing for decorative purposes was common in 1902, but then as now, it was not a commonplace medical procedure.

53. Deposition of Rosina Bonetti; Deposition of Frieda Ringler, *Corriere della Sera,* 4–5, 29–30 ott. 1902.

54. V. I *Testimoni,* 5, 13, 30 sett. 02, Esami di Picchi Ferdinando; 9 sett. 02, Ringler Frieda, Calzoni Adele; 21 sett. 02, Cervesato prof. Dante; 30 sett. 02, Biasetti Maria; 11 sett. 02, Grassi Amelia.

55. V. II *Atti*, 16 sett. 02, Esame di Ringler Frieda.

56. On October 4–5, 1902, *L'Avvenire d'Italia* reported that d'Arcangelo Simonati-Breganze, chaplain of Crosara San Giorgio, was in the trattoria Tre Spade where, on July 27, Bonmartini made the revelations; V. 1 *Atti*, 23 sett. 02, Esame di Cervesato prof. Dante (terza intervista).

57. V. 9 *Atti*, 8 aprile 03, Lettera, Bonmartini all'avv. Cosima, Venzia.

58. V. I *Testimoni*, 5 sett. 02, Esame di Picchi Ferdinando.

59. V. I *Testimoni*, 16 sett. 02, Esame di Ringler Frieda e Idem; 22 sett. 02, Esame di Antonio Massai.

Chapter 3: The Wife

1. Prof. Murri a Linda, feb., 1897, quoted in A. G. Bianchi, *Autopsia di un Delitto: Il Processo Murri* (Milano, 1904), p. 389; [Enzo Rossi] Ròiss, *Il Delitto Murri: Documenti foto e testimonianze originali con 53 lettere di Augusto Murri* (Bologna, 1974.), p. 5.; Renzo Renzi, *Il Processo Murri* (Bologna, 1974), p. 62.

2. King Umberto's wife. Umberto was assassinated in 1900 by an Italian anarchist trained in America. He was succeeded by his son, Vittorio Emanuele III. Murri also treated Princess Mafalda.

3. Luigi di San Giusto, *Memorie di Linda Murri* (Torino, 1905), unpaginated, prima parte.

4. Augusto Murri a Linda, Rapallo, domenica di Pasqua, 1903, quoted in Ròiss, *Il Delitto Murri,* pp. 249–250.

5. *Corriere della Sera* (Milano), 15 marzo 1905.

6. Augusto a Contessa Linda Bonmartini Murri, Hotel Bellevue, San Remo, 2 luglio 1899, quoted in Ròiss, *Il Delitto Murri,* pp. 228–229.

7. Augusto a Linda, 1901, ibid., p. 234.

8. Tullio offered his services free to *Verona del Popolo*, according to *Corriere della Sera*, 18 ott. 1902.

9. *Corriere della Sera,* ibid.

10. "Freedom to order his life . . ." quoted in Bianchi, *Autopsia*, p. 385; "nothing . . . but blood," 2 luglio 1899; "possesses my heart," 19 genn. 1899, *Corriere della Sera*, 18 ott. 1902.

11. A[ugusto] G[iovanni] Bianchi, acknowledged by fellow journalists as the specialist on the Murri case, *Corriere della Sera*, 17 ott. 1903.

12. *Causa Penale contro Murri, Naldi, Bonetti, e Secchi*, V. II *Atti,* 18 sett. 02, p. 99, "Rapporto Questura," Archivio di Stato di Bologna. Title of the istruttoria varies from one volume to another.

13. Prof. Murri a Linda, Rimini, 23 giugno 1900, quoted in Ròiss, *Il Delitto Murri,* pp. 7, 226ff.

14. Augusto Murri a Linda, San Marcello Pistoiese, n.d., ibid.
15. *Memorie di Linda Murri,* prima parte.
16. Giannina Murri a Secchi, 1889, quoted in Bianchi, *Autopsia,* p. 241.
17. Prosecutors mentioned the remark numerous times to show that Secchi was ready to conspire in the murder of a husband who made Linda unhappy.
18. At the time of Linda's and Secchi's separation, the Murris lived at 35 Via D'Azeglio. Even after they moved into the Murri villa at the city gates, they were still in Secchi's close vicinity.
19. The Torre degli Asinelli (four feet square by 320 feet high) and the Torre della Garisenda (4 feet by 163 feet high) were named after their builders. Dante mentioned the Torre della Garisenda in *The Inferno.* Five streets radiated from the towers to gates of the same name: Via Castiglione, Via Santo Stefano, Via Mazzini, Via San Vitale, and Via Zamboni; Karl Baedeker, *Italy: Handbook for Travellers, Part I, Northern Italy* (New York, 1903), p. 376; see also William Dean Howells, *Italian Journeys* (New York, 1907); population: Massimo Livi Bacci, *The Population of Europe* (Oxford, 2000), pp. 132–133.
20. V. IX *Atti,* 3 maggio 03, pp. 27–32, Interrogatorio Secchi Carlo.
21. *Memorie di Linda Murri,* p. 75.
22. Linda a Cesco, ruglio, 1892, quoted in Paolo Valera, *Murri e Bonmartini* (Milano, 1902), p. 203.
23. Linda a Cesco, 2 luglio 1892, ibid., pp. 192, 203.
24. Augusto a Linda, Bologna, 2 febbraio 1899, quoted in Ròiss, *Il Delitto Murri,* p. 240.
25. Tullio to an unnamed friend, 1901, quoted in Bianchi, *Autopsia,* p. 332; Karl Federn, *Un Crime Judiciaire: L'Affaire Murri-Bonmartini* (tr. from the German) (Paris, 1906), p. 57.
26. *Memorie di Linda Murri,* p. 75.
27. *L'Italia del Popolo,* (Milano), 19 sett. 1902, falsely reported that Bonmartini discovered proof of incest between Linda and Tullio.
28. Tullio a Linda, dic. 1899, quoted in Bianchi, *Autopsia,* p. 330.
29. Tullio a Linda, Hotel Bellevue, San Remo, 29 giugno 1899, quoted in full in Valera, *Murri e Bonmartini,* pp. 131–133.
30. Records of Guilio Marchi, No. 15286, 15 ottobre 1892, Archivio Notarile Distrettuale di Bologna.
31. *Memorie di Linda Murri,* p. 88.
32. Ibid., seconda parte, p. 116.
33. Ibid., p. 95.
34. Ibid., pp. 143–145.

35. Ibid., pp. 136, 140–141.
36. Prof. Murri a Contessa A.B.R., Bologna, 19 ott. 1899, quoted in Ròiss, *Il Delitto Murri,* p. 254, Valera, *Morri e Bonmartini,* p. 151.
37. *Memorie di Linda Murri,* p. 133.
38. Cesco's friend and mentor, a professor of physiology at the University of Camerino, attested to the Murris' insistence that Cesco should attain a medical degree. V. I *Testimoni,* 26 sett. 02, Esame di Gallerani cav. Giovanni.
39. *Memorie di Linda Murri,* p.152.
40. Ibid., p. 202.
41. Ibid., pp. 145, 147, 189; "Way of the Cross" remark, p. 113.
42. Quoted in Valera, *Murri e Bonmartini,* p. 212, n.d.
43. V. VIII *Atti,* 21 aprile 03, pp. 246–253, Interrogatorio Murri Teolinda.
44. Linda a Cesco, luglio 1898, in Valera, *Murri e Bonmartini,* p. 212.
45. Prof. Murri a Linda, gennaio 1899, quoted in Ròiss, *Il Delitto Murri,* p. 52.
46. Professor Murri a Linda, Bologna, 2 feb. 1899, ibid.
47. *Memorie di Linda Murri,* p. 239.
48. Linda a Battista Valvassori, 6 dicembre 1898, quoted in full in Renzi, *Il Processo Murri,* p. 65.
49. The terms of the separation can be found in V. 2 *Atti,* 20 sett. 02, pp. 154–157, Verbale di separazione coniugi, and V. VII *Atti,* n.d., p. 107, Documenti esibiti dal Cardinale Svampa.
50. V. VIII *Atti,* 30 luglio 03, p. 196, Interrogatorio Murri avv. Tullio.
51. The retreat was 2,100 feet up, situated off the main road between Florence and Modena.
52. V. I *Testimoni,* 16 sett. 02, Esame di Ringler Frieda.
53. See "Cholera," "Malaria," "Yellow Fever," and "Typhoid," *Encyclopaedia Britannica,* 11th ed. (New York, 1911); Giovanni Berlinguer, "Medicina," in Corrado Stajano, *La cultura italiana del Novecento* (Roma-Bari, 1996), pp. 445–458.
54. Professor Murri a Linda, 1901, Ròiss, *Il Delitto Murri,* pp. 233–234.
55. According to *L'Italia del Popolo,* 17 sett. 1902, Tullio had relations with Emma Grillo.
56. Augusto a Linda, n.d., Bianchi, *Autopsia,* p. 397.
57. V. VIII *Atti,* 22 aprile 03, pp. 252–253, Interrogatorio Murri Teolinda.
58. *Il Socialismo,* 10 ott. 1902.
59. The director of *L'Avvenire d'Italia* during the Murri trial was Gaetano Ercoli.
60. Helen Zimmerman, *Italy of the Italians* (New York, 1911), p. 31.
61. V. VII *Atti,* n.d., pp. 45–148, Verbale dei documenti presentati dal teste conte Gio. Battista Valvassori.

62. The two were General Panizzardi and Professor Roviglio. Roviglio testified that he had wondered how Professor Murri could speak of his daughter as being a "morally superior being" in the light of her behavior, which was common knowledge. Bianchi, *Autopsia,* pp. 421–422.

63. The name Fancini suggested was Alberto Gaspari. In 1900, Cesco had accused Fancini of the theft of some clothes in a suitcase in Cavarzere and dismissed her. Fancini threatened to sue Bonmartini for slander, but Linda reportedly defused the incident by giving Fancini 1,000 lire; Fancini's brother still wanted to file suit. After the separation, Fancini worked another two years for Linda until the reunion, making four years in all. V. I *Atti,* 9 sett. 02, pp. 112–116, Deposizione stragiudiziale di Fancini Vittoria, Rapporto Questura. See also *"furfante"* and *"birbante"* in Linda's letter to Teresa Seiler, V. IX *Atti,* 24 aprile 03, pp. 16–17.

64. In her interrogation, Linda claimed that she hired Rosina only because Cesco wanted a wardrobe mistress. She also said that Frieda was fired on Bonmartini's orders, not hers. V. I *Atti,* 14 sett. 02, p. 213.

65. Documenti di Aristide Baravelli, Matrice No. 670, 12 maggio 1900, Archivio Notarile Distrettuale di Bologna. The street was called Via Toscana when street names were assigned outside the gates, before being renamed Via Murri.

66. V. I *Testimoni,* 13 sett. 02, pp. 63–65, Esame di Borghi Teresa.

67. *Memorie di Linda Murri,* "La reunione," quoted in Ròiss, *Il Delitto Murri,* p. 327. The passages are excerpted without ellipses.

68. Corrado Stajano, *La cultura italiana,* p. 446.

69. Baedeker, *Italy,* p. 337. The "Lightning Express" to Florence (80 miles) took about three hours.

70. Linda's travels: V. III *Atti,* 27 sett. 02, pp. 86–87. Venice: V. I *Testimoni,* 30 sett. 02, p. 184, Esame di Paolucci marchesa Maria (reporting the servant's remarks).

71. The campanile of St. Mark's was begun in 888. It was 322 feet high.

72. "In defesa di Linda Murri, arringa pronunciata avanti la Corte d'Assise di Torino nelle udienze del 3–4–5 agosto 1905," Archivio di State di Torino; V. I *Atti,* 6 sett. 02, Verbale descrizione ogetti.

73. V. I *Atti,* 6 sett. 02, Verbale descrizione oggetti; V. III *Atti,* 29 sett. 02, Verbale sequestro di 15 telegrammi, and text following, esp. Rimini a Venezia, 25–8–02; V. IV *Atti,* 8, 10, 17, 20 ago. 02, Telegrammi; 14 sett. 02, Verbale descrizione e busta contenente le lettere prodotte dal Secchhi a mezzo Borghi Tisa; 9, 14 ott. 02, Nota RR. CC. Bologna, Nota direttore Poste e Telegrafi; V. IV *Atti,* 9 ott. 02, Nota RR. CC. Bologna, Castiglione a Rimini, 8–8–02; V. V *Atti,* Elenco telegrammi, 4–24 ago. 02, Venezia a

Castiglione. Coded telegram: V. I *Atti,* 3 sett. 02, Rapporto Questura, facsimile printed.

74. The girl was Nella Belisardi from Rimini; V. II *Testimoni,* 23 ott. 02, pp. 201–205, Esame de Dalla rag. Severo.

75. V. I *Testimoni,* 9 sett. 02, Esami di Bonetti Rosina; 9, 16 sett. 02, Ringler Frieda; V. I *Atti,* 4 sett. 02, Verbale di querela Linda Murri; 14, 15 sett. 02, Interrogatorio di Murri Linda; V. IV *Atti,* 10 ott. 02, Interrogatorio di Murri Linda; 16 ott. 02, Interrogatorio di Murri Tullio.

76. Besides sending several cards and letters, Linda telegraphed Antonio di Antico in Cavarzere (twice), Valvassori and Cervesato in Padua, Dr. Tranquilli in Rome, Fabio Vitali in Bologna, and the director of the Hotel Suisse in Faido; V. IV *Atti,* 7 sett. 02, p. 64, Verbale rilievo telegrammi; V. II *Atti,* 19 sett. 02, p. 130, Memoria di spedizione documenti.

77. V. IV *Atti,* 3 sett. 02, Tullio Murri a Tinti, Bologna.

78. V. I *Atti,* 9 sett. 02, Rapporto Questura, pp. 93–96; V. 1 *Testimoni,* 16 sett. 02, pp. 81–87, Esame di Ringler Frieda.

79. *Corriere della Sera,* 15–16 sett. 1902.

80. V. I *Atti,* 12 sett. 02, Rapporto Questura, Verbale arresto Bonetti, V. VI *Atti,* 13 sett. 02.

81. *Corriere della Sera,* 13–14 sett, 1902.

82. Ibid. The description of the arrest was signed "A. Bianchi," the respected crime and court reporter assigned to the Bonmartini case from the discovery of the cadaver through all the trials. Bianchi's book about the case, *Autopsia di un delitto,* is a compendium of his most important articles in *Corriere della Sera.*

83. Deposition in Turin of Public Security Officer Castagnoli, quoted in Ròiss, *Il Delitto Murri,* p. 119.

84. V. I *Atti,* 14 sett. 02, Dichiarazione stragiudizionale Pollido Giuseppe e Pedrazzi Oreste, Rapporta Questura, Verbale arresto Murri Teolinda.

85. Baedeker, *Italy,* p. 373.

86. *Corriere della Sera,* 16–17 sett. 1902.

87. V. II *Atti,* 20 sett. 02, Perizia Murri Teolinda.

88. V. IV *Testimoni,* 10 ott. 02, pp. 143–146, Interrogatorio di Murri Linda.

89. Bianchi, *Autopsia,* pp. 424–425; *Corriere della Sera,* 7–8 ott. 1902.

90. V. IV *Atti,* 5 ott. 02, Busta contenente due lettere scritte dalla Teolinda Murri ed una dalla detenuta Spinelli Teresa.

91. *Corriere della Sera,* 10–11, 12–13 ott. 1902.

92. V. I *Testimoni,* 16 sett. 02, pp. 81–87, Esame di Ringler Frieda.

93. *Corriere della Sera,* 1–10 ott. 02.

94. Murri a Linda, 2 feb. 1899, in Ròiss, *Il Delitto Murri,* p. 227.

95. 2 luglio 1899, Ròiss, ibid. See the photostatic copy of Linda's letter in Renzi, *Il Processo Murri*, Plate 39.

Chapter 4: The Brother

1. *Il Resto del Carlino* (Bologna), 13 sett. 1902; *Corriere della Sera* (Milano), 12–13 sett. 1902.
2. *Encyclopaedia Britannica*, 11th ed.,V. 15 (New York, 1910–1911), pp. 12–18.
3. Allessandro Albertazzi, *Il Cardinale Svampa e i cattolici bolognesi, 1894–1907* (Bologna, 1971).
4. For a contemporary view of the government's reaction to socialist agitation and a discussion of the career of Filippo Turati, see R. Michels, *Il Proletariato e la Borghesia nel Movimento Socialista Italiano* (Turin, 1908).
5. In 1900, there was one lawyer for every 1,300 people; Dennis Mack Smith, *Italy* (Ann Arbor, Mich., 1959), p. 246. Comment by Francesco Nitti, Radical party economist; Martin Clark, *Modern Italy, 1871–1982* (New York, 1984), p. 171.
6. M. Sylvers, "L'anticlericalismo nel socialismo italiano," *Movimento Operaio e Socialista,* 16 (1970), 187, quoted in Martin Clark, *Modern Italy,* p. 158.
7. Socialist sympathizers included Edmondo De Amicis, one of Italy's most widely read novelists; the composer Ruggiero Leoncavallo; the lawyer Enrico Ferri; the criminologist Cesare Lombroso; the historian Benedetto Croce. The party was founded in 1892; however, as early as 1879, the poet Giovanni Pascoli had gone to prison for propagating socialist doctrines. In 1904, twenty-two of the twenty-eight socialist deputies had attended universities and nine were university professors; only two had been manual laborers.
8. A. G. Bianchi, *Autopsia di un Delitto: Processo Murri-Bonmartini* (Milano, 1904), p. 340ff., quoting *La Squilla*.
9. Caffè del Corso, 33 Via Santo Stefano; Birreria Belletti, outside Porta d'Azeglio; Caffè del Commercio, 2 Via degli Orefici; Teatro del Corso, 31 Via Santo Stefano; Eden Music Hall, 69 Via dell'Indipendenza; Archivio Comunale di Bologna, Sezione mappa, Biblioteca dell'Archiginnasio, Bologna.
10. *Causa Penale contro Murri Tullio ed Altri,* V. II *Testimoni,* 29 ott. 1902, Esame Dalla Severo, Archivio di Stato di Bologna.
11. [Enzo Rossi] Ròiss, *Il Delitto Murri: Documenti foto e testimonianze originali con 53 lettere di Augusto Murri* (Bologna, 1974), p. 171.
12. V. I *Atti,* 4 sett. 02, Biglietto di Riccardo Murri al Giudice Istruttore.
13. For one of many examples of prejudice against the immigrants in America,

see reports of the lynching of Italians in Tallulah, Louisiana, *New York Times*, Dec. 6, 1899.

14. V. I *Atti*, 12 sett. 02, Verbale di perquisizione Bonetti; Pianta della casa Bonetti; V. III *Atti*, 29 sett. 02, Verbale sequestre di 15 telegrammi, Teleg. 28–8, ore 17.5 da Rimini a Bologna senza firma a Rosa Bonetti.

15. *Corriere della Sera*, 20–21 sett. 1902.

16. V. II *Atti*, 19 sett. 1902, Notizia arresto Tullio Murri; V. III *Atti*, 23 sett., 2 ott., 1902, 2 mandati cattura Tullio Murri, Interrogatorio Tullio Murri; V. IV *Atti*, 4 ott. 1902, Interrogatorio Murri avv. Tullio.

17. V. II *Atti*, 16 sett. 02, p. 21ff., Memoriale.

18. V. VII *Atti*, n.d., p. 107, Documenti esibiti dal Cardinale Svampa; p. 110, Rapporto del Capo Guardia delle Carceri.

19. *L'Avvenire d'Italia*, 19 sett. 1902. In the U.S. judges do not participate in any part of an investigation.

20. Bianchi, *Autopsia*, p. 404.

21. *La Rana*, 3–4 ott. 1902, quoted in Ròiss, *Il Delitto Murri*, pp. 135–136.

22. V. VIII *Atti*, 8 aprile 03, Interrogatorio di Murri avv. Tullio.

23. V. II *Atti*, 19 sett. 02; V. VIII *Atti*, 22 aprile 03, Interrogatorio Teolinda Murri.

24. V. III *Atti*, 28 sett. 02, Verbale descrizione indumenti Naldi; V. I *Atti*, 13 sett. 02, Mandato cattura Naldi.

25. "Traviato": Bianchi, *Autopsia*, p. 89; Ottavio Abatini, "Un mistero psicologico," *Giornale d'Italia*, 29 giugno 1903.

26. V. II *Testimoni*, 15 sett. 02, Rapporto RR.CC e dichiarazione di Benfenati Mario e Minghetti Pietro.

27. V. II *Atti*, 18 sett. 1902, Verbale sequestro degli oggetti rinvenuti indosso al Naldi, e Rapporto Questura; V. II *Testimoni*, 14 sett. 02, Esame di Benfenati Mario.

28. V. II *Atti*, 17 sett. 1902, Verbale sequestro alla Banca Popolare.

29. V. I *Atti*, 12 sett. 02, V. III *Atti*, 2 ott. 03, Interrogatorio di Naldi Pio.

30. *Corriere della Sera*, 20 maggio 1904 (dynamite); 8 maggio 1903 (publisher); assassinations: France 1894, Spain 1897, Austria 1898, King Umberto of Italy 1900.

31. V. I *Atti*, 14 sett. 02; V. IX *Atti*, 14 aprile 03, Buste e lettere dell'imp. Naldi Pio. 20 giugno 03; Interrogatorio Naldi Pio.

32. V. III *Atti*, 2 ott. 03; V. VIII *Atti*, 8–10 feb. 03, Interrogatorio di Murri avv. Tullio.

33. V. VIII *Atti*, 9–10 aprile 1903, Interrogatorio Murri avv. Tullio; V. IX *Atti*, 30 maggio 1903, Confronto Naldi-Murri; 3, 4 sett. 03, Interrogatorio Naldi Pio.

34. *Corriere della Sera,* 4–5 ott. 1902.
35. Bianchi, *Autopsia,* p. 408.
36. V.V *Atti,* 30 ott.1902,V.VIII *Atti,* 22 aprile 03, Interrogatorio Bonetti Rosina;V. IX *Atti,* 5 maggio 03, Confronto Murri-Bonetti.
37. Tullio to Linda, n.d., quoted in *Corriere della Sera,* 19 ott. 1903; Bianchi, *Autopsia,* pp. 406, 408, 416; Ròiss, *Il Delitto Murri,* pp. 185–187.
38. Rosina to Tullio, n.d., quoted in Paolo Valera, *Murri e Bonmartini* (Milano, 1902), p. 272.
39. Bianchi, *Autopsia,* p. 41. The phrase comes up repeatedly during the trial.
40. Tullio to Linda, quoted in Ròiss, *Il Delitto Murri,* p. 191.
41. V. II *Atti,* 29 sett. 02, Copia da Bologna a Rimini 28–8 colla ricevuta pure annessa di Rosina Bonetti.
42. Bianchi, *Autopsia,* p. 406ff., 411;V. II *Testimoni,* 12 sett. 02, Esame di Geniffini Vittorina.
43. Letters by Tullio in *Corriere della Sera,* 17–18, 19–20 sett. 02; Bianchi, *Autopsia,* p. 410.
44. Washing and sewing machines, dress forms, and other domestic paraphernalia were on sale in the new department stores in Bologna; advertisements quoted from the Sears Roebuck catalogue (Chicago, 1969 reprint of 1908 edition), pp. 206, 583. The design of the 1896 sewing machine would not change until the 1940s.
45. V. VI *Atti,* 25 nov. 02, Nota Direzione Ferrovie.
46. V. III *Atti,* 22 sett. 02, Elenco Frequentatori della Buvette Ponzio.
47. Ròiss, *Il Delitto Murri,* pp. 171–174.
48. Ibid., p. 250.
49. Ibid., Augusto a Linda, Belleone, 31 ago. 1902.
50. *Corriere della Sera,* 23, 25 dic. 1899; *New York Times,* Dec. 11, 1899; *Corriere della Sera,* 13–30 nov. 1899; *Encyclopaedia Britannica,* 11th ed.,V. 15 (New York, 1910–1911), pp. 7–10.
51. V. VII *Atti,* n.d., pp. 136–139, Verbale dei documenti sequestrati ott. 1902 in casa Murri in Rapagnano.
52. V. I *Atti,* 14 sett. 02, Rapporto Questura;Verbale arresto Murri Teolinda.
53. Quoted in *Corriere della Sera,* 10 ott. 1903.
54. V. III *Atti,* 2 ott. 02;V. IV *Atti,* 5, 16 ott. 02, Interrogatorio Murri avv. Tullio.
55. Tullio a Linda, n.p., 1902, Ròiss, *Il Delitto Murri,* p. 174.
56. V. I *Atti,* 14 sett. 1902;V. II *Atti,* 19 sett. 02, Interrogatorio Teolinda Murri.
57. Bianchi, *Autopsia,* p. 314.
58. See, for example,V. 10 *Atti,* 7 ago. 1903, Lettera e busta di Guiscardo Allibrante.

59. V. I *Testimoni,* 22, 23, 25, 26 sett. 1902, Esami di Cervesato prof. Dante, Valvassori n. G. Battista, Gallerani cav. Giovanni. Also see Bianchi, *Autopsia,* pp. 308, 309.
60. V. I *Testimoni,* 29 sett. 1902, Esame di Panizzardi gen. Edouardo.
61. *L'Avvenire d'Italia,* 16–17 ott. 1902; *Corriere della Sera,* 4–5, 16–17, 28–29 ott. 1902.
62. V. I *Testimoni,* 16 sett. 1902, Esame di Ringler Frieda.
63. *Corriere della Sera,* 10–11 nov. 1902; see Bianchi, *Autopsia,* appendix, for entire essay addressed to the court. V. X *Atti,* 18 ago. 03, Ordinanza contro Murri Teolinda, et al.
64. V. III *Atti,* 23 sett. 02, Verbale presentazione perizia necroscopia e risposte dei periti.
65. V. X Atti, 29 luglio 03, Nota Questura Bologna circa "Occhi" Antonio.
66. V. X *Atti,* 10 luglio 03, Lettera di Tullio Murri.
67. V. IX *Atti,* 1–4, 20–23 aprile 03, Interrogatorio Murri Tullio, Naldi Pio.
68. Ibid., 29 giugno 03, Verbale di informazioni, di descrizione, e Interrogatorio Naldi Pio, Regatorio a Pesaro; Naldi also described the details of his interrogation and attempted suicide in a letter to his aunt, *Corriere della Sera,* 26 feb. 1905.

Chapter 5: The Lover

1. *Causa Penale contro Murri Tullio ed Altri,* V. IX *Atti,* 30 giugno, 7, 28, 29 luglio 1903, Interrogatorio Murri Teolinda, Archivio di Stato di Bologna; *La Tribuna* (Roma), *Il Resto del Carlino* (Bologna), *Corriere della Sera* (Milano), 28 giunio 1903; Luigi di San Giusto (ed.), *Memorie di Linda Murri* (Roma-Torino, 1905), p. 445.
2. The composer Gioacchino Rossini built a house very near San Giovanni in 1825. The building and grounds became the Piazza Rossini, and the school Rossini attended from 1807 to 1810 was renamed Liceo Rossini.
3. The Murri case took place while the Zanardelli penal code was in effect, the code instituted in 1889 which lasted until 1931, the fascist era. For less serious crimes, the trial took place before a tribunal only. Homicide was tried in the court for serious crimes, the Corte d'Assise.
4. *Encyclopaedia Britannica,* 11th ed., V. 15 (New York, 1910–1911), p. 20.
5. V. I *Testimoni,* 13, 17 sett. 1902, V. IX *Atti,* 4 maggio 1903, V. X *Atti,* 10 luglio 1903, Esami e interrogatorio di Secchi prof. Carlo; Secchi's four examinations before his arrest are recapitulated in A. G. Bianchi, *Autopsia di un Delitto: Processo Murri-Bonmartini* (Milano, 1904), pp. 139–143, and in a very long article in *Corriere della Sera,* 5 nov. 1903. See also *Corriere della Sera,* 17–18 sett. 1902, 27 giugno 1903.

6. V. IX *Atti,* 25, 26, giugno 1903, Mandato di Cattura del Secchi, Interrogatorio Secchi dott. Carlo, Verbale di apposizione di suggelli in casa Secchi, Verbale descrizione oggetti rinvenuti addosso al Secchi, Verbale d'arresto Secchi, Nota R.R. Carabinieri, Interrogatorio Secchi dott. Carlo.

7. Louis S. Goodman, et al., *The Pharmacological Basis of Therapeutics,* 5th ed. (New York, 1997), pp. 575–588. I am indebted to Erika Green for sending me this work. Curare is used in medicine today to induce muscle relaxation in some patients undergoing general anesthesia. My thanks to Carl G. Kardinal, M.D., for his careful review of the curare information.

8. V. IX *Atti,* 27 giugno 03, Relazione sugli usi ed effetti del Curare.

9. V. X *Atti,* 13, 14, 15 luglio 1903, Verbale presentazione perizia Grixone, Relazione perizia Grixone, Verbale perizia Grixone. For a thorough recapitulation of the poison question, see Bianchi, *Autopsia,* pp. 145n., 197, 229 ff., and 166–168.

10. V. X *Atti,* 10 luglio 1903, Interrogatorio Secchi dott. Carlo.

11. V. IX *Atti,* 23 giugno 1903, Rogatorio a Pesaro, Verbali di informazioni, Verbale di descrizione; 24 giugno 1903, Interrogatorio Naldi Pio; 23 giugno 1904, Verbale di sommarie informazioni, firmato Grancesco Carro, Guardia, e avv. Augusto Stanzani.

12. *Corriere della Sera,* beginning 29 giugno 1903 and continuing for the next several months.

13. V. IV *Testimoni,* 28 giugno, 1, 2, 17 luglio 1903, Esami di Borghi Teresa; 2 luglio 1903, Confronto Dalla-Borghi. To compare press reports with the testimony, see *Corriere della Sera,* 3 sett., 7 nov. 1903; Bianchi, *Autopsia,* pp. 171, 187, 209–212.

14. V. IX *Atti,* 3 sett. 1903, Interrogatorio Secchi dott. Carlo.

15. V. IX *Atti,* 30 giugno 03, Interrogatorio Murri avv. Tullio. Interestingly, the reports of these interrogations were not released to the press until five months later; see *Corriere della Sera,* 3, 6 nov. 1903.

16. V. IV *Testimoni,* 14, 22 luglio 1903, Esami di Pacini dott. Enrico.

17. Ibid., 28 giugno, 1–3 luglio 1903, Esami Borghi Teresa; 2 luglio 03, Confronto Dalla-Borghi.

18. V. X *Atti,* 10 luglio 1903, Interrogatorio Secchi dott. Carlo.

19. For the interrogations of Tullio, Linda, Bonetti, Secchi, and the Dallas following Tisa's imputations, as well as the confrontations between them, see V. X *Atti,* throughout July 1903, pp. 17–107 *passim,* starting with 7 luglio.

20. V. IX *Atti,* 30 giugno 1903; V. X *Atti,* 28, 29 luglio 1903, Interrogatorio Murri Teolinda.

21. *Corriere della Sera,* 22 sett. 1903. V. X *Atti,* 16 luglio 1903, Lettere e cartoline del Secchi prodotte dal teste Pacini; V. IV *Testimoni,* 22 luglio 1903, Esame di Pacini dott. Enrico.

22. V. XIX *Atti,* 8 giugno 1903, Requisitoria del P.M.

23. Secchi's surviving letters are quoted in their entirety in several sources: Paolo Valera, *Murri e Bonmartini* (Milano, 1902) pp. 213ff., 435 ff; Bianchi, *Autopsia,* p. 249ff. Only Valera's letters are dated.

24. Bianchi, *Autopsia,* p. 247.

25. Valera, *Murri e Bonmartini,* in which Secchi's letters are quoted extensively.

26. *Encyclopaedia Britannica,* V. 15, p. 12–18.

27. V. X *Atti,* 10 luglio 1903, Interrogatorio Secchi dott. Carlo. The meridian line was drawn about 1500 by the astonomer Giam Domenico Cassini. In the sacristy of the cathedral, Cassini's original drawings are preserved, along with his calculations and instruments.

28. In 1902, 441,171 were drafted; 91,176 were considered physically unfit. In 1906, 476,000 were drafted; 123,000 were physically unfit. These statistics are repeated in many sources, the most convenient of which is *Encyclopaedia Britannica,* V. 15, pp. 12–18.

29. V. X *Atti,* 21 luglio 1903, Verbale consegna lettera dott. Pacini. Secchi a Pacini, 9 genn. 1903, quoted in *Corriere della Sera,* 10 nov. 1903; Bianchi, *Autopsia,* pp. 124, 223.

30. *Giornale d'Italia,* 15 luglio 1903; *Corriere della Sera,* 16 luglio 1903.

Chapter 6: The Third Accomplice

1. *Causa Penale contro Tullio Murri ed Altri,* Archivio di Stato di Bologna, Ernesto: V. IX *Atti,* 2, 3, 4, 5 luglio 1903, Interrogatorio Dalla Ernesto, Citazione, Ricognizione Dalla Ernesto, Verbale di rilievi, Verbale perquisizione casa Dalla E., Verbale perquisizione ufficio Dalla E. Richieste P.M., Ordinanza Camera di Consiglio, Atto sottomissione Dalla Ernesto; Linda: *Corriere della Sera* (Milano), 1 ott. 1903.

2. V. IV *Testimoni,* 7 feb. 1903, Esame Dalla Ernesto, Confronto Dalla-Borghi.

3. V. IX *Atti,* 2–3, 4–7, 5 sett. 1903; V. X *Atti,* 11 sett. 1903, Verbale verifica manicomio Imola.

4. Severo is often referred to in the Murri correspondence as "Riccardo," his middle name.

5. Severo was sent to talk to Frieda on the day of her dismissal by Linda, perhaps to find out what she knew; Frieda was not clear about the purpose of the interview. Severo warned Tullio that the police were about to arrest him, thus prompting Tullio's flight to Switzerland. Part of an envelope sent from Severo to Rosina Bonetti was found soaking in Rosina's bidet when

the police searched her apartment. The envelope had probably been burned that very day, along with other papers. Why would Rosina, in a hurry to escape arrest, think it important to burn a letter from Severo? While she was on the train to Switzerland with her brother, Linda sent a card to Severo warning him to tell the police that she had given Rosina a false name—Maria Pirazzoli—in order to hide from Bonmartini her identity as Tullio's lover. (Linda later insisted that she had nothing to do with Rosina's using a pseudonym.) Linda never doubted that Severo would do her bidding and tell the police whatever she wanted. From prison, Linda sent a card to Secchi warning him that the authorities knew about the little apartment. She addressed the card to Severo, who dispatched his brother to Castiglione dei Pepoli to deliver it to Secchi. "In difesa di Linda Murri, arringa pronunciata avanti la Corte d'Assise di Torino nelle udienze del 3–4–5– agosto 1905," pleadings of Cavaglià, Archivio di Stato di Torino; V. II *Atti,* 28 ott. 1902, Interrogatorio Dalla rag. Severo.

6. V. I *Testimoni,* 30 sett. 1902, Esame di Cenacci Fausto. The maid Vittoria Fancini also had keys to the little apartment. V. I *Testimoni,* 10 ott. 1902; V. X *Atti,* n.d., pp. 164–165, Ordinanza contro Dalla Ernesto.

7. *Corriere della Sera,* 30 marzo 1905.

8. V. IV *Testimoni,* 4 marzo 1903; V. IX, *Atti,* 16 luglio 1903, Nota Amministrazione Ferroviaria di Bologna; V. X *Atti,* 23 giugno 1903, Interrogatorio Dalla rag. Severo. Dalla's first trip was at the beginning of August; his second trip was from August 15 to 24.

9. V. I *Testimoni,* 17 sett. 1902, Testimoni Tosi Antonio, impiego di banca.

10. Information about Severo is contained in various places in the istruttoria: V. II *Testimoni,* n.d., Interrogatorio Dalla rag. Severo; V. V *Atti,* 10–31 ott. 1902, Banca Popolare facsimile account; Tullio's lie: V. VIII *Atti,* 8–10 aprile 1903; V. II *Testimoni,* 17 sett. 1902, Verbale sequestro alla Banca Popolare; V. X *Atti,* 10 luglio 1903.

11. The charges were dropped first against Ernesto and Riccardo, 18 August 1903; but Severo was held almost until the start of the trial. Letters to the P.M. outlining the thoughts and strategies of the investigators can be found throughout the istruttoria, as in V. IX *Atti,* 8 giugno 1903, Requisitoria del P.M.; V. X *Atti,* 13 ago. 1903, signed Liperi.

12. Parte I, V. X *Atti,* 18 ago. 1903, Ordinanza contro Murri avv. Riccardo.

13. The telegram referring to Minetta and Mariolina was sent on September 9 from Zurich to Riccardo in Fermo; V. VII *Atti,* 17 dic. 1902, Interrogatorio dell'imputato Murri avv. Riccardo.

14. V. III *Atti,* 29 sett. 1902, Verbale sequestro di 15 telegrammi; card to justice: V. I *Atti,* 19 aprile 1903, Biglietto Riccardo Murri; Prof. Murri's

response: "I don't ask for defenders, and when I do, I call lawyers and pay them. When I need colleagues, I ask them as I asked you. But I expect the truth from all of them, especially those, like you, whom I have always considered gentlemen," quoted in A. G. Bianchi, *Autopsia di un Delitto: Processo Murri-Bonmartini* (Milano, 1904) p. 253.

15. V. VII *Atti,* n.d., pp. 64–98, Interrogatorio di Riccardo Murri.

16. *Corriere della Sera,* 3 nov., 12 dic. 1903.

17. Ibid., 20 sett., 3 nov. 1903.

18. V. VII *Atti,* n.d., pp. 37–50, Lettera di Giuseppe Leti; Rogatorie a Roma; Cedola Citazione; Lettera di Manis Enrico e Bottini Salvatore, infermieri dell'Ospedale S. Spirito, Roma; Estratto dal copialettere di Giuseppe Leti.

19. V. I, Fascicolo 6, *Atti,* 4 ott. 1902, Telegrammi Murri a Vitali da San Moritz a Venezia; 28 ott. 1902, Busta con biglietto del teste Fabio Vitali; V. II *Testimoni,* 9 ott. 1902, Esame di Vitali prof. Fabio; *Corriere della Sera,* 15–16 ago, 20 sett. 1903.

20. V. VIII *Atti,* facsimile Banca Popolare, 21 ago. 1902; V. IX *Atti,* 12 giugno 1903, Banca Cooperativa di Bologna, Sovvenzioni avallate dall'avv. Tullio Murri.

21. See Prof. Murri's letter to Del Piano, 18 sett. 1903, in [Enzo Rossi] Ròiss, *Il Delitto Murri: Documenti foto e testimonianze originali con 53 lettere di Augusto Murri* (Bologna, 1974), pp. 266–267.

22. Old Murri repeatedly averred that he got his information about Bonmartini's misdeeds from his servant, Picchi. However, Ferdinando Picchi deposed that Linda was "shut up" with Rosina constantly; that Cervesato had secured Picchi's position with the count, who paid him a generous 60 lire a month, along with room and board; that the count had no women, as far as Picchi knew, and was intensely affectionate and giving toward his children, but tended to comment about small expenditures, though not insistently. V. I *Testimoni,* 30 sett. 1902, Esame di Picchi, Ferdinando; 20 sett. 1902, Esami di Murri prof. Augusto.

23. Giolitti was minister of the interior—an influential post in deciding justice issues—prior to becoming prime minister. For Crispi's letter, see Ròiss, *Il Delitto Murri,* pp. 168, 270.

24. As soon as Bonmartini's murder was announced, Massarenti repeatedly offered to testify for the prosecution; *Corriere della Sera,* 24 sett. to 2 ott. 1904; see also Dante Manetti, *Augusto Murri* (Firenze, 1923).

25. As the father was sent off to exile, Austrian soldiers came into the house and smashed all of the family's belongings, while the children watched aghast.

26. E. A. King, *Italian Highways* (London, 1896), p. 63.

27. *Corriere della Sera,* 24 sett.–8 ott. 1904, 26 genn. 1905. In the U.S. jury service was never restricted to voters or property owners.

28. *Corriere della Sera,* 8 nov. 1903.

29. The prosecution's entire case is summed up in several sources: Bianchi, *Autopsia,* pp. 116–117, gives a good chronology of the large, confusing correspondence and contacts between the conspirators up to the time of the murder; *Corriere della Sera* sums up the case 20, 21 sett., 3 nov. 1903. The case against Severo is explained in *Corriere della Sera,* 3 sett. 1903. For Riccardo, Parte I, V. X *Atti,* 18 ago. 1903, Ordinanza contro Murri, avv. Riccardo. Charges dismissed against the Dallas and Riccardo Murri: V. X *Atti,* 18 ago. 03, Ordinanza della Camera di Consiglio del Tribunale di Bologna.

30. *Corriere della Sera,* 11 luglio–30 sett. 1903 *passim.* The issue of the suspicious deaths is best summarized in Bianchi, *Autopsia,* p. 24 and note.

31. V. X *Atti,* 16 luglio 1903, Lettere e cartoline del Secchi prodotte dal teste Pacini. *Corriere della Sera,* 10 nov. 1903.

32. Prof. Murri a Linda, Belleone, 31 ago. 1902, Ròiss, *Il Delitto Murri,* pp. 245–247. Murri wrote that the judge hated his son and was a slave to his wife, accusations that his enemies might have applied to Murri himself.

Chapter 7: The Latest News

1. *Encyclopaedia Britannica,* 11th ed., V. 15 (New York, 1910–1911), p. 20.

2. See Helen Zimmern, *Italy of the Italians* (New York, 1911), p. 30, written in 1905.

3. See, for example, *Corriere della Sera* (Milano), 23 ott. 1903.

4. William Dean Howells, *Italian Journeys* (New York, 1907).

5. Literacy estimates are variable and unreliable. Martin Clark, *Modern Italy, 1871–1982* (New York, 1984), p. 36, quoting *Annuario Statistico Italiano* and *Annali di Statistica,* gives the illiteracy rate in Emilia-Romagna as 46.3 percent in 1901; but the census of 1899 showed that only 5 percent were illiterate in the province of Turin, according to *Encyclopaedia Britannica,* 14th ed., V. 15 (New York, 1906), p. 16. Four fifths of Sicily was illiterate in 1900, according to Denis Mack Smith, *Italy* (Ann Arbor, Mich., 1959), p. 234.

6. *Corriere della Sera,* 25–30 dic. 1902; 4, 14, 18, 19, 28 genn., 8, 9, 17 feb., 1–2, 5–7, 19, 21 marzo; 30 giugno 1903; 16 genn. 1–28 feb., 17 marzo, 17 ott., 1905; 27 nov. 1908. See also the Medici-Tosetti trial, 16 dic. 1904–1 genn. 1905; the Rosada case, beginning 28 ott. 1905; the Olivo case, beginning 21 nov. 1904; the Humbert-Daurignac case, beginning 9 ago. 1903, the case most similar to the Murri because it involved multiple

defendants within a family so wacky that several members eventually wound up working for Barnum and Bailey.

7. *Corriere della Sera,* 9 dic. 1904–1 genn. 1905.

8. Filippo Turati, Pietro Nenni, Enrico Ferri, Antonio Gramsci, Giovanni Giolitti, Benito Mussolini, as well as Alfredo Frassati, Luigi Albertini, Alberto Bergamini, Cesare Pavese, Benedetto Croce.

9. Ferdinando Petruccelli della Gattina, quoted in Denis Mack Smith, *Italy,* p. 202.

10. *La Stampa* (Torino), 2–4 marzo 1905.

11. Corrado Stajano, *La cultura italiana del Novecento* (Roma-Bari, 1996), "Giornalismo," pp. 349–370.

12. *Corriere della Sera,* 14 aprile 1905.

13. Ibid, 21 genn. 1903ff, 25 marzo, 8, 24 maggio 1904.

14. The Murri trial was set to begin, but for one more detail. Alessandro Stoppato was a friend of Bonmartini and the court-appointed guardian of the children during their mother's imprisonment. Stoppato wanted to sue all of the defendants on behalf of the children for depriving them of a father, though the court was not sure whether children could legally sue their mother. It cost Stoppato 70,000 lire of the children's inheritance— almost a year's worth of the Bonmartini income—to find out that they could not. If successful, that civil suit could have opened the way for the court to deny Linda the widow's portion of Bonmartini's estate. Alessandro Stoppato, *Memoria della parte civile resistente al ricorso di Tullio Murri* (Torino, 1906).

15. "In difesa di Linda Murri, arringa pronunciata avanti la Corte d'Assise di Torino nelle udienze del 3–4–5 agosto 1905," Archivio di Stato di Torino, report of nuns quoted: "[Rosina] suffered an attack of hemiplegia and anesthesia aphasica; paralysis of half of the body with insensibility of paralyzed members, including her voice."

16. Descriptions of all the defendants in *Corriere della Sera,* 24 ago., 8 ott. 1905.

17. *New York Times,* August 1–31, 1905; *Corriere della Sera,* 24 ago. 1905.

18. Causa Penale contro Tullio Murri ed Altri, V. V *Atti,* 5 dic. 1902; V. VII *Atti,* 6 genn. 1902, Lettere di Linda Murri diretta al V. Direttore delle Carceri, Archivio di Stato di Bologna; letter quoted in her lawyer Gottardi's pleadings, *Corriere della Sera,* 5 luglio 1905. A doctor ordered an armchair for Linda's cell, provoking a complaint from another prisoner who did not have such furniture.

19. Machine pictured in Cesare Lombroso and Guglielmo Ferrero, *La Donna delinquente* (Roma, 1893).

20. Ibid.; see the chapter "Anatomy and Anthropometry." Lombroso's ideas on criminality not only dominated jurisprudence, they braced the political impetus toward colonization. Italians had eagerly joined in the competition to colonize and westernize the "backward" peoples of Africa and Asia. One of the ways they convinced themselves that they could civilize benighted societies was by noting the anatomical differences between themselves and others and concluding that the physical qualities of Europeans had something to do with their high cultural achievements. People with large lips, flat noses, and abundant hair were not as intelligent or receptive to education as people with deep-set eyes and forward features, according to maxims that, though not universally accepted, were allowed to pass unchallenged in formal settings. It followed that those Italians who exhibited the racial characteristics of Africans or Asians might be impaired either mentally or morally, that is, they were abnormal and tended toward criminality.

21. Quoted in Cesare Lombroso and Guglielmo Ferrero, *Criminal Woman, the Prostitute, and the Normal Woman,* trans. Nicole Hans Rafter and Mary Gibson (Durham, N.C., 2004), p. 132.

22. Quoted in *Corriere della Sera,* 16 ott. 1904.

23. Ibid., 1 genn. 1903.

24. A wave of socialist strikes spread like a rumor across the country in September, 1904, starting in Sardinia and affecting all the industrial centers, including Venice and Bologna, and causing the deaths of workers and policemen. But Tullio was isolated from the excitement, prevented from fulminating about any situation except his own.

25. *Corriere della Sera,* 17 ott. 1905.

26. *La Stampa* (Torino), 17 ott. 1904; though Tullio complained that his idol, the lawyer Enrico Ferri, had visited him only once, briefly, he was eager for the trial to start.

27. Population as given in the *Encyclopaedia Britannica,* V. 15, p. 16. Reports vary widely.

28. *Corriere della Sera,* 19 aprile, 16 ott. 1904.

29. Giorgio Pavese, *Il Processo Murri* (Roma, 1908), p. 77.

30. Appearance of defendants: *Corriere della Sera,* 18–20 aprile 1905; documents: ibid., 19 ott. 1904.

Chapter 8: The Trial Begins

1. Official stenographic records were not usually made of court trials; the president dictated a summary of each witness's testimony to a scribe. Therefore, the entire trial—every word, every gesture—was reported by

the largest papers, especially Turin's *La Stampa,* Bologna's *Il Resto del Carlino,* and Rome's *La Tribuna.* The most fair-minded journalist was A. G. Bianchi of *Corriere della Sera,* whose reports are cited throughout because *Corriere* is the most accessible of the reliable Italian newspapers for researchers in the United States; it reported the trial in the most exhaustive detail. For the opening days, see 19 feb. 1905ff. The Court of Assize was the court of first instance for serious crimes carrying long prison terms. Everything that took place during the trial would be published immediately in the Italian press and in foreign newspapers the very next day; nevertheless, the foreign journalists were bitter about being kept out.

2. See the Milan weekly *Illustrazione Italiana* and *Secolo XX,* as well as *The Illustrated London News.*

3. *Corriere della Sera* (Milan), 19 feb. 1905.

4. Ibid., 2 feb. 1905.

5. Luigi di San Giusto (ed.), *Memorie di Linda Murri* (Roma-Torino, 1905), p. 453. Use of cages would be considered terribly prejudicial in the U.S.

6. For a thorough explanation of the procedures in 1905, see Mauro Cappelletti et al., *The Italian Legal System: An Introduction* (Stanford, 1967); G. Leroy Certoma, *The Italian Legal System* (London, 1985).

7. *Corriere della Sera,* 19, 26 feb. 1905.

8. Suicide was more common in northern Italy and most common among poor people. Suicide rates were higher in Italy than in most European countries. In both Europe and the U.S., suicide was far more common than now; see *Encyclopedia Britannica,* 11th ed., V. 15 (New York, 1910–1911), pp. 7–9; comparisons are probably fairly accurate, but the statistics given appear to be wrong; they are also questionable in Corrado Stajano, *La cultura italiana del Novecento* (Roma-Bari, 1996), pp. 193–198.

9. The scene with Stanzani was reported from Stanzani's viewpoint (since he was providing the information), *Causa Penale contro Tullio Murri ed Altri,* V. IX *Atti,* 17 ago., 23 giugno 1903, Verbale di sommarie informazioni, firmato Francesco Carro, guardia, ed Augusto Stanzani; see also Naldi's version of events written to his aunt, *Corriere della Sera,* 26 feb. 1905.

10. *Corriere della Sera,* 26 feb., 1, 2 marzo 1905.

11. Tullio's testimony, ibid., 2–4 marzo 1905.

12. He telegraphed his sister to prevent her, he said, from doing something ill advised, such as fleeing with the children. The president read the telegram: "Please delay the departure as long as possible. I await your orders. I am writing." It was signed "Borghi." Tullio then sent Linda another telegram informing her that he would arrive the next day. He signed this one "Maria

Pirazzoli" and indicated that "Maria" would be happy to accompany Linda to Switzerland.

13. *Corriere della Sera,* 1 marzo 1905.
14. V. I *Testimoni,* 3 sett. 1902, Rapporto Questura; 1 sett. 1903, Verbale di visita del cadavere, Archivio di Stato di Bologna.
15. V. II *Atti,* 20 ago. 1903. telegramma Bologna a Venezia, 31 ago. 1902. "Telegraphed Papa asking advice. I will wait for mail tomorrow in case of continued silence I will leave for Faido with Frieda informing Cervesato pass over behavior. This morning I sent cascara sagrada. Nino."
16. *Corriere della Sera,* 3 marzo 1905.
17. V. IX *Atti,* 4 maggio 1903, Interrogatorio Murri Tullio, in which he changed the order of the blows to Bonmartini and then switched back to his first account.
18. *Corriere della Sera,* 4 marzo 1905.
19. Ibid. 4–5 marzo 1905.
20. He was referring to letters written in June 1900.
21. One maid was actually a former maid, Vittoria Fancini. At the time of the reconciliation, Linda had dismissed Fancini, at Bonmartini's insistence, giving her 1,000 lire, and replacing her in the house with Bonetti.
22. *Corriere della Sera,* 5 marzo 1905.

Chapter 9: The Mystery Witness

1. *Corriere della Sera* (Milano), 15, 3 marzo 1905.
2. The appearance in court of a certain Alfredo Borghi, not related to Tisa but an acquaintance of Secchi, allowed the doctor to claim that he thought this man, and not Tullio, was the author of the telegrams sent to him after the crime.
3. *Corriere della Sera,* 12–13 marzo 1905.
4. Ibid.
5. Karl Baedeker, *Italy: Handbook for Travellers, Northern Italy* (New York, 1903), p. 362.
6. *Corriere della Sera,* neighbors: 16 marzo; Tirelli: 17 marzo; comments of Professor Boari: 15 marzo, 1905.
7. Ibid., 8 aprile; 18–19, 15 marzo, 1905.
8. Ibid., 15 marzo, 1905.
9. Ibid., 11, 15 marzo 1905.
10. The Caffè del Commercio was at 2 Via degli Orefici; *Corriere della Sera,* 24–25 marzo 1905.
11. Ibid. A telegraph operator was asked to confirm her statement that Rosina had sent Linda a message on August 28: "Everything went well." But

instead of repeating her deposition, the clerk repudiated it, saying she was influenced by what she had read in the newspapers about Rosina.

12. *Causa Penale contro Murri, ed altri,* V. IV, *Testimoni,* 7 marzo 1903, Esame Dalla rag. Severo, Archivio di Stato di Bologna.

13. Quoted in *Corriere della Sera,* 26 marzo 1905.

14. V. I *Testimoni,* 16 sett. 02, Esame Vacchi Ettore; *Corriere della Sera,* 5 maggio 1905.

15. Testimony of Prof. Boari, *Corriere della Sera,* 15 marzo 1905.

16. *La Stampa* (Torino), 30 marzo 1905.

17. All of Tisa's first appearance in court in *Corriere della Sera,* 30–31 marzo 1905.

18. Ibid.

19. Professors Romolo Albini and Alberto Pacini.

20. Because of a procedural complication, Stoppato was not allowed to take the witness chair, although he was reliably alive; *Corriere della Sera,* 15 marzo 1905.

21. Valvassori's widow testified that when the Bonmartini children first came to live with her after Linda's arrest, they had been told by the Murris that their father wouldn't give their mother any money and threatened to remove them from her; ibid., 2 aprile 1905.

22. Ibid., 6 aprile 1905.

23. *Corriere della Sera,* 25 marzo 1905.

24. Ibid., 17 aprile 1905.

25. Ibid., 9 aprile 1905.

26. Ibid., 6 aprile 1905.

27. Ibid., 9 aprile 1905, which contains all of Clelia's testimony.

28. See also V. I *Atti,* 4–6 sett. 1902, Esami di Castellani Clelia. In Bologna, Nini sang at a nice enough place: the restaurant–music hall Eden, on Via dell'Indipendenza, the main avenue.

29. *Corriere della Sera,* 15 aprile 1905.

30. Ibid., 15–16 aprile 1905; testimony of the experts.

31. Ibid.

32. All of Tisa's second appearance: *Corriere della Sera,* 27, 29 aprile 1905.

33. All of Taormina's testimony: ibid., 4, 15 maggio 1905.

34. Ibid., quoting Countess Cavazza, 15 marzo 1905.

35. Autopsy reports and arguments: *Corriere della Sera,* 8–14 maggio 1905.

36. Lorenzo Borri, *Sulla morte del conte Bonmartini: osservazioni critiche e sperimentali di medicina forense* (Modena, 1905). The prosecution maintained that Bonmartini's numerous wounds indicated that there were two assassins. But the defense pointed to other cases in which the victims

had over 70 wounds coming from all directions, yet made by a single attacker.

37. Ellero and Bellini for the prosecution; for the defense, the Lombroso collaborator Morselli, along with Toselli, Treves, and Tirelli.

38. Rosina: *Corriere della Sera,* 24–25 maggio 1905.

39. There was some discrepancy about the number of Rosina's siblings. During the trial, the number of brothers was variously given as seven, nine, or ten.

40. Tullio: *Corriere della Sera,* 25–26 maggio 1905.

41. In this, both doctors spoke the truth. According to Naldi's testimony, Tullio did sleep, but he awakened in a state of frenzy and tore through the apartment, insensible to reason. After the crime, however, he behaved with every semblance of self-possession.

42. Linda: *Corriere della Sera,* 27–31 maggio 1905.

43. Ibid., 1–4 maggio, 1905. Others defenders were also senators.

Chapter 10: The Summations

The summations are excerpted in the text without ellipses, since these would prove too distracting for the reader. The lawyers' speeches of many days are naturally much shortened in the narrative. Most of the lawyers printed their pleadings at their own expense after the trial, since no verbatim court records were made. The books published by Nasi, Morello, Sighele, Gottardi, Vecchini, Berenini, Cavaglià, Morselli, Tazzari, and Ferri are cited below. Sometimes an energetic lawyer mindful of his career would also send a printed version of his pleadings to certain newspapers, to make sure the reporters heard the speech correctly and to increase the likelihood that the pleadings would be published even if the newspaper was not among those allowed to have a representative in the courtroom. Linda's defender Berenini kept scribes and postmen busy seeing to it that a dozen or more newspapers saw his summation.

1. The president's refusal to allow an experiment with shouting from the Bonmartini apartment was one of the justifications for an appeal of the case to the Court of Cassation in Rome.

2. "Il processo per l'assassinio di Francesco Bonmartini: la 94[a] giornata . . ."; *L'Avvenire d'Italia,* 30 luglio 1905; "L'arringa dell'on. Agostino Berenini, 95[a] giornata," *Il Resto del Carlino,* 29–30 luglio 1905.

3. Alighiero Nonnis Marzano, *L'Ambiente psicopatologico nel processo Murri-Bonmartini* (Roma, 1905); L. Ellero, *Opere* (Bologna, 1926).

4. Scipio Sighele, "Processo Murri, arringa dell'avv. Scipio Sighele, Corte d'Assise di Torino, udienze del 6 e 7 giugno 1905," Riva di Trento, 1905, Pubblicistica giudiziaria.

5. These books were translated into English, but under the name of a French writer who plagiarized Sighele's work; Helen Zimmern, *Italy of the Italians* (New York, 1911), pp. 193–194.

6. Included were letters about Linda; Bonmartini a dott. Vincini, sett. 1899, *Corriere della Sera* (Milano), 7 giugno 1905.

7. Sighele, "Proceso Murri."

8. Carlo Nasi, *Processo Murri: Come e da chi fu ucciso il conte Bonmartini* (Torino, 1905).

9. The accusation began when Tullio wrote it in his memoriale; as the lawyer pointed out, it was put into circulation by friends of the Murris: Ploner—to whom Tullio lent 500 lire on the day after the murder—and Del Piano.

10. *Corriere della Sera* (Milano), 8 giugno 1905.

11. Tullio went to Ulma, Vienna, Budapest, Semlino (Zemun), Vienna again, Zurich, Costanza, Strasbourg, Paris, Strasbourg again, Munich, and Ala.

12. *Corriere della Sera,* 10–11 giugno 1905.

13. The defense lawyers eventually pointed out that the carriage driver Romagnoli at first deposed that Bonmartini arrived no later than 6:30, but on repeated questioning, he equivocated. The driver was dead by the time the trial started. Causa Penale contro Murri, Naldi ed Altri, V. I *Testimoni,* 12, 27 sett. 1902, Esame di Romagnoli Domenico, Archivio di Stato di Bologna. In the U.S. depositions by themselves are not admissible.

14. *Corriere della Sera,* 14 giugno 1905.

15. *Il Caffaro* (Genova), 14 giugno 1905.

16. Plotting the crime would have put Secchi in a special category of the criminal code, a legalism the prosecution wanted to avoid.

17. *Corriere della Sera,* 14 giugno 1905. For audience reaction, see also the long article by Scipio Sighele in *Il Nuovo Giornale* (Firenze), 24 ott. 1908.

18. It was true that Adele Calzoni claimed to have seen the package opened, Colli admitted, but Calzoni was herself involved in so many suspicious activities that her testimony was not credible, according to the prosecutor.

19. "Il processo Murri . . . in difesa di Linda Murri," *Il Momento* (Torino), 30 luglio 1905, summarizes previous arguments, including Palberti's.

20. See annotazione ms. on *Il Momento,* 28–29 luglio 1905 and on *Corriere della Sera,* 28 luglio 1905, Busta 5, Archivio di Agostino Berenini, Biblioteca Comunale di Parma.

21. *Corriere della Sera,* 17, 18 giugno 1905.

22. The deposits had actually been made by Professor Murri, through Severo Dalla; V. V *Atti,* 17 sett. 1902, Ricorso al Tribunale di Bologna del rag. Severo Dalla; V. VI *Atti,* 24 nov. 1902, Fascicolo Banca Popolare di Credito, Bologna.

23. Ferrero (1871–1942) was the author of a history of Rome, among other notable works. For his ideas, see Cesare Lombroso and Guglielmo Ferrero, *CriminalWoman, the Prostitute, and the NormalWoman* (Durham, N.C., 2004), translator's introduction by Nicole Hahn Rafter and Mary Gibson. De Amicis (b. 1846) had achieved great popular success by 1905 as a realistic novelist for *Gli Amici, Il Romanzo di un Maestro, La Carrozza di Tutti,* and other novels. He is known to American readers, if at all, through his sentimental book for boys, *Cuore,* which has long gagged intermediate-level students of Italian literature. He converted from liberalism to socialism in 1891; Ferrero Archive, Butler Library, Columbia University.

24. St. Peter was the celestial patron of Rome, St. John the Baptist of Florence, St. Ambrose of Milan; *Corriere della Sera,* 21 giugno 1905; Enrico Ferri, *Arringhe e discorsi* (Brescia, 1979 reprint).

25. *Gazzetta Ufficiale da Regno d'Italia* (Roma), no. 231, 19 sett. 1919.

26. Ferri invoked images from a painting well known to the jurors, *The Cross,* by the Turin artist Leonardo Bistolfi.

27. *Corriere della Sera,* 27–28 giugno 1905.

28. Vincenzo Tazzari, *Le dubbiezze del processo Murri: arringa pro Naldi* (Milano, 1906); *La Stampa,* 27 giugno, 1905; *Corriere della Sera,* 27 giugno, 1905. See also Vincenzo Tazzari, *Rivelazioni sul processo Murri: la riconstruzione del delitto* (Milano, n.d.).

29. *Corriere della Sera,* 27 giugno 1905.

30. Tazzari alternated with Carlo Felice Roggieri in delivering the summation for Naldi's case; ibid, 6 agosto 1905.

31. Karl Baedeker, *Italy: Handbook for Travellers* (London, 1903), p. 363.

32. Vincenzo Morello, *I delitti della gente onesta: l'arringa pro Secchi* (Roma-Torino, 1906); *Corriere della Sera,* 28–30 giugno 1905. Each lawyer was allowed two turns for summing up. In the U.S., only one turn was allowed. Morello wrote a newspaper column under the pseudonym "Rastignac."

33. *Corriere della Sera,* 30 giugno 1905.

34. Ibid., 1 luglio 1905; Giuseppe Gottardi, Arturo Vecchini, and Agostino Berenini, *Perché Linda Murri è Innocente: arringhe dei defensori* (Milano, 1906).

35. The paper referred to was *La Provincia di Padova.*

36. On August 8, for example, Tisa had written to Linda, "Carolina [Secchi] awaits your orders." This, the lawyer said, was a light-hearted reference to a coming rendezvous.

37. Gottardi et al., *Perché Linda Murri è Innocente;* Arturo Vecchini, *Arringhe penali: arringa per Linda Murri e Tarnowska* (Ancona, 1912).

38. Giannina a Linda, Rimini, 2 feb. 1900, in *Corriere della Sera,* 5 luglio 1905.

39. *Corriere della Sera,* 6 luglio 1905.
40. All of the foregoing presentations are described in full, ibid., 7 luglio–5 ago. 1905.
41. *Il Caffaro*; *La Stampa* (Torino), 30–31 luglio 1905.

Chapter 11: The Closing

1. Emanuele Gianturco, *Parere per la verità sulla costituzione di parte civile dei minori Bonmartini nel processo Murri* (Napoli, 1906).
2. *Corriere della Sera* (Milano), 19–26 luglio 1905.
3. In the U.S., a lawyer would be severly reprimanded for touching a juror.
4. Enrico Cavaglià, "In difesa di Linda Murri, arringa pronunciata avanti la Corte d'Assise di Torino nelle udienze del 3–4–5 agosto 1905," Archivio di Stato di Torino.
5. Berenini's pleadings are the easiest to procure, since he seems to have generously distributed copies to the newspapers. See *La Stampa* (Torino), *Gazzetta del Popolo* (Torino), *Il Resto del Carlino* (Bologna), *Il Momento* (Torino), *L'Avvenire d'Italia* (Bologna), and *Corriere della Sera,* 29–30 agosto, 1905.
6. 8 ago. 1905. A. G. Bianchi was the legal editor for *Corriere della Sera*. Unlike many journalists, he did not come to his post after law school but after a stint working for a railroad company. He was a staunch positivist and follower of Lombroso, and he was also a friend of Augusto Murri. Nonetheless, his pro-Murri bias rarely shows. His articles were the most complete and fair reporting of the trial.
7. *Corriere della Sera,* 10 ago. 1905.
8. Ibid., 11 ago. 1905.

Chapter 12: Tutti

1. *Corriere della Sera* (Milan), 12 ago. 1905; in the U.S. reporters may not be shut out.
2. Corte d'Assise Ordinaria di Torino, Sentenza, 11 ago. 1905, Archivio di Stato di Torino.
3. A summary of the principal questions and responses regarding Tullio: 1. Are you convinced that Tullio Murri . . . caused the death of Bonmartini . . . by stabbing him in the chest . . . and in the neck? Yes. 2. Are you convinced that he was in such a state of mental abnormality as to take away his will and liberty of action? No. 3. Are you convinced that he committed the acts . . . through the necessity of repelling an unjust attack? No. 4. Did he . . . cause others to cooperate . . . in the attack? Yes. A summary of the secondary questions regarding Tullio: 5. Did the

circumstance that Bonmartini was the brother-in-law of Tullio Murri . . .
serve to make Tullio's crime easier? Yes. 6. Did he commit the crime . . .
with premeditation? Yes. 7. At the moment he committed the act, was he
in such a state of mental infirmity as to significantly reduce his
responsibility without negating it? No. Numbers 8, 9, and 10 were
eliminated by the jury, since they dealt with the degree of violence that
might have been applied if Tullio were acting in self-defense. A summary of
more principal charges against Tullio: 11. Are you convinced that Tullio
Murri . . . dispossessed Bonmartini of money and objects? Yes. 12. Are you
convinced that in the moment of committing that crime . . . he was in a
state of . . . mental infirmity . . . ? No. 13. Are you convinced that he . . .
took away for his own profit . . . objects and documents . . . without
Bonmartini's consent? Yes. 14 and 15 eliminated without explanation. 16.
Are you convinced that he was in such a state of mental infirmity as to
lessen his responsibility [for the theft] without excusing it? No.

Each defendant's judgment required a similar number of corollary
questions to be considered.

Corte d'Assise Ordinaria di Torino, Sentenza, 11 ago. 1905, Archivio di
Stato di Torino.

4. *Corriere della Sera,* 11–12 ago. 1905.
5. Corte d'Assise Ordinaria di Torino, Sentenza, 11 ago. 1905; 1ª Sezione
   Penale Sentenza, 771/06, Archivio Centrale della Stato, Roma.
6. Giorgio Pavese, *Il Processo Murri* (Roma, n.d.), p. 88.
7. It would seem that Ferrero and the others were already in Bolgona,
   waiting for the news that reached them by telegraph; they then brought it
   to the Murri parents.
8. 12 ago. 1905.
9. "Altri commenti e impressioni sul verdetto . . . la campagna dei socialisti
   contro il verdetto . . ." *La Stampa,* 13 ago. 1905. Rome's *Giornale d'Italia*
   said the guilty verdict proved that the jury was more enlightened and
   sensible than a group of magistrates might have been. *La Tribuna* wrote,
   "We are struck with great sadness at the verdict, but a sadness that would
   not be less if the verdict had been different." *Il Giornale di Roma* exclaimed,
   "How much mud has issued from the tabernacle of justice in the 172 days
   of the trial, that the furious eloquence of the prosecution and the
   desperate eloquence of the defense could not succeed in dispersing!" *Il
   Messaggero* rejoiced that the jurors "did the right thing, . . . despite all the
   marvelous powers of the defense to depict Bonmartini as the most
   uncouth, dullest of husbands." But the socialist journal *Avanti!* headed its
   commentary "A Slaughter," referring not to the crime but to the verdict.

Condemning the judgment as "a page of terror and of death," the journal called Linda "a delicate and unfortunate creature" and Rosina "a poor mind dragged into the vortex of an inhuman passion." *Il Resto del Carlino,* aware of the divided opinion in Bologna regarding the Murris, did not debate the verdict, writing that it was not the time to second-guess the jury but to cry for the victims of the crime.

10. Incest: *Giornale di Roma,* 1 ago. 1905; press reaction: *Giornale d'Italia, La Tribuna, Giornale di Roma, Il Messaggero, Avanti!, L'Avvenire d'Italia, Il Resto del Carlino, Gazzetta dell'Emilia,* 11–12–13 ago. 1905.

11. Luigi di San Giusto, *Memorie di Linda Murri* (Torino, 1905), seconda parte.

12. For books by attorneys involved in the case, see Giuseppe Gottardi, Arturo Vecchini, and Agostino Berenini, *Perché Linda Murri è innocente* (Torino, 1906) at 910 [!] pages; Enrico Ferri, *Arringhe e discorsi* (Milan, 1979 reprint); Scipio Sighele, *Processo Murri* (Trento, 1905); Vincenzo Tazzari, *Rivelazioni sul processo Murri* (Milano, n.d.) and *Le dubbiezze del processo Murri* (Milan, 1905); Vincenzo Morello, *Il Processo Murri* (Torino, 1906), subtitled, "The Crime of Honest People"; Carlo Nasi, *Il Processo Murri* (Torino, 1905); Enrico Morselli, *Linda e Tullio Murri* (Genova, 1905). The most accessible book by a reporter covering the case is Augusto Bianchi, *Autopsia di un delitto* (Milano, 1904), written before the trial and marred by complete disorganization. A writer concocted an account supposedly offered by Tullio: Mario Casalini, *Confessioni di Tullio Murri a un compagno di cella* (Torino, 1905).

13. 1906 was a terrible year for disasters. On August 16 an earthquake struck Chile, killing 3,000 people. Roman real estate investors meanwhile were asking a teacher named Maria Montessori to organize a program for slum children whose parents were at work all day, so that the urchins would not deface the walls of public buildings.

14. "Per avv. Tullio Murri ricorrente contro la sentenza . . . della Corte d'Assise di Torino"; "Per la contessa Teolinda Bonmartini-Murri ricorrente contro la sentenza . . . ," 4 vols. (Roma-Torino, 1906), Busta 5, Archivio Berenini, Biblioteca Comunale di Parma; *Corriere della Sera,* 18 ago. 1905.

15. The Court of Cassation considered whether the assize court had been in legal error on a few minor points, such as violating the constitutional separation of Church and state by allowing a high prelate, Cardinal Svampa, to testify for the prosecution. The question was revisited as to whether the Bonmartini children, who were deprived of their father by the conspirators, could sue their mother for damages. The lawyers debated jury findings that seemed contradictory: Linda was guilty of conspiracy to kill Bonmartini, for example, but not guilty of premeditation. The defense

argued that such contradictions negated the verdicts. The prosecution reasoned that the jurors believed Linda was guilty but did not want her to suffer the severe sentence that might have been expected if they had judged her guilty on every point in the charge. Despite presentations by several lawyers, as in the first trial, the appeals trial was finished in only a week. The lawyers Palberti, Vecchini, Berenini, Calissano, Fabri, Morello, Levi, and Bernasconi took part in the appeal; G. B. Avellone was the appeals prosecutor; *Corriere della Sera,* 27 marzo, 2–8 aprile 1906; *Giornale d'Italia* (Roma), 28 aprile 1906.

16. *La Nazione* (Roma), 20 giugno 1908; *Corriere della Sera,* 7 feb. 1907.

17. Another Lombroso daughter, Paola, was once sentenced to three months in jail for writing an article protesting the dismissal of some workmen. The family thus had more than a passing interest in a proceeding widely perceived as being a socialist trial; B. King and T. Okey, *Italy Today* (New York, 1901), p. 98.

18. Despite having been highly critical of Linda, Count Mainardi, who had been keeping the children cloistered in Cavarzere, was worried about the effect the news would have on the children, especially Ninetto, who was an extremely anxious child. The children's other curator, Alessandro Stoppato, began a civil lawsuit against Secchi that lasted for many years, collecting damages from him. Stoppato was not permitted to sue Linda; he instituted a suit against Tullio, but it is not certain that he was able to collect damages. Bonetti and Naldi were too poor to be worth persecuting for compensation; *La Tribuna, Gazzetta di Torino,* 5 aprile 1905; *Corriere della Sera,* 8 aprile 1905; Alessandro Stoppato, *Memoria della parte civile resistente al ricorso di Tullio Murri* (Roma, 1906); Corte d'Assise Ordinaria di Torino, Sentenza, 11 ago. 1905 (addendum); Corte di Cassazione, 2–5 aprile, 12–16 giugno 1906, Archivio di Stato di Torino.

19. *Corriere della Sera,* 6 aprile 1905, *La Stampa,* 6 aprile 1906.

20. *Corriere della Sera,* 16 giugno 1906.

21. For a comparison of prison administration in America and some countries in Europe, see Patricia O'Brien, *The Promise of Punishment* (Princeton, 1982).

22. *Giornale d'Italia* (Roma), 8 dicembre 1906.

23. Corte d'Assise Ordinaria di Torino, Sentenza, addendum, ibid., 16 giugno 1906; *Giornale d'Italia,* 29 giugno 1906; *Corriere della Sera,* 1 luglio 1907.

24. For a typical example of press reaction, see *Gazzetta del Popolo,* 23 maggio 1906; Emanuele Gianturco, *Per una grazia . . . disgraziata! Sonnino e Giolitti . . .* (Torino, 1906); Gennaro Escobedo, *Aggravanti sub condizione (a proposito della sentenza Murri)* (Roma, 1906).

25. *Corriere della Sera,* 19 ago. 1905.

26. *La Tribuna* (Torino), 8 dic. 1906.
27. *Il Veneto* (Padova), 11 dic. 1906.
28. *Corriere d'Italia* (Roma), 12 dic. 1906; *La Tribuna* (Roma), 18 dic. 1906.
29. *Corriere della Sera,* 17 aprile 1908. In the U.S. witnesses do not wear prison garb, so as not to prejudice the jury against their testimony.
30. The suit against *La Tribuna* was withdrawn; *Corriere della Sera,* 18, 25, 26 aprile 1908.
31. *Corriere della Sera,* 17 aprile 1905.
32. See Tullio Murri, *Galera* (Milano, 1930), p. 237n. The case was reported in *Corriere della Sera* in July 1925.
33. Interview with Di Benedetto, *Corriere della Sera,* 18–19 aprile 1908.
34. Ibid., 21 aprile 1908.
35. Ibid., 25 aprile 1908. A story persists that Naldi's aunt made his lawyer, Tazzari, promise never to abandon her luckless nephew; however, according to available records, the lawyer saw neither Naldi nor his aunt after the trial in 1905 and took pains to distance himself from his former client when Naldi began making further accusations about a third accomplice. Tazzari's two books about the trial were based mainly on Naldi's depositions; see *Il Tempo,* 4 aprile 1919, clipping in the records of Raffaele Sabattini, Archivio Notarile Distrettuale di Bologna.
36. Each was to be under the supervision of the police for ten years, but that requirement was also lifted after two years for Tullio and four years for Naldi; Corte d'Assise di Torino, Sentenza, 2–5 aprile 1906, addenda, 28 aprile 1919, 27 aprile 1921, 19 febbraio 1923; Archivio di Stato di Torino. For press reaction to Tullio's release, see *Il Tempo,* 4 aprile 1919.
37. [Enzo Rossi] Ròiss, *Il Delitto Murri: Documenti foto e testimonianze originali con 53 lettere di Augusto Murri* (Bologna, 1974), p. 174ff.
38. *Il Resto del Carlino* (Bologna), 18 ott. 1908.
39. Corte d'Assise di Torino, Sentenza, addendum, n.d.
40. Luigi di San Giusto, *Una naufraga della Vita* (A Shipwrecked Life) (Torino, 1908).
41. Tullio a Dante Manetti, 20 dic. 1919, in Ròiss, *Il Delitto Murri,* p. 186.
42. *Corriere della Sera,* 9 ago. 1908.
43. The authority happened to be inspecting the prison, given in the report as the *reclusorio* of Turi, according to the story; *La Nazione* (Roma), 20 genn. 1908.
44. Valerie Paola Babini, *Il Caso Murri* (Milano, 2001), p. 294.
45. Renzo Renzi, *Il Processo Murri* (Bologna, 1974), p. 45. Renzi uses as his source the later correspondence between Tullio, Linda, and Professor Murri. See also Murri's thoughts on war; Professor Murri a Tullio, maggio 1914, p. 50.

46. See Prof. Murri a Egidi, 1908, quoted in Ròiss, *Il Delitto Murri,* p. 269.

47. Prof. Murri a Linda, Milan, 6 giugno 1919, ibid., pp. 251–252.

48. Prof. Murri a Linda, gennaio 1923 or 1922, ibid., p. 253.

49. See Anhelus (pseud.), *Metapsichica e Scienza* (Roma, 1938).

50. Ròiss, *Il Delitto Murri,* pp. 174–175.

51. Tullio Murri, *Le Carceri e le Leggi Penali* (Milano, 1920), p. 28.

52. See, for example, the letter addressed to the king of Italy by Giovanni Pascoli and signed by artists, writers, and politicians, reprinted in *Giuseppe DelVecchio* (ed.), *Dopo le tenebre: Lettere inedite di Tullio Murri* (Napoli, 1931), pp. 32–34.

53. See Tullio's lecture at a conference on penal law, published as *Le Carceri e le Leggi Penali,* and his letters to various newspapers gathered in *Scritti Vari di Tullio Murri* (Milano, 1930.)

54. Murri, *Le Carcere e le Legge Penali,* pp. 14, 17, 49–55.

55. Murri, *Galera,* 8 ed. (Milano 1930). Later editions give the actual names of inmates portrayed in the novel who Tullio alleged had suffered such mistreatment. See also Murri, *Una pagina di follia e di lacrime, appendici a "Galera,"* 2 ed. (Firenze, n.d.)

56. It would be reinstated by Mussolini in 1926.

57. Murri, *Galera,* p. 383n.

58. See Blair Niles, *Condemned to Devil's Island: The Biography of an Unknown Convict* (New York, 1928).

59. See Bino Binazzi, "Il Bilancio Morale di *Galera,*" a summary of the controversy originally written for the Milan journal *La Borghesia* included in *Scritti Vari di Tullio Murri.*

60. The suit began in 1923 and lasted three years, according to a letter of Tullio; I could locate no court record of this suit nor its outcome. Possibly it was withdrawn voluntarily; Murri, *Dopo le tenebre,* p. 52.

61. *Corriere della Sera,* 18 aprile, 28 sett. 1908.

62. Guido Guidi, *Delitti passionali* (Palermo, 1984).

63. Vidkun Quisling, *The Truth About the Ukrainian Horror, Official Report,* Fund for the Relief of Jewish Victims of the War in Eastern Europe (London, 1922).

64. "What a disappointment the twentieth century has been!" Winston S. Churchill at Dundee, Scotland, Nov. 11, 1922, quoted in Martin Gilbert, *A History of the Twentieth Century,* vol. I (Toronto, 1997), p. 648.

65. Documenti di Giovanni Mariani, 19 sett. 1928, No. 2267/11940; property transactions: 13 ott. 1923 (with Severo Dalla), No. 3723; 28 genn. 1925, No. 5599/971; 7 ott. 1925, No. 6872; 31 ott. 1925, 7065/1289; 14 maggio 1928, No. 11454; 18 sett. 1928, No. 11838; 2 nov. 1928, No. 2280/11983, Archivio Notarile Distrettuale di Bologna.

66. Tullio a Del Vecchio, 7 marzo 1929, in Murri, *Dopo le tenebre*.

67. See the extravagant praise by Mario Gastaldi, *Scrittori del tormento* (Bologna, 1929), pp. 205–246. For a summary of each of Tullio's novels, see Nanni Leone Castelli, *Tullio Murri: Profilo di un grande Uomo di fede* (Bologna, 1925.)

68. Bino Binazzi, "Il Bilancio Morale di *Galera*."

69. Antonio Fogazzaro (1842–1911) was Italy's most popular novelist, his work loved by hundreds of thousands of readers. He was so fervently Catholic that he believed in papal infallibility, though his *Il Santo* (The Saint) was placed on the Index of Prohibited Books, thereby insuring its wild success. The main character in *Il Santo* is a lay monk who battles superstition and wants church reform. A woman who was enamored of him before he became a monk continues to be in love with him. The saint dies at the end, after inspiring several conversions; his worshiper, too, rediscovers her faith. Church officials were not, however, inspired by the book. The most famous work of the very famous Edmondo De Amicis (1846–1908) was *Cuore* (Heart), known in America as the first, often despised, reading assigned to students of Italian, a collection of edifying anecdotes about a perfect ten-year-old with perfect parents and teachers growing wise in an imperfect world of school bullies and snobs.

70. Tullio a Del Vecchi, 31 ago. 1926, among many examples; Murri, *Dopo le tenebre*.

71. Tullio a Del Vecchio, 3 dic. 1927, 17 sett. 1927, 6 genn. 1928, ibid.

72. 2 dicembre 1919.

73. Dante Manetti, *Augusto Murri* (Firenze, 1923), p. 168. See also Del Vecchio's exhortations, in *Dopo le tenebre,* pp. 29–33, 52–53. Another votary was Murri's contemporary Nanni Leone Castelli; see his *Tullio Murri: Profilo di un grande Uomo di fede*.

74. Families never refused: Murri, *Dopo le tenebre,* p. 18; wanted peace: Lettere, 31 ago. 1926, 30 nov. 1929, ibid. See comments about Tullio: Vincenzo Tazzari, *Rivelazioni sul processo Murri: la ricostruzione del delitto sui confessioni del dottor Pio Naldi* (Milan, n.d.); *Le dubbiezze del processo Murri* (Milan, 1906). Tullio singled out Tazzari's books for criticism, saying "To think he was paid 300,000 lire to write that filth!"

75. King Vittorio Emanuele III yielded this power to the minister of justice in 1922, when Mussolini began gathering judicial powers into his own hands, either appointing fascists to cabinet ministries or assuming the posts himself. It was this transfer of the power of clemency that occasioned Tullio's comments. See Murri, *Scritti Vari di Tullio Murri*.

76. Gianna Murri, *La verità sulla mia famiglia e sul delitto Murri* (Bologna, 2003), unpaginated.
77. Tullio a Del Vecchio, 30 nov. 1929, in *Dopo le Tenebre,* Lettere, p. 59.
78. "Verbale d'inventario di Tullio Murri," Documenti di Giovanni Marani, 31 marzo 1930, No. 2800/15286; see also 9 giugno 1930, No. 2800/15286; 11 giugno 1930, No. 2767/15145 and 2768/15146, Archivio Notarile Distrettuale di Bologna.
79. Tullio a Del Vecchio, 30 nov. 1929, *Dopo le tenebre,* Lettere, p. 89.
80. Gianna Murri, *La verità.*
81. Documenti di Giovanni Marani, 4 giugno 1940, No. 24349, Archivio Notarile Distrettuale di Bologna. Gianna Rosa claims that Nelia even sold Tullio's letter to Linda Murri, along with the document bearing LaBella's perfunctory confession.
82. Ibid., 21 maggio 1930, No. 18619; 26 giugno 1930, No. 2781/15191. The house in Sant'Elpidio was to go to Linda, along with some lots; Gianna Rosa received other lots in Sant'Elpidio, along with stores and houses in Bologna.
83. Prof. Murri a Tullio, n.d., quoted in Renzi, *Il processo Murri,* p. 46.
84. For a discussion of the murder of Giacomo Matteotti in the context of the parliamentary collapse, see Martin Clark, *Modern Italy* (New York, 1984), pp. 224–228. For parliamentary debates of 1924–1925, see O. Barié, *Le Origini dell'Italia Contemporanea* (Bologna, 1966), pp. 164–167.
85. Murri a Paldino, 1922, quoted in Ròiss, *Il Delitto Murri,* pp. 215, 271.
86. Prof. Murri a Linda, gennaio 1923, ibid, p. 338.
87. Registro degli atti di morte del anno 1932, Comune di Bologna, documenti di Luigi Ruffini, 12 nov. 1932; Documenti di Giovanni Marani, 26 giugno 1940, No. 6119/424; "Addendum," 15 genn. 1932, Archivio Notarile Distrettuale di Bologna.

Chapter 13: Coda

1. *Corriere della Sera* (Milano), 25 marzo 1905.
2. *Causa Penale contro Murri Tullio ed Altri,* V. VI *Atti,* 17 nov. 1902, Documenti rito Murri Giannina, Archivio di Stato di Bologna.
3. *Corriere della Sera,* 18 aprile 1908.
4. Jury's reasoning: *Corriere della Sera,* 13–30 ago. 1905, *passim.* The jury found Linda guilty of conspiracy but, in a separate charge, judged her not guilty of premeditation—seemingly a contradiction; Corte d'Assise Ordinaria di Torino, Sentenza, 11 ago. 1905, Archivio di Stato di Torino.
5. To believe in her innocence, one must accept her explanations for the reconciliation; the apartment rented next to hers; the hours closeted with

Rosina; Bonmartini's intestinal illnesses; the fifteen or so telegrams sent just before the murder; the trip to Darmstadt; the postcard asking about "S" and the medicine; the money borrowed from Secchi; the money taken out of her son's account; the errands both Bonmartini and Rosina were given regarding a dress; the frantic telegrams sent to her brother about the chair incident; the likewise frantic telegram that caught up with Tullio (brought by Severo) in the train station just as he was leaving to kill Bonmartini; the telegram received by her, notifying her that the "cascara sagrada" had been sent, followed by the package supposedly containing it; the meeting at the Public Gardens in Venice; the sack of pallini from her house; the keys that turned up in Tullio's possession; the deluge of communications she sent to locate Cesco after he lay dead; the sudden trip to Switzerland for eye treatment.

6. *Fatti di Gente Perbene,* directed by Mauro Bolognini, starring Catherine Deneuve and Giancarlo Giannini.

7. Linda's lawyer, Cavaglià, in his summation finally named a woman Linda and Tullio knew; but S was only part of her long name, Adele de Witt Saladini. She was known by the name Adele de Witt, and the explanation was too late and weak to convince the jury; *In difesa di Linda Murri, arringa pronunciata avanti la Corte d'Assise di Torino nelle udienze del 3–4–5– agosto 1905,* L'Archivio di Stato di Torino.

8. As noted elsewhere, population figures vary from 105,000 for the city proper to 146,000 with the near suburbs included; U.S. prosecutors are required to turn over exculpatory evidence to the defense.

9. At various points during the istruttoria, Stanzani composed long summaries of his researches and explained his ideas and conclusions about the suspects.

10. V. IV *Testimoni,* 8 marzo 1903, Esame di Dalla rag. Severo.

11. V. I *Atti,* 10 sett. 1902, Rapporto Questura, Prof. Murri a Linda, San Moritz, 31 ago. 1902.

12. V. IV *Atti,* 27 ago. 1902, Telegramma da San Moritz da Venezia, Murri a Vitali.

13. Murri a Linda, 31 ago. 1902; Murri a Linda, San Moritz, 27 ago. 1902, quoted in [Enzo Rossi] Ròiss, *Il Delitto Murri: Documenti foto e testimoni originali con 53 lettere di Augusto Murri* (Bologna, 1974), pp. 245–262.

14. Giannina to Linda, 13 ott. 1901, quoted in Cavaglià, *Arringa.*

15. Quoted in Cavalgià, *Arringa,* p. 62.

16. Quoted in Paolo Valera, *Murri e Bonmartini* (Milano, 1902), p. 61; Ròiss, *Il Delitto Murri,* p. 164.

17. V. II *Atti,* 17 sett. 1902, Rapporto Questura.

PRONUNCIATION GUIDE

Bernasconi, Guido   Bair nah *scoh* nee, *Gwee* doh

Bianchi, Augusto   Bee *yahn* kee, Ow *goo* stoh

Bonci, Alessandro   *Bone* chee, Ah less *sahn* droh

Bonmartini, Francesco   Bone mar *tee* nee, Fran *cheh* scoh

    also called Cesco   *Chess* coh

borghesia   bor gay *zee* ah

Borghi, Tisa   *Bor* ghee, *Tee* Sah

carabiniere   kah rah bee *nyair* reh

Cavaglià, Enrico   Cah vah *lyah,* En *ree* coh

Cavarzere   Cah *vahr* zeh ray

Cenacci, Faustino   Cheh *nah* chee, Fow *stee* noh

Ceroni, Antonio   Cheh *roh* nee, An *toh* nyoh

Cervesato, Dante   Chair veh *zah* toh, *Dahn* teh

Cicognani, Teresa   Chee koh *nyah* nee, Tay *ray* zah

Corriere della Sera   Cor ree *yair* eh *del* lah *Sai* rah

Corte d'Assise   *Cor* tay dah *See* zay

Dagnini, Giuseppe   Dah *nyee* nee, Joo *zep* peh

Dalla, Severo   *Dahl* la, Seh *vair* roh

De Amicis, Edmondo   Day Ah *mee* cheess, Ed *mon* doh

Dusio, Ernesto   *Doo* zyoh, Air *neh* stoh

Egidi, Francesco   Eh *jee* dee, Fran *cheh* scoh

Ferrero, Guglielmo   Fehr *rair* roh, Gool *yell* moh

Galera   Gah *lair* ah

giudice istruttore   *joo* dee chee ee stroot *toh* reh

Gottardi, Giuseppe   Goh *tar* dee, Joo *zep* peh

istruttore	ee stroot *toh* reh
L'Avvenire d'Italia	Lah ven *neer* reh dee *tahl* ya
Municchi, Carlo	Moo *nee* kee, *Cahr* loh
Murri, Giannina	*Moor* ree, Jah *neen* nah
Murri, Tullio	*Moor* ree, *Tool* yoh
Occhi, Antonio	*Awk* kee, An *toh* nyoh
Oneglia	Oh *nay* lyah
Pacini, Enrico	Pah *chee* nee, En *ree* coh
Palazzo Bisteghi	Pah *laht* soh Bee *stay* ghee
parte civile	*pahr* tay chee *vee* leh
Piazza Maggiore	Pee *aht* zah Mah *joh* reh
Picchi, Ferdinando	*Pee* kee, Fair dee *nahn* doh
portinaia	por tee *nah* yah
pubblico ministero	*poob* blee koh mee nee *stair* oh
quesiti	*qway* zee tee
Romagnola	Roh mah *nyo* lah
Rusconi, Marchesa Paola	Roo *scoh* nee, Mar *kay* sah *Pow* lah
San Marcello Pistoiese	Sahn Mar *chel* loh Pee stoh *yay* seh
Secchi, Carlo	*Say* kee, *Cahr* loh
Sighele, Scipio	See *ghay* leh, *Shee* pyoh
Silvagni, Luigi	Seel *vah* nyee, Loo *ee* jee
Stazione Medaglie d'Oro	Stah tsee *oh* nay May *dahl* lyeh *doh* roh
Stoppato, Alessandro	Stoh *pah* toh, Ah les *sahn* droh
Svampa, Cardinal Domenico	*Zvahm* pah, Doh *meh* nee koh
Taormena, Giuseppina	Tah or *mee* nah, Joo zep *pee* nah
Tazzari, Vincenzo	Tah *tsah* ree, Veen *chen* zoh
Tutti Condannati	*toot* tee cohn dahn *nah* tee
Vacchi, Ettore	*Vah* kee, *Eh* toh ray
Valvassori, Battista	Vahl vass *soh* ree, Bah *tee* stah
Vecchini, Arturo	Veh *kee* nee, Ar *too* roh
Via d'Azeglio	*Vee* ah dah *zehl* yoh
Via Mazzini	*Vee* ah Mah *tsee* nee
Vittorio Emanuele	Vee *toh* ree oh Eh mahn *well* eh

ACKNOWLEDGMENTS

Even the most dedicated rummager in history relies almost entirely on the kindness of archivists to locate primary documents. I want to express thanks to all the staff of the Archivio Notarile Distrettuale di Bologna for their unfailing patience during an arduous month of research; my husband and I will long remember their enthusiasm. I am indebted to the staff of the Archivio di Stato di Bologna for help in consulting the very large istruttoria of the Murri case; I especially want to thank Sig. Gianni Savarese of the Sezione di Fotoriproduzione. My sincere thanks also to the gracious custodians of the Archivio di Stato di Torino, especially Dottoressa Isabella Massabò Ricci, Direttore, for trying to locate the court record of the Murri trial. These archivists went to a great deal of trouble, moreover, to make the papers of Enrico Cavaglià available to me, along with those records of the trial that remain in Turin. I received generous assistance from the staff of the Archivio Nazionale and the Archivio di Stato di Roma and from librarians and map curators in Venice, Padua, and Florence, who, like all the Italians I met, were warmhearted and diligent.

I am grateful to the libraries in the United States that allowed me extended use of valuable books, newspapers, and documents: New York Public Library; New Orleans Public Library; the Library of Congress; Widener Library and the Law Library of Harvard University, where the help of Ms. Aparna Sen was essential; Butler Library of Columbia University; the libraries of Ohio State University, Boston University, Dartmouth College, University of Kansas, Indiana

University, University of Chicago, University of Wisconsin, and Boston College. My warm thanks also to Kevin Hourihan of the Law Library and Hayden Battle of Howard-Tilton Library, both of Tulane University.

Certain individuals kindly responded when I needed their help. I want to thank my generous friend Letizia C. Hardy for countless favors. Several specialists perused the entire manuscript and offered corrections and comments: I am especially indebted to Carl G. Kardinal, M.D., Judge Dennis J. Waldron, and Judge Leon A. Cannizzaro, Jr., who cheerfully lent their expertise. My daughter Christie procured valuable materials for me. Jack Belsom, Juan Carlos De Martin, Steve Feinman, Ellen Verges, and Margaret Williams provided willing assistance. Rafael Jarpa was graciously, repeatedly helpful. William C. Davis made an unselfish contribution that I will always remember. Mazie Roy Doody and Michael Brookes read a very long first draft of the manuscript and offered suggestions, as did my cherished resident readers, Christie and Robin Vella Riehl. I appreciate the enthusiasm of my agent and friend Lane Zachary, and of my genial editor at Simon & Schuster, Bruce Nichols.

Last and most I want to thank my husband Robert Riehl, coauthor of our children and my partner in research and life. He has been, as always, my first and last reader, the final arbiter of usage, humor, and tedium. Without him, writing about the past and living the present would be more difficult and much less fun.

INDEX

387

ABOUT THE AUTHOR

CHRISTINA VELLA holds a Ph.D. in Modern European and American history. In addition to teaching and lecturing, she is a consultant to public television and to the U.S. State Department. She lives in New Orleans.